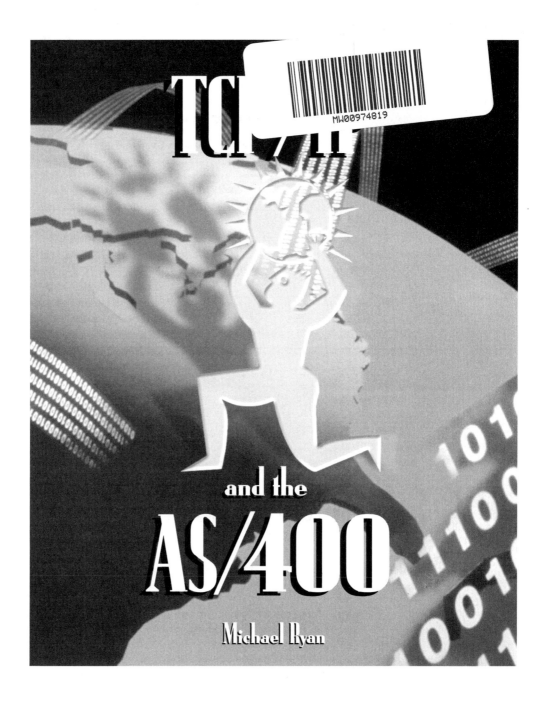

TCP/IP

and the

AS/400

Michael Ryan

A Division of
DUKE COMMUNICATIONS INTERNATIONAL

221 E. 29th Street • Loveland, CO 80538
(800) 621-1544 • (970) 663-4700 • www.29thStreetPress.com

MW00974819

Library of Congress Cataloging-in-Publication Data

Library of Congress CIP Data is available.

Published by 29th Street Press
DUKE COMMUNICATIONS INTERNATIONAL
Loveland, Colorado

Copyright © 1999 by Michael Ryan

This book was printed and bound in Canada.

ISBN 1-882419-72-3

2000 1999 1998 WL 10 9 8 7 6 5 4 3 2 1

This book is dedicated to
my sweet, loving family,
Donna and Tommy.

Thanks for your patience and support
during the long hours spent writing this book.

Acknowledgments

Many people helped me with this book. Some gave me ideas, others encouragement, but everyone played a part in putting this together. My good friend John Enck provided ideas and direction — thanks, John. Dan Riehl and Mel Beckman provided good ideas. I also thank Dan for letting me excerpt from his article "Who's Accessing My FTP Server." Robert H'obbes' Zakon provided the Internet Timeline. Trish Faubion, Barb Gibbens, and Trish McConnell provided able editing. Thanks to all!

Table of Contents at a Glance

Table of Contents

Foreword

When I first met Michael Ryan back in the late 1980s, the TCP/IP capabilities of the AS/400 were, well, "limited" is the kindest word I can think of. Both Michael and I were in the networking business, and we both realized how important TCP/IP was becoming. At that time, it seemed like every operating system vendor was making huge strides toward complete adoption of TCP/IP as the network protocol of choice.

But one obvious holdout was IBM's OS/400. Oh sure, the early releases of OS/400 had some TCP/IP capabilities — enough to offer lip service to the TCP/IP trend and qualify the AS/400 for most government bids, but not enough to make the AS/400 truly functional in a TCP/IP network. To make matters worse, IBM came up with its SNA-over-TCP/IP strategy (MPTN), an architecture that combined the worst aspects of SNA and TCP/IP.

I don't look back on those days with fondness. As consultants, we burned hours and hours struggling with the early AS/400 Telnet and FTP capabilities. Later we tested the strength of our hair roots as we strained to make MPTN connections work over LAN and WAN links. To be honest, the early TCP/IP capabilities of the AS/400 made SNA look pretty darn good — after all, we knew how to make APPC and APPN connections work.

Slowly, over the course of many years, IBM seemed to "get it." With each new release of OS/400, new and better TCP/IP capabilities came to light. Client Access moved away from SNA to full-blown TCP/IP support. The AS/400 became a Web system, a mail system, and more. Today's AS/400 supports all of the significant TCP/IP capabilities and can be compared to a Unix or Windows NT system without embarrassment.

So it is with great pleasure that I introduce Michael's book on TCP/IP for the AS/400. If you're a TCP/IP guru on another type of system, this book will show you how to configure and manage the AS/400 TCP/IP capabilities. If you're an AS/400 expert with little TCP/IP background, this book will also help you understand the importance of TCP/IP in both the world of the AS/400 and the general computing world. Any way you cut it, if you're looking for information on how to utilize the TCP/IP capabilities of the AS/400, you've got the answer in your hands.

John Enck
Director of Technology and Research, *Windows NT Magazine*

Preface

Transmission Control Protocol/Internet Protocol (TCP/IP) is fast becoming a major protocol in the AS/400 world and certainly the protocol of choice in mixed-vendor environments. TCP/IP is also the protocol for the Internet, intranets, and extranets. But why is TCP/IP becoming so popular? It is not the best protocol for an all-AS/400 network and is often less efficient than specific gateways between protocols.

The answer lies in TCP/IP's ubiquity and predominance in the networked world. Although Advanced Peer-to-Peer Networking (APPN) is still the best protocol for linking AS/400s in a network, TCP/IP is more familiar to many networking professionals, is the basis for the Internet (the most popular computer network), and is available on many more systems than APPN.

This book provides background for AS/400 professionals to understand the capabilities of TCP/IP, its strength and weaknesses, and how to configure and administer the TCP/IP protocol stack on the AS/400. The book consists of two parts — the theory and services of TCP/IP in Chapters 1 through 3 and its configuration and implementation on the AS/400 in Chapters 4 through 10.

Chapter 1 provides background on networking and some TCP/IP fundamentals. Chapter 2 expands the discussion to the standard services the TCP/IP protocol suite provides, including virtual terminal access, file transfers, and e-mail. Chapter 3 discusses TCP/IP addressing and routing, core components in a packet-switched network.

The remaining chapters discuss AS/400 TCP/IP configuration and implementation directly. Chapter 4 explains the configuration of TCP/IP on the AS/400 and provides the information you need to establish TCP/IP connectivity on your system. Chapter 5 provides details about the implementation of TCP/IP services from an AS/400 perspective. Chapter 6 discusses client configuration and includes examples of configuring TCP/IP for Win95, Client Access/400, Attachmate's Rally! product, and WRQ's Reflection for IBM software. Chapter 7 covers TCP/IP exit points, including configuration of anonymous FTP. Chapter 8 discusses TCP/IP management on the AS/400. Chapter 9 covers the implementation of the World Wide Web server on the AS/400, including the use of IBM's Net.Data database access product, Common Gateway Interface programming, and the Workstation Gateway. And Chapter 10 explains the configuration of advanced features that became available in OS/400 V4R1 and V4R2.

In addition to these ten chapters are three appendices. Appendix A discusses the history of TCP/IP. Appendix B explains how to configure the SLIP protocol. And Appendix C summarizes the major TCP/IP Requests for Comments.

Chapter 1

An Overview of TCP/IP

TCP/IP is a popular protocol, especially on the Internet, intranets, and extranets. The popularity of a technology isn't reason enough to embrace it, however, and TCP/IP has more than popularity going for it. It has been in use for more than 20 years, is familiar to many people in the data processing industry, is the basis for the Internet, and is available on almost every known computing platform.

But the best reason to use TCP/IP can be summed up in one word: connectivity. The TCP/IP protocol is growing fast and is widely used in both corporate intranets and the public Internet. Because it is implemented by so many vendors and known to so many computer professionals, TCP/IP will continue to grow and become more robust, and new applications will continue to become available.

You may be inclined to dismiss Internet access as a reason to implement TCP/IP, but that wouldn't be wise. Although the Internet is experiencing growing pains and often seems more style than substance, I am not alone in believing it will revolutionize the way we conduct business and the way we communicate.

Another reason to consider embracing TCP/IP is the support and attention IBM gives it. TCP/IP is IBM's protocol of the future, even as IBM supports the SNA and APPC of our current systems. IBM's conviction that electronic business will be the method of conducting commerce in the future is a clear indication that IBM will continue to support and enhance TCP/IP on all its platforms, from PCs to AS/400s and mainframes.

One early enhancement necessary for TCP/IP to be adopted as an AS/400 network protocol was performance. The performance enhancements and numerous other improvements made over the years strongly convey IBM's belief that TCP/IP does and will continue to play an important part in the total AS/400 communications solution, solidifying the AS/400 as the most communications-capable platform on the market today. IBM has also positioned the AS/400 as an Internet, intranet, and extranet server, with all the capabilities expected of a true TCP/IP network server.

One point key to the role TCP/IP plays on the AS/400 is that TCP/IP is a packet-switched network, as opposed to dedicated or dial-up lines, which are circuit switched. Packet-switched networks are less common on the AS/400 than circuit-switched networks, and it's important to understand how they differ.

Circuit-Switched vs. Packet-Switched Networks

Circuit switching and packet switching are the two main methods of network communication. In a circuit-switched network, a dedicated connection is made between computer systems on a leased or dial-up analog or digital line such as one obtained from a phone company. The connection is dedicated to the connected systems (Figure 1.1 illustrates a circuit-switched network), and the only traffic on the line is the traffic between those two systems.

Figure 1.1
Diagram of a Circuit-Switched Network

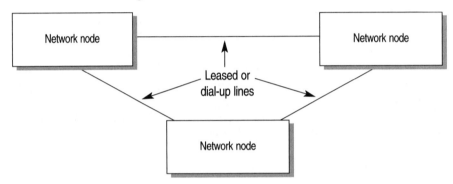

A circuit-switched environment guarantees capacity because you buy as much bandwidth as you need and have full use of that bandwidth. Of course, you also pay for that bandwidth regardless of the amount of traffic: On a dedicated line, you pay for the line whether you're using it or not; a dial-up line requires you to pay while the line is connected even if there is no traffic over it.

A packet-switched network such as TCP/IP handles traffic differently. Data to be sent over the network is encapsulated in one or more *packets*, each of which is simply a sequence of transmitted bits. When the amount of data to be sent exceeds the capacity of a single packet, the data is segmented and the pieces encapsulated in separate packets. Packets are sent over the network independently of each other and reassembled, when necessary, at the receiving end. Figure 1.2 illustrates a packet-switched network.

Each packet includes information such as source and destination addresses, all or part of the actual data being transmitted, error recovery information, and information regarding the network protocol. The address information in the packet enables the network to route the packet to the correct destination. The protocol information lets the systems involved agree on a protocol implementation so they can correctly segment and reassemble large packets.

FIGURE 1.2
Diagram of a Packet-Switched Network

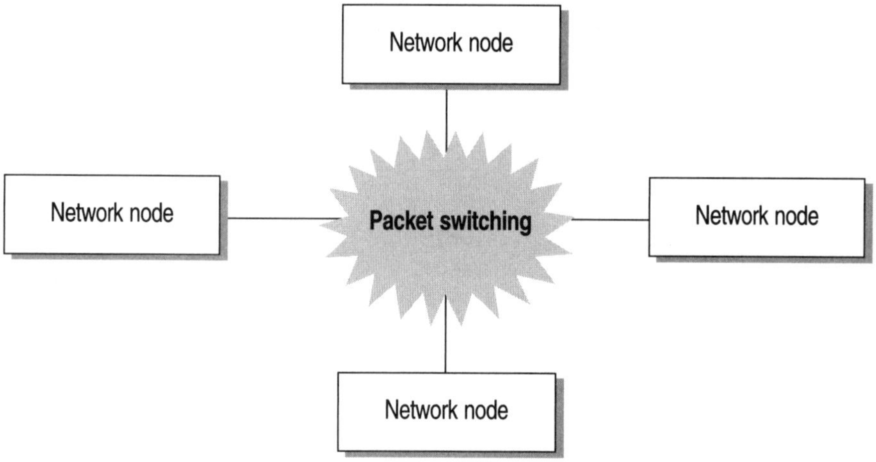

A packet-switched network can interleave packets for multiple destinations over the same physical connection, meaning that multiple users (or systems) can multiplex over the same line at the same time. The cost-efficiency of network sharing is one of the primary advantages to packet switching. A drawback of network sharing is that network capacity cannot be guaranteed as it can with a circuit-switched network.

PORTS

Because multiple stations can use a packet-switched network at the same time and any given station can use multiple concurrent services from a server, there must be a method of determining the specific logical connection point between two systems. Packet-switched networks use ports to identify specific network connections, usually for specific services.

The term *port* originated in the Unix world and indicates the socket used to establish a connection between a client and a server. A *socket* is a TCP/IP logical connection point — the interface a program uses to send and receive information. A TCP/IP server "listens" at a socket for an incoming connection. Both the client and the server use ports; the client port is logically connected to the server port when a connection is made.

The client system initiates a connection across a network by specifying two pieces of information — the Internet Protocol (IP) address and the server port (interface) with which the client wants to connect. Of course, the client also sends many other pieces of information to the server, but the IP address and the port are necessary to establish communications.

Figure 1.3 illustrates the concept of clients and servers listening at ports.

Illustration of a Client Sending a Telnet Connection Request

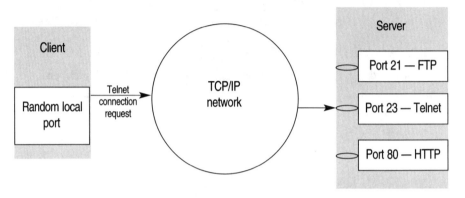

The diagram shows a client sending a Telnet connection request for virtual terminal access to a server across a TCP/IP network. The server is listening concurrently to several ports — port 21 for File Transfer Protocol (FTP), port 23 for Telnet, and port 80 for Hypertext Transfer Protocol (HTTP, the protocol used for Web access) services. When the server detects a packet containing the IP address and port (socket) number the server is monitoring, the server makes the connection. If the IP address is incorrect or the port isn't one the server is monitoring, no connection is made.

The same is true from the client perspective, although a client connection to a server actually uses two ports — the client port and the server port. A client executing multiple applications across a TCP/IP network may have multiple connections (perhaps to different servers), each of which might have a different destination IP address and port number. All the related processing is transparent to the user. The user simply requests a service; the underlying TCP/IP protocol suite handles the processing.

Port numbers are arbitrary — you can create a client/server program using any port numbers you wish. However, the concept of *well-known ports* has become established over time. Well-known ports are socket numbers below 1024 that are standard across different vendors' implementations of TCP/IP. All major and minor services that comprise the TCP/IP protocol suite are assigned socket numbers, and vendors usually include these ports in both client and server implementations of TCP/IP.

For instance, the well-known port for Telnet is 23, and that for HTTP is 80. Well-known port numbers are defined in Request for Comment (RFC) 1060. (Changes to the TCP/IP protocol suite are made through the RFC process. For more information about this process and a list of some of the major RFCs, see Appendix D.) Table 1.1 lists some well-known ports.

TABLE 1.1
A Partial List of Well-Known Ports

Port	Keyword	Description
5	RJE	Remote Job Entry
7	ECHO	Echo
11	USERS	Active System Users
17	QUOTE	Quote of the Day (an interesting Unix facility)
20	FTP-DATA	File Transfer Protocol Data Portion
21	FTP	File Transfer Protocol Control Portion
23	Telnet	Virtual Terminal Processing
25	SMTP	Simple Mail Transfer Protocol
37	TIME	Current Time
53	DOMAIN	Domain Name Server
67	BOOTPS	Bootstrap Server
68	BOOTPC	Bootstrap Client
69	TFTP	Trivial FTP
79	FINGER	Finger Utility (Information)
80	HTTP	Hypertext Transfer Protocol (WWW)
109	POP2	Post Office Protocol 2
110	POP3	Post Office Protocol 3
113	IDENTD	Identification
144	NEWS	Usenet News
161	SNMP	Simple Network Management Protocol
162	SNMP-TRAP	Simple Network Management Protocol Trap
1080	SOCKS	Socks Server

The server ports are the well-known ports, while the client port number is a random, locally available port number above 1023. You should select a port number above 1023 for any custom client/server programs you write that use TCP/IP ports.

THE CLIENT/SERVER MODEL

Much has been written about the client/server model of computing. The model has been hailed as a panacea for today's business problems and a solution for computing in the future. However, as with many concepts trumpeted by IS (remember artificial intelligence?), the implementation falls short of the goal.

This shortfall doesn't mean that the client/server model is invalid, merely that it is difficult to create and may be expensive to maintain.

Client/server computing is simply the ability for an application system's processing to be spread across more than one system. In other words, the workload is shared between a client system and a server system. There are different implementations of the client/server model, but all can be pigeonholed into one of three broad categories: distributed process, distributed data, or distributed display. A given client/server application may use one or more of these concepts.

Distributed process means that the actual processing — the executable programs — are divided between the client and the server, with each doing the parts it does best. In other words, complementary executable programs exist on both platforms and work together to accomplish the objective. The benefit of this approach is that the workload is shared between the client and server systems. The distributed process model requires program-to-program connections between server processes and client processes.

Distributed data entails sharing data between the client and the server. This model can be difficult to exploit fully because of database synchronization issues and network bandwidth constraints.

Distributed display means that the client and server share the responsibility for displaying information. The server sends a data stream to the client, which interprets it in a format appropriate for the client's display capabilities.

The TCP/IP protocol suite uses the client/server model extensively. Each client application establishes a connection to a server, and related processing occurs on each platform. For instance, an FTP data transfer occurs when the client FTP program interacts with the server FTP program. The two programs communicate, passing data and control information between them. Distributed display is also common with display-oriented applications such as Telnet and HTTP. Because the client system's display capabilities may not match those assumed by the server process, the client may modify the data stream sent by the server before displaying it.

In a peer environment, either system may be the client or the server. In fact, the roles may change several times during a connection between two systems. The TCP/IP protocol suite supports such interaction and role switching.

NETWORK PROTOCOLS

A network protocol is a structured method of enabling communications between two or more computer systems. It consists of a set of rules, processes, and procedures that enable the communication. For communication to be successful, the systems involved in the network must agree upon many aspects of the communication process, such as the type of physical transmission to be used, the error recovery and correction to be used, the pacing, and the application services to be used. All protocols handle the same issues, differing only in how they implement the solutions.

Most protocols are proprietary. For example, IBM's Systems Network Architecture (SNA) has become the most widely implemented Wide Area Network (WAN) protocol in business, and Novell's Internetwork Packet Exchange (IPX), the foundation of the Netware protocol suite, has become the most popular Local Area Network (LAN) protocol. Other protocols, such as TCP/IP, are standards based. Unlike SNA and IPX, no one vendor or organization controls TCP/IP; rather, the people in the TCP/IP community have input to and can influence the decision-making process. As a result, TCP/IP is widely implemented on many different hardware and software platforms.

The Open Systems Interconnection (OSI) Protocol

Although this book is about the TCP/IP protocol, you'll find it easier to understand with a little background in other protocols and how they compare. The Open Systems Interconnection (OSI) model is the standard to which all other protocols are compared. The OSI model clearly delineates the functions of a network protocol, enabling better understanding of the inner processing of network communications.

Like TCP/IP, OSI is a standards-based protocol. Although never attaining the critical mass in the marketplace that its founders expected, OSI is popular with multinational organizations and is especially important in standards definition and as a model for other protocols. Some of the protocols and applications within OSI have become more widely used than OSI itself. Notable examples are X.400 (a directory service) and X.500 (an e-mail service).

OSI is the model to which other protocols are compared. The OSI model consists of seven layers that encompass the requirements for a protocol. These layers constitute the *protocol stack*. Figure 1.4 illustrates the model and the component services within it.

FIGURE 1.4
The OSI Reference Model

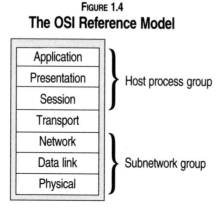

The OSI model implements a framework to provide communications between any two or more systems that use the same model. The model's seven layers are an abstraction. All protocols must perform the same services and functions, although other protocols may have different names for these functions and perform them at different levels.

The lowest layer, the physical layer, handles bit transmission between nodes in the network. This layer defines the attributes of the physical network. The functions in this layer include interfacing with the transmission media (the cabling), encoding the data signal, defining the allowable range of voltage on the media, and defining connector sizes, shapes, and pinouts.

The data link layer maintains a reliable link between adjacent nodes on the network. The data link layer deals only with adjacent nodes; another layer (the transport layer) ensures reliable transmission from end to end. The data link layer assumes that the physical layer is error prone and that the data link layer must itself handle errors. This layer also performs bridging functions. Bridging is a technique for linking LANs; it can also be used to logically isolate or separate networks ("Physical Connections, Routing, and Bridging" in Chapter 3 covers bridging in detail). The data link layer includes such functions as providing the reliable mechanism for packet delivery, inserting source and destination addresses in the data packet, and providing error control and recovery.

The network layer performs routing functions — that is, it establishes a path for the packet from the source to the destination. Routing links LANs and provides routes for TCP/IP packets to find other networks (routing is covered at length in "Physical Connections, Routing, and Bridging" in Chapter 3). The network layer provides networking functions such as routing and network congestion control.

The transport layer provides reliable delivery of messages originating in the application layer. The transport layer is similar to the data link layer in that it delivers packets, but the data link layer delivers only between adjacent nodes on a network, while the transport layer delivers packets from the source to the destination. The transport layer includes such functions as packet segmenting and reassembly.

The session layer establishes and terminates process-to-process communication between nodes in a network. The nodes could be clients, servers, or peers. The session layer also provides translation and synchronization functions.

The presentation layer establishes the form in which data is exchanged between nodes. This layer provides data manipulation functions, including data compression and encryption.

The seventh and highest layer, the application layer, is where user interaction occurs. The application layer provides end-to-end services such as virtual terminal access, file transfers, and mail exchange.

The OSI model's seven layers are considered to consist of two main groupings. The three lowest layers, the physical, data link, and network layers, are the subnetwork group. The top three layers, the session, presentation, and application layers, are the host process group. The transport layer is the lowest end-to-end layer in the model and divides the two groups.

Vital to an understanding of the OSI model (or any protocol, really) is the concept of layers communicating with each other. An application communicates down through the protocol stack from the application layer, where the user interacts, to the physical layer, where the data is actually converted to electrical signals. The electrical signals are sent across the media (the cabling) to the physical layer at the destination node (or system). In the destination protocol stack, the process is repeated in reverse order — the electrical signals are received at the physical layer and sent up through the protocol stack to the application layer.

Although this process explains the application-layer-to-application-layer interaction, another important communication process also takes place. Each layer on the source node communicates with the corresponding layer on the destination node. In other words, the presentation layer on the source node communicates with the presentation layer on the destination node, the session layer on the source communicates with the session layer at the destination, and so on. This communication doesn't occur directly, but rather through the packet as it traverses the protocol stack. Each source layer adds to the packet unique information that is read and used by the corresponding layer on the destination system. For example, the physical layers exchange electrical signals that indicate the type of physical connection used, such as RS-232 or V.35. The data link layers exchange information such as the "burned in" address of an Ethernet card. The network layers exchange source and destination address information. Realize that the roles of the stations will be reversed during communication: The initial sending station will receive packets from the original destination station that indicate successful packet transmission.

The TCP/IP Protocol Stack

As I've mentioned, not all protocols implement their layers and services in the same manner as the OSI model. The TCP/IP protocol stack is a 4-layer stack. Figure 1.5 shows how TCP/IP's layers correspond to the OSI model. As you can see, the layers are different, but the overall functions of the TCP/IP stack are the same.

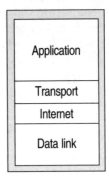

FIGURE 1.5
Comparison of OSI and TCP/IP Protocol Stacks

The TCP/IP application layer provides the interaction between TCP/IP services such as Telnet or FTP and the rest of the stack. This interaction takes the form of the user presentation, such as displaying a screen or accepting commands for a file transfer session. The transport layer controls the end-to-end data transfer. This layer comprises the Transmission Control Protocol portion of the TCP/IP stack and provides for accurate and reliable packet delivery.

The Internet layer links the logical network (addresses, system names, and services) with the physical network (the wires and data communication devices). The logical network is composed of the nodes that can be reached through routing or bridging; the physical network is composed of the wiring, hubs, and concentrators. The logical network uses the physical network to deliver information between the nodes. The Internet layer encompasses the IP portion of the TCP/IP protocol stack and provides routing for packets.

The data link layer provides the interface to the network hardware, including the electrical signals on the physical media. TCP/IP does not need a specific type of network — the protocol is independent of the underlying physical protocol and media.

The SNA Protocol Stack

In contrast to both OSI and TCP/IP, SNA is a 5-layer protocol stack. Figure 1.6 illustrates the SNA protocol stack in comparison with the OSI stack. The figure appears to show a 7-layer SNA stack, but notice that the application and physical layers are in italics. Although analogous to OSI's application and physical layers, these layers are not part of the SNA protocol stack; their functions are performed in other layers or outside the SNA model.

FIGURE 1.6
Comparison of OSI and SNA Protocol Stacks

OSI protocol stack

SNA protocol stack

OSI protocol stack
Application
Presentation
Session
Transport
Network
Data link
Physical

SNA protocol stack
Application
Function management
Data flow control
Transmission control
Path control
Data link control
Physical

The physical layer missing from the SNA model is not encompassed by any other SNA layer. SNA implementation assumes that the physical layer functions and components are in place and made available to the stack. SNA uses the data flow control and path control layers to provide packet sequencing and reassembly services (similar to OSI's network layer) and to control data transmission over a physical link (similar to the OSI data link layer). The transmission control layer provides several of the same functions as OSI's transport layer, such as session level pacing and sequencing of data units.

SNA's data flow control layer is similar to the OSI session layer in that both deal with synchronization issues such as data flow interruption. They differ, however, in exception reporting and security, which are handled in the session layer in OSI and in the transmission control layer in SNA. The SNA function management layer encompasses OSI's presentation layer and portions of its application layer. OSI (and TCP/IP) define a set of application services for virtual terminal access, file transfers, and other services, whereas the SNA protocol stack does not define application-level services. Both the OSI presentation layer and the SNA function management layer provide services for session establishment and disconnection.

The IPX Protocol Stack
Netware is a network operating system created by Novell in the early 1980s. Unlike a networking protocol, which uses an operating system for system-level services, a network operating system provides a complete environment, including system-level services such as file and print sharing (Netware's claim to fame), e-mail, and messaging, as well as other services for local and remote users. This is an important distinction — Netware provides services for which protocols such as OSI, TCP/IP, and SNA rely on the underlying operating system.

Netware uses Internetwork Packet Exchange/Sequenced Packet Exchange (IPX/SPX) as a networking protocol under the network operating system. Because Netware is a network operating system and not a protocol, it provides different services at different levels than the OSI protocol.

Figure 1.7 compares the layers of the Netware operating system to the OSI protocol. A server responding to client requests uses the Netware Core Protocol. SPX is the transport protocol; it supplements the datagram (packet) service provided by the underlying network layer protocol. SPX guarantees delivery, sequences packets, detects errors, and suppresses packet duplication.

FIGURE 1.7

Comparison of OSI and the Netware Operating System

OSI protocol stack   Netware operating system

OSI protocol stack	Netware operating system
Application	Netware Core Protocol
Presentation	
Session	
Transport	SPX
Network	IPX
Data link	Physical media
Physical	

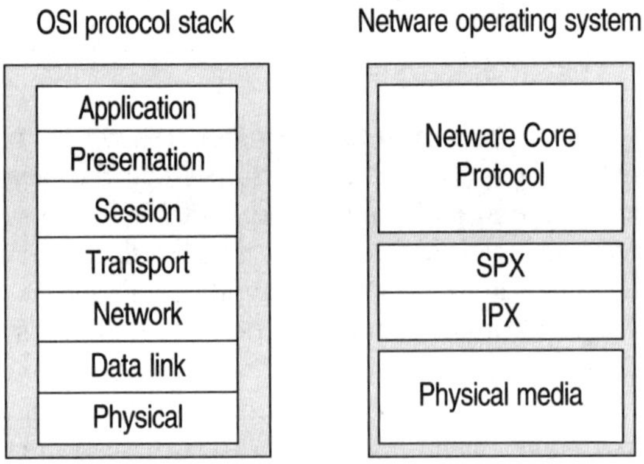

IPX is the network layer protocol used to transfer data between the server and clients. IPX supports addressing and routing in a Netware network, but it uses addresses differently than does IP. An IPX network uses the data link and physical layers to provide node addressing rather than the IP method of assigning addresses and using Address Resolution Protocol to determine the physical address. Consequently, the abstraction that exists in a TCP/IP network, which uses a logical address instead of the physical address of the network interface card, does not exist in an IPX network. (The TCP/IP addressing method is covered in Chapter 2 under "Internet Protocol Addresses.")

The AnyNet Framework

AnyNet is the AS/400 implementation of IBM's Multiprotocol Transport Networking (MPTN) architecture. AnyNet enables applications written for one network protocol to be used over other network protocols.

Multiple-protocol environments are difficult to integrate. Proprietary protocols are not designed to interoperate. Although you can enable connectivity between different proprietary protocols using gateways, they can be expensive and difficult to manage. For example, consider an environment in which IBM AS/400 systems and Digital Equipment Corporation (DEC) VAX systems coexist. The AS/400 might be running SNA and the DEC VAX could be running DECNet. You could use a gateway to allow the AS/400 and the VAX to communicate. But add a Hewlett Packard HP9000 running TCP/IP, and now you'd need three gateways to provide complete connectivity. Adding a fourth host with a different protocol would require six gateways, and so on.

You might instead consider using TCP/IP (or OSI) on all the hosts. Although at first glance this may seem to be the best solution, some hosts in the environment (especially older, legacy systems) may not be able to use TCP/IP, or the decision may be made not to purchase TCP/IP based on cost or other factors. Another consideration is whether the existing network infrastructure supports TCP/IP. Although the protocol does not require a specific network type, vendors have not implemented TCP/IP on all devices — it is not available on IBM 5494 remote workstation controllers, for example. If the existing network is an SNA network that supports distributed computing between AS/400 systems, that network might have been designed for a specific set of applications, none of which support TCP/IP. The cost of changing such a network to provide the necessary support might well be prohibitive. And even if it's not, making a wholesale change to a networking environment does not give you the flexibility to use the more correct — and far easier — approach of gradually implementing the new networking protocol.

The MPTN architecture — and its AS/400 implementation, AnyNet — lets you access applications regardless of the underlying network protocol. MPTN supports the following implementation techniques:

- SNA over TCP/IP
- Sockets over SNA
- NetBEUI over SNA
- Sockets over NetBIOS

With MPTN, you can develop "best of breed" applications without concern about which network protocol is being used. MPTN also lets you deploy existing applications to new locations on the network.

AnyNet provides MPTN capabilities essentially by encapsulating one protocol inside another. The most important AnyNet encapsulations are SNA over TCP/IP and sockets over SNA. Figure 1.8 illustrates how SNA is encapsulated over TCP/IP.

FIGURE 1.8

Encapsulation of SNA over TCP/IP

Header information	TCP/IP packet data portion	Trailer information
	SNA data contained within the TCP/IP packet	

Support for SNA over TCP/IP is important when you need to use legacy applications over a TCP/IP network. SNA over TCP/IP is most commonly used with Client Access/400. This encapsulation enables a Client Access/400 workstation to communicate over a TCP/IP network while providing full Client Access functionality. Client Access/400 is only one example of SNA over TCP/IP support; any SNA application, including APPC applications, can use AnyNet support.

Encapsulation of sockets over SNA lets Unix-like socket programs communicate over an SNA network. Socket programs implement program-to-program communications (i.e., direct communication between a program on a source system and one on a target system), which is widely used by client/server applications to integrate client and server activities. Socket programming is a mainstay in the TCP/IP world, especially on Unix systems, although most computer systems that support a TCP/IP protocol stack also support sockets. AnyNet enables socket programs to communicate over a legacy SNA network.

AnyNet support provides clear advantages in a multiprotocol environment. However, these advantages are not without cost. Encapsulation adds overhead because the packets of one protocol must be bundled and unbundled from the data portion of another. AnyNet is essentially a method of combining protocol usage. Before you decide to use AnyNet, you should closely examine your need for it and determine whether moving to one particular protocol (with the possible resulting requirement to rewrite applications) might be a more efficient way to provide the necessary interconnectivity.

AS/400 TCP/IP IMPLEMENTATIONS

TCP/IP has a long history on the AS/400. When introduced with V1R2 in the late 1980s, TCP/IP was written in Pascal ported from an IBM VM-type system. That early version of the protocol "ran above the MI layer." A discussion of the MI layer is important at this point, especially to understand the strides IBM has made with TCP/IP since V3R1.

The MI layer is a (somewhat inaccurate) reference to a dividing point between the operating system and applications. *MI* refers to the Machine Interface — the programming language in which the operating system was written. Newer versions of OS/400 are written in C++, so the MI reference is a bit outdated but still illustrative of the placement of TCP/IP within OS/400.

The Licensed Internal Code (LIC) resides below the MI layer. The LIC interacts with the operating system and the hardware and can access those resources directly, whereas programs that exist above the MI layer must undergo additional processing to access operating system services and hardware resources. This "translation" process between application programs and the operating system services and hardware resources adds overhead. Although this additional processing is normal and expected for application programs, it's undesirable for processes such as terminal access and file transfers, which must interact closely with the operating system and hardware. Such processes must exist below the MI layer for optimum performance.

Until V3R1, TCP/IP on the AS/400 was written to be processed above the MI layer, making it essentially another application that competed for resources. It's not surprising, then, that the performance of those early versions could not match that of SNA, which was written to be executed below the layer. A secondary reason for TCP/IP's relatively poor performance was that it was written in Pascal and ported from a mainframe. Neither Pascal nor VM architecture is native to the AS/400, so porting-related issues further inhibited TCP/IP's performance.

This situation changed with V3R1 of OS/400, which brought extensive functional improvements to the TCP/IP protocol stack, removed some of its restrictions, and increased its performance on the AS/400 eightfold. The performance of TCP/IP is now equivalent to that of SNA.

One restriction removed from TCP/IP was the 160-session limit. Before V3R1, only 160 sessions were available on any AS/400, regardless of the machine's size, amount of memory, or processor speed. This restriction was part of the TCP/IP architecture and its implementation as a viable AS/400 communication protocol. The 160-session limit was particularly a problem for large shops that communicated with non-AS/400 hosts. Although Telnet requires only one session, FTP requires two: one for data and another for control. Consequently, a user accessing a host using TCP/IP could often use three sessions for one connection. V3R1 and subsequent implementations of TCP/IP have removed this restriction.

The other major early restriction was the 16 MB file-size limit for information transfers, which limited both FTP file transfers and Simple Mail Transport Protocol (SMTP) e-mail transfers. Because large files could not be transferred, the ability of AS/400 installations to fully implement TCP/IP was hampered. Again, V3R1 and later versions of TCP/IP removed this restriction.

V3R1 also added functions to the AS/400 implementation of TCP/IP. The early versions of TCP/IP were part of the TCP/IP Connectivity Utilities Licensed Program Product (LPP), which was optional and had to be purchased separately. Pre-V3R1 versions had the following components:

- The TCP/IP protocol stack and configuration support for TCP/IP
- Pascal-based Transmission Control Protocol (TCP) and User Datagram Protocol (UDP) APIs
- The NETSTAT command (for obtaining network status information)
- The PING command (for the Packet InterNet Groper process, a TCP/IP-based service for determining whether a remote system is reachable across a network)
- A Telnet client and server (for virtual terminal access)
- An FTP client and server (for file transfers)
- A Line Printer Requester (or Line Printer Remote — LPR) client (for printing in a TCP/IP network)
- A Line Printer Daemon (LPD) server (for processing incoming print requests from the TCP/IP network)
- An implementation of SMTP (for e-mail)

V3R1 and later TCP/IP is part of the operating system and has the following components:

- The TCP/IP protocol stack and configuration support for TCP/IP
- The NETSTAT command
- The PING command
- A Simple Network Management Protocol (SNMP) agent for use in an SNMP-managed-environment network, and the configuration support for SNMP
- AnyNet support for SNA (APPC) application execution over a TCP/IP network
- AnyNet support for TCP/IP socket application execution over an SNA network, including IBM-supplied socket programs such as FTP, LPR, LPD, and SMTP
- The C programming language sockets API

The V3R1 and later TCP/IP Connectivity Utilities LPP is now included with OS/400 at no charge and contains the following components:

- A Telnet client and server
- An FTP client and server
- An LPR client

- An LPD server
- An implementation of SMTP
- The Pascal TCP/IP API

The changes accompanying V3R2 (for CISC systems) and V3R7 (for RISC) brought even more function to the TCP/IP suite of applications. The changes in these releases of the operating system and the TCP/IP Connectivity Utilities LPP include

- HTTP for serving World Wide Web pages to TCP/IP network users with a Web browser
- A 5250/Hypertext Markup Language (HTML) gateway to translate standard 5250 "green screens" to HTML pages viewable with a Web browser (this feature is also known as the Workstation Gateway)
- User-defined exit points for security with FTP and the Workstation Gateway
- Anonymous FTP access
- A Post Office Protocol Version 3 (POP3) server for serving e-mail to POP3-compliant clients
- Serial Line Internet Protocol (SLIP) support for dial-in and dial-out access with the TCP/IP protocol

Continuing the expansion of TCP/IP on the AS/400, with more features targeting security in general and secure commerce in particular, additional HTTP server function, and enhanced routing capabilities, V4R1 signifies IBM's enduring interest in and support of the e-business arena and the continued move to RISC technology. Enhancements available with V4R1 include

- Electronic commerce security with Secure Sockets Layer and public key cryptography and encryption (128-bit data encryption for use in the U.S. and Canada and 40-bit data encryption for export)
- A firewall implemented on the Integrated PC Server (IPCS) that provides both AS/400 and network security. Features of the IPCS firewall include
  - IP packet filtering
  - proxy servers for HTTP, FTP, and Gopher (a tool to access textual information)
  - a Secure Sockets (SOCKS) server (for disguising the internal address of a client when it accesses information on a network such as the Internet)

- — a Domain Name Service server
- — a mail server
- — security logging and monitoring capabilities
- Additional HTTP server capabilities with support for multiple HTTP server instances and user authentication with Access Control Lists
- The use of a Web browser to administer the Internet Connection Server, the IPCS-based firewall, and network stations
- Routing support with the Routing Information Protocol (RIP)
- Enhanced Net.Data support with the Web Registry and flat file support

Chapter 2

TCP/IP Services

Well-understood services, including well-defined data streams and methods of processing, enable TCP/IP to be used on many systems with complete inter-operability. Adherence to the standards for these services is what makes TCP/IP so popular. Although vendors may extend the services in TCP/IP (IBM's Client Access Telnet processing, for instance, provides a fixed work-station ID, unlike other vendors' Telnet implementations), all vendors support the same set of basic services.

The standard TCP/IP protocol suite includes application services that address the information needs of most organizations, and almost all vendors' implementations embrace the features of virtual terminal access, file transfers, mail transfer, mail access, network management, and printing. This chapter helps you identify the requirements of these common services and understand the behind-the-scenes processing and data flow associated with them.

The TCP/IP services discussed here are the most common and widely used. Other services may exist that provide the same or similar function, but not all vendors embrace other services. For instance, rlogin (remote login) is a terminal access method, but it is not as widespread as Telnet and is not sup-ported on the AS/400. Although the application services discussed in this chapter are the user's interface to the TCP/IP protocol, the information pro-vided is not intended for users. Rather, this information gives the system administrator background for understanding the processing of the services and for troubleshooting.

VIRTUAL TERMINAL ACCESS — TELNET

Accessing other systems with a terminal session was one of the first capabilities demonstrated over an early version of the Internet. Although that implementa-tion was not Telnet, it clearly indicated that virtual terminal access would be an important part of the TCP/IP protocol suite.

Telnet is simply a connection from a client across a network to a well-known port on a server. The user enters the Telnet (or TN, TN3270, TN5250, or similar) command, and the underlying TCP/IP protocol suite handles the rest.

Although Telnet is well defined, it is not necessarily network efficient. When the user enters a keystroke at the terminal or PC, the operating system delivers that keystroke to the client Telnet program, which sends it across the network to the server. The server's Telnet program echoes the keystroke back to the client and then sends it on to the server's application program. Although this character-mode method of processing keystrokes has a distinct advantage with applications that require validation of each key pressed, that advantage may well be overshadowed, especially over slow lines, by the method's inefficiency and large network bandwidth requirements. Block-mode Telnet clients, such as TN5250 and TN3270, send keystrokes in a block rather than singly, reducing bandwidth requirements and increasing efficiency.

Telnet involves much more than a simple connection. Telnet uses three services or features to effect a connection between a client and a server: Network Virtual Terminal (NVT) definition, option definition or specification, and option negotiation.

Network Virtual Terminal Definition

Telnet's NVT definition service defines an NVT model to provide a standard interface to the target system or server. The NVT model is a theoretical model that symbolizes a standard network terminal. Both the client and the server systems convert their data streams to NVT format, so any type of system that supports Telnet can communicate with any other system that supports Telnet.

For instance, the NVT construct lets a Digital Equipment Corporation VT100 terminal implementation (a standard in the TCP/IP world) access an IBM AS/400, even though the two systems have nothing in common. Both systems change their data streams to the NVT format (also known as *canonical form*) for transmission across the network. The target client or server program then translates the NVT data back to its own proprietary format. Figure 2.1 illustrates the process of NVT format conversion that occurs during a Telnet session.

FIGURE 2.1
Network Virtual Terminal Format Conversion

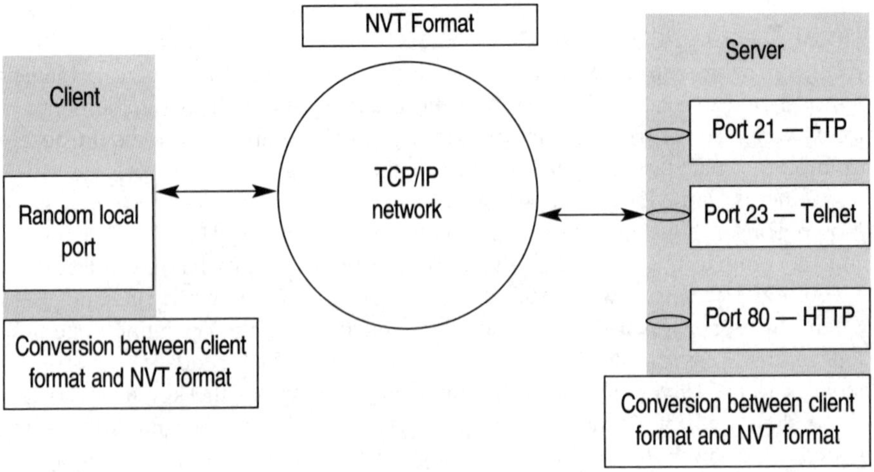

Option Definition

Telnet's option definition feature lets the client and server agree on the options to be used between them. Both systems must agree on such options as the character code to be used (e.g., ASCII or EBCDIC) and the control characters to be used to interrupt the Telnet process and to erase characters and lines.

The client and the server Telnet programs identify specific options they would like to use for the connection. Two negotiation requests and two responses are available: DO, DON'T, WILL, and WON'T. DO requests the other system to use a certain option; DON'T requests the other system not to use a specified option. WILL or WON'T is sent as an acknowledgment of a particular DO or DON'T request. WILL indicates the program will perform the requested option; WON'T indicates the program will not (or cannot) perform the option.

This negotiation is critical, especially when older clients (or servers) interact with newer programs. When a newer Telnet implementation requests an option unavailable to an older implementation, the older version simply returns a WON'T response. Option definition allows different versions of Telnet client and server programs to coexist. Because all Telnet implementations understand the basic NVT format, communication can occur, although it might not be as efficient as if the client and server understood all of each other's options.

Option Negotiation

Option definition and negotiation work hand in hand. When the service is established, the defined options (those that the client and server can support) are negotiated. Both the client and the server have the right to negotiate the options for a Telnet session. The right of both to negotiate is known as *symmetry*.

An option is implemented as part of a Telnet command. Telnet commands consist of at least a two-octet sequence. (An octet is an 8-bit byte; *octet* is a more precise term than *byte* because the ASCII format uses 7 bits for a byte, whereas the AS/400's EBCDIC data stream uses 8 bits.) The first octet is always the Interpret As Command (IAC) code, which indicates the bytes that follow are to be interpreted as a command and executed accordingly. The second octet is the command itself, implemented as a code. Table 2.1 lists the decimal representations of the Telnet command codes (which are actually sent in hexadecimal format).

TABLE 2.1
Telnet Commands

Command	Code	Description
SE	240	End of negotiation parameters
NOP	241	No operation
Data Mark	242	Marks the end of urgent processing caused by the Synch mechanism
*Break	243	BRK NVT function
*Interrupt Process	244	IP NVT function
*Abort Output	245	AO NVT function
*Are You There	246	AYT NVT function
*Erase Character	247	EC NVT function
*Erase Line	248	EL NVT function
*Go Ahead	249	GA NVT function
SB	250	Option subnegotiation to follow
WILL	251	WILL perform the option
WON'T	252	WON'T (or can't) perform the option
DO	253	DO perform the option
DON'T	254	DON'T perform the option
IAC	255	Interpret the following as a command

*Specifies a command that is actually an NVT function, standard in all vendors' Telnet implementations. These commands execute functions such as stopping the transmission, erasing characters or lines, and continuing the transmission after it has been halted.

Some commands have an optional third octet, which is the option to be negotiated when the command regards negotiation. Table 2.2 shows the Telnet options that can be negotiated.

TABLE 2.2
Telnet Options

Option	Name
0	Binary transmission
1	Echo
2	Reconnection
3	Suppress go ahead
4	Approximate message size negotiation
5	Status
6	Timing mark

continued

TABLE **2.2** *CONTINUED*

Option	Name
7	Remote controlled transmission and echo
8	Output line width
9	Output page size
10	Output carriage return disposition
11	Output horizontal tab stops
12	Output horizontal tab disposition
13	Output formfeed disposition
14	Output vertical tab stops
15	Output vertical tab disposition
16	Output linefeed disposition
17	Extended ASCII
18	Logout
19	Byte macro
20	Data entry terminal
21	SUPDUP
22	SUPDUP output
23	Send location
24	Terminal type
25	End of record
26	TACACS user identification
27	Output marking
28	Terminal location number
29	Telnet 3270 regime
30	X.3 PAD
31	Window size negotiation
32	Terminal speed
33	Remote flow control
34	Line mode
35	X display locations
255	Extended options list

A sample negotiation might be

255 253 24 IBM-5251-11 (IAC DO TERMINAL-TYPE-IS IBM-5251-11)

which means that one system is instructing the other to use the IBM 5251
Model 11 terminal type. The other system might respond

255 252 24 IBM-5251-11 (IAC CAN'T TERMINAL-TYPE-IS IBM-5251-11)

meaning that it can't accommodate that terminal type.

Telnet's value derives from its ability to embrace many vendors' client implementations and provide a common method of access to multiple servers. The NVT model provides a level of abstraction that enables clients and servers to communicate, regardless of the vendor or the age of the client or server program. And because Telnet can define and negotiate options, the client and the server will perform at the highest level of efficiency at which they can agree. Although much of the attention paid to the TCP/IP protocol suite recently has focused on graphical user interfaces, such as HTTP for browsing Web pages, Telnet will continue to be used as an interface to server-resident applications.

FILE TRANSFERS

File transfer was another early application on the Internet and remains an important method of sharing information between computer systems. As the term implies, file transfer involves transferring complete files from one system to another using a method such as File Transfer Protocol (FTP) in the TCP/IP world or SNA Distribution Services in the IBM SNA world. File transfers are used to update files, synchronize databases, and satisfy many other needs for information sharing.

File Transfer Protocol (FTP)

The most widely used TCP/IP file transfer service is File Transfer Protocol (FTP). The ubiquity of FTP, which is part of every implementation of the TCP/IP protocol suite, lets systems of different types share information with little regard to the underlying file structure. The tradeoff is that FTP must use a low common denominator of file formats, which can be a distinct disadvantage when one of the systems has a well-developed file structure such as the AS/400's.

FTP is a relatively simple protocol. Unlike other TCP/IP applications, FTP requires two connections between the client and the server processes. The first connection, which uses well-known port 21 on the server, is initiated by the client and controls the FTP process by exchanging commands between the client and server systems. The second connection, also client initiated, contacts the server using well-known port 20 and is used for the data portion of the file exchange.

Figure 2.2 illustrates the FTP connection between a client and server. The client decides which local port to use for the data portion of the file transfer process and passes that information to the server to ensure synchronization of the transfer. Interestingly, FTP uses a base NVT implementation of Telnet to pass information across the control connection.

FIGURE 2.2
FTP Connection Between a Client and Server

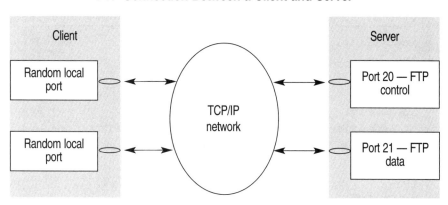

FTP is essentially an interactive process, although it can be executed in batch by redirecting the input for the process from a file. A user initiates an FTP connection by using the FTP command and (usually) specifying the server with which to connect (specifying the server is not required when an FTP OPEN command is used). The user then signs on to the server (actually, to the server's FTP program or process) and issues FTP commands that control the transfer operation. Usually only a few commands are needed, but FTP provides a complete set of commands to access the server and control the transfer. The user usually issues PUT or GET commands to transfer files to or from the server. The user may also change the data representation — translating between ASCII and EBCDIC, for example. To end the connection, the user usually executes a QUIT command, which ends both the server and client FTP process.

Commands fall into two main categories: client commands and server commands. Client commands are fairly standard across implementations of FTP. Vendors, however, extend their implementation of FTP through the use of server commands. The AS/400, for example, has CRTL (Create Library), CRTF (Create File), and RMVM (Remove Member) FTP commands to adapt the standard FTP process to the AS/400's unique library/file/member structure. Not all systems recognize all commands, especially when the command does not work in the context of the other system. Table 2.3 lists some of the more standard FTP commands. This is not an exhaustive list, and server commands depend on the server's implementation.

TABLE 2.3
Standard FTP Commands

Command	Description
open <server>	Open a connection to a server
close	End a connection to a server
quit	End the FTP process
user <user id>	Specify the user ID
pass <password>	Specify the password
get <fromfile> <tofile>	Transfer a file from the server to the client
put <fromfile <tofile>	Transfer a file from the client to the server
ascii	Transfer the file in ASCII format
ebcdic	Transfer the file in EBCDIC format
binary (or image)	Transfer the file with no translation
cd <directory>	Change directories on the server
lcd <directory>	Change the local (client) working directory
pwd	Show the present working directory
ls (or dir)	Display the contents of the server directory
mget (and mput) <file spec>	Multiple gets and puts with wildcard characters
quote <command>	Send a command to the server
mkdir <directory>	Make a directory on the server
rmdir <directory>	Remove a directory on the server
type <type code>	Representation type (ASCII, EBCDIC, image)
help <topic>	Show help
server <command>	Issue a server FTP process command
dele <file>	Delete file on the server
appe <file>	Append the transferred file to an existing file
verbose	Use verbose mode (see the messages)

FTP issues return codes or replies to each command entered, even though the user usually doesn't see commands the client FTP process sends to the server process. When the user enters a command, the server FTP process acknowledges the outcome of the command whether it was valid and executed or invalid or unable to be executed. It's interesting to issue the VERBOSE command after invoking FTP and watch the message interaction between the client and the server.

Other file transfer or information sharing mechanisms in the TCP/IP protocol suite are Trivial File Transfer Protocol (TFTP) and the Network File System (NFS).

Trivial File Transfer Protocol (TFTP)

Trivial File Transfer Protocol (TFTP) was developed because full-blown implementations of FTP are more than is needed for certain applications. The protocol name does not indicate that the information being shared is trivial, but
that the FTP implementation is "trivial" compared to a complete FTP package.

A complete implementation of FTP is fairly large for some applications of
information sharing. For example, "thin" clients such as network stations (or
network computers), which must download their operating system from a
server, don't require all the bells and whistles of FTP, such as the ability for a
user to sign on or the ability to change data representations. Rather, such
clients must simply be able to transfer information between two nodes on a
network. Thin clients commonly use TFTP, as do X-stations (special, graphically oriented workstations with multiple windows) and data communications
equipment such as routers.

You'll recall that communication between a client and a server with a
complete implementation of FTP requires two connections, whereas TFTP uses
one connection. Furthermore, TFTP uses unreliable User Datagram Protocol
(UDP) over IP rather than reliable TCP over IP. UDP is unreliable because it
lacks TCP's error checking and recovery capability, using instead time-outs and
retransmissions to ensure that data is transferred. TFTP also uses five types of
packets, unlike FTP, which uses the same packet structure regardless of the
action being performed. The TFTP packet type depends on the action being
performed and is indicated by a two-byte op code at the front of the packet: 1
(Read Request), 2 (Write Request), 3 (Data packet), 4 (Acknowledgment
packet), or 5 (Error packet).

A client initiates a connection by issuing a Read (or Write) Request packet
to well-known port 69 of the server. The request includes the name of the file
to be read or written, terminated by the 0 (zero) character. The packet's Mode
field contains one of three codes: a code for NETASCII (a special form of the
ASCII character set), one for raw data, or one for mail. TFTP is not often used
to transmit mail, but when it is, the mail code indicates that the data is to be
sent to a user rather than to a system. The Mode field is also terminated by a 0.

When each 512-byte block is received, the TFTP client acknowledges it
with an Acknowledgment packet that includes a block number. Once a connection has been made via a Read or Write Request, further communication
regarding that connection is identified by using the block number. If a problem
occurs in the communication, an Error packet is sent containing an error code
and error message.

Network File System (NFS)

The NFS allows information on one system to be shared with other systems in
the network but accessed as if the data resided on the local system. Any system
that completely implements NFS can function as a client or a server — that is,

the system can allow its file system to be mounted on another system, and it can mount remote file systems locally. The operating system used by either the client or server system is relatively unimportant — the client accesses the server system using the client's native file management commands. Unlike most other TCP/IP services, not all systems implement NFS completely — the AS/400, for example, for years could be an NFS server but not a client.

Sun Microsystems developed NFS based on the IP and UDP protocols. Sun also developed three modules that reside above the IP and UDP layers: Remote Procedure Call (RPC), External Data Representation (XDR), and Network File System. The RPC module establishes a logical IP connection between the client and server at the IP and UDP layers. The XDR module describes and encodes data between the client and the server to implement the presentation layer services as defined in the OSI model ("The Open Systems Interconnection (OSI) Protocol" in Chapter 1 provides details about the OSI model). The NFS layer defines the file structures of the client and the server. The importance of this layered design is that neither the client nor the server needs to know details of the other's file system — RPC handles the communication, and XDR handles the representation of the data.

Custom-written programs can use the RPC and XDR layers to provide the same encoding and data representation functions used in the overall NFS application. RPC in particular is a target for hackers (see "RPC Security" for more information on this exposure), and many network managers do not allow RPC or XDR on their networks.

RPC Security

RPC is a big security risk because the default authorization for RPC is none. For authorization to be required, it must be implemented on the client that issues the RPC request. The server must also be able to understand the client's authorization scheme and accommodate the authorization request.

Even when RPC does provide some level of authorization through the client, it has no provisions for access control — it doesn't provide resource security at the file level, for example. The server application must provide access control. The server application must also take the responsibility for validating an incoming connection (if such validation is necessary). This is usually done with an application password that the server application uses to determine the level of access to be granted to the incoming application.

Mail Transfer — Simple Mail Transfer Protocol (SMTP)

From the standpoints of bandwidth and function, e-mail is one of the Internet's "killer apps." In fact, the two applications on the Internet that use the most bandwidth are HTTP and Simple Mail Transfer Protocol (SMTP), the TCP/IP-standard tool for exchanging e-mail between servers.

Another mail protocol, Post Office Protocol 3 (POP3, discussed in the next section), is used to transfer mail between a server and a client. Most Internet mail client software packages used for dial-in access to the Internet (such as Netscape Navigator and Eudora) have settings for both SMTP and POP3 servers.

TCP/IP-based e-mail using SMTP operates in the traditional client/server model. Like Telnet and FTP, a client SMTP process issues a request to a server SMTP process. However, SMTP must provide for mail storage when the user for whom the mail is intended is not online. Other TCP/IP-based applications work on a principle of direct communication. SMTP provides for direct interaction but also has a spooling component to hold the mail until it is requested.

SMTP is also unique in that it does not care about the format of the mail message. The SMTP process is concerned solely with transferring mail from one system to another — nothing in the process specifies anything about the presentation of the mail to the user, how the system accepts mail from the user, how the mail is to be stored, or how frequently the mail is checked to send messages. These processes are part of the mail client (for user interaction) or the underlying operating system (for mail storage and timing issues).

SMTP sends the information in human-readable text. Network managers beware — anyone can read unencrypted SMTP traffic over a network. The transfer mechanism is reminiscent of FTP, extending even to similar commands between the two applications.

The SMTP command set is simple, as Table 2.4 shows. SMTP commands need not be sent in uppercase, but they often are.

Table 2.4
SMTP Commands

Command	Description
HELO <domain>	Identify the sender to the receiver
MAIL FROM: <user address>	Deliver the mail to the mailbox
RCPT TO: <user address>	Identify the mail recipient
DATA	Mail information (the message)
RSET	Abort the current mail transaction
SEND FROM: <user address>	Deliver mail
SOML FROM: <user address>	Send or mail

continued

TABLE 2.4 CONTINUED

Command	Description
SAML FROM: <user address>	Send and mail
VRFY <info>	Verify that the user exists
EXPN <info>	Verify a mailing list exists
HELP	Send help information
NOOP	No operation
QUIT	Send acknowledgment, then end the session
TURN	Switch sender/receiver roles (not often used)

Interaction between the sending and receiving systems is straightforward. The sender establishes a TCP/IP connection with the receiver and waits for the receiver to send a 220 Ready For Mail message. The sender then sends a HELO command to identify itself to the receiver, and the receiver returns a 250 OK message. Next, the sender sends a MAIL command followed by a series of RCPT commands to identify the recipients of the mail message. Each recipient must be known to the receiving system. If a recipient is unknown, the receiver answers with the message 550 No Such User Here and returns the e-mail message to the sending system.

The sender then issues a DATA command, which the receiver answers with a 354 Start Mail Input reply. The receiver also sends the termination characters that should be used to identify the end of the message: a carriage return/line feed, a period, and another carriage return/line feed. Client mail software prevents a mail message from having a period alone on a line because the receiver interprets it as the end of the message.

Finally, the sender sends the mail data followed by the termination characters. To terminate the session, the sender issues a QUIT command to close the connection.

The format of a mail message is also straightforward. Essentially, a mail message consists of a header (which contains a number of fields), a blank line separator, and the message text. Table 2.5 shows some of the header fields; others are defined in the RFC that defines the format of the message (RFC 822), but not all implementations of SMTP use those fields.

TABLE 2.5
SMTP Header Fields

Field	Description
Date	Date the message was sent
From	The sender
Subject	Message subject
Reply-To	User address to which to reply
To	The recipient
cc	Recipients of message copies

An Infamous Unix Hack

A famous sendmail hack was created in the late 1980s by Robert Morris, a student at MIT. The son of a noted computer security expert, Morris unleashed a program on the Internet community that exploited a "back door" in the Unix sendmail program. Morris's worm (a program designed to infiltrate or "worm" into a system) sent itself to other systems, which it found by checking certain system files that contain host addresses, by using the Unix netstat program to check the network status, and by trying random IP addresses.

Once the worm was on a new system, it used the Unix sendmail program to mail a program to a process, which in turn passed the incoming code to the operating system to be executed. This back door was a known issue on some systems, but was normally not considered a threat. Morris's worm did not delete files, compromise passwords (except for its own use), or intercept private mail, but it did increase system utilization to the point that performance on the infected system was extremely degraded.

E-mail is and probably will remain one of the most ubiquitous applications, and SMTP is likely to continue in its role of one of the most widely used TCP/IP services. The ability to send a message to someone across the room or across the world simply, easily, and cost effectively makes e-mail popular with individuals as well as businesses.

MAIL ACCESS — POST OFFICE PROTOCOL 3 (POP3)

Just as SMTP handles the transfer of e-mail between servers, POP3, another TCP/IP standard tool, provides mail transfer between a server and a client. The POP3 process assumes that the server maintains the mail for the client. POP3 accesses and downloads the mail dynamically when the user on the client system wants to receive it. POP3 usually removes the mail from the server after downloading it, but the user can direct POP3 (and most mail packages) to leave the mail on the server after download.

The server monitors well-known port 110 for an incoming POP3 connection. After making a TCP connection to this port, the client sends a greeting to the server. The server issues a response — essentially any positive response, such as +OK POP3 Server Ready — and the client and server exchange commands (from the client) and responses (from the server) until the mail session is complete. All commands are case insensitive and terminated by a carriage return/line feed (CRLF) combination. A command may be followed by parameters, which are separated from the command by a space.

The POP3 protocol includes several commands, as shown in Table 2.6. Responses from the server consist of a status indicator — either +OK (positive response) or –ERR (negative response) — and a keyword, and possibly additional information; the complete response may be up to 512 characters long.

TABLE 2.6
POP3 Commands

Authorization State Commands

Command	Parameters	Description
USER	User ID	Sends the user ID to the server
PASS	Password	Sends the password to the server
APOP	Name digest	A more secure (encrypted) method of logging on to the server
QUIT	None	Ends the POP3 session with no updates

Transaction State Commands

Command	Parameters	Description
LIST	Msg Nbr (opt)	Returns the size of one or more messages
UIDL	Msg Nbr (opt)	Returns a unique identifier for one or more messages
DELE	Msg Number	Marks a message as deleted on the server
RETR	Msg Number	Retrieves the message from the server
RSET	None	Unmarks deleted messages
NOOP	None	No operation — server returns a positive response
TOP	Msg Nbr	Sends the top portion of the specified message
STAT	None	Returns the number and size of messages
QUIT	None	Ends transaction state

A POP3 connection proceeds through three states during a session: Authorization, Transaction, and Update. The Authorization state occurs when the client connects to well-known port 110 and exchanges greetings with the server. The client identifies itself to the server using the USER and PASS commands or the APOP command. During this process the user enters the user ID and password assigned by the mail administrator. (Sometimes the user ID and password are entered during the setup of the software and are not entered every time a POP3 connection is made.) The user's mail files and folders on the server are associated with the user during the Authorization state. The server locks the files and folders and assigns a sequential number to each message in the mail area.

The Authorization state is followed by the Transaction state, where the POP3 session spends most of its time. During the Transaction state, the client sends requests (commands) to the server for processing. The client software — not the user — issues the commands. POP3 is similar to SMTP in that no user interaction is needed to send mail — the client software sends messages to the POP3 process, which sends the mail on behalf of the client software. There is no provision for sending messages from the client to the server — SMTP handles that process.

When the client software issues the QUIT command during the Transaction state, the POP3 session enters the Update state. The server releases any resources (file, folders, processes) used during the POP3 session, deletes messages marked for deletion, and sends a goodbye message to the client. The client then ends the TCP connection.

POP3 is a simple and widely used application that brought mail client software to a wide variety of platforms, including the AS/400 with V3R2/V3R7 and higher versions of OS/400.

NETWORK MANAGEMENT — SIMPLE NETWORK MANAGEMENT PROTOCOL (SNMP)

Few experiences in this modern world are more frustrating than network downtime. A number of problems can arise with networks, such as physical problems (e.g., a defective piece of data communications equipment, failing cables, electrical interference), logical problems (incorrect routing, invalid gateway information, unavailable resources), and application problems (inability to access the resource due to an authorization failure). The TCP/IP protocol suite includes provisions for a network management service, Simple Network Management Protocol (SNMP). SNMP can help solve physical problems and, to a lesser degree, logical problems.

Management software lets you gather and display statistics, identify problems such as a failed device or communications line, and reset devices on the network. SNMP is a client/server-based application, although SNMP uses the terms *agent* and *manager* instead of client and server. The agent is also known as the managed system, and the manager is also termed the managing system. We have discussed clients as intelligent devices, whether they are mainframes, minicomputers, workstations, or PCs. SNMP's agent concept takes that client definition a bit further: Any device capable of supporting SNMP can be a managed system. By this definition, a managed system can be a bridge, router, switch, or hub, as well as any of the types of systems mentioned above.

SNMP is not the only network management tool available for TCP/IP-based networks. Another, the Common Management Information Protocol (CMIP), is used primarily by OSI-based networks but has had an effect on part of the SNMP standard, as we'll see in a moment. This section discusses only SNMP.

SNMP separates network management into two distinct areas — the Management Information Base (MIB) for communicating management information to a managing system, and the Abstract Syntax Notation (ASN), which deals with the names and syntax used in the communication. Standards are in place for both portions, but ASN is of concern only to vendor programmers who create MIBs for their products. System administrators deal with the MIB, and it is the focus of the following discussion.

SNMP Management Information Base

The Management Information Base (MIB) is a standard that specifies the type of information SNMP must keep about the network devices and the operations allowed on those devices. The MIB standard divides the management information into the 10 categories shown in Table 2.7.

TABLE 2.7
The MIB Categories of Network Information

Category	Description
system	Information about the managed system
interfaces	Network interfaces that can use TCP/IP
addr.trans	Physical and network address translation
ip	IP routing and datagram information
icmp	Internet Control Message Protocol (ICMP) information and statistics
tcp	TCP information and statistics
udp	UDP information and statistics
egp	Exterior Gateway Protocol (EGP) information and statistics
transmission	Physical transmission information
snmp	SNMP information

Keeping the definition of the MIB separate from the SNMP protocol lets vendors extend their own MIB definitions (essentially extending the features of SNMP) to incorporate the specific needs of their hardware and software. Every

SNMP-compliant vendor has added its own extensions. Vendors usually supply an MIB database to be incorporated (through a compilation process) with the network management software's existing MIB database.

Eight of the MIB standard categories were part of the original MIB definition. The transmission and snmp categories were added as part of the MIB-II definition, which came about as a result of a difference of opinion between participating SNMP vendors and users and their CMIP counterparts regarding extensions to the MIB standard. The two groups formed two MIBs. The SNMP MIB is known as MIB-II, and the CMIP MIB, which includes more extensions, is known as MIB-II-OIM. The TCP/IP management world uses SNMP much more than CMIP; this detail is fairly esoteric, but you should be aware of which standard your network management package supports.

The notation used to represent data in the MIB is known as Abstract Syntax Notation 1, or ASN.1. This notation is in two forms — a human-readable format and a more compact representation maintained by the managed device. Because the notation is formal and strict, no ambiguity is involved, allowing the SNMP software to adhere to standards that ensure its interoperability with other software.

The SNMP Process

The SNMP process is a simple one, and in that simplicity lie advantages and disadvantages. SNMP uses only the five commands shown in Table 2.8 and uses those commands in a get/put fashion.

TABLE 2.8
SNMP Commands

Command	Description
get-request	Get a value from an MIB variable
get-next-request	Get a value from a list or table of values
get-response	The response to a get or put command
set-request	Put a value in a variable
trap	A reply triggered by an event in the managed device

SNMP polls the devices it knows about on a network to obtain errors and alerts. The system administrator can explicitly define devices to SNMP, or SNMP can learn about them by searching the network. Because polling messages are short, polling does not significantly slow performance even over large networks. Most implementations of network management software automatically discover SNMP-compliant devices in the network and provide a network map of all devices the software knows about.

Devices respond to the managing station poll using well-known port 161. Traps, which indicate an error or a warning condition on the device, use well-known port 162. SNMP can change the state of a device by assigning a specific value to a specific variable. By changing device states, SNMP can reboot a router, reset a printer, disable a port on a hub, or do almost anything else that can be done manually or by connecting to the device. Most SNMP implementations also support alerts, which provide information regarding device problems, network congestion problems, and down systems or links. SNMP can display this information graphically on a network map, usually using different colors to represent different conditions.

SNMP has some inherent disadvantages. Because it uses UDP rather than TCP over IP, SNMP traffic is not as reliable as traffic carried by TCP. Another disadvantage is that information is not filtered — the managing software must check each response to determine whether it is important. However, in spite of the disadvantages, SNMP is by far the most widely used network management protocol for TCP/IP networks on the market and is supported by every major computer manufacturer, including IBM for the AS/400.

LINE PRINTER REMOTE/LINE PRINTER DAEMON

Line Printer Remote (LPR) is a Unix program that assigns printed output to an output queue. The AS/400 supports a version of LPR to communicate with printers that implement the server process Line Printer Daemon (LPD). The AS/400 also supports a version of LPD so it can print files sent to it by LPR-capable systems.

The TCP-based LPR process communicates with the LPD process using well-known port 515. LPR sends commands to the LPD as a series of 1-octet codes followed by the name of the printer queue and by parameters associated with the command. A line feed (LF) character specifies the end of the command. Table 2.9 shows the commands the LPR process can send to the LPD process (the printer queue name follows every command and is not shown in the parameter list). Note that the 02 command, Receive a printer job, uses subcommands to control the printing process.

TABLE 2.9
LPR Commands and Subcommands

Command	Parameters	Description
01	None	Print waiting jobs
02	None	Receive a printer job — uses subcommands
Subcommand 01	None	Removes queue entries created in this session
Subcommand 02	Size/Name	Sends a control file of the specified size and name
Subcommand 03	Size/Name	Sends a data file of the specified size and name
03	Job Nbr/User Name	Send the queue state (short list)
04	Job Nbr/User Name	Send the queue state (long list)
05	Job Nbr/User Name	Removes entries from the queue

After a connection is made and the 02 command is sent (and acknowledged) to cause the LPD process to receive a print file, the LPR process sends subcommands to control printing. The control file sent by subcommand 02 can contain specific directives for formatting the associated data file — for example, the directives can specify banner pages, indenting, titles, and width of the printed output. Many of these directives are fairly esoteric and are used only with Unix implementations.

LPD is also implemented on PCs, directly in network-ready printers, and on printer interface equipment (such as a Hewlett-Packard JetDirect device) that provides a limited implementation of LPD. Most printing needs do not require a complete implementation of LPR or LPD.

Chapter 3

Addressing and Routing

A TCP/IP network revolves around addressing and routing. Because nodes on the network are not connected directly, packets must include the address of both the source and destination node, and a route from the source to the destination must be found or stated to allow the nodes to communicate with each other.

This chapter examines the lower levels of TCP/IP, beginning with a discussion of the IP address, physical frames, and some of the most widely used physical network implementations. We cover the characteristics and structure of UDP, TCP, and IP packets and explain the TCP/IP processing flow — the process of sending application information from one system to another.

No discussion of TCP/IP addressing would be complete without a look at Domain Name Service (DNS), which acts like a "telephone directory" to the Internet, and at Address Resolution Protocol (ARP), which maps the logical IP address to the physical address of the network interface card. We conclude this chapter by discussing physical connections and the routers and bridges that provide connections between networks.

INTERNET PROTOCOL ADDRESSES

TCP/IP addressing is the foundation of a TCP/IP network. Every intelligent device on a network, be it a router, a PC, an AS/400, or something else, has an IP address. Only one device on a network may have a particular IP address, so that IP address uniquely identifies that device on the network.

Although most devices have only one IP address, some have more than one. Routers, for example, have an IP address for each connection to a network. In fact, an IP address is not truly associated with a host or device, but with an interface — a connection to a TCP/IP-based network. Most hosts and PCs have only one connection to a network, and so have only one interface and one IP address. But a host may have more than one interface connecting to the same or different networks, in which case each interface has its own IP address. Such a host is said to be multihoming — that is, it has multiple IP addresses to which other network nodes can attach.

Most IP addresses are hierarchical, consisting of a network identifying portion and a host identifying portion. All IP addresses are 32 bits long, although the explosive growth of the Internet has led to a move toward longer addresses. Addresses consist of four octets (8-bit bytes), each having a value of from 0 to 255, as in the following example:

11000110 01001001 01010101 01100110

Typically, addresses are represented in dotted decimal (also known as "dotted quad") notation, which expresses each octet in base 10 and separates it from neighboring octets with periods. For the above example, the dotted decimal notation is 198.73.85.102; each of the four numbers in the notation is also known as a "quad." Dotted decimal notation is a bit more illuminating than its binary equivalent. Later in this chapter, in the section "Domain Name Service," we'll see another method of expressing host names that is much easier to remember.

IP Next Generation

The current version of TCP/IP addressing, IP Version 4, uses 32 bits for each IP address. But the phenomenal growth of the Internet over the past few years has made it apparent that 32 bits is insufficient to provide the number of IP addresses we're going to need. IP Version 6, also known as IPv6 or IP Next Generation, became a Proposed Standard for TCP/IP on September 18, 1995.

IPv6 has many new features, one of the most important being that it extends the length of the address to 128 bits, ensuring a supply of addresses for many years. Other changes incorporated in IPv6 are simplification of the IP packet header, better support for extensions and options, flow labeling for quality of service, and authentication and privacy capabilities.

IPv6 accommodates evolution from IPv4. Data communications devices and host implementations of TCP/IP will be able to use IPv4, IPv6, or a combination of the two, even in the same network. IPv6 will be implemented over the next few years, with a full implementation across the Internet by 2005. Because the implementation of IPv6 is evolutionary rather than revolutionary (due to the coexistence of IPv4 and IPv6), IPv6-enabled devices such as routers will soon appear in the marketplace.

IP addresses fall into three main categories: Class A, Class B, and Class C, plus specialized categories D and E (see "Class D and E Addresses" for more about these two categories). The 32 IP address bits have different meanings depending on the class of network in which the address is to be used. Each class has a different number of network and host ID bits that together encompass all valid addresses within that class.

You can determine into which of the three primary classes an IP address falls from the address's first two bits. A Class A address begins with a 0 bit, a Class B address begins with bits 10, and a Class C address begins with bits 11. Figure 3.1 illustrates the five classes of IP addresses; note how the host ID portion of the three primary classes becomes progressively smaller. A Class A address uses 7 bits to identify the network and 24 bits to identify the host, a Class B address uses 14 bits to identify the network and 16 bits to identify the host, and a Class C address uses 21 bits to identify the network and only 8 bits to identify the host.

There are different classes of addresses because there are different sizes of networks. Large organizations with many hosts need Class A addresses. The

FIGURE 3.1

IP Address Classes

Class A Address — 7 network bits, 24 host bits

0	Net ID	Host ID

Class B Address — 14 network bits, 16 host bits

1	0	Net ID	Host ID

Class C Address — 21 network bits, 8 host bits

1	1	0	Net ID	Host ID

Class D Address — 4 identifying bits

1	1	1	0	Multicast address

Class E Address — 4 identifying bits

1	1	1	1	Reserved for future use

Class A address space allows for 128 networks, each accommodating up to 16,777,216 hosts. Network addresses 0 and 127 are reserved (for network identification and for multicasting, respectively), leaving 126 usable Class A networks. The Class B address space provides for up to 16,384 networks with up to 65,536 hosts each. Network addresses 0 and 16,384 are reserved, leaving 16,382 usable networks. The Class C address space provides for up to 2,097,152 networks, each having up to 256 hosts. Again, the first and last network addresses are reserved, leaving 2,097,150 usable networks.

In dotted decimal notation, addresses with a first quad in the range of 0 to 127 are Class A addresses, those in the range of 128 to 191 are Class B addresses, and those from 192 to 223 are Class C. Currently, no Class A or B addresses are available. The Internet Network Information Center (InterNIC), the governing body of IP address (and domain name) assignment, is assigning only Class C addresses at this time.

Because only Class C addresses are available, organizations that have more than one network face a problem. Each Class C address provides up to 254 host addresses but only one network ID. One way to obtain another network ID is to acquire another Class C address from InterNIC. That solution can waste IP addresses, however, especially if the total number of addresses needed over all your networks falls short of the 254 addresses available in one Class C address.

Class D and E Addresses

There are also Class D and E addresses, but they are specialized. Class D addresses are used for multicasting, in which a single packet is transmitted to multiple selected recipients. Multicasting differs from broadcasting, in which a transmission is sent to all systems. Some examples of multicasting are delivery of live stock quotes, multiparty videoconferencing, and shared whiteboard applications.

The first 4 bits of a Class D address are 1110; the next 28 bits contain a multicast group ID. Group IDs are registered with the Internet Assigned Name Authority (IANA — the group within the Internet community that tracks such things) and relate to certain types of transmissions. Recipient systems register for the type of transmission (through the appropriate software program) and can then receive multicast transmissions.

A Class E address begins with 1111. Class E addresses are reserved for future or experimental use. You should never see a packet with a Class E address.

Subnetting is another way of supporting more than one network with a single Class C address. Subnetting lets you divide a single address space into multiple smaller address spaces. A standard address consists of a network portion and a host portion. With subnetting, you can add a third dimension — the logical subnetwork — as we explain in a moment. This additional dimension lets you support several subnetworks using your Class C address space.

Figure 3.2 illustrates subnetting. This example shows three subnetworks comprising a single logical network, which could consist of one or more physical networks. The subnetworks are connected by routers, which determine whether the standard hierarchical addressing scheme has been changed. The routers are configured with routing tables that identify the subnetworks, providing the information needed to route packets correctly. Subnetting affects only the devices in your own network. The network portion of the IP address does not change, so systems outside your own local network continue to forward packets to the same network ID.

Subnetting uses a *subnet mask* to turn part of every host identifier into a subnetwork identifier. Depending on the number of networks you want to support, the subnet mask for a Class C address uses the first one to several bits of the final octet to identify the subnetwork, leaving fewer bits for identifying the host.

The subnet mask is a 4-octet number that looks like an IP address and, like an IP address, is usually expressed in dotted decimal format. The subnet mask consists of a network portion, a subnet portion (derived from the host portion), and an abbreviated host portion. The bits in the subnet mask "overlay" those in the IP address and enable the host's IP software to determine

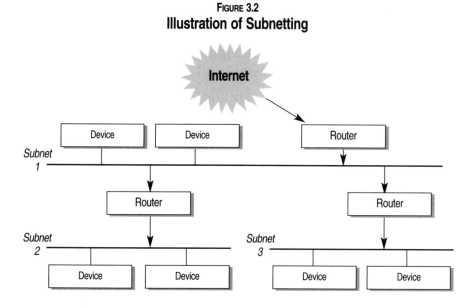

FIGURE 3.2
Illustration of Subnetting

whether the destination address is located on the same subnetwork as the host address.

An octet of all 1 bits (255) in the subnet mask means that the corresponding octet of the address should not be considered — in other words, it does not factor into the subnet mask. Because the first three octets of a Class C address comprise the network ID, which is not affected by subnetting, all Class C subnet masks begin with 255.255.255, meaning that the network portion of the IP address is not to be used for subnet identification.

An octet of all zero bits (0) means that the corresponding portion of the address should be maintained as it is with no changes. A common subnet mask for Class C networks is 255.255.255.0. The 0 in the last octet means that the host portion of the address is unchanged. In other words, a subnet mask of 255.255.255.0 for a Class C network means no subnetting is in effect.

When the final subnet mask octet is neither all ones nor all zeros, the final octet masks the corresponding octet of the IP address. Table 3.1 shows all possible subnet masks for a Class C network with the resulting number of logical networks, the number of hosts per network, and the binary equivalent of the mask octet. Note that the number of available hosts decreases as the number of subnets increases, because the first and last address of each subnet are reserved for the address of the subnetwork and the broadcast address, respectively. As you can see from the table, a mask with a last octet of 0 causes no subnetting, and a mask with a last octet of 254 provides no hosts (a pretty useless situation). Usable subnets are somewhere between these two extremes. Subnet masks 255.255.255.224 and 255.255.255.192 are widely used because they provide a reasonable number of hosts and networks.

TABLE 3.1
Possible Subnet Masks for a Class C Network

Subnet mask (in decimal)	Number of networks	Number of hosts per network	Binary equivalent
255.255.255.0	1	254	00000000
255.255.255.128	2	126	10000000
255.255.255.192	4	62	11000000
255.255.255.224	8	30	11100000
255.255.255.240	16	14	11110000
255.255.255.248	32	6	11111000
255.255.255.252	64	2	11111100
255.255.255.254	128	0	11111110

Let's look at an example of subnetting. Say we have a Class C license that covers the IP addresses from 200.1.2.0 to 200.1.2.254. Because our organization has four small networks, we want to subnet this address space into four separate address spaces. The above table shows that a subnet mask of 255.255.255.192 provides four subnetworks, each with 62 hosts. The IP addresses produced by using this subnet mask over the original address of 200.1.2.0 are as follows:

Subnet Address	First Host	Last Host	Broadcast
200.1.2.0	200.1.2.1	200.1.2.62	200.1.2.63
200.1.2.64	200.1.2.65	200.1.2.126	200.1.2.127
200.1.2.128	200.1.2.129	200.1.2.190	200.1.2.191
200.1.2.192	200.1.2.193	200.1.2.254	200.1.2.255

Keep in mind that subnetting is not required. If your network has no need for subnetting, it's much less complicated not to subnet. If you don't use subnetting and are asked to enter a subnet mask (e.g., during configuration of a client software package), simply use the mask 255.255.255.0.

Network Address Translation

If you need more addresses than are available with a single Class C license, one solution is to obtain multiple Class C addresses. Another way to make available more addresses than a single license provides is to use network address translation (NAT), a function that masks internal IP addresses from the external network.

NAT lets you translate the addresses of your internal network to addresses you can use on the Internet. The system administrator maintains a pool of InterNIC-registered addresses in a NAT device or a firewall. When an outgoing request (from your internal network to the Internet) occurs, the NAT device dips into the pool of registered addresses, selects one, and uses it for the outgoing connection.

The NAT device maps the return flow of traffic in reverse, translating the external address to the internal address using a table to match up the incoming and outgoing addresses. The internal address still uniquely identifies a device on the internal network, but NAT masks the internal address from the external network, providing security benefits. This technique is especially helpful when a large number of devices need access to the Internet, but relatively few of them need access simultaneously.

PHYSICAL FRAMES

The IP address is only part of the required addressing solution. Another critical piece of the address is the physical network address, which identifies the actual hardware device (the network interface card, or NIC) for which a packet is destined. As we explain a little later in this chapter, the TCP packet or User Datagram Protocol (UDP) packet that contains the data to be transmitted over the network is placed into an IP packet, which in turn is put into a network packet (or frame) for transmission across the physical media to the destination. Figure 3.3 shows a generalized representation of a physical frame.

FIGURE 3.3
Diagram of a Physical Frame

Header	Data (IP packet)	Trailer

As you can see, a frame contains header information, a data portion (consisting of the IP packet), and trailer information. The header contains the physical network address (e.g., the Media Access Control (MAC) address in an 802 network) for both the source and destination systems. The trailer contains check-sum information used to ensure that the transmitted data packet is received without corruption or error.

The addressing scheme depends on the type of physical medium used. Possibilities include Ethernet, Token-Ring LAN, and WAN connections. In the next few sections we examine the contents of various TCP/IP packets and physical frames in detail; this information is necessary for troubleshooting low-level problems. If you prefer to skip the technical details of TCP/IP packets and frames, you can jump ahead to the section on Domain Name Service.

Let's begin with an examination of one of the most popular physical network implementations — Ethernet.

Ethernet

Today, Ethernet is used as a generic term, like "kleenex" for tissues or "xerox" for copies. This section discusses the original Ethernet standard. In the next section we cover the Institute of Electrical and Electronic Engineers (IEEE) 802 series of standards, which is usually what people mean when they refer to Ethernet today.

Ethernet was developed in 1973 by a consortium consisting of Digital Equipment Corporation (DEC), Intel, and Xerox, collectively known as DIX. DIX created a LAN system known as Experimental Ethernet. This original version of Ethernet transmitted information at the stellar speed of 3 Mbps and used 8-bit addresses, which severely limited the address space for a message. Experimental Ethernet was followed by Ethernet Version I, which refined the standard, and then by Ethernet Version II, which remains in use today. Ethernet Version II operates at a speed of 10 Mbps and uses 48-bit addressing.

An Ethernet frame (Figure 3.4) consists of a preamble, destination and source addresses, a type field, a data portion (which includes the IP packet), and a checksum area. Let's look at each area in a little more detail.

FIGURE 3.4
Ethernet Version II Frame

Preamble	Destination address	Source address	Type	Data	Checksum (Frame Check Sequence)

The preamble is a specific bit pattern that serves to synchronize the Ethernet data packets. The destination and source addresses, each 48 bits long, are the physical addresses of the destination and source Ethernet NIC, respectively. (We discuss the mechanism for mapping the IP address in the TCP/IP packet to the actual hardware address in the "Address Resolution Protocol" section later in this chapter.)

The 48-bit Ethernet II addresses are represented as 12 hexadecimal digits and raise an interesting question. All Ethernet NICs have a "burned-in" address assigned by the manufacturer when the NIC is made. The first three bytes are unique to the manufacturer and are assigned by the IEEE. For example, IEEE assigned X'08005A' to IBM and X'080009' to Hewlett-Packard. The last three bytes of the address are a serial number assigned by the manufacturer. NIC cards from different manufacturers may have the same serial number, but because of the manufacturer number still have a unique address.

Because each NIC address is unique, why is it necessary to override the burned-in address and assign a different Ethernet address? The reason is for maintenance. In the event that the Ethernet card fails (which does occasionally happen), the new NIC can be given the same Ethernet address so no network changes are required.

The type field of the Ethernet II frame usually identifies the contents of the data portion of the frame. Some common Ethernet II type-field values are X'0800' for IP and X'0805' for ARP. In the 802.3 IEEE standard, however, this field instead identifies the length of the following data packet, so proper configuration of the drivers associated with the NIC is critical.

The data field contains the IP packet (which in turn contains the TCP packet and application data). The data portion of an Ethernet frame is between 46 and 1,500 bytes long. Later in this chapter, in the section "TCP/IP Processing Flow," we discuss in detail the encapsulation of the TCP packet within the IP packet.

At the end of the Ethernet frame is the checksum field. Also known as the Frame Check Sequence (FCS), this portion of the frame is created by the source system and used by the destination system to ensure the accuracy of the frame contents.

In the early 1980s, responsibility for the further development of the Ethernet II standard was transferred from DIX to the IEEE. In 1983, the IEEE produced the 802.3 specification, which further developed the Ethernet II standard.

IEEE 802 Series

The IEEE created several of the LAN standards in use today. The three IEEE protocol standards we're primarily concerned with are

- 802.2 — Logical Link Control
- 802.3 — Carrier Sense Multiple Access with Collision Detection access method
- 802.5 — Token-Ring access method

802.2 — Logical Link Control

The basis for the 802 series protocols is in layer 2 of the OSI model, the data link layer (for a discussion of the OSI model, see "The Open Systems Interconnection (OSI) Protocol" in Chapter 1). In the 802 series, the data link layer consists of two functions: Logical Link Control (LLC) and Media Access Control (MAC). Every LAN protocol implements the LLC function as defined in 802.2 and a media-dependent MAC function defined by one of the other 802.x standards. Because of this dichotomy in the data link layer, people often speak of the two functions as separate sublayers of OSI layer 2.

The LLC portion of an 802 frame, defined by IEEE standard 802.2, is the upper sublayer of the data link layer and provides the physical addressing function for all 802 series protocols, ensuring delivery of packets to the correct physical address. The LLC has three components — the Destination Service Access Point (DSAP), the Source Service Access Point (SSAP), and a Control field. Together, these components identify the type of frame being transmitted or received (e.g., Ethernet Version II, Token-Ring).

SSAPs are rather like ports in TCP/IP. An SSAP identifies the point at which the line "listens." A protocol that uses an SSAP that is not configured on the AS/400 line cannot be "heard" or used with the AS/400. The most important SSAP in TCP/IP processing is AA, which is required for standard TCP/IP processing on the AS/400. (An SSAP of AA actually indicates the use of the Subnetwork Access Protocol or SNAP. SNAP allows an Ethernet II frame to be transmitted with 802.2 information.) When you create an AS/400 Ethernet line description, you specify the SSAPs that can be used on the line by indicating which Ethernet standard is used for the line description. For example, if you specify Ethernet II as the Ethernet standard for the line description, SSAPs 04 and 08 are used by default. If you specify the 802.3 standard, SSAPs 04, 12, AA, and C8 are used by default.

The MAC sublayer provides the interaction between the physical layer and the data link layer of the OSI model. The MAC standard identifies the framing for the packet with synchronization and checksum information, as well as the discipline used to establish communication on the physical network. The MAC sublayer is media-type dependent, meaning that a different MAC sublayer standard exists for each IEEE 802 series network (the 802.3 standard for Ethernet and the 802.5 standard for Token-Ring).

802.3 — Carrier Sense Multiple Access with Collision Detection

Carrier Sense Multiple Access with Collision Detection (CSMA/CD) is the technology implemented in Ethernet. 802.3 is the standard for the IEEE implementation of CSMA/CD.

The IEEE is just one developer of standards for communications protocols. There are other standards organizations, and companies or even individuals can also devise ad-hoc standards and make them freely available for others to use. Ethernets I and II came about that way, and many computer companies have followed Ethernet II for years.

Eventually, the IEEE decided that a more formal, vendor-independent standard was needed. Rather than follow the Ethernet II standard exactly, though, IEEE made some subtle but critical modifications. Now, some vendors follow the IEEE standard and many others the Ethernet II standard. Ethernet II is the prevailing implementation today, but enough vendors follow the IEEE standard that all vendors implement both in all their products.

The CSMA/CD method of transmission lets multiple network stations use the network concurrently. The stations "listen" to network transmissions and transmit their signal when the network has no traffic. You can liken CSMA/CD to merging onto an expressway: You wait for a break in traffic, and then you merge into the flow of traffic. This "merging" is the Carrier Sense Multiple Access portion of CSMA/CD.

The Collision Detection portion of CSMA/CD handles collisions on the network. A collision, which occurs when more than one station transmits information at the same time, results in an unsuccessful transmission. When that happens, the involved stations wait for a random period of time (measured in milliseconds) and then retransmit their information.

Figure 3.5 depicts an 802.3 frame. At first glance, the 802.3 frame and Ethernet II frame seem similar. But important differences exist between the frame types and can cause network problems if the drivers for the NICs are not implemented correctly. For instance, as we mentioned earlier, an Ethernet II frame's type field is in the same position as the length field in an 802.3 frame.

FIGURE 3.5
Diagram of an 802.3 Frame

Preamble	Start Frame Delimiter	Destination address	Source address	Length	Data	Pad	Checksum (Frame Check Sequence)

The first portion of the 802.3 frame is the 7-byte preamble, which, like the 8-byte preamble of Ethernet II, synchronizes the frames across the network. The preamble is followed by the Start Frame Delimiter field, which indicates the start of the frame.

The next two fields are the destination and source addresses. Don't confuse these with the LLC DSAP and SSAP, which come later in the frame. The standard specifies that the destination and source address fields may be two or six bytes long, but they are usually six bytes, to match the Ethernet II standard. As in the corresponding Ethernet II fields, the source and destination addresses contain the addresses of the NICs.

The next field in the frame contains the length of the data field, which may be from 46 to 1,500 bytes long. The data field itself contains the IP datagram (the terms datagram and packet are synonymous in the TCP/IP world) in both the 802.3 and the Ethernet II frame. However, the 802.3 data field contains much more information than the Ethernet II field.

Figure 3.6 shows the data field for an 802.3 frame. The field consists of the LLC header, the SNAP header, and the IP datagram. The LLC header comprises three 1-byte fields: the DSAP, the SSAP, and the Control field. The SNAP header consists of a 3-byte protocol identifier and a 2-byte Ethernet type field.

FIGURE 3.6
Data Portion of an 802.3 Frame

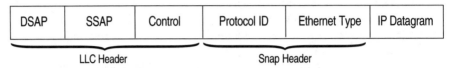

DSAP	SSAP	Control	Protocol ID	Ethernet Type	IP Datagram

LLC Header   Snap Header

The pad field follows the data field in the 802.3 frame. When necessary, this field pads the data to reach the minimum frame size. The FCS field is used for cyclic redundancy check error checking.

Because it has no additional overhead, CSMA/CD has an advantage over other network media sharing techniques such as token passing because it has no additional overhead. However, this advantage exists only when the network load is no more than approximately 40 percent of capacity. Network load levels above 40 percent cause more collisions, decreasing the throughput of the network.

802.5 — Token-Ring

Token-Ring is a physical network protocol that predates Ethernet's early 1970s development. Token-Ring was developed in 1969 but did not receive much attention until 1982, when IBM presented its Token-Ring implementation to the IEEE. In 1984, IBM announced its own standard of wiring for Token-Ring, a step that helped IBM take the lead in Token-Ring development. 1985 brought IBM's official announcement of its Token-Ring network and began the implementation of Token-Ring products.

The Token-Ring access method is significantly different from CSMA/CD. In the Ethernet or 802.3 standard, collisions are expected, and the physical network protocol automatically retransmits any frames involved in a collision. CSMA/CD doesn't work well under heavy loads because there are too many collisions.

Token-Ring uses a token passing technique, which is designed to eliminate collisions. One station, known as an active monitor, initiates Token-Ring activity by sending a 24-bit token onto the network. The token is passed continuously from station to station — unlike an 802.3 network, an 802.5 network is never idle. When a station needs to transmit information, the station acquires the token, places information in it, and releases the token to continue around the network to the destination. The destination station copies the information from the frame and releases the token back onto the network. The source station then acquires and reads the frame for acknowledgment that the information was successfully received and again releases the token, allowing another station to acquire it. Only one station on the network "owns" the token, and only one station can "talk" at a time. Any given station may hold the token only for a certain amount of time so as not to prevent other stations from acquiring it.

In addition to initiating Token-Ring activity, the active monitor performs several other functions, including

- monitoring for lost tokens
- identifying other active monitors
- handling a short-ring situation
- providing the clocking for token passing

A token can become lost if the station that transmitted it develops a problem and removes itself from the network or is shut down. A short-ring situation develops when the ring has such a small amount of delay that it cannot hold a token. This might be the case if Token-Ring is implemented on a high-speed network but uses slower technology and equipment. The clocking function is important because Token-Ring is built on clock synchronization rather than on 802.3-style frame synchronization.

The IEEE 802.5 standard was developed for Token-Ring. As one of the 802 series of network protocols, the 802.5 frame (illustrated in Figure 3.7) contains much the same information as the 802.3 frame.

FIGURE 3.7

Diagram of an 802.5 Frame

Starting delimiter	Access control	Frame control	Destination address	Source address	Routing information	Information	FCS	Ending delimiter	FS

The frame begins with a 1-byte starting delimiter that indicates the start of the frame. The subsequent 1-byte access control field contains several pieces of information:

- frame priority
- frame type, indicating whether the frame is a token frame (meaning the token is available) or a data frame (meaning the token is in use)
- an indication of network health, such as whether there is a bad (malformed) token or inoperable or "chattering" adapters
- whether the frame is reserved, indicating it is part of an ongoing conversation and is not available to another station

The frame control field, also one byte long, indicates whether the frame contains data or is a MAC-level maintenance frame. The destination and source address fields contain the address of the destination and source NICs, respectively, and may be two or six bytes in length (6-byte address fields are more common).

The next field is the routing information field. This field, which may be from 0 to 30 bytes long, contains information regarding the route to be taken from the source to the destination. This field is used when the Source Route Bridging method of routing is implemented for the network. Source Route Bridging allows rings to be connected by bridges. When a Token-Ring frame determines the path from the source to the destination, the routing information field is set for each frame and enables the frame to use that path.

The information field is similar to the 802.3 data field but has no set length limit. According to the Token-Ring standard, the maximum length of the data field, and thus the 802.5 frame, depends on the speed of the network. For example, a 4 Mbps network has smaller frame sizes than a 16 Mbps network. We explain the token passing concept in more detail in the next section.

The 4-byte FCS field uses a cyclic redundancy check to verify the integrity of the transmitted frame. The ending delimiter field indicates the end of the Token-Ring frame. The last field in the frame, the frame status (FS), contains two pieces of information — whether the destination station recognizes the destination address, and whether the destination node has successfully copied the frame.

Token-Ring provides excellent inherent diagnostics, such as identification of the nearest upstream neighbor. Another advantage of Token-Ring is that a station will remove itself from the network if the station develops a problem that compromises its ability to function correctly. Token-Ring also is ideal for heavily loaded networks because the token is owned by only one station at a time and cannot have collisions.

So why don't more networks use Token-Ring? One problem is price — Token-Ring NICs, Multistation Access Units (MAUs — the equivalent of an Ethernet repeater), and other data communications equipment is significantly more costly than corresponding Ethernet equivalents. Another problem is with marketing — IBM was the main proponent of Token-Ring, while other manufacturers embraced Ethernet. So although Token-Ring is faster and more efficient than Ethernet, the cost of Token-Ring and its lack of market share means that the Ethernet or 802.3 physical networks are and will remain more popular.

PACKET STRUCTURE

UDP and TCP packets can both be used with IP. The UDP or TCP packet is put into an IP packet, which in turn is placed into the data (802.3) or information (802.5) field in the physical network frame. Here we look at the structure of UDP, TCP, and IP packets.

User Datagram Protocol Packet

As mentioned in Chapter 2 (in "Trivial File Transfer Protocol — TFTP"), UDP is an unreliable transfer mechanism. UDP assumes that the underlying protocol is IP and that the higher-level application that uses the UDP protocol monitors for successful packet transfer and retransmits the packet if an error occurs. Some applications that use UDP include Domain Name Service (DNS), the Bootstrap Protocol (BOOTP), and Sun's Remote Procedure Call (RPC). UDP, like IP, is a connectionless protocol.

Connection-oriented vs. Connectionless Protocols

A connection-oriented protocol is one that requires a connection be kept open from the source to the destination. SNA is an example of a connection-oriented protocol: A connection must be in place for SNA to function, and packets must flow over that connection between the source and the destination systems, or the connection will time out and will need to be reestablished.

A connectionless protocol, such as TCP/IP, establishes a dynamic connection. Packets are not necessarily sent along a preestablished path, but are routed to the destination. Packets in the same session are not guaranteed to follow the same path (although they usually do). Consequently, response time is also not guaranteed. However, dynamic rerouting of packets in the event of a network problem is much easier than reestablishing a connection and rerouting packets in other protocols.

Figure 3.8 illustrates a UDP packet. The first two fields in the packet are the 2-byte source port and destination port. The source port is optional and is filled with zeros when it is not used. The destination port identifies the port on the destination system to which the UDP packet is sent. UDP ports are similar to TCP ports and often use the same number as their TCP counterparts.

FIGURE 3.8
UDP Packet

Source port	Destination port
Length	Checksum
Data	

The 2-byte length field identifies the length of the UDP datagram. The checksum field is optional and is not used when the higher-level application process manages the validity of the packet information. When a checksum is used, it is calculated using a "pseudo" UDP header, which consists of the source and destination addresses, the protocol, and the UDP length fields from the IP packet.

Transport Control Protocol Packet

The TCP packet contains the application data, port information, and error checking and sequencing information. Remember that TCP provides a connection-oriented service (unlike UDP and IP) and is responsible for the end-to-end validity of the data.

The TCP packet serves six basic functions:

- basic data transfer
- reliability
- flow control
- multiplexing
- identifying port number for connections
- maintaining packet precedence

Figure 3.9 illustrates the packet, which consists of a header portion and the application data. The header comprises all the fields that precede the application data.

FIGURE 3.9

TCP Packet

Source port							Destination port
Sequence number							
Acknowledgment							
Offset	Reserved	U	A	P	R	S	F	Window
Checksum							Urgent pointer
Options and padding							
Data							

The first two fields are the 2-octet source and destination port numbers, which identify the process using the TCP packet. The client determines the source port. The destination port either is a well-known port (in which case it identifies the process using the TCP packet) or is programmer-defined for a custom application.

The next field in the TCP packet is the 4-octet sequence number field. Initialized when the connection is made, this field identifies the sequence number of the first TCP packet of the transmission. The field is incremented by 1 for each data packet transmitted. Sequencing is critical for end-to-end reliability of the connection and is used in conjunction with the acknowledgment field.

The 4-octet acknowledgment field contains the next sequence number the destination expects. TCP requires that each packet sent be acknowledged; if an acknowledgment is not received, the source system times out and retransmits the missing packet. A flag is set when an acknowledgment is being processed. The acknowledgment field is bidirectional: Both systems involved in the connection must acknowledge the other system's packets.

TCP packet headers can vary in length, so an offset is needed to locate the data portion of the packet. The 4-bit offset field contains this offset. The six bits that follow the offset field are reserved for future use and are set to zeros.

The next series of fields are 1-bit flags that control the connection between the source and destination systems. In order, the fields are

- URG — urgent pointer field is significant
- ACK — acknowledgment field is significant
- PSH — push function is in use
- RST — reset the connection
- SYN — synchronize sequence numbers
- FIN — no more data to be sent from the sender

Window is a 2-octet field that controls the flow of packets between the source and destination systems. A window is the number of packets that may be sent before an acknowledgment must be received. The window value is large when the network is robust and has little interference (e.g., on a LAN) but is small when the network requires many retries, such as a WAN connection that uses unreliable or "noisy" lines.

The window field is bidirectional, meaning either system in the conversation can change its value. The field is initialized to 1 when the connection is made and is adjusted upward. If either side determines that the window should be smaller, the value is adjusted downward. The buffers on each system may also affect the size of the window: A system with large buffers (perhaps with more memory) allows a larger window because the system can store more information. A system with smaller buffers requests a smaller window.

The next field in the TCP packet is the 2-octet checksum. Like the UDP pseudo header checksum calculation, this value is calculated over a pseudo TCP header, which is composed of the source and destination addresses and the protocol and length fields from the IP packet.

The 2-octet urgent pointer field in the TCP packet works with the URG control flag. When the URG flag is set, the urgent pointer field contains the sequence number of the first packet that contains nonurgent data. Therefore, the packets before the number specified in the urgent pointer field are urgent and, with most implementations of TCP/IP, are sent before other information.

The 4-octet options and padding field provides two functions. One function is to send to the destination system options (e.g., security, source routing, timestamp information) that system requires. The other function is to pad the header portion of the packet so the packet ends on a 32-bit boundary.

The data portion of the packet contains the data from the application, such as a Telnet or FTP data stream.

Internet Protocol Packets

The IP packet is every bit as complex as the TCP packet. The IP packet contains the TCP or UDP header and the application data. The packet header is composed of all the fields in the IP packet before the start of the TCP or UDP packet. Figure 3.10 shows a diagram of the IP packet.

FIGURE 3.10
Diagram of an IP Packet

Version	IHL	Type of service	Total length	
Identifier			Flags	Fragment offset
Time to live		Protocol	Header checksum	
Source address				
Destination address				
Options and padding				

The first field in the IP header is the 4-bit version, which should have a value of 4. The 4-bit Internet header length field contains the length of the IP header in 32-bit words and can be used as an offset to the start of the TCP header. The 1-octet type-of-service field identifies the precedence, delay, throughput, and reliability requested by the client or server for this IP datagram.

The two octets of the total length field indicate the length of the entire IP packet, from the header through the application data. An IP packet can be from 576 to 65,535 octets long.

The next three fields in the packet deal with packet fragmentation. Different networks may have different requirements for the size of a packet. Generally, a fast, robust LAN can use a large packet size, while a slower WAN connection may require a smaller packet. The standard for each media type (e.g., Ethernet, Token-Ring) determines the maximum physical frame size and therefore the maximum IP packet size, which in turn determines the maximum TCP packet size, which then determines the maximum amount of application data that can be sent in one datagram.

There are two ways of accommodating variable packet size across a group of interconnected networks. One way is to use a lowest-common-denominator approach. When an IP packet traverses the networks from the source to the destination system, the minimum packet size on any network along the path could be used to determine the packet size. This approach would often be inefficient, though, because it would force fast LANs to use much smaller packets than they can accommodate.

The method actually used to accommodate variable frame sizes is known as *fragmentation*. Fragmentation, which is part of the specifications for the IP protocol, means that the IP packet is broken down into multiple smaller IP packets that are then sent across the network. Fragmentation is often done at the point two networks meet to allow each network to use the most efficient frame size (and thus IP packet size) for that network. The source and destination systems may not know the IP packet is being fragmented, assuming the fragmentation and reassembly are not done on either system.

The fragment size is determined by the physical network frame in which the fragment is transported. The identifier field provides a unique identifier for every fragment between the source and the destination. The flags field contains three bits. The first bit is reserved and is always 0. A value of 0 in the second bit means the packet may be fragmented; 1 means the packet may not be fragmented. When the third bit is a 0, it means this fragment is the last (or only) fragment; a value of 1 means that more fragments follow. The fragment offset is 13 bits long and contains an offset (in 64-bit words) identifying the fragment's position in the datagram.

The header of a fragmented IP packet contains all the information that would be included if the packet were not fragmented. In other words, the complete IP header (with appropriate identifier field bits) is transmitted along with the TCP header and as much of the application data as can be accommodated. It's the responsibility of the gateway or the destination host to reassemble the packets into the complete datagram. Fragmentation and reassembly obviously incur overhead on the source system, the destination system, or the gateways between the source and destination and cause more network traffic than would exist between networks with the same physical frame sizes.

The next field in the IP packet is the time-to-live octet, which is used to identify "lost" packets. Packets can be lost because of a wrong address, a system being down, there being no available route to the destination, or for other reasons. The time-to-live field was designed to hold a value indicating the length of time a packet could exist on the network before it was considered lost and would be discarded. As it's actually used, however, this field contains a number of "hops" allowed before the packet is considered lost. A hop refers to the number of times the packet leaves a network in search of its destination. The time-to-live field is decremented every time a packet hops from one network to another.

The protocol octet identifies the protocol used for the datagram being transported by the IP packet. For example, a value of 1 indicates Internet Control Message Protocol (ICMP, used for the Packet Internetwork Groper, or PING), 6 indicates TCP, and 17 indicates UDP. The protocol field enables encapsulation of other protocols as well, such as Novell's IPX or IBM's SNA. Such encapsulation is useful when you want to use just one protocol across a WAN but multiple protocols in different LANs. Although performance issues can arise as a result of encapsulation, the cost savings of encapsulation generally outweigh any decrease in performance.

The 2-octet header checksum field is used to verify the contents of the packet. The 32-bit source and destination address fields that follow contain the IP address of the source and destination, respectively. The options and padding field contains any optional values needed by the source or destination systems (e.g., security information, source route information, timestamp information) and any padding needed to ensure the IP packet ends on a 32-bit boundary.

Figure 3.11 shows all the components of a physical network frame, including the IP header, the TCP header, the application data, and the network trailer (mentioned in the section "Physical Frames" earlier in this chapter).

Figure 3.11
Complete Frame with IP and TCP Information

Network header	IP header	TCP header	Data	Network trailer

TCP/IP Processing Flow

The process of sending application information from one system to another is straightforward. The application process delivers the application data to the Transport layer, which provides the TCP header. The Transport layer then delivers the TCP packet (containing the TCP header, the application data, and the checksum information) to the Internet layer. The Internet layer adds the IP header and additional checksum information and passes the IP packet (containing the source and address information and the TCP packet) to the Data Link layer. The Data Link layer places the IP packet into the physical frame, adding the MAC address of the source and target systems.

The physical frame, containing the IP and TCP headers and the application data, is sent across the physical network (the wire). The actual method of sending the packet is determined by the type of network in use (e.g., Ethernet, 802.3, or 802.5). Regardless, the packet is either delivered to the destination or target system or is lost. We'll discuss routing issues later in this chapter, but for the time being, let's assume the packet reaches its destination.

When the packet arrives at the destination, the system receives it at the Physical layer. The process discussed above now takes place in reverse order, with lower-layer information being stripped and higher-level information proceeding up the protocol stack. The destination system's Data Link layer removes the MAC address and other physical information and sends the remaining portion (the IP packet) to the Internet layer. The Internet layer removes the IP address information and sends the TCP packet to the Transport layer. The Transport layer removes the TCP information and sends the application data to the Application layer, which then provides the data to the actual application, such as Telnet or FTP. Figure 3.12 illustrates the entire process.

FIGURE 3.12
TCP/IP Processing Flow

Source System		Destination System	
Application	Application data is sent to the Transport layer	Application	Application data is delivered to the application
Transport	Transport layer adds TCP header	Transport	Transport layer removes the TCP header
Internet	Internet layer adds the IP header	Internet	Internet layer removes the IP header
Data Link	Data Link layer adds the physical frame information	Data Link	Data Link layer removes the physical frame information

Physical Media

To reiterate, the application data from the source system traverses the TCP/IP protocol stack from the Application layer to the Data Link layer. The physical frame is then sent across the physical media (a LAN or WAN connection) to the destination system, where the packet traverses the layers of the destination protocol stack in reverse order until the data is presented to the application.

DOMAIN NAME SERVICE (DNS)

To call someone on the telephone, you must know or find the telephone number for that person. Typically, if you don't already have this essential piece of information, you at least know the party's name. Having that, you find the telephone number in a telephone directory (either a personal directory or the phone book) or get it from directory assistance or from someone else who you know has it. The key is that although you need a telephone number, you can find it by knowing the name of the party you want to call. For most of us, a name is easier to remember than a number.

A similar situation exists with TCP/IP addresses. Although you need the 4-octet IP address to access a system, it's much easier to remember a name — you're far less likely to remember 198.47.212.83, for example, than as400.ibm.com. Domain Name Service (DNS) acts like a "telephone directory" to IP addresses. Included with most versions of TCP/IP, DNS lets you access a system using a (relatively) easily remembered name rather than an IP address.

For DNS to find an IP address based on a name, the name must be associated with the address (an address can be associated with more than one name). One method of associating a host name with an IP address is through a host table. All implementations of TCP/IP provide for a host table. TCP/IP processes can examine the host table to resolve the host name to an IP address. Figure 3.13 shows a sample AS/400 host table accessed using the CL CFGTCP (Configure TCP/IP) command, option 10, Work with TCP/IP Host Table Entries.

FIGURE 3.13
Sample AS/400 Host Table

```
              Work with TCP/IP Host Table Entries
                                            System: DEVL400
     Type options, press Enter.
       1=Add    2=Change   4=Remove   5=Display   7=Rename


            Internet         Host
     Opt    Address          Name
      _
      _     127.0.0.1        LOOPBACK
                             LOCALHOST
      _     198.0.0.1        AS400.400SCHOOL.COM
                             AS400
      _     198.0.0.2        MRPC
                             CLIENTPC.400SCHOOL.COM
```

As you can see, this host table defines three hosts (or interfaces). The first entry, IP address 127.0.0.1, is a standard TCP/IP entry on most systems and is associated with the names LOOPBACK and LOCALHOST. This entry serves as an internal IP address used only by internal TCP/IP processes. The first octet for a loopback address must be 127.

The next entry, with IP address 198.0.0.1 and names AS400.400SCHOOL.COM and AS400, associates an IP address with two names. In this case, the IP address belongs to the host. A host-table entry that associates the host with an

IP address is important on all AS/400s so the host system can be identified, especially for proper e-mail processing. This entry shows the fully qualified host name (AS400.400SCHOOL.COM) and a "nickname" for the same system (AS400). The next entry, IP address 198.0.0.2, illustrates that alternative names associated with an IP address need not be related — the entries MRPC and CLIENTPC.400SCHOOL.COM both refer to the same IP address even though they are not similar names. Either name can serve as a target for a TCP/IP client/server request, such as a Telnet or FTP request. When multiple names are associated with an IP address in a host table, all of the names will be resolved to that particular address. In a *reverse lookup*, however, in which the system starts with an IP address and tries to find the associated name, the system always returns the first name specified in the host table.

Because there were far fewer networks and hosts in the early days, users could easily remember the IP addresses they most frequently needed and use host-table lookups for the rest. In fact, the Internet Network Information Center used a flat namespace — basically a large host table — to resolve addresses for the entire Internet. Host tables were transferred to different hosts, and system administrators updated their own host tables. (The AS/400 still has an option to merge host tables from different sources.)

As the Internet grew, however, a better method of name and address resolution was needed. At the rate new hosts were being added to the Internet, system administrators couldn't keep up with the changes, and ultimately the namespace itself became too large to maintain. The namespace was declared obsolete around 1990, when there were about 140,000 Internet hosts (IP addresses). It was replaced by DNS. Although the AS/400 does still have an option to merge host tables from different sources, the search order to resolve an IP address based on a system name is usually customizable — you can specify that either the host table or a DNS server be the first (or only) avenue for searching.

DNS is based on the hierarchical structure of domain names. A domain is a logical grouping of hosts that provides structure for TCP/IP host names. Domains are hierarchical — related domain names are grouped together in subdomains (often geographic or organizational) within higher-level domains. For instance, the domain name IBM.COM identifies subdomain IBM within the higher-level domain COM. There are many subdomains within the COM domain, and many sub-subdomains within IBM.COM (e.g., AS400.IBM.COM). The hierarchical structure enables DNS to search from a high-level domain through levels of subdomains to a specific host.

A host or system name usually consists of three sections: a host name, one or more subdomain names, and a high-level domain name. The host name identifies a particular host. When you qualify the host name by adding a domain name, the qualified name uniquely identifies a host within that domain. A fully qualified domain name includes all host, subdomain, and domain information. DNS names (host, subdomain, and domain) are not case sensitive; however, user names (for e-mail) may be, depending on the system type. Unix systems, for example, are case sensitive.

Domain names are read from left to right — from the most specific (the host) to the most general (the highest-level domain). An example of a fully qualified domain name is ftp.400school.com, where ftp is the name of a host (perhaps an anonymous FTP server), 400school is a subdomain, and com is the highest-level domain. Another example is www.us.pc.ibm.com (an IBM server used for IBM PC and ThinkPad patches and information). Here, the host (www) is in a subdomain (us) that is part of another subdomain (pc), which is part of yet another subdomain (ibm) within the high-level domain com. Although there is no limit to the number of subdomains (and sub-subdomains) that can be used, subdomains are usually limited to two levels to keep the fully qualified domain name short. You must specify a fully qualified domain name for your local AS/400 to be able to resolve its own address, especially for e-mail.

The highest-level domain names are standard across the Internet. There are two main categories of domain names: organizational and geographical. The organizational domain names are probably the most familiar to readers in the United States, whereas the geographical domain names may be more familiar to readers in other countries. The organizational domain names are

- com — commercial organizations
- edu — educational institutions
- gov — government entities
- mil — military organizations
- net — network (Internet) support organizations
- org — organizations (usually nonprofits)
- int — international organizations (obsolete)
- arpa — temporary ARPANet domains (obsolete)

A geographic domain name consists of a country code and provides a way to identify the location of the host but gives no information regarding its nature or function. Some examples are

- us — United States (the highest subdomain within this domain is a state code)
- ca — Canada
- ch — Switzerland
- es — Spain

- it — Italy
- de — Germany
- jp — Japan

An example of a fully qualified geographic domain name is the address for Lansing Community College (a fine institution) in Lansing, Michigan. The school's public Web server is www.lansing.cc.mi.us, which means that a host named www (obviously a Web server) is in a domain named cc (which stands for "community college") in a domain named mi (Michigan, my Michigan) in the highest-level domain us (United States). Note that, as an educational institution, LCC could have used the more common edu domain. The use of geographic domain names is growing, albeit slowly, in the United States.

Even if your network isn't attached to the Internet, you should adopt one of the standard naming conventions to ensure that the addresses will work when the network is eventually attached to the Internet. I also recommend registering a domain for your organization, even if the network is not connected to the Internet. This inexpensive ($50 per year) safeguard ensures that the domain name is available when the organization decides to go online.

We've discussed the concept of host tables and the hierarchical structure of domain names that serves as the foundation of DNS; now let's look at how it works. Because a detailed discussion is far beyond the scope of this book (several complete books have been devoted to the topic) and because you can remain blissfully ignorant of DNS's complexities without jeopardizing your effectiveness in the least, we will limit ourselves to a broad overview of the mechanics of DNS and how it resolves addresses.

Consider a device, host, or system that needs to resolve a name to an IP address. The request for resolution could originate with a client requesting Telnet or FTP services or from "behind the scenes" when the SMTP e-mail process needs to forward mail to another system. In any case, the search for the IP address associated with a name usually begins on the system's host table, if there is one. If no match is found there, if no host table is present, or if DNS is the preferred method of address resolution, the search sends a request to a DNS server, which is often on the local network.

If the DNS server can't resolve the address (in other words, the DNS server doesn't have the name and IP address information), the request is forwarded to a higher-level DNS server. This higher DNS server may be part of the same network as the original DNS server, it may be on another network within the same organization, or it may be maintained by an Internet Service Provider (ISP). The higher-level DNS server attempts to resolve the address, but if it can't, it sends the request to another higher-level DNS server.

The uppermost DNS servers (those that contain information about the highest-level domains, such as COM and EDU) are located at several points around the world. The highest-level DNS servers are the court of last resort; if they cannot resolve the address, the address is considered unresolvable and the system that originated the request is notified that the host name cannot be resolved. This process continues until the request is resolved or until all available DNS servers in the domain are searched. This hierarchical address resolution requires that all DNS servers in the domain are properly configured.

With the standard implementation of TCP/IP, pre-V4R1 AS/400s cannot be DNS servers. They can use a DNS server to resolve host names but cannot respond to other systems' requests to provide DNS resolution. This limitation is overcome with OS/400 V4R1 and V4R2. Beginning in V4R1, the AS/400 firewall can provide DNS services to an outside network (one on the unsecure side of the firewall). V4R2 systems have DNS built in to the operating system, so the AS/400 can provide standard DNS services to any device that can connect to the network on which the AS/400 resides. The best implementation of firewall and DNS technology is to use a firewall — either the AS/400's or a stand-alone firewall — to provide DNS services to the unsecure network and to use the AS/400 or some other device to provide DNS services to the internal network.

Like other TCP/IP services, such as Telnet and FTP, DNS has its own packet structure. The system requesting name resolution services sends to the DNS server a DNS packet containing information such as the name of the requested host, and the DNS server returns its response in a DNS packet. The initiating system must know the address of the DNS server; supplying that address is part of the TCP/IP configuration on any system.

Configuration of DNS, and the related SMTP, is a very complex and involved subject and beyond the scope of this book. Readers interested in a greater level of detail can find many excellent books on these subjects.

ADDRESS RESOLUTION PROTOCOL

Regardless of whether a client request for TCP/IP services uses an IP address directly, searches the host table, or uses a DNS search, the IP address must be mapped to the physical address of the NIC. Address Resolution Protocol (ARP) is the method used for this mapping.

When the requesting system knows the destination system's IP address (perhaps through a host table lookup or a DNS search), the sending system examines its ARP cache for the target system's physical hardware address. If the hardware address is not in the cache, the system broadcasts an ARP packet containing the target system's IP address to all other systems on the network. Upon receiving the broadcast, the target system recognizes its own IP address and returns an ARP packet containing its hardware address to the sending system. The sending system then incorporates that hardware address into the physical frame that contains the message or data.

The sending system maintains the target system's physical address information in its ARP cache for a certain length of time. Thus, a system that communicates frequently with a particular destination system usually has the necessary physical address in its cache. Packets destined for a network beyond the local network use the same process, but in those cases the router at the remote network provides the ARP broadcast, discovery, and caching functions.

Reverse Address Resolution Protocol (RARP) is similar to ARP but is used when a system knows its own hardware address but not its own IP address. This situation arises with systems, such as diskless workstations, X-stations, and network stations, that must download an operating system from a server. The RARP process is similar to the ARP process: The device broadcasts an ARP packet with its hardware address set to the proper value and its own IP address and the target's hardware and IP address set to zeros. The system that recognizes the RARP broadcast is known as a RARP server. The RARP server processes the request, inserts the sending device's IP address into the packet, and returns it to the device.

Physical Connections, Bridging, and Routing

Higher-level search techniques, such as host table lookups, DNS searches, and ARP resolution, provide name resolution and physical address resolution. But how are packets physically moved from the source system to the target system? Here we discuss the two components of physical packet movement: physical connections, such as wiring, and logical connections, such as bridging and routing, which link networks together and provide the logical connections from a source to a target system.

Wiring and Physical Connections

The network topology and associated cabling are part of the physical layer of the OSI Reference Model. A network topology is the geometric configuration in which the network devices (or nodes) are connected. The three main network topologies used today are the star, ring, and bus. Any of these topologies can be used with TCP/IP (or any networking protocol); the decision of which to use is generally based on existing wiring or the physical protocol (Ethernet or Token-Ring) to be used.

The star topology is probably the oldest on the market and the most common. In a star topology, network nodes are connected to a common point, such as a hub or repeater. The cabling most often used with a star topology is unshielded twisted pair, which is relatively inexpensive (compared to the coaxial cable used for older Ethernet networks), easy to implement, and flexible. Figure 3.14 illustrates a star topology network.

The most significant advantage of a star over other topologies is that failure of a node or of the cabling to a node does not cause problems elsewhere in

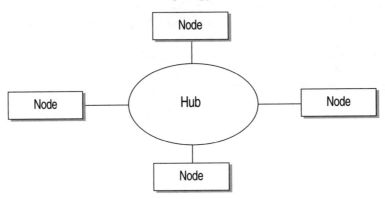

FIGURE 3.14
A Star Topology Network

the network. The node is out of commission, but other nodes are not affected. This characteristic decreases network downtime due to cabling problems.

The ring topology is most often used with Token-Ring networks. In a ring topology, as you'd expect, each node is connected to two others in a ring configuration. A signal beginning at the source system is passed from node to node until it reaches the destination system. Each station on the ring repeats the signal as it travels around the ring, thus regenerating the signal as it traverses the network. An advantage of the ring topology is that only one station can communicate at any given time, eliminating contention and collisions. Figure 3.15 shows a ring topology network.

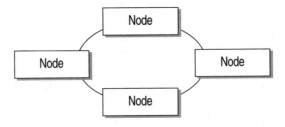

FIGURE 3.15
A Ring Topology Network

As you might suspect, a ring topology also has an inherent disadvantage: If the cable is broken at any point, the signal cannot traverse the network and *all* stations are unable to communicate. Although a Token-Ring network uses a ring topology, it also usually borrows from the star topology to create a "star ring." A star ring connects all stations through a special repeater. Rather than the stations being physically connected, the repeater completes the ring, thus eliminating this topology's biggest disadvantage.

Less popular than either the ring or star is the bus topology. This topology was used for Ethernet networks in the past, and some implementations still exist. The bus topology is very simple, but may be more costly to implement than a star network. Nodes on a bus network are connected in a "daisy chain" fashion to the same cable, usually coaxial for 10Base2 networks (known as "thinnet") or a thicker cable for 10Base5 networks (known as "thicknet"). The cable that connects the nodes must be terminated on each end with a special connection that contains a resistor. Figure 3.16 shows a diagram of a bus topology network.

FIGURE 3.16
A Bus Topology Network

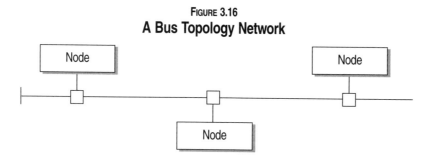

The main advantage of a bus network is its simplicity. The primary disadvantage is that a broken cable disables all nodes. Bus networks are not as popular as they were in earlier networking days, but they still have a role as backbones for other networking topologies, notably the star topology.

Bridges and Routers

Bridges and routers are devices used to form logical connections between LANs and between LANs and WANs. Such logical interconnections between networks are the basis of the Internet. Bridges and routers can logically isolate or separate networks from each other as well as link networks together, as we'll see.

The difference between bridges and routers is the level at which they operate. As Figure 3.17 illustrates, bridges interconnect networks at the data link layer of the OSI Reference Model (more specifically, at the MAC sublayer), whereas routers operate at the network layer.

Because bridges operate at the data link layer, they are not concerned with higher-level protocols (e.g., TCP/IP, IPX), which operate at the network layer. Bridges can connect networks of the same physical protocol — for instance, an Ethernet bridge can connect two Ethernet networks — and networks of dissimilar physical protocols, such as Ethernet and Token-Ring. Bridges can also logically isolate networks, and this isolation or separation is a primary reason for bridging.

FIGURE 3.17
Bridging and Routing

Application		Application
Presentation		Presentation
Session		Session
Transport		Transport
Network	— Routing —	Network
Data Link	— Bridging —	Data Link
Physical		Physical

Although the primary purpose for bridges in the past was network interconnection, a more important use for them actually is to selectively prohibit traffic from flowing across a WAN link. A bridge can "learn" (or be "taught") the IP addresses on the other side of a WAN link. Once the bridge knows those addresses, it can decide, based on the address, whether to prohibit traffic (because the address needed does not appear on the other side of that link) or allow traffic across a particular WAN link. Regulating the flow of traffic across WAN links can greatly improve network performance. And because bridges need only see the MAC address in a packet to decide whether to forward it, they can move packets quickly.

Routers direct packets to the correct destination by knowing the location of — or a route to a location for — all nodes on a network. The router may not actually know of each individual node on the network, but it can send packets to the network on which the node is located or to a network that has a router that knows of the destination. In other words, a router may not itself know of the actual destination, but it knows of other routers that can "figure it out."

Routers contain routing tables that learn the addresses of other networks and let the router forward TCP/IP packets to networks without knowing the explicit path to the network. The routing table usually includes a default entry that allows packets to be forwarded even if the routing table has no information about the remote network. Routers are used on large or complex networks for which multiple or redundant paths are needed. Multiple and redundant paths provide additional connections in the event of a failure in any one path.

Because routers operate at the network layer, the networks being connected must use the same networking protocol, such as TCP/IP. This does not mean that a separate router is needed for each networking protocol — routers usually accommodate multiple protocols. However, a router cannot forward a packet that uses a protocol the router does not accommodate. Routers must identify the actual network address of the packet to determine whether the packet should be forwarded, so the speed of the router determines the performance of packet filtering and forwarding.

Routers and bridges are becoming increasingly similar in function. In fact, you can now obtain data communications devices known as brouters that combine the features of a bridge and a router. Although the distinctions between bridges and routers are becoming blurred, the simplest way to understand the differences is to know that a bridge operates at the data link layer and a router at the network layer.

Many vendors offer bridging and routing products. Along with switches and gateways, routers and bridges are some of the most popular products on the data communications market. You should deal with an established vendor that can support the protocols you use. If you also use SNA, make sure the vendor supports SNA and provides appropriate mechanisms for connecting the SNA environment as well as the TCP/IP environment.

Chapter 4

Configuring the AS/400 for TCP/IP

The AS/400 provides a strong implementation of TCP/IP. From a simple Local Area Network (LAN) TCP/IP configuration to a complicated network configuration involving intranets and the Internet, the AS/400 has the configuration options needed to ensure its participation in the network.

However, you must configure the AS/400 to use the TCP/IP protocol suite. (Doing so doesn't mean that the AS/400 will be unable to communicate using other protocols, including Advanced Program to Program Communications (APPC), the "mainstay" AS/400 networking protocol. Multiple protocols can (and often do) operate at the same time on an AS/400.) The minimal configuration needed for TCP/IP communications requires that you create a line (with the network controller and network device automatically created), specify the host and domain name, and issue the STRTCP (Start TCP/IP) command. This minimal configuration by default allows Telnet and File Transfer Protocol (FTP) processing, which are key components in TCP/IP networking. Further configuration provides support for the other services, such as Line Printer Daemon (LPD) and Simple Mail Transfer Protocol (SMTP).

This chapter covers the configuration of TCP/IP on the AS/400 from the bottom up — from the physical layer to the application layer. We first cover creating a line description for Ethernet and Token-Ring lines. Then we look at the CFGTCP (Configure TCP/IP) menu, discuss each menu option, and identify appropriate entries. We cover the necessary SMTP options to configure the AS/400 for e-mail support. And although most installations won't need advanced configuration options, we also cover the following topics, but more briefly:

- TCP/IP attributes
- Port restrictions
- Remote system information
- Merging TCP/IP host tables
- Configuring TCP/IP-related tables
- Configuring point-to-point TCP/IP

We conclude the chapter with a discussion of configuring AnyNet, the IBM framework that allows encapsulation of TCP/IP packets in SNA packets and the encapsulation of SNA packets in TCP/IP packets.

CONFIGURING THE LINE, CONTROLLER, AND DEVICE

The AS/400 can use TCP/IP over Ethernet, Token-Ring, and X.25 protocols and asynchronous lines. This section describes configuring the AS/400 for a LAN TCP/IP connection with both Ethernet and Token-Ring. We won't discuss X.25 line configuration because it is used much less often than a LAN connection, and we discuss asynchronous line configuration in Appendix C.

A LAN configuration for a TCP/IP connection is simple. Use the CRT-LINETH (Create Line Description — Ethernet) or CRTLINTRN (Create Line Description — Token-Ring) command, or take option 6 from the Main menu, then option 4 from the Communications menu, option 1 from the Configure Communications menu, and then press F6 to create a new line description for the LAN line. You can accept most of the default parameter values for configuring a LAN connection, but let's look at both line types and discuss the parameters used for each line.

Configuring an Ethernet Line Description

You create an Ethernet line description by typing the CRTLINETH command on a command line and pressing F4 to prompt the command. The prompted command is shown in Figure 4.1.

FIGURE 4.1

Create Ethernet Line Descripton Prompt Screen — Screen 1

```
                        Create Line Desc (Ethernet) (CRTLINETH)

 Type choices, press Enter.

 Line description  . . . . . . . .            Name
 Resource name  . . . . . . . . .            Name, *NWID, *NWSD




                                                                        Bottom
 F3=Exit   F4=Prompt   F5=Refresh   F10=Additional parameters   F12=Cancel
 F13=How to use this display     F24=More keys
```

The Line description (LIND) specifies a name for the line. You may choose any name up to 10 characters long. I usually use a name such as ETHLINE so that I can quickly identify the line when I use the WRKCFGSTS (Work with Configuration Status) command.

The Resource name (RSRCNAME) parameter specifies the resource name associated with the connection. The resource is the name of the communications adapter that will be used to connect the AS/400 to the network. This resource will be an Input/Output Adapter (IOA) and will be different depending on the communications hardware available on the specific AS/400. This parameter can have several different values depending on the type of physical connection. A value of *NWID indicates that a network interface description for frame relay will be used. A *NWID description is a special type of description that provides support for a frame relay interface. A value of *NWSD, which we will specify for this example, indicates that a network server description will be used. Network server descriptions are used for File Server Input-Output Processors (FSIOP) and Integrated PC Servers (IPCS). Using either *NWID or *NWSD leads to additional parameter prompts that must be completed for the specific interface used. Consult the *OS/400 Communications Configuration* manual for more details.

If you don't use a special value of *NWID or *NWSD, you need to enter the specific name of the communications resource, which you can find using the WRKHDWRSC (Work with Hardware Resources) command (see "The WRKHDWRSC Command" below).

Typing the resource name — in this case *NWSD — and pressing Enter brings up more parameters (Figure 4.2). We look at only those required for an Ethernet line description for TCP/IP.

The On line (ONLINE) parameter (which appears after you type other parameters and press Enter) determines whether the line should be brought online when an IPL is performed. The default value is *YES, indicating that the line will be brought online when the system is IPLed. This value is usually acceptable unless special processing considerations dictate otherwise.

The Vary on wait (VRYWAIT) parameter specifies whether the system should wait until the line is varied on before ending the VRYCFG (Vary Configuration) command. A value of *NOWAIT (meaning no wait time) is the default and is usually acceptable. Specifying a vary-on wait time (from 15 to 180 seconds) can increase the IPL time but is useful when an application acquires or opens an ICF file after varying on the line.

The Network server description parameter specifies the network server description to which this nonswitched line is attached. You can find this description using the WRKHDWRSC command (see "The WRKHDWRSC Command" below). The second element of this parameter, Port number, specifies the network server port to which the line is attached. Valid values are 1, 2, and 3.

FIGURE 4.2

Create Ethernet Line Description Prompt Screen — Screen 2

```
                    Create Line Desc (Ethernet) (CRTLINETH)

 Type choices, press Enter.

 Line description . . . . . . . . > ETHLINE        Name
 Resource name  . . . . . . . . > *NWSD           Name, *NWID, *NWSD
 Vary on wait . . . . . . . . .   *NOWAIT         *NOWAIT, 15-180 seconds
 Network server description:
                                  *NONE           Name, *NONE
   Port number  . . . . . . . .                   1-3
 Local adapter address  . . . .   *ADPT           020000000000-7EFFFFFFFFFF...
 Exchange identifier  . . . . .   *SYSGEN         05600000-056FFFFF, *SYSGEN
 Ethernet standard  . . . . . .   *ALL            *ETHV2, *IEEE8023, *ALL
 Line speed . . . . . . . . . .   10M             Character value, 10M, 100M...
 Duplex . . . . . . . . . . . .   *HALF           Character value, *HALF...
 SSAP list:
   Source service access point .  *SYSGEN         02-FE, *SYSGEN
   SSAP maximum frame . . . . . .                 *MAXFRAME, 265-1496, 265...
   SSAP type                                      *CALC, *NONSNA, *SNA, *HPR
             + for more values
                                                                   More...
 F3=Exit   F4=Prompt   F5=Refresh    F10=Additional parameters   F12=Cancel
 F13=How to use this display    F24=More keys
```

The Local adapter address (ADPTADR) lets you specify the LAN adapter address for the Ethernet line. The default value is *ADPT, meaning that the manufacturer's address should be used. See Chapter 3 for a detailed description of Network Interface Card (NIC) addresses. *ADPT may be satisfactory, but if the numbering conventions of your network require certain addresses, you may specify the hexadecimal-number (12-digit) address to be used.

The Ethernet standard (ETHSTD) parameter identifies the Ethernet standard to be used with this line. The default is *ALL, meaning that both the Ethernet Version II and the Institute of Electrical and Electronic Engineers (IEEE) 802.3 standards are supported. Consult Chapter 3 for more information regarding Ethernet standards. Other possible values are *ETHV2 for Ethernet II only and *IEEE8023 for the 802.3 standard. Because *ALL enables the use of any of the Ethernet standards, I always use *ALL.

The Source service access point (SSAP) parameter specifies the hexadecimal logical channel addresses used to route incoming data off the network to the correct user. The default value of *SYSGEN, meaning system-generated SSAP values, is probably the most appropriate choice because it ensures that the critical SSAP value of AA will be assigned to the line description (an SSAP of AA lets TCP/IP applications run over the Ethernet line). Other SSAPs are also associated with the line description when the *SYSGEN special value is used, including 04, 12, and C8. SSAP 04 is used for SNA applications, 12 is used for LAN printing, and C8 is used for Advanced Peer-to-Peer Networking (APPN) High Performance Routing (HPR).

Other SSAP list parameters (this parameter is a complex parameter) are the SSAP Maximum frame size and the SSAP type. The former specifies the maximum data field that can be transmitted or received, and the latter specifies whether the SSAP will be used for SNA or non-SNA applications. For TCP/IP, these parameters should be left at their default values of *MAXFRAME and *CALC, respectively.

The other parameters on this screen, as well as several more, are available for Ethernet line creation, but the default values are appropriate for most implementations of Ethernet connectivity.

The WRKHDWRSC Command

You can find the specific name of a communications resource using the WRKHDWRSC (Work with Hardware Resources) command and specifying *CMN as the hardware parameter. Figure 4A shows an example of the list screen for the WRKHDWRSC *CMN command.

FIGURE 4A
Work with Communication Resources Screen

```
                    Work with Communication Resources
                                                   System:    S1029F3R
 Type options, press Enter.
   5=Work with configuration descriptions   7=Display resource detail

 Opt   Resource      Type  Status           Text
  _    CMB01         6756  Operational      Combined function IOP
  _      LIN01       2720  Operational      Comm Adapter
  _        CMN01     2720  Operational      V.24 Port Enhanced
  _      LIN02       2850  Operational      File Server IOA
  _        CMN02     2838  Operational      Ethernet Port
  _        CMN03     6B00  Operational      Virtual Port
  _      LIN03       285A  Operational      LAN Adapter




                                                               Bottom
 F3=Exit    F5=Refresh    F6=Print    F12=Cancel
```

Network hardware varies depending on the model of AS/400 you are using. However, the resource for the type of attachment you are configuring will be (more or less) clearly identified. The resource name is shown in the Resource column. In this example, a 6756 Combined Function IOP will be used for the Ethernet connection. You would specify LIN02 in the Network server description parameter in Figure 4.2. Another type of Ethernet resource is a 2617 card, which is an Ethernet card without the FSIOP or IPCS processor.

Configuring a Token-Ring Line Description

You create a Token-Ring line description by typing the CRTLINTRN command on a command line and pressing F4 to prompt the command. The prompted command is shown in Figure 4.3.

FIGURE 4.3

Create Token-Ring Line Description Prompt Screen — Screen 1

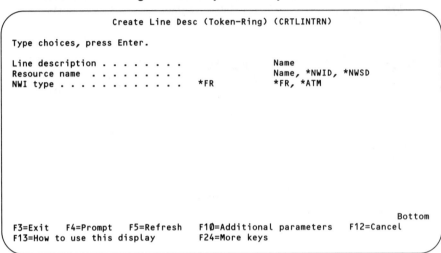

```
                  Create Line Desc (Token-Ring) (CRTLINTRN)

Type choices, press Enter.

Line description . . . . . . . .              Name
Resource name  . . . . . . . . .              Name, *NWID, *NWSD
NWI type . . . . . . . . . . . .    *FR       *FR, *ATM




                                                                    Bottom
F3=Exit    F4=Prompt    F5=Refresh    F10=Additional parameters    F12=Cancel
F13=How to use this display         F24=More keys
```

With a couple of minor exceptions, the parameters for creating a Token-Ring line are the same as for an Ethernet line.

The Line description and Resource name parameters are exactly the same as for an Ethernet line creation. Remember that the WRKHDWRSC command can help you identify the Token-Ring adapter in your system. Typing the resource name and pressing Enter brings up a second screen of parameters (Figure 4.4).

The Online at IPL, Vary on wait, Local adapter address, and SSAP list parameters are the same as for an Ethernet line. See the previous section for details regarding these parameters.

An important Token-Ring-specific parameter is Line speed (LINESPEED), which specifies the speed of the line on the network. The default value is 4M — 4 megabits per second (Mbps). Most Token-Ring installations now operate at 16 Mbps. It is critical to have this value set to the speed of the network because a Token-Ring adapter operating at the wrong speed in a network can cause physical damage to other NICs or other Token-Ring network equipment.

FIGURE 4.4
FIGURE 4.4
Create Token-Ring Line Description Prompt Screen — Screen 2

```
                    Create Line Desc (Token-Ring) (CRTLINTRN)

 Type choices, press Enter.

 Line description . . . . . . . > TRNLINE        Name
 Resource name  . . . . . . . . > *NWSD          Name, *NWID, *NWSD
 NWI type . . . . . . . . . . .   *FR            *FR, *ATM
 Vary on wait . . . . . . . . .   *NOWAIT        *NOWAIT, 15-180 seconds
 Maximum controllers  . . . . .   40             1-256
 Network server description:
                                  *NONE          Name, *NONE
   Port number  . . . . . . . .                  1-3, *INTERNAL
 Line speed . . . . . . . . . .   4M             4M, 16M, *NWI
 Duplex . . . . . . . . . . . .   *HALF          Character value, *HALF, *FULL
 Maximum frame size . . . . . .   1994           265-16393, 265, 521, 1033...
 Local adapter address  . . . .   *ADPT          400000000000-7FFFFFFFFFFF...
 Exchange identifier  . . . . .   *SYSGEN        05600000-056FFFFF, *SYSGEN




                                                                    More...
 F3=Exit   F4=Prompt   F5=Refresh   F12=Cancel   F13=How to use this display
 F24=More keys
```

The other parameters shown in Figure 4.4, as well as several more, are available for creating a Token-Ring line description, but the default entries are appropriate for most implementations of Token-Ring connectivity.

Network Controllers and Devices
The AS/400 automatically configures a network controller and a network device when TCP/IP is first started. The network controller and the network device provide the interaction between the LAN line and the network. The controller and device are needed to provide the standard line, controller, and device configuration.

BASIC TCP/IP CONFIGURATION OPTIONS
The heart of configuring TCP/IP is the Configure TCP/IP menu (Figure 4.5), which you access with the CFGTCP command. Although this menu has several options, you need only a few to configure TCP/IP on your system. In this section, we discuss the basic TCP/IP configuration options and the associated parameters, highlighting the most common and important ones. In "Advanced TCP/IP Configuration Options" later in this chapter, we briefly cover the more advanced options.

FIGURE 4.5
Configure TCP/IP Menu

```
CFGTCP                          Configure TCP/IP
                                                        System:    S1029F3R
Select one of the following:

    1. Work with TCP/IP interfaces
    2. Work with TCP/IP routes
    3. Change TCP/IP attributes
    4. Work with TCP/IP port restrictions
    5. Work with TCP/IP remote system information

   10. Work with TCP/IP host table entries
   11. Merge TCP/IP host table
   12. Change TCP/IP domain information

   20. Configure TCP/IP applications
   21. Configure related tables
   22. Configure point-to-point TCP/IP


Selection or command
===>  _____

 F3=Exit    F4=Prompt    F9=Retrieve    F12=Cancel
```

Working with TCP/IP Interfaces

You use option 1 on the Configure TCP/IP menu to work with TCP/IP interfaces. This menu option lets you to specify the IP address (or addresses) for your AS/400, which is critical to the success of a TCP/IP implementation. Remember that an IP address identifies the connection to a system, not the system itself. The AS/400 is multihomed, meaning that it may have multiple interfaces to the TCP/IP network. Entering option 1 from the CFGTCP menu brings up a screen similar to the one in Figure 4.6. This display shows the IP address, subnet mask, line description, and line type for each interface defined on your system. As shown in Figure 4.6, when there is a TCP/IP interface defined on your system, one interface entry should always be present — the loopback entry with an IP address of 127.0.0.1, a subnet mask of 255.0.0.0, a line description of *LOOPBACK, and a line type of *NONE. This entry is used for internal TCP/IP processes and for testing. *Do not remove or modify this entry.*

From this screen, you may add, change, remove, display, start, or end TCP/IP interfaces. The available options (and their associated CL commands, where applicable) are

- Option 1, Add an interface — ADDTCPIFC
- Option 2, Change an interface — CHGTCPIFC
- Option 4, Remove an interface — RMVTCPIFC
- Option 5, Display an interface

FIGURE 4.6
Work with TCP/IP Interfaces Screen

```
                       Work with TCP/IP Interfaces
                                                      System:    S1029F3R
   Type options, press Enter.
    1=Add    2=Change   4=Remove   5=Display   9=Start   10=End

        Internet           Subnet            Line       Line
   Opt  Address            Mask              Description Type

   _    127.0.0.1          255.0.0.0         *LOOPBACK   *NONE
   _    198.0.0.20         255.255.255.0     ETHLINE     *ELAN




                                                                 Bottom
   F3=Exit       F5=Refresh    F6=Print list   F11=Display interface status
   F12=Cancel    F17=Top       F18=Bottom
```

- Option 9, Start an interface — STRTCPIFC
- Option 10, End (stop) an interface — ENDTCPIFC

Adding a TCP/IP Interface

To add an interface, you enter a 1 in the option field on the top, blank line of the display. You may also enter the IP address at this time, or simply press Enter for the entire prompt display (Figure 4.7). For the Internet address (INT-NETADR) parameter, you specify the IP address, which must follow the requirements for IP address assignment within your organization and must also follow the format for a proper IP address. See "Internet Protocol Addresses" in Chapter 3 for more information about IP addresses. Note that multiple IP addresses may be specified (beginning in V4R1) for the same description. In other words, the AS/400 can be a multihomed system, in that it can support multiple IP addresses for the same physical interface. This feature can be helpful when you want the AS/400 to be known to different hosts by different IP addresses.

The Line description (LIND) parameter lets you identify the line description associated with this IP address and interface. You must have already created this line description (see "Configuring an Ethernet Line Description" or "Configuring a Token-Ring Line Description" earlier in this chapter).

The Subnet mask (SUBNETMASK) parameter is required and identifies the subnet mask that will be used with the specified IP address. "Internet Protocol Addresses" in Chapter 3 has information regarding subnet masks, but networks

FIGURE 4.7
Add TCP/IP Interface Prompt Screen

```
                   Add TCP/IP Interface (ADDTCPIFC)

 Type choices, press Enter.

 Internet address . . . . . . . . >  ' '
 Line description . . . . . . . .              Name, *LOOPBACK
 Subnet mask . . . . . . . . . .
 Associated local interface . . .  *NONE
 Type of service  . . . . . . . .  *NORMAL   *MINDELAY, *MAXTHRPUT...
 Maximum transmission unit  . . .  *LIND      576-16388, *LIND
 Autostart . . . . . . . . . . .   *YES       *YES, *NO
 PVC logical channel identifier               001-FFF
                + for more values
 X.25 idle circuit timeout  . . .  60         1-600
 X.25 maximum virtual circuits  .  64         0-64
 X.25 DDN interface . . . . . . .  *NO        *YES, *NO
 TRLAN bit sequencing . . . . . .  *MSB       *MSB, *LSB




                                                           Bottom
 F3=Exit    F4=Prompt    F5=Refresh    F12=Cancel   F13=How to use this display
 F24=More keys
```

that don't require subnetting and are using a Class C address (which covers most networks) can use a subnet mask of 255.255.255.0. This subnet mask doesn't provide any subnetting capability. If a value other than the standard 255.255.255.0 (no masking) is required for your specific network, enter it here.

You can usually leave the remaining parameters at their default values, but let's briefly look at three others. The Type of service (TOS) parameter lets you specify a service level for TCP/IP transmissions using this interface. This feature is similar to the APPN Class of Service capability. TOS allows specification of *NORMAL for normal service, *MINDELAY for minimum delays, *MAXTHRPUT for maximum throughput, *MAXRLB for maximum reliability, and *MINCOST for minimum cost. These features do not actually change the characteristics of the AS/400's TCP/IP transmission; rather they identify the desired characteristics to other network devices, usually routers. Not all hosts and network devices can implement Type of service.

The Maximum transmission unit (MTU) parameter defaults to a value of *LIND indicating that the maximum transmission unit for the type of line (including the Ethernet standard and the Token-Ring speed) will be used. MTU is the TCP/IP nomenclature for the size of the physical frame. Generally speaking, a larger MTU provides greater throughput. However, on a noisy line, a larger MTU actually causes less throughput because of the retransmission needed if interference corrupts a physical frame. (Because less information is contained in a smaller physical frame, a smaller MTU or physical frame size means that less information needs to be retransmitted if a burst of noise or interference is encountered on the line.) Another important point regarding MTU sizes is that if a system using a large MTU is communicating across a network where data communications devices (such as routers) use a smaller MTU, the packets must be fragmented to accommodate the smaller MTU, then reassembled when they arrive at the destination node. This causes more overhead on the nodes or the intermediate data communications devices. In general, you should select an MTU that is the same as the MTU for all the interfaces on a network. Doing so ensures that fragmentation doesn't occur. Understand that the specified MTU may or may not be the actual MTU size used. Negotiation between the two communicating systems at the start of a TCP/IP session determines the actual MTU size used for the connection.

The Autostart (AUTOSTART) parameter defaults to a value of *YES, indicating that this interface will be started automatically when TCP/IP is started with the STRTCP command. Normally you would want the interface to start automatically, but for security reasons or for performance reasons, you may want to start the interface manually with the STRTCPIFC (Start TCP/IP Interface) command. In either case, the line description associated with the interface will be varied on (if needed) and the appropriate routing will be associated with the interface.

The remaining parameters for this option relate to X.25 traffic.

Working with TCP/IP Routes

AS/400s running V4R1 of OS/400 support version 1 of the Routing Information Protocol (RIP), which enables the AS/400 to learn about routes to other networks from other RIP-capable systems, such as other hosts — or more probably — routers. Option 2 on the Configure TCP/IP menu (Figure 4.5) lets you specify or modify *static* routes to other networks and hosts — that is, routes that cannot be learned, either because an earlier version of OS/400 is in use or because other hosts or routers cannot be known to the local network (e.g, the other network is available only when a dial-up connection is made). Obviously, if the AS/400 doesn't need to communicate with networks or hosts outside of the network to which it is logically attached, no routes are needed. However, if static routing is required, you use option 2 to specify the routing information to the AS/400. Entering option 2 from the CFGTCP menu brings up a Work with TCP/IP Routes screen similar to the one in Figure 4.8.

The initial display shows the static routes known to the AS/400 and the following information about them: the route destination, the associated subnet mask, and the next hop address. Figure 4.8 shows an example of the default routing often used with TCP/IP networks. A default route indicates that if a connection is desired between the AS/400 and a system on another network, the connection should be established through the device with the address specified in the next hop column. In other words, a router on the local network

FIGURE 4.8
Work with TCP/IP Routes Screen

```
                         Work with TCP/IP Routes
                                                    System:     S1Ø29F3R
Type options, press Enter.
  1=Add    2=Change   4=Remove   5=Display

       Route             Subnet            Next            Preferred
Opt  Destination         Mask              Hop             Interface

  _
  _  *DFTROUTE           *NONE             192.168.1.22Ø


                                                                  Bottom
 F3=Exit       F5=Refresh   F6=Print List   F11=Display type of service
 F12=Cancel    F17=Top      F18=Bottom
```

that would know of other networks (and hosts) will connect the local network
to other networks (including the Internet).

From the screen in Figure 4.8, you may add, change, remove, or display
TCP/IP routes. The available options (and their associated CL commands,
where applicable) are

- Option 1, Add a route — ADDTCPRTE
- Option 2, Change a route — CHGTCPRTE
- Option 4, Remove a route — RMVTCPRTE
- Option 5, Display a route

Adding a TCP/IP Route

To add a route to your system, you enter a 1 in the option field on the top,
blank line of the display. You may also enter the IP address (either host
address or network address) of the route destination, the subnet mask, and the
IP address of the next hop, or simply press Enter for the entire prompt display
(Figure 4.9). You use the Route destination (RTEDEST) parameter to specify
the IP address of the route destination. This parameter identifies the destination
address of the host or network to which a route is desired. You may enter the
special value of *DFTROUTE as the default route destination. As we explained
above, the default route is convenient when only one route exists to go outside the local network, which is often the case when a router is attached to

FIGURE 4.9

Add TCP/IP Route Prompt Screen with
*DFTROUTE as the Route Destination

```
                        Add TCP/IP Route (ADDTCPRTE)

Type choices, press Enter.

Route destination  . . . . . . . > *DFTROUTE
Subnet mask  . . . . . . . . . . > *NONE
Type of service  . . . . . . . .   *NORMAL        *MINDELAY, *MAXTHRPUT...
Next hop . . . . . . . . . . . . > 192.168.1.220
Preferred binding interface  . .   *NONE
Maximum transmission unit  . . .   576            576-16388, *IFC
Route metric . . . . . . . . . .   1              1-16
Route redistribution . . . . . .   *NO            *NO, *YES
Duplicate route priority . . . .   5              1-10




                                                             Bottom
F3=Exit    F4=Prompt    F5=Refresh    F12=Cancel    F13=How to use this display
F24=More keys
```

the local network and any networks or hosts that must be reached have a route destination available through the router connection — normally to a wide area network (WAN) or to another LAN. If you specify *DFTROUTE for the RTEDEST parameter, you must enter special values for other parameters (explained below). You can specify and define up to eight default routes, with the appropriate default route chosen based on a match with the type of service (TOS) and next hop (NEXTHOP) parameters. In many cases, only one default route is defined for a network.

If you enter a specific address for the RTEDEST parameter, the destination address follows the normal IP addressing scheme, but take particular note that the IP address of a destination network should have a value of zero (0) for the fourth (or second and/or third) octet. The placement of zeroes for the ending octets depends on the class of IP address for the destination network. In a normal situation (no special subnetting), the placement of zeroes would be as follows:

- A class A address would have the last three octets zero.
- A class B address would have the last two octets zero.
- A class C address would have the last octet zero.

Any combination of valid numbers (1 through 255) may be used for any of the four octets to accommodate subnetting within the address space. A route to a specific host on a network would have the complete IP address of the host specified for the RTEDEST parameter.

If there is only one route out of our local network, we could use a default route as shown in Figure 4.9. But let's look at an example of connecting to a remote network where we specify the actual network address. We will establish a route to another network in our Paris, France, office. First the facts:

- Our local host address is 192.168.1.200.

- The network in Paris is another Class C network, with a network address of 200.1.2.0. (We received this information from the system administrator in Paris.) Remember, a Class C network address always has a last octet of 0. A router (or gateway) on our network has a WAN connection to the Paris office. Note that this connection could be over a leased line, ISDN line, dial-up line, or frame relay — the connection type doesn't matter. The AS/400 is not providing a connection to the Paris office; the router is providing the connection.

- The LAN interface IP address of the router (on our local network) is 192.168.1.230.

- We are not subnetting on our networks.

We now have all the facts we need to establish a static route to the AS/400 in Paris. The screen in Figure 4.10 shows the information entered into the appropriate parameters of the Add TCP/IP Route prompt screen.

The Subnet mask (SUBNETMASK) parameter defines the subnet mask to be used to "mask" the RTEDEST parameter to identify the correct address of the destination host or network. Remember that the subnet mask causes the 1s in the mask to be applied to the specified address. An octet in the mask of 255 (all binary 1s) indicates that that portion of the address is not modified for the purpose of subnetting. Octets in the subnet mask that are some other number than 255 mask the binary 1 bits in the mask octet with the corresponding octet in the host or network IP address.

If you specify *DFTROUTE for the RTEDEST parameter, you must specify the special value *NONE for the SUBNETMASK parameter as shown in Figure 4.9. Another SUBNETMASK special value, *HOST, indicates that the RTEDEST parameter identifies a host and not a network. In this case, the subnet mask applied to the RTEDEST IP address is 255.255.255.255, indicating no masking because all the octets in the subnet mask are all binary 1s.

The Type of service (TOS) parameter defines the type of service for the specified route. The parameter has the same values as the TOS parameter for the interface definition: *NORMAL (the default), *MINDELAY, *MAXTHRPUT, *MAXRLB, and *MINCOST. See the Type of Service discussion in "Adding a TCP/IP Interface" earlier in this chapter.

Figure 4.10
Add TCP/IP Route Prompt Screen with a
Network Address Route Destination

```
                    Add TCP/IP Route (ADDTCPRTE)

 Type choices, press Enter.

 Route destination  . . . . . . . > 200.1.2.0
 Subnet mask  . . . . . . . . . . > 255.255.255.0
 Type of service  . . . . . . . .   *NORMAL      *MINDELAY, *MAXTHRPUT...
 Next hop . . . . . . . . . . . . > 192.168.1.230
 Preferred binding interface  . .   *NONE
 Maximum transmission unit  . . .   576          576-16388, *IFC
 Route metric . . . . . . . . . .   1            1-16
 Route redistribution . . . . . .   *NO          *NO, *YES
 Duplicate route priority . . . .   5            1-10




                                                               Bottom
 F3=Exit    F4=Prompt    F5=Refresh    F12=Cancel    F13=How to use this display
 F24=More keys
```

The Next hop (NEXTHOP) parameter identifies the IP address of the next hop to the destination, usually a router. The next hop system must be a system the local network can access directly. In other words, the next hop system must be attached to the local network and must have an address that is accessible from the local network.

The Maximum transmission unit (MTU) parameter defines the physical frame size for packets that will be sent to the route destination. Recall from the discussion under "Adding a TCP/IP Interface" that an MTU value that is larger than other hosts or routers can accommodate causes the packets to be fragmented. The default of 576 is a small MTU value that most hosts and routers in a network should be able to accommodate. A special value of *IFC indicates that the MTU associated with the interface should be used. Note that the MTU value cannot exceed the MTU of the next hop system being defined.

Other parameters are also available on the Add TCP/IP Route prompt screen but may easily be left at their default values. The Preferred interface parameter lets you specify an IP address when a router or gateway has more than one IP interface. The Route metric parameter lets you specify a relative weight to this route, with a value of 1 meaning very desirable and a value of 16 meaning not reachable, therefore not desirable. The Route redistribution parameter determines whether information regarding this static route should be shared with other routers. A value of *NO reduces the traffic on this system; a value of *YES causes the network served by this static route to be known to other routers in the network. The Duplicate route priority parameter is a relative weighting that helps identify a route — a route with a high duplicate priority is chosen over a route with a lower duplicate priority.

Working with TCP/IP Host Table Entries

The host table concept is included with most vendors' implementations of TCP/IP because the host table is a convenient method of establishing the names and IP addresses of commonly accessed hosts. Use of a host table doesn't preclude the use of Domain Name Service (DNS). A host table search is, however, quicker (and less network bandwidth intensive) than a DNS search unless the host table is inordinately large. Because the table's size affects the search time and a host table can't realistically contain all the host names and IP addresses that a given system could conceivably access, I find that using the host table for the most commonly used entries and DNS for less frequently used entries is the best approach.

Option 10 on the Configure TCP/IP menu (Figure 4.5) lets you specify or modify host table entries. Entering option 10 from the CFGTCP menu brings up a Work with TCP/IP Host Table Entries screen similar to the one in Figure 4.11.

FIGURE 4.11
Work with TCP/IP Host Table Entries Screen

```
                    Work with TCP/IP Host Table Entries
                                                   System:    S1029F3R
      Type options, press Enter.
        1=Add    2=Change    4=Remove    5=Display    7=Rename

           Internet          Host
      Opt  Address           Name
       _   _____           ____
       _   127.0.0.1         LOOPBACK
                             LOCALHOST
       _   198.0.0.20        AS400E.RYANTECH.COM
                             AS400E
                             AS400



                                                                 Bottom
       F3=Exit    F5=Refresh    F6=Print list    F12=Cancel    F17=Position to
```

This display shows the current host names and associated IP addresses defined on your system. The LOOPBACK entry is always present — it is used for internal processing. Also note that, for SMTP processing, one instance of the fully qualified domain name of the local system and its associated IP address must be entered into the host table.

From the screen in Figure 4.11, you may add, change, remove, display, and rename a host table entry. The available options (and their associated CL commands, where applicable) are

- Option 1, Add a host table entry — ADDTCPHTE
- Option 2, Change a host table entry — CHGTCPHTE
- Option 4, Remove a host table entry — RMVTCPHTE
- Option 5, Display a host table entry
- Option 7, Rename a host table entry — RNMTCPHTE (Despite its name, the RNMTCPHTE command — or the associated option — doesn't rename the host table entry; it only lets you change the IP address of the host table entry.)

Adding a TCP/IP Host Table Entry

To add a host table entry, you enter a 1 in the option field on the top, blank line of the display. You may also enter the IP address of the host you are adding. In either case, pressing Enter displays an Add TCP/IP Host Table Entry prompt screen similar to the one in Figure 4.12.

FIGURE 4.12
Add TCP/IP Host Table Entry Prompt Screen

```
                  Add TCP/IP Host Table Entry (ADDTCPHTE)

 Type choices, press Enter.

 Internet address . . . . . . . . >  '  '
 Host names:
   Name . . . . . . . . . . . . .



                   + for more values
 Text 'description' . . . . . . .





                                                               Bottom
 F3=Exit    F4=Prompt    F5=Refresh    F12=Cancel   F13=How to use this display
 F24=More keys
```

For the Internet address (INTNETADR) parameter, you need to enter the dotted-decimal notation IP address of the host. Note that you can enter an IP address for a service such as Telnet or FTP. Then, for the next parameter, you can specify a host name for that service, and the host table (through an internal search procedure that is transparent to the user) will provide the corresponding IP address.

You use the Host names (HOSTNAME) parameter to specify the name of the host. You can specify up to four host names for a given IP address by entering a plus (+) in the field supplied for additional host names. Being able to specify multiple names lets you refer to the same IP address with different names, perhaps a shorter name or a name with more meaning. For instance, I could specify the host name for a specific IP address as SERVER1.RYAN-TECH.COM. I could also specify (for the same IP address) names such as SERVER1, ACCT, and NEWSYS. Any of these names could be used to access the host containing the interface identified with the IP address.

Changing TCP/IP Domain Information

Option 12 of the Configure TCP/IP menu (Figure 4.5) has been significantly modified with V4R2 of OS/400. Using this option or its associated CL command — CHGTCPDMN (Change TCP/IP Domain) — you can now specify or modify the local host and domain names as well as specify or modify DNS servers. In earlier releases, you used an additional option on the CFGTCP menu — option 13 — to do the latter.

Local Host and Domain Names

The local host and domain names are critical to a successful TCP/IP implementation because several TCP/IP services, especially SMTP and Line Printer Remote (LPR) services, need the local host and domain name information. SMTP needs this information to identify the local host in the network for mail transfers and as the return address for outgoing mail. LPR needs this information to send in the control file to the Line Printer Daemon process at the printer. Simple Network Management Protocol (SNMP) also needs this information for the Management Information Base (MIB) used for SNMP processing. Recall from the discussion of host table entries that the local host and domain names must also be entered in the host table to provide appropriate addressing for this system.

In V4R2, entering option 12 from the CFGTCP menu brings up a Change TCP/IP Domain prompt screen similar to the one in Figure 4.13.

Only the first two parameters on this screen are associated with specifying the local host and domain names. If the local host and domain are already named, this display shows the current host and domain names. To change or specify the host name, for the Host name (HOSTNAME) parameter, you enter the local host name that uniquely identifies this specific AS/400 system. It must be different from every other host or system name in your network.

FIGURE 4.13
Change TCP/IP Domain Prompt Screen

```
                    Change TCP/IP Domain (CHGTCPDMN)

 Type choices, press Enter.

 Host name  . . . . . . . . . .   'AS400E'

 Domain name  . . . . . . . . .   'RYANTECH.COM'


 Host name search priority  . . .   *LOCAL        *REMOTE, *LOCAL, *SAME

   Internet address . . . . . . .   *NONE




                                                              Bottom
 F3=Exit    F4=Prompt    F5=Refresh   F10=Additional parameters   F12=Cancel
 F13=How to use this display     F24=More keys
```

To change or specify the domain name, for the Domain name (DMNNAME) parameter, you enter the local domain name assigned to the domain that contains the nodes in your network. Remember that a domain is not limited to a specific LAN — it is instead related to an organization. See "Domain Name Service" in Chapter 3 for more information regarding domain name conventions.

DNS Server Information

As we mentioned earlier, as of V4R2, on the Change TCP/IP Domain prompt screen, you can also specify or modify DNS server information. A DNS server resolves host names to their IP addresses. Using DNS in a network is optional and may be unnecessary if the network is small or is not likely to change much. In such cases, host table entries can provide the name resolution processing needed. However, if the network is large or dynamic or if it will be connected to the Internet, DNS services are probably needed. Here we look briefly at the parameters associated with DNS servers.

In Figure 4.13, for a DNS server, neither a host name value nor a domain name value is needed. However, you need a value for the Host name search priority (HOSTSCHPTY) parameter to specify the order the AS/400 uses to resolve a name to an IP address. A value of *REMOTE indicates the AS/400 should first search the DNS server (or servers) to attempt to resolve the address. If the address cannot be resolved, the host table is then searched. A value of *LOCAL indicates the reverse — the host table will be searched first, and then the DNS servers. The proper setting for this parameter should be determined by the type of connections most common in your network (local or remote), whether the AS/400 is connected to the Internet (indicating that many connections will need to be resolved by DNS), and how much time you want to spend maintaining the local host table.

For the Internet address (INTNETADR) parameter, you specify the IP address of the name server(s). You can specify up to three addresses for a primary and two secondary name servers. Name servers may be part of your network or may be maintained by an Internet Service Provider (ISP). If *REMOTE is specified for the HOSTSCHPTY parameter, a request from the AS/400 for name resolution is sent to the primary name server first. The name server is searched in an attempt to resolve the name specified in the request to that host's IP address. If the primary name server is unavailable or unable to resolve the address, the request is sent to a secondary name server (if one is specified). If all name servers have been searched and the name is still not resolved to an IP address, a DNS message is sent to the requesting system indicating that the name cannot be found. Then the host table will usually be searched to determine whether the address is specified locally.

For the rest of the parameter prompts for DNS servers, you need to press F10 from the Change TCP/IP Domain prompt screen to display additional parameters. Doing so brings up the additional prompts shown in Figure 4.14.

FIGURE 4.14
Change TCP/IP Domain Prompt Screen with Additional Parameters

```
                    Change TCP/IP Domain (CHGTCPDMN)

 Type choices, press Enter.

 Host name . . . . . . . . . .     'AS400E'

 Domain name . . . . . . . . .     'RYANTECH.COM'


 Host name search priority . . .   *LOCAL       *REMOTE, *LOCAL, *SAME

   Internet address . . . . . . .  *NONE



                         Additional Parameters

 Port . . . . . . . . . . . . . .  53           1-65535, *SAME
 Protocol . . . . . . . . . . . .  *UDP         *UDP, *TCP, *SAME
 Domain name server retry:
   Number of retries . . . . . .   2            1-99, *SAME
   Time interval . . . . . . . .   2            1-99, *SAME

                                                               More...
 F3=Exit   F4=Prompt   F5=Refresh   F12=Cancel   F13=How to use this display
 F24=More keys
```

The Port (PORT) parameter specifies the remote port number used for DNS queries. The default is port 53 and should not be changed unless there is a specific security reason for doing so or there is a conflict with another service. I don't know of any networks for which the DNS port number has been changed, primarily because 53 is a well-known DNS server port number, so a change would likely disable DNS processing with name servers outside your local network.

The Protocol (PROTOCOL) parameter defaults to *UDP, indicating that User Datagram Protocol will be used. Because most DNS servers use UDP, changing this value from the default would likely disable DNS processing with name servers outside of your local network.

The Domain name server retry (DMNSVRRTY) parameter is a complex parameter that defines the number of times each name server will be queried for DNS resolution and the length of time (in seconds) the AS/400 will wait for a response from each name server. The default for the number of retries is 2, with a range of 1–99. The default value is probably sufficient, but may need be increased if the network becomes overloaded or your DNS servers are accessible only across a slow-speed link. The default for the time interval is 2 seconds, with a range of 1–99 seconds. The default value is probably sufficient, but may need to be increased if the network becomes overloaded. Note that the wait time is doubled after each unsuccessful retry up to the limit of the Number of retries element.

Configuring TCP/IP Applications

You use option 20 on the Configure TCP/IP menu (Figure 4.5) to configure a wide array of TCP/IP applications. In the sections that follow, we discuss the eight applications that most installations will find useful:

- Simple Network Management Protocol (SNMP)
- File Transfer Protocol (FTP)
- Telnet
- Simple Mail Transfer Protocol (SMTP)
- Line Printer Daemon (LPD)
- Hypertext Transfer Protocol (HTTP)
- Workstation Gateway (WSG)
- Post Office Protocol (POP)

Entering option 20 from the Configure TCP/IP menu brings up the Configure TCP/IP Applications menu (Figure 4.15).

FIGURE 4.15
Configure TCP/IP Applications Menu

```
                    Configure TCP/IP Applications
                                              System:    S1029F3R
Select one of the following:

    1. Configure SNMP agent
    2. Configure RouteD
    3. Change Trivial FTP Attributes
    4. Configure BOOTP
    5. Change DDM TCP attributes
    6. Change DHCP attributes

   10. Change FTP attributes
   11. Configure TELNET
   12. Configure SMTP
   13. Change LPD attributes
   14. Configure HTTP
   15. Configure workstation gateway
   16. Change POP attributes
                                                          More...
Selection or command
===> _____

 F3=Exit   F4=Prompt   F9=Retrieve   F12=Cancel
```

The options available from this menu primarily allow changes to the operational attributes of the servers for TCP/IP applications. (As with most AS/400 menu options, there are CL commands to change the attributes directly. Where applicable, we provide the CL command.)

Configuring SNMP Agents
Recall from Chapter 2 that SNMP provides network management capabilities. The AS/400 can be a managed system in an SNMP managed network, but the AS/400 can't be an SNMP manager. Although most AS/400 TCP/IP installations don't use SNMP, those of you who do would use option 1 on the Configure TCP/IP Applications menu to configure SNMP-specific parameters and attributes, such as system location and autostart, for the SNMP agent. Entering option 1 (or the CFGTCPSNMP command) brings up another menu, the Configure TCP/IP SNMP menu (Figure 4.16).

From this menu, you have two options — you can change SNMP attributes or work with communities for SNMP.

Changing SNMP Attributes
Entering option 1 from the Configure TCP/IP SNMP menu (or the CHGSNMPA command) brings up the Change SNMP Attributes prompt screen (Figure 4.17).

You use the System contact (SYSCONTACT) parameter to identify the name of a contact person for SNMP processes. You may specify the contact person's name, *NONE for no contact person, or *CNTINF to indicate that the

FIGURE 4.16
Configure TCP/IP SNMP Menu

```
                        Configure TCP/IP SNMP
                                                    System:    S1029F3R
    Select one of the following:

        1. Change SNMP attributes
        2. Work with communities for SNMP










    Selection or command
    ===>
    F3=Exit    F4=Prompt    F9=Retrieve    F12=Cancel
```

FIGURE 4.17
Change SNMP Attributes Prompt Screen

```
                    Change SNMP Attributes (CHGSNMPA)

    Type choices, press Enter.

    System contact . . . . . . . . . SYSCONTACT      *NONE



    System location  . . . . . . . . SYSLOC          *NONE



    Send authentication traps  . . . SNDAUTTRP        *YES
    Automatic start  . . . . . . . . AUTOSTART        *NO
    Object access  . . . . . . . . . OBJACC           *READ
    Log set requests . . . . . . . . LOGSET           *NO
    Log get requests . . . . . . . . LOGGET           *NO
    Log traps  . . . . . . . . . . . LOGTRP           *NO


                                                              More...
    F3=Exit    F4=Prompt    F5=Refresh    F12=Cancel    F13=How to use this display
    F24=More keys
```

system should use the name and telephone number obtained from the WRK-CNTINF (Work with Contact Information) command.

The System location (SYSLOC) parameter identifies the physical location of the AS/400 for SNMP processes. You may specify the system's location, *NONE to indicate that no system location information exists, or *CNTINF to indicate that the system should use the mailing address obtained from the WRKCNTINF command.

The Send authentication traps (SNDAUTTRP) parameter specifies whether the AS/400 should send authenticationFailure traps to an SNMP managing system. An authenticationFailure occurs when an SNMP managing system with a community name not known to the AS/400 issues a request to the AS/400 for SNMP information. The default value of *YES specifies that the AS/400 will send an authenticationFailure trap to the managing system in its community indicating that an unknown SNMP managing system requested information. Specifying *NO lets unknown SNMP managing systems access information on the AS/400. You should use the default value of *YES to help minimize security risks.

The Automatic start (AUTOSTART) parameter specifies whether the SNMP agent processes on the AS/400 should start automatically when the STRTCP command is issued. The default value of *NO is probably appropriate for most AS/400 TCP/IP installations because most sites don't use SNMP. But if your site uses SNMP, change this parameter's value to *YES so the SNMP agent processes will start automatically as soon as the STRTCP command is issued.

The Object access (OBJACC) parameter specifies the MIB database access available from an SNMP managing system that is part of the AS/400 community. The default value of *READ allows read-only access. *WRITE allows an SNMP managing system that is part of the AS/400 community to modify MIB objects. *NONE prohibits read and write access to MIB objects. The default value of *READ is probably the best bet to ensure that change-access to the MIB database is prohibited.

Three parameters — Log set requests (LOGSET), Log get requests (LOGGET), and Log traps (LOGTRP) — specify whether SNMP set, get and get-next, and trap requests from an SNMP managing system in the AS/400's community will be logged to the QUSRSYS/QSNMP journal. The default value of *NO is appropriate for most installations because it reduces the amount of unneeded information. This value could be changed, especially for debugging an AS/400 SNMP implementation.

Pressing Roll up (or Page down) from the prompt screen in Figure 4.17 brings up the Trap manager (TRPMGR) parameter, a complex parameter that lets you specify the IP address for the SNMP station that will manage the AS/400, the managing system's community name, and whether the community name should be translated to ASCII. *NONE, the default value, specifies that no SNMP managing system will receive traps generated by the AS/400. If you specify an IP address instead, you must also specify the SNMP managing system's community name. You use the default value of *YES for the last element in the parameter, Trap community name, unless the community name has characters that can't be displayed.

Working with SNMP Communities

An SNMP community is the logical entity that comprises the SNMP managing station and managed systems that interact to form a managed network. An SNMP managed system uses a community profile — which consists of a community name, an object-access specification, and a list of SNMP managers that are part of the community — to determine whether to honor a request from an SNMP man-aging station. The default community is the public community. Administrator-defined communities could include Marketing, Production, Research & Development, or other groups that it makes sense to monitor as a group.

Entering option 2 from the Configure TCP/IP SNMP menu (Figure 4.16) brings up a Work with Communities for SNMP screen similar to the one in Figure 4.18.

FIGURE 4.18
Work with Communities for SNMP Screen

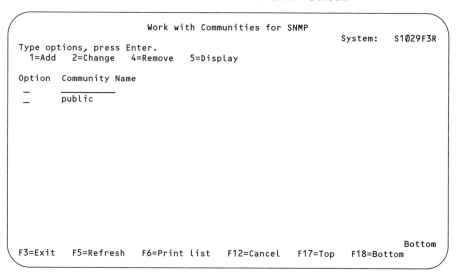

This display shows the communities that have already been defined. The AS/400 ships with the default community — public — defined for SNMP because many SNMP installations (regardless whether an AS/400 is involved) use the public community. This default setting can be a security exposure because hackers know that many SNMP implementations use the default public community. If your AS/400 is connected to the Internet and your firewall and SNMP configurations aren't correct, an SNMP managing station from outside your enterprise could access information on your AS/400. I recommend that no SNMP traffic from outside the secure network cross the firewall and that you change your community name from "public" to something less obvious.

From the screen in Figure 4.18, you may add, change, remove, or display a community. The available options (and their associated CL commands, where applicable) are

- Option 1, Add an SNMP community — ADDCOMSNMP
- Option 2, Change an SNMP community — CHGCOMSNMP
- Option 4, Remove an SNMP community — RMVCOMSNMP
- Option 5, Display an SNMP community

To define an SNMP community and add it to the SNMP community on your system, you enter a 1 in the option field on the top, blank line of the display. Pressing Enter displays the Add Community for SNMP prompt screen (Figure 4.19).

FIGURE 4.19
Add Community for SNMP Prompt Screen

```
                   Add Community for SNMP (ADDCOMSNMP)

 Type choices, press Enter.

 Community name . . . . . . . . . COM          > ' '


 Translate community name . . . . ASCIICOM     *YES
 Manager internet address . . . . INTNETADR    *ANY
                      + for more values
 Object access  . . . . . . . . . OBJACC       *SNMPATR
 Log set requests . . . . . . . . LOGSET       *SNMPATR
 Log get requests . . . . . . . . LOGGET       *SNMPATR




                                                               Bottom
 F3=Exit   F4=Prompt   F5=Refresh   F12=Cancel   F13=How to use this display
 F24=More keys
```

For the Community name (COM) parameter, you specify the name of the SNMP community you're adding. The name must be unique among other community names defined on the AS/400, and it may contain EBCDIC characters or characters that can't be displayed.

With the Translate community name (ASCIICOM) parameter, you specify whether the community name should be translated to ASCII. The default of

*YES is appropriate if the community name you specified in the COM param-
eter is entirely ASCII characters. Because most SNMP managing stations are
Unix based and, therefore, ASCII based, you will probably use the default
value most of the time. You specify *NO if the community name you specified
in the COM parameter contains EBCDIC characters or characters that can't be
displayed.

For the Manager internet address (INTNETADR) parameter, you specify the
IP address, in dotted-decimal notation, of the managing station or stations. You
may specify up to 300 IP addresses to accommodate multiple managing stations. You may also specify a special value of *ANY to indicate that any managing station may be a member of this SNMP community, but doing so is a
security exposure, especially if you use the default SNMP community name of
"public." As I suggest above, you should change the default SNMP community
name, and you should specify IP addresses for managing stations instead of
using the *ANY special value.

The next three parameters — Object access (OBJACC), Log set requests
(LOGSET), and Log get requests (LOGGET) — all default to the special value
*SNMPATR, indicating that the corresponding value from the SNMP attributes
should be used. The SNMP attributes are set with the CHGSNMPA (Change
SNMP Attributes) command or using option 1 on the Configure TCP/IP SNMP
menu (Figure 4.16). See "Configuring SNMP Agents" earlier in this chapter for a
description of these parameters and their values.

Changing FTP Attributes

Normally, you don't need to change the AS/400's FTP server configuration. However, you may want to change the autostart parameter, the number of FTP
servers, or the timeout value for an inactive connection. If changes are required,
option 10 from the Configure TCP/IP Applications menu (Figure 4.15) supports
making such changes. Entering option 10 or the CHGFTPA command brings
up the Change FTP Attributes prompt screen (Figure 4.20).

The Autostart servers (AUTOSTART) parameter lets you specify whether
the FTP servers should start automatically when the STRTCP command is
issued. Because FTP is usually an integral part of an AS/400 TCP/IP implementation, the default value of *YES, which causes the servers to begin automatically in the QSYSWRK subsystem, is usually appropriate. However, if you don't
need file transfer capability or if you want to control the server initiation manually, you should specify *NO. Although I am very comfortable with AS/400
resource security (especially level 40 security) with FTP, if you are not as
comfortable, you could start the FTP server only when another system needs
to initiate a file transfer to the AS/400. Note that the FTP server does not need
to be active for the AS/400 to initiate a file transfer, either to or from the
AS/400. The only need for the FTP server to be active on the AS/400 is for a
remote system to initiate a file transfer to or from the AS/400. The FTP server

FIGURE 4.20

Change FTP Attributes Prompt Screen

```
                        Change FTP Attributes (CHGFTPA)

 Type choices, press Enter.

 Autostart servers  . . . . . . .   *YES          *YES, *NO, *SAME
 Number of initial servers  . . .   3             1-20, *SAME, *DFT
 Inactivity timeout . . . . . . .   300           0-2147483647, *SAME, *DFT
 Coded character set identifier      00819         1-65533, *SAME, *DFT
 Server mapping tables:
   Outgoing EBCDIC/ASCII table  .   *CCSID        Name, *SAME, *CCSID, *DFT
     Library . . . . . . . . . .                  Name, *LIBL, *CURLIB

   Incoming ASCII/EBCDIC table  .   *CCSID        Name, *SAME, *CCSID, *DFT
     Library . . . . . . . . . .                  Name, *LIBL, *CURLIB




                                                                     Bottom
 F3=Exit   F4=Prompt   F5=Refresh   F12=Cancel   F13=How to use this display
 F24=More keys
```

will listen for the incoming connection, and assuming proper authorization, allow the remote system access to transfer files.

The Number of initial servers (NBRSVR) parameter specifies the number of FTP servers to be started when the STRTCP command or the STRTCPSVR (Start TCP/IP Server) command is issued. The default is three FTP servers to be started automatically. From one to twenty servers may be started automatically. Having a greater number of servers active decreases the amount of time needed to process an incoming FTP request. The trade-off is that more active servers require more processing power, therefore potentially decreasing system performance for other applications and server jobs. The balance between good FTP server performance and overall system performance is dependent on the number of file transfers involving your system, the type of processor and amount of memory on your system, and your overall system load. I suggest starting with a value of 3 (the default) and adjusting as needed. If FTP server performance is poor, try increasing the number of servers. Remember to monitor overall system performance while increasing the number of FTP servers to provide that proper balance.

With the Inactivity timeout (INACTTIMO) parameter, you specify the number of seconds that an FTP connection can remain idle before the AS/400 disconnects the FTP connection. The default value is 300 seconds or five minutes. The valid range for this parameter is from 0 seconds (meaning idle connections will not be broken) to an incredible value of 2,147,483,647 seconds, which is more than 68 years. The default value of 300 seconds is reasonable for most FTP servers.

You can usually leave the last three parameters, which specify how ASCII to EBCDIC (and vice versa) translations are performed for file transfers, set at their default values. The Coded character set identifier (CCSID) parameter's default value of 00819, specifying use of the ISO 8859-1 8-bit ASCII set for ASCII-to-EBCDIC and EBCDIC-to-ASCII mapping, is appropriate for most FTP implementations. If your translation needs are different (e.g., if you have a unique need to translate certain characters in a different format than IBM's default or different national language considerations), change the CCSID parameter to an appropriate value.

The Outgoing EBCDIC/ASCII table (TBLFTPOUT) and Incoming ASCII/EBCDIC table (TBLFTPIN) parameters let you specify a custom translation table for outgoing and incoming file transfers, respectively. The default value of *CCSID specifies that the CCSID parameter value will be used to determine the mapping. Normally, you won't need custom translation tables, so the default value is appropriate. However, as mentioned earlier, this does give you the capability for a custom translation if needed.

Configuring Telnet

Normally, changes don't need to made to the Telnet server configuration of the AS/400. Telnet is a standard TCP/IP service, and accessing the AS/400 through Telnet (or TN5250) requires that the server process be made active. However, you may wish to change the Telnet server configuration for security reasons (e.g., not wanting to provide the capability to interactively access the AS/400), to change the timeout value for an inactive session, or to change translation tables. If changes are required, option 11 from the Configure TCP/IP Applications menu (Figure 4.15) supports making such changes. Entering option 11 or the CFGTCPTELN command brings up the Configure TCP/IP Telnet menu (Figure 4.21).

Three options are available from this menu. Option 1 lets you change Telnet attributes. Options 10 and 11 let you change Telnet-related system values.

FIGURE 4.21
Configure TCP/IP Telnet Menu

```
                       Configure TCP/IP TELNET
                                                    System:    S1029F3R
   Select one of the following:

      1. Change TELNET attributes

    Associated system values:
      10. Work with autoconfigure virtual devices
      11. Work with limit security officer device access




   Selection or command
   ===>  _____

 F3=Exit   F4=Prompt   F9=Retrieve   F12=Cancel
 (C) COPYRIGHT IBM CORP. 1987, 1998.
```

Changing Telnet Attributes

Entering option 1 or the CHGTELNA command brings up the Change Telnet
Attributes prompt screen (Figure 4.22).

FIGURE 4.22
Change Telnet Attributes Prompt Screen

```
                   Change TELNET Attributes (CHGTELNA)

   Type choices, press Enter.

   Autostart server . . . . . . . .   *YES          *YES, *NO, *SAME
   Inactivity timeout . . . . . . .   0             0-2147483647, *SAME, *DFT
   Timemark timeout . . . . . . . .   600           0-2147483647, *SAME, *DFT
   Default NVT type . . . . . . . .   *VT100        *SAME, *VT100, *NVT
   Coded character set identifier     *MULTINAT     1-65533, *SAME, *MULTINAT...
   ASCII fullscreen mapping:
     Outgoing EBCDIC/ASCII table .    *CCSID        Name, *SAME, *CCSID, *DFT
       Library  . . . . . . . . . .                 Name, *LIBL, *CURLIB

     Incoming ASCII/EBCDIC table .    *CCSID        Name, *SAME, *CCSID, *DFT
       Library  . . . . . . . . . .                 Name, *LIBL, *CURLIB



                                                                       Bottom
    F3=Exit    F4=Prompt   F5=Refresh   F12=Cancel   F13=How to use this display
    F24=More keys
```

The Autostart server (AUTOSTART) parameter lets you specify whether the Telnet server should start automatically when the STRTCP command is issued. Unlike FTP, Telnet initially has only one server started — QTGTelnetS, which runs in the QSYSWRK subsystem. Normally, the TCP/IP support on the AS/400 creates new Telnet server jobs as needed. However, if you want to start additional Telnet servers (perhaps because session initiation time is slow), you can use the STRTCPSVR command with a parameter of SERVER(*Telnet).

With the Inactivity timeout (INACTTIMO) parameter, you specify the number of seconds that a Telnet connection can remain idle before the AS/400 disconnects the Telnet connection. The default value is 0 seconds, meaning idle connections will not be broken. The valid range for this parameter is from 0 seconds to 2,147,483,647 seconds. This is the only point where an incoming Telnet (or TN5250) session can be checked for an inactive condition — system value QINACTITV does not control Telnet sessions. I recommend a value of 300 seconds, meaning that a connection that is inactive for 5 minutes (300 seconds) will be deactivated.

The Timemark timeout (TIMMRKTIMO) lets you specify the amount of time between the AS/400 sending timemarks. A Telnet timemark is a signal sent from the server to the client at a specified interval. If the server cannot send the timemark, the connection is closed. The range is from 0 to 2,147,483,647 seconds, with the default of 600 seconds being a reasonable number.

The Default NVT type (DFTNVTTYPE) parameter specifies the default type of network virtual terminal (NVT) to be used if the client and the AS/400 server can't negotiate a terminal type. The default value of VT100 specifies that the pseudo-standard DEC VT100 terminal type should be used. The other special value, *NVT, indicates that network virtual terminal mode will be used. The use of *NVT requires a program to be written on the AS/400 to work with NVT devices.

You can usually leave the next three parameters, which specify how ASCII to EBCDIC (and vice versa) translations are performed for virtual terminal access when using VT-style terminals, set at their default values. The Coded character set identifier (CCSID) parameter's default value of *MULTINAT, specifying that the DEC Multinational replacement character set should be used, is appropriate for most Telnet implementations.

The Outgoing EBCDIC/ASCII table (TBLFTPOUT) and Incoming ASCII/EBCDIC table (TBLFTPIN) parameters let you specify a custom translation table for outgoing and incoming full screen terminal access, respectively. The default value of *CCSID specifies that the CCSID parameter value will be used to determine the mapping. Normally, you won't need custom translation tables, so the default value is appropriate. If your translation needs are different (e.g., a unique need to translate certain characters in a different format than IBM's default or different national language considerations), you may need to change the translation table parameters.

Changing Telnet-related System Values

Entering option 10 from the Configure TCP/IP Telnet menu (Figure 4.21) invokes the WRKSYSVAL (Work with System Value) command to modify the QAUTOVRT system value, which determines the number of virtual devices that may be created automatically. The range is from 0 through 9999, with 0 specifying that no virtual devices should be created. You may want to set this system value to some nonzero number to automatically create the virtual devices that you need. Then set the value to zero after the devices have been created to prohibit future automatic creation of new virtual devices. If you allow virtual devices to be created automatically and the value for QMAXSIGN (maximum number of signon attempts) is greater than zero, the number of attempts a hacker has to try to break into your system is QAUTOVRT × QMAXSIGN.

Entering option 11 from the Configure TCP/IP Telnet menu invokes the WRKSYSVAL command to modify the QLMTSECOFR system value, which controls system access by users with a high level of authority (*ALLOBJ — all object — or *SERVICE — service functions). If you have Telnet installed on your system, you should set this value to 1 (on) to prohibit users without explicit authority from accessing the system remotely, thereby limiting the power of potential intruders.

Changing SMTP Attributes

Option 12 from the Configure TCP/IP Applications menu (Figure 4.15) provides a convenient way to modify the SMTP server configuration as well as the tables that support SMTP use. Entering option 12 or the CFGTCPSMTP command brings up the Configure TCP/IP SMTP menu (Figure 4.23).

Six options are available from this menu. Here we focus on changing SMTP attributes (option 3). In "E-mail — SMTP and POP3," later in this chapter, we cover the other SMTP-related menu options.

Entering option 3 or the CHGSMTPA command brings up the Change SMTP Attributes prompt screen (Figure 4.24).

The Autostart server (AUTOSTART) parameter specifies whether the SMTP server process should start automatically when the STRTCP command is issued. The default of *YES specifies that the SMTP server should start automatically. If you are not running SMTP on your AS/400, you should ensure that this value is set to *NO to reduce demand on system resources (because a server job isn't being executed) and to reduce your security exposure.

The Retries by minute (RTYMIN) and Retries by day (RTYDAY) parameters specify the number of attempts and the amount of time between attempts for SMTP to distribute mail and to retry the remote name server. The RTYMIN parameter's valid range for the number of retries is 0 to 99, with a default value of 3 retries; its valid time interval range is 0 to 99 minutes, with a default value of 30 minutes. If the SMTP doesn't succeed in the specified number of

FIGURE 4.23
Configure TCP/IP SMTP Menu

```
                         Configure TCP/IP SMTP
                                                    System:    S1029F3R
 Select one of the following:

     1. Work with system alias table
     2. Work with personal alias table
     3. Change SMTP attributes

  SNADS related options:
    10. Work with directory entries
    11. Work with distribution queue for SMTP
    12. Configure distribution services




 Selection or command
 ===> _____

 F3=Exit    F4=Prompt    F9=Retrieve    F12=Cancel
 (C) COPYRIGHT IBM CORP. 1987, 1998
```

FIGURE 4.24
Change SMTP Attributes Prompt Screen

```
                       Change SMTP Attributes (CHGSMTPA)

 Type choices, press Enter.

 Autostart server . . . . . . . .   *NO        *YES, *NO, *SAME
 Retries by minute:
   Number of retries  . . . . . .   3          0-99, *SAME, *DFT
   Time interval  . . . . . . . .   30         0-99, *SAME, *DFT
 Retries by day:
   Number of retries  . . . . . .   0          0-9, *SAME, *DFT
   Time interval  . . . . . . . .   0          0-9, *SAME, *DFT
 Retry remote name server . . . .   *NO        *YES, *NO, *SAME
 Automatic registration . . . . .   *NO        *NO, *YES, *SAME
   User ID prefix . . . . . . . .   QSM        Name, *SAME, *DFT
   Address  . . . . . . . . . . .   QSMRMTAD   Name, *SAME, *DFT
   System name  . . . . . . . . .   TCPIP      Character value, *SAME, *DFT
   Alias table type . . . . . . .   *SYSTEM    *SAME, *SYSTEM, *PERSONAL
 User ID delimiter  . . . . . . .   '?'        *SAME, *DFT, ?, =, ., &, $...

                                                                    More...
 F3=Exit    F4=Prompt    F5=Refresh    F12=Cancel   F13=How to use this display
 F24=More keys
```

retries, the daily retries specified in the RTYDAY parameter are attempted. The RTYDAY parameter's valid range for the number of retries is 0 to 9, with a default value of 0; its valid time interval range is 0 to 9 days, with a default value of 0 days. If the remote name server can't be contacted and SMTP mail can't be distributed in the limits imposed by these two parameters, a note is sent to the sender indicating that the mail could not be delivered. Retries to contact the name server are usually not needed, so the default values are appropriate for most installations.

The Retry remote name server (RTYRMTSVR) parameter works with the RTYMIN and RTYDAY parameters. The default value of *NO specifies that the remote name server will not be retried. A value of *YES specifies that the values in the RTYMIN and RTYDAY parameters will be used to retry contacting the name server if needed.

The next several parameters work together to provide automatic e-mail name and address registration for incoming mail so users can automatically reply to incoming mail without putting the sender's e-mail name and address in the system directory. Although it's a fine concept, it lacks a bit in implementation. The IBM method of registering the name and address on incoming mail creates an entry in the system directory that has no connection with the sender's actual e-mail name and address, so you find system directory entries such as QSM?12345 QSMRMTAD. Although you can modify the naming convention somewhat, the address that is created is difficult to understand. I usually don't have OS/400 automatically add addresses for me; instead I manually add the sender's address to my personal alias table.

The Automatic registration (AUTOADD) parameter specifies whether incoming senders' names and addresses will be added automatically to the system directory and an alias table. The default value of *NO specifies that names and addresses will not be added automatically. You specify the next five parameters only if the AUTOADD parameter has a value of *YES.

The User ID prefix (USRIDPFX) parameter specifies the 3-character user ID prefix to be used for automatically added entries. The default value is QSM, but you may specify any three characters. The remaining portion of the added address will contain a system-generated 5-digit number.

The Address (ADDRESS) parameter specifies the SNADS address to be generated for automatically added entries. The default value is QSMRMTAD; you may specify up to 8 characters.

The System name (SYSNAME) parameter specifies the system name that will be used for mail routing. This name must correspond with the SNADS routing table entry associated with the QSMTPQ SNADS distribution queue.

The Alias table type (TBLTYPE) parameter specifies whether the system alias table (the default) or the personal alias table should be updated with an automatic address addition.

Finally, the User ID delimiter (USRIDDELIM) parameter specifies the character used to delimit the portions of the user name/address that is generated by the AS/400. The default is the question mark (?). Other allowable delimiters are =, ., +, &, _, -, $, #, *, and ".

Changing LPD Attributes

The LPD process allows incoming LPD print requests (from other AS/400s, Unix systems, or any system that supports LPR) to be printed on AS/400 printers. Option 13 on the Configure TCP/IP Applications menu (Figure 4.15) lets you modify the LPD server attributes. Entering option 13 or the CHGLPDA command brings up the Change LPD Attributes prompt screen (Figure 4.25).

FIGURE 4.25
Change LPD Attributes Prompt Screen

```
                     Change LPD Attributes (CHGLPDA)

 Type choices, press Enter.

 Autostart servers  . . . . . . .   *NO          *YES, *NO, *SAME
 Number of initial servers  . . .   2            1-20, *SAME, *DFT

 

 

 

 

 

                                                            Bottom
 F3=Exit   F4=Prompt   F5=Refresh   F12=Cancel   F13=How to use this display
 F24=More keys
```

On this screen, you can modify two parameters — Autostart servers (AUTOSTART) and Number of initial servers (NBRSVR).

Like all the AUTOSTART parameters we've covered, this one specifies whether the LPD server(s) should start automatically when the STRTCP command is issued. The default value of *YES specifies that the server(s) start automatically. If you don't implement LPD on your AS/400, change this value to *NO to eliminate unnecessary use of system resources.

The NBRSVR parameter specifies the number of servers that will be started when LPD is started. The valid range of values is 1 to 20; the default value of 2 is appropriate for most installations that implement LPD. At least two servers should be started to accommodate multiple jobs. If only one server is started, additional LPD jobs must wait until the previous job completes. If the AS/400 is the target of many incoming print requests, you may want to start additional servers initially.

HTTP Server Attributes

The HTTP protocol lets the AS/400 function as a Web server. Entering option 14 from the Configure TCP/IP Applications menu (Figure 4.15) or the CFGTCPHTTP command brings up the Configure TCP/IP HTTP menu (Figure 4.26).

FIGURE 4.26
Configure TCP/IP HTTP Menu

```
                        Configure TCP/IP HTTP
                                                System:     S1029F3R
Select one of the following:

   1. Change HTTP attributes
   2. Work with HTTP configuration

 Related options:
   10. Configure workstation gateway




Selection or command
===>  _____

F3=Exit   F4=Prompt   F9=Retrieve   F12=Cancel
```

Three options are available from this menu. Here we focus on the HTTP server attributes (option 1). In Chapter 9, we provide a complete description of the Web-serving capabilities of the AS/400, including an explanation of the WRKHTTPCFG (Work with HTTP Configuration) command, the HTTP directives, and WSG. Entering option 1 or the CHGHTTPA command brings up the Change HTTP Attributes prompt screen (Figure 4.27).

As before, the Autostart (AUTOSTART) parameter specifies whether the HTTP server processes should start automatically when the STRTCP command is issued. The default is *YES; you should change this value to *NO if you want to start the HTTP server jobs manually or if you don't implement HTTP on your AS/400.

The Number of server jobs (NBRSVR) parameter specifies the minimum and maximum number of server processes. The minimum number of server jobs defaults to 3 in a range of 1 to 200. The maximum number of server jobs can range from 1 to 200, with a default value of 5. The HTTP server allocation process is quite clever — the number of server jobs specified in the minimum portion of the NBRSVR parameter start automatically when the STRTCP command is issued, and additional server jobs (to the maximum number in the

FIGURE 4.27
Change HTTP Attributes Prompt Screen

```
                    Change HTTP Attributes (CHGHTTPA)

 Type choices, press Enter.

 Autostart  . . . . . . . . . .   *YES          *YES, *NO, *SAME
 Number of server jobs:
   Minimum  . . . . . . . . . .   3             1-200, *SAME, *DFT
   Maximum  . . . . . . . . . .   5             1-200, *SAME, *DFT, *NOMAX
 Coded character set identifier   00819         1-65533, *SAME, *DFT
 Server mapping tables:
   Outgoing EBCDIC/ASCII table  .  *CCSID       Name, *SAME, *CCSID, *DFT
     Library  . . . . . . . . . .               Name, *LIBL, *CURLIB

   Incoming ASCII/EBCDIC table  .  *CCSID       Name, *SAME, *CCSID, *DFT
     Library  . . . . . . . . . .               Name, *LIBL, *CURLIB




                                                                     Bottom
 F3=Exit   F4=Prompt   F5=Refresh   F12=Cancel   F13=How to use this display
 F24=More keys
```

NBRSVR command) start when needed. When the HTTP activity drops, the number of HTTP servers also decreases. Be aware that specifying a large minimum number of servers may impact system performance. I generally start out with the default of 3 for the minimum and 20 for the maximum and then monitor performance. Every site will be different — monitor the performance and adjust the number of servers based on your system requirements.

The next three parameters specify how ASCII to EBCDIC (and vice versa) translations are performed for Web access to the HTTP server. Normally the browser's MIME header contains the character set and code page information. However, if the browser doesn't supply this information, these parameters determine the translation.

The Coded character set identifier (CCSID) parameter's default value of 00819, specifying use of the ISO 8859-1 8-bit ASCII set for ASCII-to-EBCDIC and EBCDIC-to-ASCII mapping, is appropriate for most HTTP implementations. If your translation needs are different, for a unique translation or for national language considerations, change the CCSID parameter to an appropriate value.

The Outgoing EBCDIC/ASCII table (TBLHTTPOUT) and Incoming ASCII/EBCDIC table (TBLHTTPIN) parameters let you specify a custom translation table for outgoing and incoming HTTP access, respectively. The default value of *CCSID specifies that the CCSID parameter value will be used to determine the mapping. Normally, you won't need custom translation tables, so the default value is appropriate. If you do have unique considerations (as mentioned above), you may need to change the translation tables.

WSG Attributes

WSG enables access to the AS/400 from a standard Web browser. Entering option 15 from the Configure TCP/IP Applications menu (Figure 4.15) or the CFGTCPWSG command brings up the Configure TCP/IP Workstation Gateway menu (Figure 4.28).

FIGURE 4.28
Configure TCP/IP Workstation Gateway Menu

```
                   Configure TCP/IP Workstation Gateway
                                                    System:     S1029F3R
Select one of the following:

    1. Change workstation gateway attributes

  Related options:
    10. Configure HTTP

  Associated system values:
    11. Work with autoconfigure virtual devices
    12. Work with limit security officer device access





Selection or command
===>  _____
      _____
F3=Exit    F4=Prompt    F9=Retrieve    F12=Cancel
```

Four options are available from this menu. Here we focus on the WSG attributes (option 1). In the previous section, we covered configuring HTTP, which is required to provide WSG access. In Chapter 9, we provide a complete description of WSG and the HTTP directives needed for WSG configuration. Entering option 1 or the CHGWSGA command brings up the Change WSG Attributes prompt screen (Figure 4.29).

The Autostart (AUTOSTART) parameter specifes whether the WSG server processes should start automatically when the STRTCP command is issued. The default value is *YES to automatically start the WSG servers. Specify *NO if you want to start the servers manually or if you don't want to implement the WSG function.

The Number of clients per server (NBRCLT) parameter specifies the number of client sessions that each WSG server job will handle. With the default value of 20, the AS/400 manages the number of WSG server jobs to ensure that at least 20 client sessions are always available for use. This number of server jobs either increases or decreases depending on the activity for the WSG server. The valid range for this value is 1 to 50. Start with the default value of 20 and monitor performance for your site.

FIGURE 4.29
Change WSG Attributes Prompt Screen

```
                    Change WSG Attributes (CHGWSGA)

 Type choices, press Enter.

 Autostart  . . . . . . . . . . .    *YES          *YES, *NO, *SAME
 Number of clients per server . .    20            1-50, *SAME, *DFT
 Inactivity timeout . . . . . . .    10            0-60 minutes, *SAME, *DFT
 Data request timeout . . . . . .    10            1-1200 seconds, *SAME, *DFT
 Display sign on panel  . . . . .    *YES          *SAME, *NO, *YES
 Access logging . . . . . . . . .    *NO           *SAME, *NO, *YES
 Top banner URL . . . . . . . . .    *NONE



 Bottom banner URL  . . . . . . .    *NONE




                                                            More...
 F3=Exit   F4=Prompt   F5=Refresh   F12=Cancel   F13=How to use this display
 F24=More keys
```

The Inactivity timeout (INACTTIMO) parameter specifies the amount of time a WSG session connection can remain idle before the system disconnects it. The default value is 10 minutes, with a valid range of 0 (specifying that no timeouts will occur) to 60 minutes.

The Data request timeout (DTARQSTIMO) parameter specifies the amount of time between an initial WSG client connection and the WSG server receiving all the request data. If the amount of time elapsed between these events exceeds the value specified for the DTARQSTIMO parameter, a timeout occurs and the connection is broken. The valid range is 0 (specifying that no timeouts will occur) to 1,200 seconds, and the default value is 10 seconds. The default value is probably appropriate — make this timeout value larger if you have delays on your network, or make it shorter to minimize overall system resource utilization. Monitor the performance of your system and adjust this timeout value accordingly.

The Display sign on panel (DSPSGN) parameter specifies whether the AS/400 sign-on panel will be displayed when a WSG request comes in from a Web browser. The default value of *NO indicates that a sign-on screen will not be displayed; a value of *YES causes a sign-on screen to be displayed to the user. Specify *YES to allow the workstation gateway to provide a sign-on screen to the incoming request from a Web browser. IBM states that the WSG will work with the standard sign-on panel — be sure you test this sign-on capability if you have a modified sign-on panel.

The Access logging (ACCLOG) parameter specifies whether access to the AS/400 using the WSG will be logged. The default value of *YES specifies that access information will be logged to file QUSRSYS/QATMTLOG. Logging can be helpful in determining who is accessing your AS/400 through the Workstation Gateway, but I find that I normally don't log incoming connections.

The Top banner URL (TOPBNRURL), Bottom banner URL (BOTBNRURL), and Help panel URL (HLPPNLURL) parameters specify the URLs to be used to display a top or bottom banner and/or WSG online Help information, respectively. (Press Roll down (Page up) from the prompt screen in Figure 4.29 to display the HLPPNLURL and remaining parameter prompts.) The default value for all three parameters is *NONE, specifying that no banners will be displayed and no online help will be available. If you want a banner or online help, enter a fully qualified URL in the standard URL format. I find I don't usually specify a URL for the top, bottom, or help banners. I prefer to have the screen look as similar to an AS/400 screen as possible. Adding the banners does, however, allow the screen to look more like a Web page than an AS/400 screen — the choice is yours.

The last three parameters specify how ASCII to EBCDIC (and vice versa) translations are performed for WSG server access. Normally the browser's MIME header will contain character-set and code-page information. However, if the browser does not supply the information, these parameters determine the translation.

The Coded character set identifier (CCSID) parameter's default value of 00819, specifying use of the ISO 8859-1 8-bit ASCII set for ASCII-to-EBCDIC and EBCDIC-to-ASCII mapping, is appropriate for most HTTP implementations. If your translation needs are different (e.g., you need a unique translation or have national language considerations), change the CCSID parameter to an appropriate value.

The Outgoing EBCDIC/ASCII table (TBLWSGOUT) and Incoming ASCII/EBCDIC table (TBLWSGIN) parameters let you specify a custom translation table for outgoing and incoming WSG server access, respectively. The default value of *CCSID specifies that the CCSID parameter value will be used to determine the mapping. Normally, you won't need custom translation tables, so the default value is appropriate.

Changing the POP Server Attributes

The POP server is the AS/400 implementation of the POP3 mail interface. The POP server lets an AS/400 act as a POP server for any clients that support the POP mail interface (e.g., Netscape Messenger, Microsoft Mail, Eudora). Option 16 from the Configure TCP/IP Applications menu (Figure 4.15) provides the ability to change the POP attributes. Entering this option or the CHGPOPA command brings up the Change POP Server Attributes prompt screen (Figure 4.30).

FIGURE 4.30
Change POP Server Attributes Prompt Screen

```
                Change POP Server Attributes (CHGPOPA)

Type choices, press Enter.

Autostart servers  . . . . . . . AUTOSTART       *NO
Number of initial servers  . . . NBRSVR          3
Inactivity timeout . . . . . . . INACTTIMO       600
Message split size . . . . . . . MSGSPLIT        128
MIME CCSID:                       MIMECCSID
  Coded character set identifier                 00819
  When to use  . . . . . . . . .                 *BESTFIT
Allow standard POP connection  . ALWSTDCNN       *YES
Host server connection . . . . . HOSTSVRCNN      *NONE
                       + for more values
Address book:                     ADRBOOK
  Enabled  . . . . . . . . . . .                 *NO
  Refresh interval . . . . . . .


                                                          Bottom
F3=Exit    F4=Prompt    F5=Refresh    F12=Cancel   F13=How to use this display
F24=More keys
```

The Autostart servers (AUTOSTART) parameter specifies whether the POP server processes should start automatically when the STRTCP command is issued. The default value is *YES to specify that the POP servers should start automatically. Specify *NO if you want to start the servers manually or if you don't want to implement POP mail serving.

The Number of initial servers (NBRSVR) parameter specifies the number of POP servers to start when the STRTCP command is issued. You can specify that multiple servers should start so that multiple mail clients can access the AS/400 without OS/400 starting additional server jobs. The valid range is 1 to 20 servers, with a default value of 3, which is a good place to start. Then monitor your system's performance, and make changes based on gained knowledge.

The Inactivity timeout (INACTTIMO) parameter specifies the amount of inactive time that may elapse before the server assumes the client has stopped communicating and disconnects from the client. If a timeout condition occurs, the connection is broken, but no mail is removed from the user's mail area on the AS/400. The default value is 600 seconds (10 minutes), with a valid range of 10 to 65,536 seconds. This default value is a good place to start — monitor the activity at your site and make changes as needed.

The Message split size (MSGSPLIT) parameter is used only for remote mail delivery. It specifies the maximum size (in kilobytes) that a message can be without being split. If a message exceeds the specified size, it will be split into smaller blocks. Systems such as routers and gateways across the network must be able to accommodate the specified size. The valid range is 32K to 2048K, with a default size of 128K, which is generally applicable. If you know that the routers in your environment (such as a private intranet) can accommodate a larger size, make the change and monitor the effect.

The MIME CCSID (MIMECCSID) complex parameter has two parts: Coded character set identifier and When to use. The CCSID portion specifies the CCSID that should be used for ASCII-to-EBCDIC translations. The default is 00819 (ISO 8859-1 8-bit ASCII). The "When to use" portion specifies when translation should be used. The default value is *BESTFIT, meaning that the Mail Server Framework (MSF) will decide when it must translate, and is generally appropriate unless you have a need to limit the character set that should be used for translation.

The Allow standard POP connection (ALWSTDCNN) and Host server connection (HOSTSVRCNN) parameters are related. ALWSTDCNN specifies whether standard mail clients (that is, non-Client Access clients) are allowed to connect to the POP server using standard POP (TCP/IP) connection protocol. The default value of *YES specifies that the POP connection will be used. HOSTSVRCNN specifies the types of connection protocols to be supported for Client Access clients connected to the POP server. You can specify any of the following values: *IP (TCP/IP), *IPX (IPX/SPX), *SNA (SNA), *ALL (all three protocols). Select the appropriate value based on the networking protocol used by the Client Access systems in your network. The default value of *NONE specifies that none of the connection protocols for Client Access clients are supported. In many cases, the ALWSTDCNN parameter should have a value of *YES, and the HOSTSVRCNN parameter should have a value of *NO. However, IBM recommends that if you plan to use only Client Access clients, you set the ALWSTDCNN parameter value to *NO to conserve system resources.

The address book (ADRBOOK) parameter is a complex parameter that specifies whether the POP address book will be made available to mail clients that request it. The address book contains information about the POP user names extracted from the AS/400 System Distribution Directory. If you are using POP across the Internet, I recommend the default value of *NO, specifying that client requests for the address book will be denied. I don't make the POP address book available in this situation because it gives information about system users to the "outside world." If you are using POP across an intranet, the POP address book information may be helpful; a value of *YES enables support for the address book. If you specify *YES for the first element, you must specify a refresh interval (in minutes) to indicate how often the address book information should be refreshed from the AS/400 System Distribution Directory. The default value is 60 minutes, which I would specify if I wanted to use this feature.

E-MAIL — SMTP AND POP3

In this section, we step through configuring the AS/400 for e-mail support. The AS/400 has supported SMTP since V3R1, but it was used primarily as an Internet mail interface to standard OS/400 mail products, such as OfficeVision and JustMail. V3R2 and V3R7 introduced support for Post Office Protocol Version 3 (POP3), the standard for clients to access mail on a server, and since then, e-mail has been implemented quite well in OS/400.

SNADS is a vital component for e-mail on the AS/400, regardless of whether OfficeVision (or any other SNA-based mail product) is used. As a result, you need SNADS distribution queues and routing table entries for proper processing of incoming and outgoing mail. You configure these SNADS-related objects, as well as system distribution directory entries, using three options on the Configure TCP/IP SMTP menu (Figure 4.23). The available options (and their associated CL commands) are

- Option 10, Work with directory entries — WRKDIRE
- Option 11, Work with distribution queue for SMTP — WRKDSTQ
- Option 12, Configure distribution services — CFGDSTSRV

In addition, you need to use the WRKSMTPNAM (Work with SMTP Names) command to add entries to the system alias table for e-mail support.

Working with Directory Entries

Option 10 from the Configure TCP/IP SMTP menu enables modifications to the system distribution directory, which contains information regarding users on the system. Every user who will use e-mail on the AS/400 must have a system distribution directory entry, whether the user is an OfficeVision user or an SMTP/POP3 user. Entering option 10 (or the WRKDIRE command) brings up a Work with Directory Entries screen similar to the one in Figure 4.31.

Initially, this display lists the current directory entries, several of them beginning with the letter Q, indicating that they are IBM-supplied. From this display, you can perform a number of actions, including adding, changing, and removing directory entries.

To create a new directory entry for an e-mail user, enter a 1 in the option field on the top blank line of the display. You may also enter the user ID and address at this time or simply press Enter for the entire interactive display (Figure 4.32). This display shows entry fields for a wealth of information, but only a small part of the information is needed to enable e-mail.

The User ID/Address (USRID) parameter is required and specifies the user ID and address to associate with this directory entry. The User ID portion may be up to eight characters and is usually the user-profile name. The Address portion may also be up to eight characters and is usually the system name.

FIGURE 4.31
Work with Directory Entries Screen

```
                    Work with Directory Entries

Type options, press Enter.
  1=Add      2=Change   4=Remove   5=Display details   6=Print details
  7=Rename   8=Assign different ID to description   9=Add another description

Opt  User ID   Address   Description
 _   BILLW     S1Ø98765  Bill Wilson
 _   MICHAEL   S1Ø98765  Michael Ryan
 _   QDFTOWN   QDFTOWN   Default Owner
 _   QDOC      QDOC      Internal Document Owner
 _   QFAXMSF   FAX       QFAXMSF Entry
 _   QLPAUTO   QLPAUTO   Licensed Program Automatic User
 _   QLPINSTL  QLPINSTL  Licensed Program Install
 _   QSECOFR   QSECOFR   Security Officer
 _   QSYS      QSYS      Internal System User Profile
 _   QUSER     QUSER     Default user for PC Support
 _   TOMMY     S1Ø98765  Tommy Ryan

                                                                    Bottom
F3=Exit      F5=Refresh   F9=Work with nicknames   F11=Sort by description
F12=Cancel   F13=Work with departments   F17=Position to   F24=More keys
```

FIGURE 4.32
Add Directory Entry Interactive Display — Screen 1

```
                        Add Directory Entry

Type choices, press Enter.

    User ID/Address . . . .
    Description . . . . . .
    System name/Group . . .   S1Ø29F3R        F4 for list
    User profile . . . . .                    F4 for list
    Network user ID . . . .

    Name:
      Last  . . . . . . . .
      First . . . . . . . .
      Middle  . . . . . . .
      Preferred . . . . . .
      Full  . . . . . . . .

    Department  . . . . . .                   F4 for list
    Job title . . . . . . .
    Company . . . . . . . .
                                                        More...
F3=Exit   F4=Prompt   F5=Refresh   F12=Cancel   F18=Display location details
F19=Add name for SMTP
```

The Description (USRD) parameter is also required to specify the description (e.g., the e-mail user's full name) to associate with the user ID and address specified in the first parameter. You may specify up to 50 characters.

The System name/group (SYSNAME) parameter specifies the name of the system on which the e-mail user works. The value defaults to the system name.

The User profile (USER) parameter is required and specifies the user profile to associate with this directory entry. A user profile must be associated with each directory entry. As a security note, the user need not have the ability to sign on to the AS/400 and create an interactive session. When you create the user profile (using the CRTUSRPRF command), specify *SIGNOFF for the initial menu (INLMNU) parameter to cause the user to be signed off the system if (s)he attempts to establish an interactive session. Doing so won't affect his/her ability to send and receive e-mail.

The remaining fields on this screen are fairly straightforward, and none are required parameters. However, two more parameters are needed for implementing e-mail. Press the Roll down (Page up) key four times to reach the display that contains the fields for the Mail service level (MSFSRVLVL) parameter and the Preferred address (PREFADR) parameters (Figure 4.33).

FIGURE 4.33
Add Directory Entry Interactive Display — Screen 5

```
                      Add Directory Entry

  Type choices, press Enter.

    Mail service level  . .   2                   1=User index
                                                  2=System message store
                                                  4=Lotus Domino
                                                  9=Other mail service
      For choice 9=Other mail service:
        Field name  . . . .                       F4 for list

    Preferred address . . .   3                   1=User ID/Address
                                                  2=O/R name
                                                  3=SMTP name
                                                  9=Other preferred address
      Address type  . . . .                       F4 for list
      For choice 9=Other preferred address:
        Field name  . . . .                       F4 for list


                                                            More...
  F3=Exit   F4=Prompt   F5=Refresh   F12=Cancel   F18=Display location details
  F19=Add name for SMTP
```

The MSFSRVLVL parameter specifies where this user's e-mail should be stored. You must use a value of 1 (*USRIDX), which specifies that the mail should be stored in a user index, for OfficeVision users; a value of 2 (*SYSMS), which specifies that the mail should be stored in a system area where mail clients can access it, for SMTP/POP3 users; a value of 4 (*DOMINO), which specifies that the mail should be stored in the Lotus Domino mail database, for Domino users; or a value of 9 for a custom mail service.

The PREFADR parameter specifies the address scheme to be used for this e-mail user. You must use a value of 1 (*USRID), which specifies that the user ID/address is the preferred address, for OfficeVision/400 users; a value of 2 (*ORNAME), which specifies that the X.400 originator/recipient name is the preferred address, for the user to whom the incoming mail is addressed; a value of 3 (*SMTP), which specifies that the SMTP name (userid@host.domain) is the preferred address, for POP3 and SMTP mail services; or a value of 9, which specifies that another preferred address (e.g., the user name or telephone number) will be used.

Distribution Queue and Routing Table Entry

Distribution queues and routing table entries, together with the system distribution directory, create the relationship among an outgoing or incoming SMTP-based e-mail message, the sending or receiving mail server, and the AS/400. SMTP mail messages are sent to a system (TCPIP) defined in a routing table entry. (This is kind of a "fake" system — nothing is actually sent to a system named TCPIP. It instead indicates that SMTP and SNADS will interoperate to provide the appropriate mail handling.) The routing table entry associates TCPIP with distribution queue QSMTPQ, which sends the message to a special location named TCPIPLOC that interacts with the SNADS and SMTP support to send or receive the message.

The distribution queue and routing table entry are created automatically when the TCP/IP Connectivity Utilities are installed. The characteristics of the QSMTPQ distribution queue and the TCPIP routing table entry are shown in Figures 4.34 and 4.35, respectively.

If you need to send, hold, release, or reroute the QSMTPQ queue or work with its entries, you can use option 11 from the Configure TCP/IP SMTP menu (Figure 4.23) or the WRKDSTQ command to bring up the Work with Distribution Queues display for the QSMTPQ queue. If for some reason the QSMTPQ distribution queue and/or the TCPIP routing table entry are not present on your system (or you need to create another QSMTPQ), you can use option 12 from the Configure TCP/IP SMTP menu to invoke the CFGDSTSTV (Configure Distribution Services) command to create either or both.

FIGURE 4.34
QSMTPQ Distribution Queue Characteristics

```
                    Display Details of Distribution Queue          Page 1 of 2

Queue . . . . . . . . . . . :    QSMTPQ
Queue type  . . . . . . . . :    *RPDS
Remote location name  . . . :    TCPIPLOC
Mode  . . . . . . . . . . . :    *NETATR
Remote net ID . . . . . . . :    *LOC
Local location name . . . . :    *LOC
Normal priority:
  Send time:
    From/To . . . . . . . . :         :          :
    Force . . . . . . . . . :         :
  Send depth  . . . . . . . :    1
High priority:
  Send time:
    From/To . . . . . . . . :         :          :
    Force . . . . . . . . . :         :
  Send depth  . . . . . . . :    1


Press Enter to continue.
                                                                  More...
F3=Exit      F12=Cancel
```

FIGURE 4.35
TCPIP Routing Table Entry Characteristics

```
                    Display Details of Routing Table Entry

Destination system
  name/Group . . . . . :    TCPIP
Description  . . . . . :    TCP/IP Routing
Service level:
  Fast:
    Queue name . . . . :    QSMTPQ
    Maximum hops . . . :    *DFT
  Status:
    Queue name . . . . :    QSMTPQ
    Maximum hops . . . :    *DFT
  Data high:
    Queue name . . . . :    QSMTPQ
    Maximum hops . . . :    *DFT
  Data low:
    Queue name . . . . :    QSMTPQ
    Maximum hops . . . :    *DFT


Press Enter to continue.

F3=Exit      F12=Cancel
```

System Alias Table

The WRKSMTPNAM command is used to add entries to the system alias table for equating system directory names with their corresponding SMTP name. There are actually two SMTP alias tables available — the system alias table and a personal (by user) alias table. Although the ability to have separate tables has some value, I find that I use only the system alias table. Using the personal alias table identifies only an SMTP address for a given user, while use of the system alias table identifies the address for all users. Both tables allow the same options for the associated list of users.

You can enter the WRKSMTPNAM command on a command line or select option 1 or option 2 from the Configure TCP/IP SMTP menu (Figure 4.23). From the Work with Names for SMTP list screen, you may add, change, remove, display, or print the alias table entries.

Entering a 1 in the Option field on the top blank line brings up the Add Name for SMTP prompt screen (Figure 4.36).

FIGURE 4.36

Add Name for SMTP Prompt Screen

```
                              Add Name for SMTP
                                                    System:   LAB400
  Type choices, press Enter.

    User ID . . . . . . . . .   MICHAEL    Character value, *ANY, F4 for list
    Address . . . . . . . . .   S1098765   Character value, F4 for list


    SMTP user ID  . . . . . .   michael
    SMTP domain . . . . . . .   ryantech.com



    SMTP route  . . . . . . .
```

The User ID and Address parameters specify the name of the user as defined in the system directory. You may prompt these parameter to produce a list of all the directory entries. (If you enter this screen by pressing function key F19 from the ADDDIRE or CHGDIRE screen, the system fills in this information.) The SMTP user ID parameter specifies the name to which other users (on the LAN, the intranet, or the Internet) will send their e-mail. You can specify a name of your choosing.

The SMTP domain essentially specifies the name of your system. Remember in the TCP/IP configuration, option 10 from the Configure TCP/IP menu (Figure 4.5) allowed changes to the host table, and option 12 allowed changes to the local domain and host names. Generally, the values for these two entries would be the same, and you would specify the domain for the SMTP Domain parameter on this screen. You may also add other names (both host and domain) for your system in the host table, and one of these names could also be specified for the SMTP Domain. However, it is much more common to have the same host and domain name specified in both locations.

The SMTP Route parameter establishes the path a message must take when the message is to be routed through multiple systems in an SNA environment. This parameter is usually not needed, but could be used in the case of a private intranet where systems are connected and e-mail is routed through different systems. An example of an entry for this parameter could be RED,GREEN:MICHAEL@BLUE, which would indicate user MICHAEL on system BLUE can be reached by routing e-mail through systems RED and GREEN.

Once the AS/400 has been properly configured for e-mail, interaction with the system is the same interaction as with any mail server. A mail client, such as Eudora, Microsoft Mail (or Exchange), Netscape Communicator, or any of the many other client mail packages may be used. Simply configure your mail client to use the AS/400 system (identified by the host and domain name) as the POP3 and SMTP server.

ADVANCED TCP/IP CONFIGURATION OPTIONS

Now that we've covered the basic TCP/IP configuration options, let's look at some of the advanced options. Although most installations won't need these configuration options, we briefly cover TCP/IP attributes and port restrictions, remote system information, merging host tables, configuring TCP/IP-related tables, and configuring point-to-point TCP/IP.

Changing TCP/IP Attributes

You use option 3 on the Configure TCP/IP menu (Figure 4.5) , to change a variety of protocol-layer attributes. Use this menu option carefully because changes you make to these attributes can cause poor performance or even an inability to use TCP/IP. I recommend changing these attributes only when instructed by IBM or if you fully understand TCP/IP at a protocol level and understand the ramifications of such changes. Entering option 3 or the CHGTCPA command brings up the Change TCP/IP Attributes prompt screen (Figure 4.37). Initially, this display shows the current value of 11 TCP/IP attributes.

The TCP keep alive (TCPKEEPALV) parameter specifies the amount of time that TCP/IP waits before sending a probe to an idle system with which a connection has been established. The valid range is 1 through 40,320 minutes, with a default value of 120 minutes.

The TCP urgent pointer (TCPURGPTR) parameter specifies the method used to determine the byte to which the urgent pointer in the TCP/IP header should point. Two methods are available — the Berkeley Software Distribution

FIGURE 4.37
Change TCP/IP Attributes Prompt Screen

```
                    Change TCP/IP Attributes (CHGTCPA)

 Type choices, press Enter.

 TCP keep alive . . . . . . . . . TCPKEEPALV    120
 TCP urgent pointer . . . . . . . TCPURGPTR     *BSD
 TCP receive buffer size  . . . . TCPRCVBUF     8192
 TCP send buffer size . . . . . . TCPSNDBUF     8192
 UDP checksum . . . . . . . . . . UDPCKS        *YES
 IP datagram forwarding . . . . . IPDTGFWD      *NO
 IP source routing  . . . . . . . IPSRCRTG      *YES
 IP reassembly time-out . . . . . IPRSBTIMO     10
 IP time to live  . . . . . . . . IPTTL         64
 ARP cache timeout  . . . . . . . ARPTIMO       15
 Log protocol errors  . . . . . . LOGPCLERR     *NO




                                                          Bottom
 F3=Exit   F4=Prompt   F5=Refresh   F12=Cancel   F13=How to use this display
 F24=More keys
```

(*BSD) method where the urgent pointer points to the byte following the last byte of urgent data, or the Request for Comment (*RFC) method where the urgent pointer points to the last byte of urgent data. Associated nodes must use the same method for communications to occur properly. The default value is *BSD.

The TCP receive buffer size (TCPRCVBUF) and TCP send buffer size (TCPSNDBUF) parameters specify the receive and send buffer size, respectively, for each TCP/IP connection. The buffer size determines the number of bytes that may be held in memory on the AS/400. When the amount of data exceeds these buffer sizes, retransmission of the TCP/IP data occurs. A larger buffer size allows more data to be received or sent before an acknowledgement occurs. A smaller buffer size is useful when many retransmissions occur because more data is being received or sent than the AS/400 can handle. The initial value is 8K, with valid values in a range of 512 bytes to 8 MB; a buffer of the specified size will be created for every TCP/IP connection. Realize that the more memory allocated to buffer sizes, the less memory is available for other jobs.

The UDP checksum (UDPCKS) parameter specifies whether User Datagram Protocol (UDP) checksum processing will be used. Because UDP does not have the error recovery capabilities of TCP/IP, IBM recommends a value of *YES (the default) so that UDP checksum processing is used. A value of *NO disables UDP checksum processing but provides improved performance.

While the AS/400 does not support complete routing capabilities, IP datagram forwarding between different networks is available and specified with the

IP datagram forwarding (IPDTGFWD) parameter. The default value of *NO is generally appropriate: The AS/400 should not forward IP datagrams; a router or bridge is much more cost-effective and should be used for this process. However, if an organization uses both Ethernet and Token-Ring networks and the AS/400 has both types of network cards, allowing the AS/400 to forward IP datagrams may be a cost-effective solution, especially if traffic volumes are fairly low.

The IP reassembly time-out (IPRSBTIMO) parameter specifies the amount of time the system will expend reassembling a fragmented IP datagram. If the time limit is exceeded, a timeout message is sent to the sending system. The default value of 10 seconds is the upper limit of the value you should specify for this parameter, although values of 5 through 120 seconds are valid.

The IP time to live (IPTTL) parameter name can be misleading. Basically, it is a counter that specifies the number of hops over which an IP datagram can be processed. It acts as a hop counter and is reduced by one for each router (or host) through which the IP packet passes. When the time-to-live (TTL) value equals zero, the packet is assumed undeliverable and is discarded. The range of valid values for the IPTTL parameter is 1 to 255. The default value of 64 is large — many systems implement a value of 32 for TTL. The only drawback to having a large IPTTL value is that packets with incorrect addresses bounce around the network longer, causing more network traffic and overhead.

The ARP cache timeout (ARPTIMO) parameter specifies the number of minutes the system will wait before flushing or purging entries in the Address Resolution Protocol cache. Valid values are in the range of 1 through 1,440 minutes. The default value is 15 minutes, which is usually sufficient time to flush old values and not allow the ARP cache to become too large.

The Log protocol errors (LOGPCLERR) parameter specifies whether IP, ICMP, ARP, and NAM protocol errors are to be logged. If *YES is specified, errors are logged to the system error log and may be valuable in determining the cause of network problems. The default value of *NO specifies that protocol-level error messages will not be written to the error log. Although the AS/400 provides this limited capability to log protocol errors (TCP/IP and UDP errors are not logged), any significant effort to identify protocol error problems usually requires some type of packet and protocol analyzer or sniffer.

Working with TCP/IP Port Restrictions

Option 4 on the Configure TCP/IP menu (Figure 4.5) lets you control user profile access to TCP/IP ports. This feature provides some measure of increased security, but you shouldn't view it as a replacement for firewalls or other data communications security schemes. Entering option 4 brings up the Work with TCP/IP Port Restrictions screen (Figure 4.38).

FIGURE 4.38

Work with TCP/IP Port Restrictions

```
                       Work with TCP/IP Port Restrictions
                                                     System:    LAB400
     Type options, press Enter.
       1=Add   4=Remove

             --Port Range--                  User
     Opt    Lower    Upper      Protocol      Profile
      _               *ONLY
      _     2000      *ONLY       *TCP        TCPUSER
```

This display shows the port restrictions currently in effect. The port range, the protocol, and the user profile associated with the restriction are shown on this display. From this screen, you may add or remove port restrictions. The available options (and their associated CL commands) are

- Option 1, Add TCP/IP port restriction — ADDTCPPORT
- Option 4, Remove TCP/IP port restriction— RMVTCPPORT

To add a restriction to a port or range of ports, you type a 1 on the top, blank line of the display. You may enter the port range, protocol, and user profile at this time, or press Enter to bring up the Add TCP/IP Port Restriction prompt screen (Figure 4.39).

FIGURE 4.39

Add a TCP/IP Port Restriction Prompt Screen

```
                    Add TCP/IP Port Restriction (ADDTCPPORT)

     Type choices, press Enter.

     Range of port values:
       Lower value  . . . . . . . . > 2000         1-65535
       Upper value  . . . . . . . . > *ONLY        1-65535, *ONLY
     Protocol . . . . . . . . . . . > *TCP         *UDP, *TCP
     User profile . . . . . . . . . > TCPUSER      Character value
```

The Range of port values (PORT) parameter specifies the port number or range of port numbers to be restricted. The first element in this complex parameter specifies the lower range, and the second element specifies the upper range of ports. The second element of the parameter defaults to *ONLY, specifying that the port specified in the first element is the only port to be considered for this restriction. An upper and lower limit to the range of ports may be specified.

The Protocol (PROTOCOL) parameter specifies the protocol, either TCP/IP or UDP, for which the port is being restricted. Recall from Chapter 1 that both TCP/IP and UDP use the concept of ports. The combination of the port number (or range) and the protocol uniquely identifies the port(s) to be restricted.

The user profile (USRPRF) parameter specifies the user profile to which the port restriction is being applied. This user profile can be an individual user profile or a group profile. When the port restriction is in effect, only users using the specified user profile (or part of the specified group profile) may access the restricted port(s).

Working with TCP/IP Remote System Information

With option 5 on the Configure TCP/IP menu (Figure 4.5), you specify remote system information. This information must be specified for systems connecting over a public or private X.25 network. Because our focus is LAN connections, the most common for TCP/IP on the AS/400, I refer you to the *AS/400 TCP/IP Configuration* manual for detailed information regarding X.25 connections.

Merging TCP/IP Host Tables

Option 11 on the Configure TCP/IP menu (Figure 4.5) is used to merge host tables from different systems. You use this option if you have not implemented DNS in your network. Recall from "Working with TCP/IP Host Table Entries" earlier in this chapter that if DNS isn't implemented, host tables are used to resolve IP addresses from host names. With option 11, you can merge host table entries from another system into the host table on the AS/400 or you can completely replace the host table on the AS/400. Host table entries are merged by IP address, adding any host names and comments. Entering option 11 or the MRGTCPHT command brings up the Merge TCP/IP Host Table prompt screen (Figure 4.40).

The From file (FROMFILE) and From member (FROMMBR) parameters specify the physical file that contains the host table information to be merged into the AS/400 host table. The FROMFILE parameter identifies the file (and library) of the host table information, while the FROMMBR parameter identifies the member containing the information.

The File format (FILEFMT) parameter specifies whether the physical file member to be merged with the local host table is *AS400, *AIX, or *NIC format. A value of *AS400 specifies that the file containing the host table information was produced on an AS/400 running OS/400 V3R1 or later. A value of *AIX specifies that the host table information was created on an RS/6000 running AIX or an AS/400 with an operating system release earlier than V3R1. A

FIGURE 4.40
Merge TCP/IP Host Table Prompt Screen

```
                    Merge TCP/IP Host Table (MRGTCPHT)

  Type choices, press Enter.

  From file  . . . . . . . . . . .  FROMFILE
    Library  . . . . . . . . . . .                    *LIBL
  From member  . . . . . . . . . .  FROMMBR           *FIRST
  File format  . . . . . . . . . .  FILEFMT           *AS400
  Replace host table . . . . . . .  REPLACE           *NO




                                                              Bottom
  F3=Exit   F4=Prompt   F5=Refresh   F12=Cancel   F13=How to use this display
  F24=More keys
```

value of *NIC indicates that the file is in Internet format, specifically the format used by a Network Information Center (NIC) or an ISP.

The Replace host table (REPLACE) parameter specifies whether the host table information should be merged with the AS/400 host table or should replace the AS/400 host table. This is not an option that you will be using. You will not be merging host tables, but using DNS.

Configuring TCP/IP-related Tables
Option 21 on the Configure TCP/IP menu (Figure 4.5) lets you modify the service table, which contains a list of ports and their names; the protocol table, which contains a short list of the protocols (e.g., TCP, UDP) and the protocol numbers; and the network table, which can contain information about networks in your environment. These tables should rarely be changed.

Configuring Point-to-Point TCP/IP
Option 22 on the Configure TCP/IP menu enables configuration of Serial Line Internet Protocol (SLIP) for dial-in and dial-out TCP/IP connections. We cover this topic in detail in Appendix B.

AnyNet/400
AnyNet/400 is shipped with OS/400. As part of the family of AnyNet products, AnyNet/400 is based on the Multiprotocol Transport Network (MPTN) architecture and lets application programs written for one protocol run over another

protocol. In other words, with AnyNet/400 enabled, SNA applications — such as Client Access or Distributed Data Management (DDM) — can run across a TCP/IP network, and TCP/IP applications, such as FTP, can run across an SNA network. AnyNet/400 supports the following protocol combinations:

- SNA over TCP/IP (SNA over IP) for applications such as
  - DB2/400 for DDM
  - Display Station Passthrough (DSPT)
  - Distributed Relational Database Architecture (DRDA)
  - SNADS
  - SNA-based Client Access
- SNA over IPX
- TCP/IP Sockets over IPX
- TCP/IP Sockets over SNA (IP over SNA) for applications such as
  - FTP
  - TCP/IP-based Client Access
  - SMTP
  - SNMP
  - PING

Note that the SNA support includes APPC as well as Common Programming Interface — Communications (CPI-C) applications.

In this section we cover TCP/IP over SNA and SNA over TCP/IP, with an emphasis on the latter. Many organizations are establishing routed, TCP/IP-based WANs, which are great for such applications as e-mail, data transfer, and virtual terminal access. However, some legacy applications, such as custom APPC or CPI-C programs or traditional Client Access support, require APPC or SNA, making SNA over TCP/IP the most common implementation of AnyNet/400.

The TCP/IP over SNA implementation, on the other hand, is less common and would be used in an organization that has an established SNA network and wants to deploy TCP/IP (socket) applications. SNA can be used as a transport with the TCP/IP data encapsulated with the SNA packet.

AnyNet/400 Configuration

The configuration of AnyNet/400 varies depending on the type of encapsulation desired. However, regardless of what type of encapsulation you plan to implement, for any type of AnyNet/400 configuration, you must first enable AnyNet/400 support by changing the ALWANYNET (Allow AnyNet) attribute.

OS/400 ships with this attribute set to its default, *NO, because according to IBM, TCP/IP socket applications run more slowly if AnyNet/400 support is enabled, even if TCP/IP over SNA is not being used. This means a socket program, even communicating directly with another socket program (with no AnyNet/400 involved) performs more poorly if this network attribute is set to *YES. To enable any and all AnyNet/400 support, you use the following CHGNETA (Change Network Attributes) command:

```
CHGNETA ALWANYNET(*YES)
```

Configuring IP over SNA

Configuring IP over SNA requires that the IP addresses that will be routed across the SNA network be identified and a Logical Unit (LU) name be associated with each IP address. An LU name defines a point in an SNA network. On the AS/400, LU names are defined in device descriptions as the Local Location Name (LCLLOCNAME) and the Remote Location Name (RMTLOCNAME). These LU names must be matched to the IP address of the remote system that will be communicating with your AS/400. Usually there will be a one-to-one correspondence between a remote system with which you want to communicate and an LU name, but you may wish to designate multiple LUs for a given system if you need to associate a specific application with a specific LU or if you need to balance the load across LUs.

The first step in configuring AnyNet/400 IP over SNA support is to add an interface for IP over SNA using the ADDIPSIFC (Add IP over SNA Interface) command. The prompt screen for this command is shown in Figure 4.41.

Two parameters are needed — the Internet Address (INTNETADR) of the interface and the associated Subnet mask (SUBNETMASK). Each interface must have a unique Internet address — one that is not the same as any defined TCP/IP interface Internet address. In other words, this IP address is to be used just for IP over SNA.

The next step is to associate IP addresses with an LU name using the ADDIPSLOC (Add IP over SNA Location) command. The prompt screen for this command is shown in Figure 4.42. The first two parameters on this display define the TCP/IP side, while the third and fourth parameters define the SNA side.

The Remote destination (RMTDEST) parameter specifies the IP address (or addresses) of the remote host or the remote network. The address should be specified in standard dotted-decimal format. You may specify an IP address for a single host or a network address for a range of hosts.

The Subnet mask (SUBNETMASK) parameter specifies the subnet mask to be used with the RMTDEST parameter to identify the remote system or group of systems. Standard subnetting considerations apply.

FIGURE 4.41
Add IP over SNA Interface Prompt Screen

```
                    Add IP over SNA Interface (ADDIPSIFC)

Type choices, press Enter.

Internet address . . . . . . . .
Subnet mask  . . . . . . . . . .





                                                             Bottom
F3=Exit    F4=Prompt    F5=Refresh    F12=Cancel    F13=How to use this display
F24=More keys
```

FIGURE 4.42
Add IP over SNA Location Prompt Screen

```
                    Add IP over SNA Location (ADDIPSLOC)

Type choices, press Enter.

Remote destination . . . . . . . RMTDEST
Subnet mask  . . . . . . . . . . SUBNETMASK
Remote network identifier  . . . RMTNETID          *NETATR
Location template  . . . . . . . LOCTPL




                                                             Bottom
F3=Exit    F4=Prompt    F5=Refresh    F12=Cancel    F13=How to use this display
F24=More keys
```

The Remote network identifier (RMTNETID) parameter specifies the name of the remote SNA network associated with the IP network or IP address specified by the remote route destination. The default is *NETATR, specifying that the remote network identifier specified in the network attributes is used.

Specify the network ID of the remote system if it is different than the local system's network ID.

The Location template (LOCTPL) parameter specifies the LU associated with the IP network or subnetwork specified by the remote route destination. You can specify the LU name in one of two ways: specify the LU name to be used for a specific host, or specify an 8-character template that the AS/400 will use to generate remote LU names based on the remote IP address specified on socket system calls. The template would consist of characters (and the wild card character ?) that would be used to identify a group of hosts. An example might be LU?SYS?A, where the connection could be made to any LU that fits the pattern.

The last step in creating an IP over SNA connection is to define the route to the remote system with the ADDIPSRTE (Add IP over SNA Route) command. The prompt screen for this command is shown in Figure 4.43.

FIGURE 4.43
Add IP over SNA Route Prompt Screen

```
                  Add IP over SNA Route (ADDIPSRTE)

Type choices, press Enter.

Route destination  . . . . . . . RTEDEST
Subnet mask  . . . . . . . . . . SUBNETMASK
Next hop . . . . . . . . . . . . NEXTHOP




                                                              Bottom
F3=Exit   F4=Prompt   F5=Refresh   F12=Cancel   F13=How to use this display
F24=More keys
```

The routing is straightforward — you need to specify the address of the gateway system (router) that will route the TCP/IP socket packets to the correct destination over the SNA network.

The Route destination (RTEDEST) parameter specifies in dotted-decimal notation the route destination as either the IP address of the remote system or the address of the network that contains the remote system.

The Subnet mask (SUBNETMASK) parameter specifies the subnet mask to be used with the RTEDEST parameter to identify the remote system or network.

The Next hop (NEXTHOP) parameter specifies the IP address of the gateway or router that will provide the route to the destination system or network. The important consideration with this parameter is that the IP over SNA interface address and the next hop address must be on the same network and must have IP addresses that are from the same network.

Configuring SNA over TCP/IP

Configuring SNA (APPC) over TCP/IP is similar to configuring TCP/IP itself. The line, network controller, and network device descriptions for TCP/IP communications are created as part of standard TCP/IP configuration (see "Configuring the Line, Controller, and Device" earlier in this chapter). The main differences are work that needs to be done on the host table (or a domain name server) and two APPC configuration objects — an APPC controller description and a configuration list for APPN remote locations — that need to be created.

The host table (or a domain name server) needs an entry for each system that will be communicating using SNA over TCP/IP. The name of the remote system must be unique and in the form *luname.netid*.SNA.IBM.COM, where *luname* is the APPC remote location name (LU name), and *netid* is the network ID of the remote location. This naming convention is critical to the success of the SNA over TCP/IP connection. The remote system name should be associated with the IP address of the remote system either as a host table entry or by specifying the information in a name server (see " Working with TCP/IP Host Tables" and "Changing TCP/IP Domain Information" earlier in this chapter).

You use the CRTCTLAPPC (Create Controller APPC) command to create the controller description required for SNA over TCP/IP. The following five parameters are needed:

- Controller description name (CTLD) — may be any valid name
- Link type (LINKTYPE) — must be *ANYNW
- Use APPN functions (APPN) — must be *YES
- Remote network ID (RMTNETID) — defaults to *NETATR, indicating the network ID of the local system
- Remote control point name (RMTCPNAME) — must be unique

A sample command to create an APPC controller with a link type of *ANYNW is shown below:

```
CRTCTLAPPC CTLD(ANYNWCTL) LINKTYPE(*ANYNW) APPN(*YES) +
           RMTCPNAME(TCPIP)
```

For the controller description created above, you need to add an entry to the APPN remote configuration list — TYPE(*APPNRMT) — to identify the controller description that an incoming SNA over TCP/IP request for a session should use. Only one remote configuration list exists on a system. You can use the CHGCFGL (Change Configuration List) command to change the existing configuration list or the CRTCFGL (Create Configuration List) command to create a new list. A sample command to add an APPN remote configuration list entry is shown below:

```
CHGCFGL TYPE(*APPNRMT) +
        APPNRMTE((RMTLOC RMTNET LCLLOC TCPIP))
```

This command specifies the remote location name as RMTLOC, the network identifier of the network in which the remote location resides as RMTNET, the local location name as LCLLOC, and the remote control point that will provide network functions for the remote location as TCPIP. The remote control point name specified in the remote APPN configuration list must match the remote control point name in the controller description that has the line type of *ANYNW.

When to Use AnyNet/400

In many environments, one of the main reasons for using AnyNet is to provide APPC-based services, especially Client Access, in a TCP/IP network. While the Windows version of Client Access is supported over TCP/IP and performs quite well, there are two areas where TCP/IP-based Client Access does not provide the functionality needed in some installations:

- TCP/IP-based Client Access doesn't support a fixed workstation ID for terminal access.
- You can't print to locally attached printers through TCP/IP-based Client Access.

Note that both of these features are available with OS/400 versions V3R2/R7 and later, Client Access version V3R1M3 and later, and the appropriate PTFs and ServicePacks. The use of AnyNet/400 provides this functionality in a TCP/IP environment regardless of OS/400 or Client Access version.

Another reason to use AnyNet/400 is to support APPC applications, especially custom applications that may be used in a client/server environment. APPC provides several Application Programming Interfaces (APIs) that have been used in APPC/APPN environments for many years. Changing an organization's network to use TCP/IP may provide several advantages, but, without AnyNet/400, the custom APPC applications would be unuseable across the network.

AnyNet/400 support is included as part of OS/400, so no additional licensed program product charges apply. However, the increased functionality gained in these situations by using AnyNet/400 is not without associated costs.

AnyNet/400 consumes system resources. As we mentioned earlier, use of AnyNet/400 causes socket applications to run slower, even if the applications are not used across the network. APPC applications (in the case of SNA over TCP/IP) also run slower because of the inherent overhead involved with encapsulation. In addition, use of AnyNet/400 requires additional configuration effort. While AnyNet/400 does provide a method of encapsulation and the ability to run applications over a network with less regard for the underlying network protocol in use, I recommend that either the applications be changed to use the underlying network protocol or routers be used to provide the encapsulation needed. Either alternative decreases the load on the AS/400 and may well provide better performance.

SUMMARY

Configuring the AS/400 for TCP/IP is a straightforward proposition. The main elements of configuration include specifying the IP address for the interface, specifying the host and domain name, specifying the routing (if needed), and placing an entry in the host table — that's all that's needed to enable TCP/IP on your AS/400. You usually take a few additional steps, such as determining the TCP/IP servers to autostart, identifying the number of servers, and perhaps changing a timeout value. Many more steps may be taken — such as working with port restrictions, changing attributes, fine tuning the characteristics of servers — but these steps are usually not needed and should be approached with caution.

Chapter 5

AS/400 TCP/IP-Based Services and Examples

TCP/IP services on the AS/400 provide virtual terminal access, file transfers, printing, and e-mail. These services are all part of the operating system, so other products are not required. You may need client software for printing (an LPD client) or e-mail (a POP3 client), but the core TCP/IP processing software is available free in OS/400.

Using AS/400 TCP/IP services is similar to using them on other systems, although there are some minor differences due to the AS/400's unique architecture. For example, virtual terminal processing to an AS/400 is best with TN5250 emulation, and file transfers let you choose between name format 0 for the traditional library structure and name format 1 for the Integrated File System (IFS). The AS/400 supports both LPD and LPR, so incoming and outgoing print requests can use the TCP/IP standard for printing. The e-mail capability interacts with SNADS, but no OS/400 mail software, such as JustMail/400 or OfficeVision/400, is required.

This chapter explores AS/400-based TCP/IP services with discussions of

- Telnet virtual terminal access, including coverage of TN5250 and standard 5250 access
- file transfers with FTP, including access to the IFS
- printing with LPR and LPD, including using the SNDTCPSPLF (Send TCP/IP Spooled File) command and configuring an output queue for remote printing
- e-mail with SMTP and POP3

TELNET

Virtual terminal processing with Telnet gives the AS/400 access to non-AS/400 hosts on a LAN or WAN. This openness is in both directions — other devices may also access the AS/400. For host environments such as the AS/400 that are heavily terminal-oriented, Telnet is critically important because it gives local terminals access to other TCP/IP hosts and permits various types of remote terminals to access the local host.

When it was originally designed and implemented more than 20 years ago, Telnet was oriented toward simple "dumb" terminal types, such as teletypes or limited-function ASCII displays, because those were the types of devices commonly used for interactive I/O. In retrospect, these devices were remarkable for their sheer simplicity — I/O was performed either on a character-at-a-time or a line-at-a-time basis. All output was "raw" and presented without benefit of display highlights (e.g., bold, reverse video, blinking) or graphical aids. These "dumb" devices provided a simple interface for simple times.

As the terminal market matured and progressed, so did Telnet. Thus, when the Digital Equipment Corporation (DEC) VT series of terminals became immensely popular in the ASCII terminal market, Telnet adopted the characteristics of the VT terminal, allowing users to continue to use Telnet and still enjoy the benefits of the VT terminals (e.g., display highlights, more sophisticated screen handling, improved keyboard functions). Similarly, when users needed access from TCP/IP networks to IBM mainframes, a version of Telnet was developed to provide the capabilities of an IBM 3270 workstation. More recently, a version supporting IBM 5250 workstation functions was introduced to facilitate access from TCP/IP networks to the AS/400 environment.

As with any TCP/IP-based application, Telnet operates on a client/server model: A user initiating a Telnet request uses client software, and the request is received by server software operating in the background of the target system. Note that the server does not need to be on the local network — it might reside on a network on the other side of the world. The client accesses the server using well-known port 23, and the server begins the communication with the client.

When the server receives a client request for a Telnet socket connection, the server normally starts a new copy of the Telnet server program to handle the new client connection. The client and server then establish a dynamic "side-channel" on the socket they use to communicate with one another. This architecture allows multiple client/server conversations to occur concurrently over the same socket.

Once the client and server programs have established a link, they can start interacting. In the case of the AS/400 Telnet server, the initial interaction involves terminal negotiation, a process the client and server modules use to agree on the special terminal functions or capabilities to be made available during the session (we discuss terminal negotiation in more detail in "Telnet Terminal Negotiation" later in this chapter). After the option negotiation has taken place, the user can log on to the target AS/400 and perform interactive terminal functions.

Telnet Client Operation

Before Telnet client and server programs can begin to communicate, the user must execute a Telnet client program. Most Telnet client programs have two modes of operation — input mode and command mode. The standard operational mode for a Telnet client, input mode lets the client interact with the target system. In command mode, the client can control Telnet operations and perform functions such as initiating a new connection, closing an open connection, or exiting the client program.

The Telnet client's start-up mode usually depends on how the client is initiated. In particular, if you direct the client to connect to a specific host upon connection (via a command line option, a dialog box, or a prompted menu), the client program initiates the connection to the target system and goes into input mode. In this case, the next thing you see after initiating the client is the server's log-on screen.

The look, feel, and availability of Telnet command mode depends on the client environment. At one extreme, some Telnet implementations don't allow interactive command mode — the client opens the connection at initiation time and shuts it down when you log off the host. At the other extreme, Telnet clients that run in the Microsoft Windows environment often incorporate all command-mode functions into Windows command or dialog boxes. In this case, you simply select a drop-down box to invoke a Telnet command.

Most DOS-mode and Unix-based Telnet clients are between these two extremes. With these clients, you typically invoke command mode either by invoking the client without parameters or by entering an Escape command (normally Ctrl-[ ) while connected to a system. When you request command mode, the Telnet client responds with a command line prompt (e.g., telnet>), at which you can then enter commands. Normally you can toggle between command and input mode as needed. (Not all DOS and Unix clients follow these rules exactly, but most have corresponding capabilities.)

Although the look and feel of command mode depends on the characteristics of the client environment, the look and feel of input mode depends on the characteristics of the terminal type the client and server agree on during terminal negotiation.

Telnet Network Virtual Terminal

As we mentioned earlier, Telnet's designers developed the Telnet client and server program based on a generic terminal model called the Network Virtual Terminal (NVT), which provides a set of primitive terminal functions.

The NVT functions comprise two groups — a core set of mandatory functions and a set of optional functions. Any terminal that performs Telnet activity must be able to perform the mandatory functions, shown in Table 5.1.

TABLE 5.1

NVT Core Functions

CR	Carriage return
LF	Line feed
NUL	No operation

Table 5.2 lists the optional functions in the NVT model. Both groups of functions come into play whenever a Telnet client is in input mode. While in input mode, the client translates keys the user presses into these functions and passes the function (not the key) on to the Telnet server. For example, Wyse, Televideo, and DEC terminals all have a Tab key, but each terminal may produce a different internal value when the user presses that key. To compensate for these differences, the Telnet client program traps the value generated by the terminal and passes it to the Telnet server as an HT function, thus isolating the server from the unique characteristics of the user terminal.

TABLE 5.2
NVT Optional Functions

BEL	Audible alert
BS	Destructive backspace
FF	Form feed
HT	Horizontal tab
VT	Vertical tab

As you can imagine, this approach greatly simplifies the server's job because the server need not know the specific characteristics of each type of terminal that may interact with it. By the same token, this approach makes the job of the Telnet client a little more difficult because the Telnet client must be able to translate the key values generated by different types of terminals into core NVT functions.

Another area where the NVT model helps neutralize the differences between physical terminal types is end-of-line processing — specifically, what happens when the user presses Return or Enter. As with the Tab key, there is a lack of consistency between different terminal types. Some terminals generate a single carriage return (CR), some generate a line feed (LF), and others generate both. Under the Telnet NVT model, however, the Telnet client always sends a combined CR-LF function to indicate that the Enter or Return key has been pressed.

When Telnet was first deployed in the early 1970s, the NVT model incorporated a rich set of functions that pretty well covered the capabilities of the terminals on the contemporary market. But terminal manufacturers have produced several generations of terminals since then, each more sophisticated than the last, and today's terminals offer features and functions far beyond the basic functions of the NVT model. That's where the need for terminal negotiation comes in.

Telnet Terminal Negotiation

The explosion of interactive terminal usage that began in the 1970s resulted in literally hundreds of different types of terminals. Rather than expand the NVT model, the Telnet developers decided to let the Telnet client and server programs determine additional terminal capabilities dynamically during the initial connection dialogue. Under this approach, in a process referred to as option negotiation, the client or server can ask its counterpart whether it supports a particular function.

Some options handle straightforward, easily understood functions such as character echo, support for extended ASCII characters (including line-drawing characters), and the maximum message size the client or server can handle. The most significant option, however, is the terminal type. This option lets the client and server agree on a specific terminal type that both systems support. Once the two sides are in agreement, the operator can use all the native features and functions of that terminal.

Both sides must support the desired terminal for a terminal type to be negotiated successfully. In other words, the client must be able to interface with the physical terminal (or terminal emulation package) and recognize that terminal's operational and functional keystrokes. Similarly, the server side must be able to handle those terminal characteristics. If the client supports a specific terminal type but the server side does not, the server rejects any attempt to negotiate that terminal type.

For example, most Telnet implementations support the VT100 terminal type. Therefore, when a client connects to a server, it can ask "Do you do VT100?" Most servers will respond with "Yes, I do." Once all other option negotiation is complete, the Telnet client operation can interface with applications on the Telnet server system and use native VT100 functions such as Select, Remove, and function keys PF1 through PF4. Also, the server-side applications can send display highlights (e.g., blinking, bold, underline) for display on the Telnet client terminal.

What terminal types are supported on which systems? The answer depends mostly on the computer platform and operating system. Unix systems support a wide variety of terminal types through the TERMCAPS and TERM-INFO facilities. Non-Unix systems tend to support a narrower range of terminal types; many non-Unix systems support only the VT100 and IBM 3270 terminal types. The IBM 3270 terminal (used with mainframe systems) and the IBM 5250 terminal (used with AS/400s) are not in the traditional Telnet style and require different data streams than VT devices.

The IBM 3270 Terminal

In most TCP/IP environments, Telnet functions as an interactive, character-level service: When you type a character on the terminal, the Telnet client sends that character or function over the network to the Telnet server, which then passes it on to the application. Furthermore, Telnet was designed with the ASCII character code in mind, so clients assume they will communicate with the server using ASCII encoding.

But the ASCII character set and character-level operation are contrary to the way IBM terminals function in mainframe, S/3X, and AS/400 environments. IBM 3270 (mainframe) and 5250 (S/3X and AS/400) terminal types use the EBCDIC character code instead of ASCII. IBM terminals are also oriented toward block-mode operation instead of character-mode operation. In the IBM environment, information entered at the keyboard is stored locally until the user presses Enter or a function key. At that point, the system transmits the input data as a block of information.

These two differences affect how IBM devices operate in the Telnet environment from both the client and server perspective. For example, if an IBM terminal initiates a Telnet client connection using VT100 emulation, the client must translate EBCDIC characters to ASCII and provide terminal emulation to translate display highlights and function key operations and to compensate for the difference between block-mode and character-mode operations. From a purely technical perspective, EBCDIC-to-ASCII translation is a minor issue, while terminal emulation is significantly more difficult (but certainly not impossible).

Using an IBM mainframe, S/3X, or AS/400 as a Telnet server for VT100-style traffic introduces similar difficulties. The IBM server must provide EBCDIC-to-ASCII translation and terminal emulation for data it serves to the client. But for data it receives from the client, the server must also translate display-highlight sequences into IBM highlight attributes, keystrokes into standard IBM function keys (e.g., PF1 through PF24), and character-mode operations into block-mode operations. This overhead consumes CPU cycles that affect the performance of the system overall. Furthermore, because Telnet is character oriented, much unnecessary traffic is generated on the network. From a networking perspective, the overhead of sending characters one at a time is much higher than sending them out as a block (the traditional IBM approach).

To alleviate many of these difficulties, IBM developed a 3270 terminal type for the Telnet environment. Released in 1988, the 3270 terminal type is a negotiated option between the server and client that addresses many of the incompatibilities between the Telnet and IBM environments. The Telnet 3270 client program has been instilled with a greater awareness of the IBM environment. Some of the benefits of the IBM Telnet 3270 solution are

- support for block-mode operations — the 3270 client collects keystrokes and forwards them to the server as a block when the user presses a trigger key (e.g., Enter or a function key)
- flexible mapping — keyboard mapping files allow mapping of terminal keys to IBM 3270 keys (including function keys) as desired

- translation of display attributes — the Telnet 3270 client translates IBM field attributes into the appropriate highlight sequences for the client terminal

- EBCDIC-to-ASCII translation — the Telnet 3270 client can translate and switch between EBCDIC and ASCII character codes as needed

These features work together to create a Telnet client environment with the look and feel of an IBM 3270 terminal: The user can enter information into structured display forms, use Tab to move from field to field, and change incorrect input before transmission.

The Telnet 3270 solution can be used by ASCII terminals accessing IBM systems, IBM terminals accessing Unix systems, and IBM terminals accessing IBM systems over a TCP/IP network. By far the most popular scenario is to use Telnet 3270 to accommodate ASCII terminal access. IBM 3270 support is typically included in a separate Telnet program, usually named TN3270. Consequently, it's not uncommon to find Telnet client environments that feature multiple Telnet programs. For example, the IBM RS/6000 includes both Telnet and TN3270 programs. The Telnet program negotiates for the current terminal type, while TN3270 negotiates for the IBM 3270 terminal type.

The TN5250 Terminal

When TCP/IP connectivity was introduced to the AS/400 environment, the AS/400 supported VT100 and 3270 Telnet terminal types. Telnet access using the VT100 terminal type posed the same difficulties found in the mainframe environment (ASCII instead of EBCDIC translation and character-mode instead of block-mode operation), so Telnet 3270 access seemed the logical choice. But 3270 access to the AS/400 had its own set of conflicts, the most bothersome being keyboard and display-attribute differences. Another conflict was that 3270 terminals do not support "numeric-only" input fields. In the 3270 environment, all fields can be used for alphanumeric or numeric input. The AS/400, however, depends on the terminal to restrict data entry in numeric-only fields. The 3270-to-5250 translation does enforce the numeric-only rule, but it does so on the AS/400, eating up valuable AS/400 CPU cycles in the process.

To address these conflicts, IBM developed a definition for a new Telnet terminal type, the 5250 terminal. Introduced in 1991, Telnet 5250 (often called TN5250) operation provides all the benefits of Telnet 3270 operation and addresses the limitations of the 3270-to-5250 translation process by making the Telnet client program aware of the unique characteristics of the 5250 terminal. Thus, a Telnet 5250 client provides the following features not found in a Telnet 3270 client:

- support for 5250-specific keys. Like Telnet 3270, the TN5250 client permits flexible keyboard mapping and provides client-based emulation of unique 5250 keys such as Roll up, Roll down, Field exit, Field +, and Field −.

- enforcement of numeric-only fields. The TN5250 client recognizes numeric data-entry fields and restricts data access locally.

- support for the full range of display attributes. The TN5250 client provides direct translation between 5250 display attributes and display attributes on the actual terminal running the Telnet client program.

The enhancements available in the TN5250 solution make it superior to Telnet 3270 for accessing an AS/400. Is TN5250 as good as using a native IBM 5250 terminal? That depends. The quality of the TN5250 client functions depends on the terminal running the client program.

- TN5250 access from terminals that have few function keys and that don't support a full range of display attributes is compromised by awkward keyboard mapping and unnatural-looking displays.

- A TN5250 client program running on a terminal that features lots of function keys for mapping and supports the full range of display attributes has the look and feel of real 5250 terminal access.

- TN5250 running on a PC or Macintosh is as good as any native 5250 terminal emulation package.

As you can see, the functionality and viability of TN5250 is strongly tied to the flexibility of the client. If TN5250 is run from a PC or a high-function terminal, it can certainly achieve the look and feel of a native 5250 terminal.

The AS/400 Telnet Server

The Telnet server on the AS/400 is a full-function server within the screen capabilities of the AS/400 — in other words, the server supports 5250 capabilities fully but does not expand on that support. The AS/400 Telnet server supports the following Telnet modes:

- 5250 full-screen mode
- 3270 full-screen mode
- VT220 full-screen mode
- VT100 full-screen mode
- ASCII line mode (similar to a teletype device)

The best of these is TN5250 emulation: It provides the look and feel of a 5250 display, including screen colors and, more important, keyboard mapping. The 3270 full-screen mode is also useful, but its keyboard mapping is not as precise as 5250 mapping. VT100 and VT220 full-screen modes may be the most common method of accessing AS/400s, especially those in mixed-system networks. ASCII line mode is offered as a lowest-common-denominator choice for terminal negotiation with older clients and should be avoided when possible.

An incoming Telnet connection (regardless of the emulation) uses virtual controller and virtual device descriptions. When a Telnet session is initiated on the AS/400, job QTGTelnetS (running in subsystem QSYSWRK) creates a controller description using a name of the form QPACTL*xx*. The same job either selects (if available) or creates the device description using names of the form QPADEV*xxxx*

You can have the Telnet server start automatically when you execute the STRTCP (Start TCP/IP) command by specifying AUTOSTART(*YES) on the CHGTELNA (Change Telnet Attributes) command. Alternatively, you can start the Telnet server (or an additional Telnet server job) manually by executing the command STRTCPSVR SERVER(*Telnet).

Some system values affect the Telnet server, especially the creation of virtual devices. System value QAUTOVRT determines the number of virtual devices you can create. The shipped value is 0, indicating that virtual devices may not be created automatically; a value of up to 9999 is allowed. System value QMAXSIGN determines the maximum number of invalid sign-on attempts allowed at a given device before the system takes action. QMAXSGNACT

The Telnet Disaster Formula

The values you choose for QAUTOVRT, QMAXSGNACT, and QMAXSIGN are vital to the security of your system when you allow Telnet access to it. The following formula quantifies the effect of the values you assign:

$$NISOA = NUVD * NSOA$$

where

NISOA = the maximum number of invalid sign-on attempts a hacker has to break into your
   AS/400 via Telnet

NUVD = the number of unused virtual devices (QAUTOVRT less the number of virtual devices
   currently in use)

NSOA = the maximum number of sign-on attempts allowed (QMAXSIGN)

This formula assumes that QMAXSGNACT is set to either 1 (to disable the device) or 3 (to disable the device and profile) when a user reaches QMAXSIGN number of invalid sign-on attempts. If QMAXSGNACT doesn't disable the device, the number of invalid log-in attempts is limitless.

As an example, let's set QMAXSIGN to 5 (which seems like a reasonable number) and QAUTOVRT to 500. Let's also say that 100 virtual devices are currently in use by authorized users. With these values, a hacker can try 2,000 (5 * 400) profile/password combinations before being disallowed further attempts.

determines the action the system will take when that maximum number is reached. For security considerations related to these system values, see "The Telnet Disaster Formula," page 141.

VT100 Terminal Keyboard Mapping

There are some major differences between the keys on a VT-style keyboard and those on a 5250-style keyboard. For instance, the VT keyboard does not have a Field exit key, and the 5250 keyboard does not have a Ctrl (Control) key. The AS/400 provides VT100 terminal keyboard mapping, which you can change through the use of the keyboard mapping commands. Keyboard mapping lets you associate the function of a particular key on one terminal type with another key on another terminal type. For example, you can map the Enter key on a PC keyboard to the AS/400 Field Exit function and the right Control key to the AS/400 Enter function.

The keyboard mapping commands are

- CHGVTMAP (Change VT Keyboard Map)
- DSPVTMAP (Display VT Keyboard Map)
- SETVTMAP (Set VT Keyboard Map)

The CHGVTMAP and SETVTMAP commands let you assign up to four VT key combinations to an AS/400 keyboard action, so you can provide (for instance) both a Control key map and an Escape key map to accommodate different VT keyboard types.

The DSPVTMAP printout in Figure 5.1 shows the keyboard mapping between a VT terminal and an AS/400 terminal. ESC indicates the escape key, CTL indicates the control key, and keys such as NXTSCR (next screen) and PRVSCR (previous screen) are specific to the VT keyboard.

The mapping shown in the figure is for all VT100 terminals, not just for PCs. The mapping is functional but not graceful — it takes some familiarity. For instance, as you can see from the figure, the F3 key (CF03) is mapped to the ESC (escape) key and the 3 key, meaning that on a VT100 keyboard, you would press ESC and then press 3 to emulate the CF03 function key. Some important VT100 mappings to remember are

- Ctrl-B — roll down
- Ctrl-F — roll up
- Esc + number — function key
- Ctrl-R — error reset
- Enter — enter

FIGURE 5.1
AS/400 VT Terminal Keyboard Mapping

```
Display VT Keyboard Map

5250 Function                    VT Key(s)
    5250 Attention . . . :       *CTLA        *ESCA
    5250 Help  . . . . . :       *CTLQST      *ESCH
    Page Down (Roll Up) :        *CTLD        *CTLF        *NXTSCR
    Page Up (Roll Down) :        *CTLB        *CTLU        *PRVSCR
    System Request . . . :       *CTLC        *ESCS
    Insert . . . . . . . :       *ESCI        *ESCDLT      *INS
    Delete . . . . . . . :       *DLT         *RMV
    Enter  . . . . . . . :       *RETURN
    Backspace  . . . . . :       *BACKSPC
    Duplicate  . . . . . :       *ESCD
    Erase Input  . . . . :       *CTLE
    Error Reset  . . . . :       *CTLR        *ESCR
    Field Exit . . . . . :       *CTLK        *CTLX        *ESCX
    Field Minus  . . . . :       *ESCM
    Home . . . . . . . . :       *CTLO
    New Line . . . . . . :       *ESCLF
    Print  . . . . . . . :       *CTLP        *ESCP
    Field Advance  . . . :       *TAB
    Field Backspace  . . :       *ESCTAB
    Cursor Up  . . . . . :       *CSRUP
    Cursor Down  . . . . :       *CSRDOWN
    Cursor Left  . . . . :       *CSRLEFT
    Cursor Right . . . . :       *CSRRIGHT
    Clear Screen . . . . :       *ESCC
    Test Request . . . . :       *CTLT
    Toggle Indicator
      Lights . . . . . . :       *ESCT
    Redraw Screen  . . . :       *CTLL        *ESCL
    F1 . . . . . . . . . :       *ESC1        *PF1         *F1
    F2 . . . . . . . . . :       *ESC2        *PF2         *F2
    F3 . . . . . . . . . :       *ESC3        *PF3         *F3
    F4 . . . . . . . . . :       *ESC4        *PF4         *F4
    F5 . . . . . . . . . :       *ESC5        *F5
    F6 . . . . . . . . . :       *ESC6        *F6
    F7 . . . . . . . . . :       *ESC7        *F7
    F8 . . . . . . . . . :       *ESC8        *F8
    F9 . . . . . . . . . :       *ESC9        *F9
    F10  . . . . . . . . :       *ESC0        *F10
    F11  . . . . . . . . :       *ESCMINUS    *F11
    F12  . . . . . . . . :       *ESCEQ       *F12
    F13  . . . . . . . . :       *ESCEXCL     *F13
    F14  . . . . . . . . :       *ESCAT       *F14
    F15  . . . . . . . . :       *ESCPOUND    *F15
    F16  . . . . . . . . :       *ESCDOLLAR   *F16
    F17  . . . . . . . . :       *ESCPCT      *F17
    F18  . . . . . . . . :       *ESCCFX      *F18
    F19  . . . . . . . . :       *ESCAMP      *F19
    F20  . . . . . . . . :       *ESCAST      *F20
    F21  . . . . . . . . :       *ESCLPAR
    F22  . . . . . . . . :       *ESCRPAR
    F23  . . . . . . . . :       *ESCUS
    F24  . . . . . . . . :       *ESCPLUS
```

You may find (depending on how long you've worked with the AS/400) that the Esc-number key combination for function keys is not difficult to pick up; many old 5250 terminals used similar CMD-number key combinations.

Ending a Telnet-to-AS/400 session depends on the type of client being used. Signing off the AS/400 does not end the connection; it just displays the sign-on screen. A standard method of signing off and disconnecting a session on the AS/400 is to use SIGNOFF ENDCNN(*YES). Windows-based clients usually have a drop-down menu that enables disconnecting a session.

The AS/400 Telnet Client

The AS/400's client Telnet capability lets your AS/400 initiate a virtual terminal session to systems in a TCP/IP network. The Telnet client can access any system that supports full-screen Telnet. Although the AS/400 Telnet server supports ASCII line mode, the client does not — it supports only full-screen modes.

The AS/400 Telnet client can use the following screen modes (negotiated in this order):

- 5250 full-screen mode with TN5250
- 3270 full-screen mode with TN3270
- VT220 full-screen mode
- VT100 full-screen mode

The client's full-screen 5250 mode lets you access another AS/400 in the network with the full capability of a 5250 terminal. Of course, SNA-based Display Station Passthrough provides this ability, but that approach requires using the SNA protocol. In a TCP/IP-only environment, TN5250 between AS/400 systems provides the functionality needed for reliable and accurate communications.

Sniffing for Passwords

A "sniffer" is a network monitoring tool that typically provides diagnostics and throughput analysis. But sniffers also let the user view network traffic. It is this capability that, in the wrong hands, can compromise network security. Telnet sessions are not encrypted, meaning that passwords and user profile names are transmitted on the network "in the clear." A simple sniffer can catch this information.

You might think there are no sniffers on your network. But as anyone familiar with the AS/400's communications trace capability knows, the AS/400 itself is a network sniffer. Although the AS/400 communications trace is provided as a network troubleshooting tool, only effective AS/400 security, such as allowing only certain users to have *SERVICE authority (which enables them to use the trace function), can prevent the communications trace from being used to sniff network data such as passwords. Other LAN-based network troubleshooting tools normally have similar sniffing capabilities.

We earlier discussed the differences between a 5250 terminal and a VT-style terminal — EBCDIC vs. ASCII character sets and block mode vs. character mode. The character set issue is not difficult to resolve — the AS/400 does a good job of translation, and translation tables can resolve any unique considerations. The block mode issue is a much more important consideration. When an AS/400 client accesses a system that supports character mode, the user must press a key that sets the Attention Identifier (AID) byte to tell the remote system that information has been entered and to transmit the block. This requirement may cause a problem when the remote system is validating information character by character as it is entered. The 5250 workstation keys that cause the AID byte to be set are

- Attention
- Clear
- Command keys (CF01–CF24)
- Enter
- Help
- Print
- Record backspace
- Roll up
- Roll down

Other keys, such as the arrow and cursor control keys, do not cause the entered information to be sent to the remote host.

The block mode issue aside, the AS/400 Telnet client works well. To initiate a Telnet connection, enter the Telnet command (or the STRTCPTELN (Start TCP/IP Telnet Connection) command) and either the host name or its IP address. Figure 5.2 shows how to enter a Telnet command on the command line at the AS/400 main menu. If you enter a host name, either that name must be in the host table or the host's IP address must be available through a name server. In either case, you then press Enter to establish a connection between the AS/400 and the remote host.

Figure 5.3 shows a connection with the host of the online card catalog at the University of Michigan library. Although this system does not require the user to enter a user ID or password, most systems require both. Most clients automatically suppress the display of a password as it's typed so passersby cannot see it. However, the AS/400 must be told not to display information. To hide the password (or other entered information), the user must press the CF06 key before typing the information.

FIGURE 5.2
Initiating an AS/400 Telnet Connection

```
MAIN                        AS/400 Main Menu
                                                      System:    S1029F3R
Select one of the following:

     1. User tasks
     2. Office tasks
     3. General system tasks
     4. Files, libraries, and folders
     5. Programming
     6. Communications
     7. Define or change the system
     8. Problem handling
     9. Display a menu
    10. Information Assistant options
    11. Client Access/400 tasks

    90. Sign off

Selection or command
===> telnet mirlyn.telnet.lib.umich.edu

F3=Exit   F4=Prompt   F9=Retrieve   F12=Cancel   F13=Information Assistant
F23=Set initial menu
```

FIGURE 5.3
AS/400 Telnet Client Accessing a Remote Host

```
                 University of Michigan Libraries             V023
                    DATABASE SELECTION MENU
You may search the databases listed below and on the next screens. Type FOR
or press <F8> to move forward to the next screen.  To select a database, type
its abbreviated name and press <ENTER>.  To leave MIRLYN, type STOP <ENTER>.
If you press <ENTER> without typing anything, MCAT will be selected.

     MCAT        UMich Online Catalog
     FLNT        UMich-Flint Catalog
     CLEM        UMich Clements Library
     BUSI        UMich Kresge Business Library
     DRBN        UMich-Dearborn Catalog

     REMOTE      Online Catalogs from libraries outside of UMich
     INDEXES     Indexes and databases such as WILS, PSYC, etc.



---------------- + Page 1 of 13  ----------------------------
     HELp           Select a database label from above     <F8>  FORward
                    NEWs  (Library System News)


Database Selection: MCAT
```

Navigation through a system such as this is easy, as Figure 5.4 shows. Simply enter the option for the appropriate menu and press Enter. The menu in this figure includes an option to disconnect the session. If you access a system that does not provide a disconnect option, you can press the Attention key and enter 99 to end the Telnet session. The Attention key provides a small menu of options (Figure 5.5) that may be useful in a Telnet session. You can use these Telnet control functions to interrupt the current process, query the connection status with an "Are You There" command, discard the host output data, and clear the data path.

FIGURE 5.4
AS/400 Telnet Client Executing a Remote Application

```
                                                        UMich Online Catalog
                                                                 Introduction
--------------------------------------------------------------------------------
     Welcome to MCAT, the online catalog of the University of Michigan
(c)1998 by The Regents of the University of Michigan.  All rights reserved.
You can use MCAT to identify books and other materials owned by the UM
Libraries (UL) and the Bentley Library (Michigan Historical Collection) (XB).
Type NEWS for library hours.

TO SEARCH BY:      TYPE THE COMMAND:       EXAMPLE:
   Author                  a=                 a=king stephen
   Title                   t=                 t=catcher in the rye
   Subject                 s=                 s=animation
   Medical Subject         sm=                sm=mitosis
   Keyword                 k=                 k=mutation and radiation
   Call Number             c=                 c=pn 2287 m 39
   Supt. of Documents      cs=                cs=y 4.Ap 6/1:H 81/2/988
                       Enter a search, or press <ENTER> for other options.
------------------------------------------------- + Page 1 of 3 -------------
STArt over       Enter search command              <F8>  FORward page
                 NEWs            CHOose
                 CR for Course Reserve

NEXT COMMAND:
```

FIGURE 5.5
AS/400 Telnet Client Attention Key Options

```
                    Send TELNET Control Functions
                                                    System:   S1029F3R
Select one of the following:

    1.  Interrupt process - IP
    2.  Query connection status - AYT
    3.  Discard host output data - AO
    4.  Clear the data path - SYNCH

    6.  Change VT100 (Primary) keyboard map
    7.  Change VT100 (Alternate) keyboard map

    99. End TELNET session - QUIT

===> _____

 F3=Exit     F12=Cancel
Primary keyboard map active.
```

Another option on the Attention key menu lets you change the primary and alternate keyboard maps. The keyboard map used (the primary map) depends on whether VT100 or VT220 emulation was negotiated. Figure 5.6 shows the keyboard mapping for a VT100 connection. On this map, each 5250 function key (CF01 to CF24) corresponds to a specific key or function. The first four function keys are mapped to PF1 to PF4. CF05 emulates the Escape key, while CF06 provides the Hide function for nondisplay fields.

FIGURE 5.6

AS/400 Telnet Client VT100 Keyboard Mapping

```
                      Change VT100 Primary Keyboard Map

  Type changes, press Enter:

  5250 key                        VT100 function
    Function Key 1   . . . .      *PF1
    Function Key 2   . . . .      *PF2
    Function Key 3   . . . .      *PF3
    Function Key 4   . . . .      *PF4
    Function Key 5   . . . .      *ESC
    Function Key 6   . . . .      *HIDE
    Function Key 7   . . . .      *TAB
    Function Key 8   . . . .      *CTLA
    Function Key 9   . . . .      *CTLB
    Function Key 10  . . . .      *SHIFTDSP
    Function Key 11  . . . .      *SENDWOCR
    Function Key 12  . . . .      *CTLC
    Function Key 13  . . . .      *CSRUP
    Function Key 14  . . . .      *CSRDOWN
    Function Key 15  . . . .      *CSRRIGHT
    Function Key 16  . . . .      *CSRLEFT
                                                           More...

    F3=Exit    F6=Save    F12=Cancel
  Primary keyboard map active.
```

Because many keys on a 5250 keyboard do not set the AID byte, other VT functions are provided, such as Tab (CF07) and the cursor control keys (CF13 to CF16). CF11 provides a Send Without Carriage Return (SENDWOCR) function, which lets the user enter information and send it to the host without causing a carriage return. This function may be needed for character validation at the remote host.

If you change the keyboard map, you can save the changes by pressing CF06. Press CF03 to return to the client session.

FILE TRANSFER PROTOCOL (FTP)

FTP operates in the same client/server model as most other TCP/IP-based applications. The client issues a request to a server's port 21. The server listens at this port and establishes a connection with the client, letting the client control the interaction with a series of commands. The client then establishes another connection at server port 20. Data is transferred using port 20, the FTP data port, while control information is passed between the client and the server using port 21, the control port. The control port passes information using TCP/IP's NVT capabilities.

FTP can operate as either a client or a server. A system is designated as the client or the server depending on where the commands originate, not on where the data resides or will be placed. When a system initiates an FTP conversation with another system, the initiating system issues the commands and is the client; the system that responds to the commands is the server. The client system may transfer data to the server (with the Put command) or from the server (with the GET command).

The client and server modes are quite distinct, and different commands are available in each mode. FTP client commands are somewhat standard across platforms, but FTP server commands are often unique, due to differences in system architecture, particularly in file systems and file structure. We discuss the AS/400's server commands in "The AS/400 FTP Server" below.

An interesting point regarding file transfers is the conversion between character sets used by different systems. The FTP process on the AS/400 automatically (and by default) converts between the EBCDIC and ASCII character sets. You can also transfer data without converting it.

Another conversion issue relates to packed numeric information. When transferring EBCDIC data to an ASCII file, the AS/400 converts the data byte by byte. This approach works fine with character or zoned-numeric information, but unexpected results can occur when transferring packed or signed information. For instance, the packed number 1234 is represented in EBCDIC internally as 01 23 4F. This representation is not translated properly to ASCII, however. Rather, it is translated as SOH ETB O — not the desired value! The same number in zoned format in EBCDIC is F1 F2 F3 F4, which is translated appropriately to 31 32 33 34 (1234 in ASCII).

A similar problem arises when transferring negatively signed information, because ASCII translation changes the last high-order half byte (nibble) of a signed zoned-decimal value from an F to a D, again resulting in an incorrect value.

Tip!

If you transfer numeric data from AS/400 files to an ASCII-based system, make sure the data is first converted to unsigned zoned-decimal format. Conversion is not an issue for FTP transfers between two AS/400 systems, as no translation is needed.

FTP Operation

FTP is primarily an interactive process. A typical FTP session proceeds as follows:

1. The client system invokes FTP and specifies (opens) a server.
2. The client sends FTP subcommands (GETs and PUTs) to the server.
3. The server responds to the subcommands by performing actions (sending data or control functions).
4. The process continues until the data transfers are complete.
5. The client sends a request to the server to end the FTP session.

This process is normally performed by a user issuing FTP subcommands at a terminal. However, FTP transfers can also be done in batch mode, as we'll explain in "FTP as a Batch Process" later in this chapter.

As we've noted, some FTP commands are specific to the type of server being accessed, with the AS/400 supporting commands that deal with its unique file structure. But most FTP subcommands are the same across systems, regardless whether you're accessing the AS/400 from a client or accessing a remote system from an AS/400 terminal.

The AS/400 FTP Server

When the AS/400 acts as a server, it allows clients to access physical, logical, source, and save files and members stored on the system. When files are transferred to a client system, the AS/400 automatically translates them from EBCDIC to ASCII, but files can also be transferred without translation.

Invoking FTP on a client system is dependent on the client's operating system. Windows, for example, may use graphical FTP software, while a Unix machine may use command-line FTP. Most clients provide the features and functions needed to transfer files, but some clients (especially some Windows-based GUI clients) cannot accommodate an AS/400. I've found that command-line (nongraphical) FTP clients work well with the AS/400. Let's look at FTP processing with a Windows 95 client.

Basic FTP Processing

When invoking FTP with a command-line interface, you can specify FTP either with or without a host name (or IP address). Specifying FTP with a host name takes you directly to the user ID and password prompts. Invoking FTP without a host name puts you in FTP command mode, as in the following example:

```
C:\WINDOWS>ftp
ftp> open as400e.ryantech.com
Connected to AS400E.RYANTECH.COM.
220-QTCP at AS400E.RYANTECH.COM.
220 Connection will close if idle more than 5 minutes.
User (AS400E.RYANTECH.COM:(none)): michael
331 Enter password.
Password:
230 MICHAEL logged on.
ftp>
```

Here, I execute three FTP subcommands. The first, OPEN, establishes a connection from the client to the server. The command

```
open as400e.ryantech.com
```

opens the host known on my network as as400e.ryantech.com. The network
resolves this name using either the host table or DNS. I could have specified
an IP address instead of the host name.

The other two subcommands executed, USER and PASS, are not displayed
because they are executed "under the covers" when the FTP connection is
established. The USER subcommand specifies a user ID on the system, and the
PASS subcommand specifies the associated password. The USER and PASS
subcommands must be user-entered only to change users. Thus, while in an
FTP session, you can close the connection with a given server (by executing
an FTP CLOSE command) and then open another connection with a different
user ID by entering USER and PASS subcommands. You may also need to
use the USER and PASS commands if you make a keying error and need to re-
enter the user ID and password.

We listed many of the common FTP commands in Table 2.3. Table 5.3
lists some FTP subcommands not included there that are helpful in understanding the connection between the client and server or that provide other
connection functions. You can usually view this list by either entering the
HELP subcommand from a command line or pressing the appropriate button
in a Windows interface.

TABLE 5.3
FTP Subcommands

Command	Function
Debug	Toggles debug mode
Status	Shows the status of the session
Prompt	Toggles prompting with m commands
Trace	Shows the commands being issued by the client
Verbose	Toggles verbose mode to provide more trace-type information
Remotehelp	Causes the server to display server help — good for server-specific commands
rename <fromfile <tofile>	Rename a file on the server
Append	Append the new information to the end of a file
!	Exit to the operating system (return to FTP with exit)
?	Show the client help screen

After establishing a connection to the server, the client can transfer data between the systems. In the following dialog between the client and the server, the client transfers a file to the server:

```
ftp> put d:\xfer400\empmast.txt michael/empmast
200 PORT subcommand request successful.
150 Sending file to member EMPMAST in file EMPMAST in
library MICHAEL.
250 File transfer completed successfully.
1288 bytes sent in 0.06 seconds (21.47 Kbytes/sec)
ftp>
```

The PUT command specifies the path and name of the file (d:\xfer400\empmast.txt) to be transferred from the client system and names an existing receiving file (michael/empmast) on the AS/400. Although you can direct the AS/400 to create a new file to hold the transferred data, transfers are much quicker when the receiving file already exists. Another advantage to creating an AS/400 file ahead of time to hold the transferred data is that you can use DDS to describe the fields in the receiving file. When you transfer the data, it is then formatted correctly in the externally defined file on the AS/400.

Transferring the same file from the client to a file that does not already exist on the AS/400 is similar. However, the file the AS/400 creates to hold the data contains only one field, and that field is the same length as the record. In other words, an AS/400 file created at the time of transfer looks as though it were created using the CRTPF (Create Physical File) command and specifying the record length. If you must transfer data without first defining the target AS/400 file, you can format the data by then copying it to an externally

Tip!

When you use FTP to copy a file to the AS/400 and the target file does not already exist, the system uses the record length of the client file as the record length for the new physical file. The AS/400 determines the record length of the client file by examining the last used byte of the client record. In other words, the AS/400 creates the target file with a record length equal to the position of the last nonblank byte in the longest client record. Consequently, these records may very well not be fixed length.

If you find yourself in this situation, place a nonblank character into the last position of at least one of the client records to make a record length that is equal to or greater than the AS/400 record length. You can then execute a CPYF command to copy the records to the AS/400 physical file without losing information.

defined file. Simply execute the CPYF (Copy File) command, specifying the externally defined target file and FMTOPT(*NOCHK).

Transferring a file from the AS/400 to the client is the same process in reverse. Specify the GET subcommand to retrieve the file from the AS/400 to the client (remember that the client issues the commands and the server processes the commands, regardless of direction of the flow of data). Here's a sample dialog for transferring a file from the AS/400 to the client:

```
ftp> get michael/empmast d:\xfer400\newmast.txt
200 PORT subcommand request successful.
150 Retrieving member EMPMAST in file EMPMAST in library
MICHAEL.
250 File transfer completed successfully.
1288 bytes received in 0.44 seconds (2.93 Kbytes/sec)
ftp>
```

The GET command specifies the path and name for the new file on the client (d:\xfer400\newmast.txt) and the name of the AS/400 file to be transferred (michael/empmast).

There are two ways to close the connection between the client and the AS/400. Issuing the CLOSE command closes the connection to the AS/400 but leaves the user in FTP. The user can create a new connection (with the OPEN command) to the same AS/400 or to any other FTP server in the network. Executing the QUIT command closes the connection and exits FTP.

Wildcard and Multiple-File Processing

The FTP MGET and MPUT commands let you get and put multiple files using wildcard processing. Simply specify the appropriate command with a wildcard pattern, and the files are transferred accordingly. The following sample dialog transfers multiple files with an MGET command:

```
ftp> mget michael/x*
200 PORT subcommand request successful.
150 Retrieving member X1 in file X1 in library MICHAEL.
250 File transfer completed successfully.
778 bytes received in 0.00 seconds (778000.00
Kbytes/sec)
200 PORT subcommand request successful.
150 Retrieving member X2 in file X2 in library MICHAEL.
250 File transfer completed successfully.
1663 bytes received in 0.16 seconds (10.39 Kbytes/sec)
200 PORT subcommand request successful.
150 Retrieving member X3 in file X3 in library MICHAEL.
250 File transfer completed successfully.
963 bytes received in 0.00 seconds (963000.00
Kbytes/sec)
200 PORT subcommand request successful.
150 Retrieving member TST in file X4 in library MICHAEL.
250 File transfer completed successfully.
1319 bytes received in 0.00 seconds (1319000.00
Kbytes/sec)
ftp>
```

The "m commands" actually transfer the specified files one at a time. In the above example, the MGET command transfers four members: X1, X2, X3, and X4. An interesting phenomenon of file transfers under the traditional AS/400 file system is that the FTP process transfers members in an AS/400 file, not the file itself.

Tip!

The PROMPT subcommand toggles interactive prompting on and off. When interactive prompting is on, the user must acknowledge every file that fits the wildcard pattern before it is transferred. When prompting is off, files are transferred without user intervention.

On multiple transfers using wildcards, you cannot specify the receiving file name. Rather, when you use the m commands to transfer files to any system that uses file-name extensions, such as Unix, PC, and DEC OpenVMS systems, FTP gives the target file the same name as the AS/400 file and an extension based on the name of the AS/400 member. Figure 5.7 shows a directory listing

FIGURE 5.7
Directory Listing of Transferred Files

```
D:\xfer400>dir

 Volume in drive D has no label
 Volume Serial Number is 2565-11E2
 Directory of D:\xfer400

 .                 <DIR>        02-16-98  1:50p .
 ..                <DIR>        02-16-98  1:50p ..
 EMPMAST  TXT          1,288    02-18-98  9:45a empmast.txt
 X1       X1             778    05-26-98 10:44a X1.X1
 X2       X2           1,663    05-26-98 10:44a X2.X2
 X3       X3             963    05-26-98 10:44a X3.X3
 X4       TST          1,319    05-26-98 10:44a X4.TST
 NEWMAST  TXT          1,288    05-26-98 10:41a newmast.txt
          6 file(s)         8,587 bytes
          2 dir(s)     343,818,240 bytes free

D:\xfer400>
```

of files that our examples have transferred to or from the client. Note the extension of the client file names.

If a number of similarly-named members are transferred from the same AS/400 file, the file names on the receiving system are modified to maintain uniqueness. For example, AS/400 file NETDATA.EXECMAIN becomes NETDAT~1.EXE on the target system and NETDATA.EXECPROD becomes NETDAT~2.EXE.

Using Other File Systems

Up to this point, we've transferred files in the traditional *library/file.member* structure of the AS/400. But the AS/400 also supports other file systems through the IFS. The IFS provides a method of storing and accessing files not part of the traditional file structure, such as executable PC files and graphics

Tip!

If you need to transfer information between an AS/400 that is on the Internet and one that is not, consider using a save file and a PC. Simply create a save file on one AS/400, save the objects you want to transfer to the save file, and transfer the save file to a PC (or some other client system) using FTP. Then create a save file on the receiving AS/400 and use FTP again to transfer the save file from the PC to the AS/400. Ensure that the transfers from the sending AS/400 and to the receiving AS/400 are in binary format, because no translation is desired. You can transfer any object that can be saved in this fashion — even program objects.

files in JPEG format. Thanks to the IFS, the AS/400 can participate as a file server or Web server in a network.

Standard file systems on the AS/400 include

- QSYS.LIB
- Root (/ or \)
- QDLS
- QOpenSys

Other file systems may also exist depending on the specific hardware and software on your AS/400. For instance, the QOPT file system exists if you have a RISC-based system with a CD-ROM, the QLANSrv file system is present if you have a File Server Input-Output Processor (FSIOP) or Integrated PC Server (IPCS), and the QNETWARE file system exists if you're using Novell Netware on your AS/400.

The file system you're likely most familiar with is QSYS.LIB, which provides the standard library, file, and member structure used on the AS/400 since its inception. The QSYS.LIB file system enables access to the physical and logical files in the AS/400 database, as well as to save files and source physical files.

The root, or slash (/) file system is the one used by PCs and Unix systems. Stream files (those such as Unix files, without a fixed record format) are stored in the AS/400's root file system, which is the parent to all other AS/400 file systems. The root file system on the AS/400 is similar to that on a PC, including directories and subdirectories. On an AS/400, the root file system holds files that can be served to a PC or Unix client.

The QDLS file system holds documents and folders. Subdirectories in this file system are actually folders that can be used with OfficeVision/400 or with the shared-folders component of Client Access. The QDLS file system can contain Office Vision mail and documents as well as files that can be served to a PC or Unix client.

QOpenSys is a Unix look-alike file system used mainly to maintain compatibility with Unix systems. This file system helps vendors port applications from Unix to the AS/400.

Any of these file systems may be targets for file transfers from another system. However, the naming conventions for these file systems are different from the AS/400's traditional *library/file.member* naming convention. For this reason, the AS/400 implementation of FTP supports two naming formats: name format 0 and name format 1. Name format 0 is the naming format for the AS/400's traditional file structure. Name format 1 was established to accommodate the IFS and the different file systems now available on the AS/400.

Name format 1 syntax is similar to the syntax on a PC or Unix system, with the different components separated by a slash (/). The QOpenSys, QDLS, and root file systems all use the directory/subdirectory.../file syntax. You can also access the AS/400's traditional (QSYS.LIB) structure through name format 1 and the IFS, but in that case the naming convention is a bit ... interesting.

Accessing files in the QSYS.LIB file system using name format 1 requires a full path name to the file. The path name identifies the file system, library, file, and member. The file system is QSYS.LIB, the library name is *library*.LIB, the file name is *file*.FILE, and the member name is *member*.MBR. So, for instance, the full path name to access file EMPMAST in library MICHAEL is /QSYS.LIB/MICHAEL.LIB/EMPMAST.FILE/EMPMAST.MBR. The member name is optional; if you don't specify it, FTP attempts to transfer a member with the same name as the file (which is the default member name when a file is created).

Similarly, you can access other types of objects in the traditional file structure using the IFS. Again, you must use the object's full path name and an appropriate extension from the following list:

- .LIB — library
- .FILE — file (any type)
- .PF — physical file
- .LF — logical file
- .SRCPF — source physical file
- .SAVF — save file
- .MBR — member

You can use the .FILE extension instead of the more specific extension for any file type — physical, logical, source, or save file.

To switch from name format 0 (the default when you access the AS/400 from a client using FTP) to name format 1, execute FTP subcommand QUOTE as shown in the following dialog:

```
ftp> quote site namefmt 1
250 Now using naming format "1".
ftp>
```

You can use the FTP DIR command to view a directory listing of the root file system like the one in Figure 5.8. The listing shows the different file systems (e.g., QOpenSys, QDLS) under the root file system, as well as other directories (e.g., home, tmp, rtrnfs) accessible on the system. To access a file under another file system, simply specify the path name beginning with a slash (/), the file system name, and the name of the file to be accessed.

FIGURE 5.8
Root File System Directory Listing

```
ftp> dir /
200 PORT subcommand request successful.
125 List started.
QSYS              19456 03/18/98 05:04:47 *DIR      /QOpenSys/
QDOC               8192 01/01/70 00:00:00 *FLR      /QDLS/
QSYS                  0 05/25/98 15:08:19 *LIB      /QSYS.LIB/
QDFTOWN      2147483647 01/01/70 00:00:00 *DDIR     /QOPT/
QSYS               1920 05/18/98 15:22:22 *DDIR     /QFileSvr.400/
QSYS              23552 03/18/98 05:39:46 *DIR      /dev/
QSYS              23552 03/18/98 05:04:36 *DIR      /home/
QSYS              29184 03/18/98 05:04:37 *DIR      /tmp/
QSYS              23552 05/15/98 10:54:55 *DIR      /etc/
QSYS              23552 03/18/98 05:04:42 *DIR      /usr/
QSYS              23552 03/18/98 05:04:45 *DIR      /QIBM/
QSECOFR           23552 03/28/98 17:47:19 *DIR      /QSR/
QSYS              23552 03/18/98 05:50:44 *DIR      /QCA400/
QTCP              23552 03/18/98 06:06:11 *DIR      /QTCPTMM/
QSYS              23552 03/28/98 17:37:30 *DIR      /QISAFIX/
QSECOFR           23552 05/15/98 11:43:25 *DIR      /rtrnfs/
250 List completed.
965 bytes received in 0.00 seconds (965000.00 Kbytes/sec)
ftp>
```

The AS/400 FTP server provides a number of commands unique to the file structure of the AS/400. Some of these AS/400-specific commands are listed below.

Command	Function
addm	Add a member to a physical file
addv	Add a variable-length member to a physical file
crtl	Create a library
crtp	Create a physical file
crts	Create a source physical file
dltf	Delete a file
dltl	Delete a library
rcmd	Execute a command on the AS/400

You can view these commands by using the REMOTEHELP command (or the QUOTE HELP command string) to access the help available on the AS/400 FTP server.

The AS/400-specific commands let you manipulate the files and libraries in the traditional file system. When you work in the IFS, you must use the standard FTP processing.

The AS/400 FTP Client

The AS/400 FTP client behaves like any other FTP client. Entering the FTP command (or the STRTCPFTP (Start TCP/IP File Transfer Protocol) command) on the AS/400 displays a screen like the one in Figure 5.9.

FIGURE 5.9
AS/400 STRTCPFTP Command Prompt

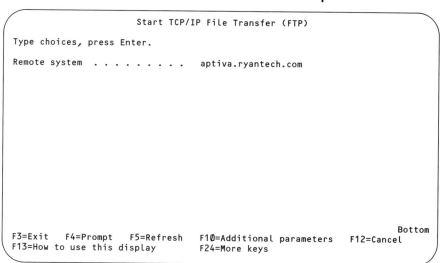

```
                    Start TCP/IP File Transfer (FTP)
Type choices, press Enter.

Remote system . . . . . . . . .   aptiva.ryantech.com

























                                                             Bottom
F3=Exit    F4=Prompt    F5=Refresh   F10=Additional parameters   F12=Cancel
F13=How to use this display       F24=More keys
```

After you enter the remote system name and sign on to the FTP server with a valid user ID and password, you can transfer files between the AS/400 client and the FTP server using standard FTP commands. However, the AS/400 client also uses AS/400 standards and provides AS/400 commands.

One of the most beneficial AS/400 standards the client adheres to is the use of F9 to retrieve a previous command, which makes it easy to retrieve and modify the command just entered and reissue it. Users can also press F6 to print the "scroller" — IBM's term for the commands and responses used in the FTP session. By giving you a way to document sessions, the scroller helps you find and solve problems. F21 provides a CL command line.

The commands available with the AS/400 FTP client are the same standard commands used with any FTP client, with some exceptions. Executing the HELP command during an AS/400 FTP client session provides a hypertext display of all FTP client subcommands, as shown in Figure 5.10.

One command in particular is unique to the AS/400 client: The SYSC command lets the user execute any interactive system (CL) command on the AS/400 from the client session. F3 exits the command and returns the user to the client FTP session.

FIGURE 5.10
AS/400 FTP Client Help Display

```
┌─────────────────────────────────────────────────────────────────────────┐
│ ▫▫Session A - [24 x 80]                                       _ □ ✕      │
│ File  Edit  Transfer  Appearance  Communication  Assist  Window  Help     │
│ ┌──┐ ┌──┐ ┌──┐ ┌──┐ ┌──┐ ┌──┐ ┌──┐ ┌──┐ ┌──┐ ┌──┐ ┌──┐ ┌──┐ ┌──┐ ┌──┐  │
│ │  │ │  │ │  │ │  │ │  │ │  │ │  │ │  │ │00│ │00│ │00│ │00│ │  │ │  │ ││ ││
│ └──┘ └──┘ └──┘ └──┘ └──┘ └──┘ └──┘ └──┘ └──┘ └──┘ └──┘ └──┘ └──┘ └──┘  │
│ PrtScrn Copy Paste Send Recv Display Color Map Record Stop Play Quit Clipbrd Index │
│                    File Transfer Protocol                                 │
│ ......................................................................... │
│ :                                                                       : │
│ :              FTP Client Subcommands - Help                            : │
│ :                                                                       : │
│ : . !____ . ?____ . ACCT___ . APpend__ . AScii__ . Binary_             : │
│ : . CD____ . CDUp___ . CLose__ . DEBug___ . DELete__ . DIr____         : │
│ : . EBcdic . Get____ . Help___ . LCd_____ . LOCSIte_ . LOCSTat         : │
│ : . LPwd__ . LS_____ . LType__ . MDelete_ . MGet____ . MKdir__         : │
│ : . MOde__ . MPut___ . NAmefmt . NOop____ . Open____ . PAss___         : │
│ : . PUt___ . PWd____ . QUIt___ . QUOte___ . REInitialize               : │
│ : . REName . RESet__ . RMDir__ . SENDPAsv                              : │
│ : . SENDPOrt___ . SENDSite____ . SIte___ . STAtus__                    : │
│ : . STRuct___ . SUnique___ . SYSCmd___ . SYStem___ . TYpe____ . User___ : │
│ : . Verbose___                                                         : │
│ :                                                                       : │
│ : You can abbreviate subcommands to the most unique series of characters. : │
│ : For example, you can type AP for the APPEND subcommand.               : │
│ :                                                                       : │
│ :                                                         More...        : │
│ :                                                                       : │
│ : F2=Extended help   F3=Exit help    F10=Move to top    F12=Cancel      : │
│ : F13=Information Assistant           F14=Print help     F20=Enlarge     : │
│ ......................................................................... │
│ MA▌    a                                                        17/049   │
└─────────────────────────────────────────────────────────────────────────┘
```

FTP as a Batch Process

I've mentioned that FTP is normally an interactive process. A user invokes FTP from the client, signs on to an FTP server session, transfers files, and issues the quit command to leave the session. Interactive sessions work well for ad hoc file transfers, but batch or scheduled transfers do not work well within an interactive construct.

IBM provides a method of processing FTP in batch by using a script file to supply the FTP commands from the client to the server. A standard CL program first overrides the input to and the output from the FTP process. Inputs to the FTP process are the user ID, password, and commands such as GET, PUT, and QUIT. Figure 5.11 shows FTPCLPGM, a simple CL program to process an FTP file transfer in batch.

The associated script file that provides the FTP commands to the FTP process is

```
FTPuser FTPpass
get empmast.txt rtr/testfile
quit
```

The output from the FTP process consists of the messages received — the same messages displayed on the screen during interactive FTP processing. Program FTPCLPGM overrides the output from the FTP process to physical file FTPOUTPUT. After the batch FTP process is executed, FTPOUTPUT would contain something like

```
Output redirected to a file.
Input read from specified override file.
Connecting to host FTPSERVER at address 198.0.0.2
Not logged in
Enter login ID (michael):
331 User OK, Send PASS
230 Password Successful - User logged in
Enter an FTP subcommand.
> get empmast.txt rtr/testfile
200 Port command Successful
150 opening data connection
226 Retrieve successful
1288 bytes transferred in 10.911 seconds.
Transfer rate 0.118 KB/sec.
Enter an FTP subcommand.
> quit
221 Close connection
```

This message file shows that the output was redirected to a file and the input was redirected from a file. The brackets (>) show the commands issued from the script file. The user was logged in with the appropriate user ID and password, and the GET command transferred files from the server to the client.

FIGURE 5.11

Sample CL Program to Process an FTP File Transfer in Batch

```
          PGM

/*   Clear FTP messages output file                          */
          CLRPFM     FILE(RTR/FTPOUTPUT)

/*   Override the input (commands) and output (messages) files     */
          OVRDBF     FILE(INPUT) TOFILE(RTR/QTXTSRC) MBR(FTPSCRIPT)
          OVRDBF     FILE(OUTPUT) TOFILE(RTR/FTPOUTPUT)

/*   Transfer the file using the commands in the FTPSCRIPT member */
          FTP        RMTSYS(FTPSERVER)

/*   Delete the overrides                                     */
          DLTOVR     FILE(INPUT)
          DLTOVR     FILE(OUTPUT)

          RETURN

          ENDPGM
```

This is a simple example, but you can accomplish any FTP process in batch as well as in interactive mode.

LPR AND LPD

The primary method of printing in a TCP/IP environment is Line Printer Remote (LPR) and Line Printer Daemon (LPD). These two processes work hand in hand to let users transfer print streams across a TCP/IP network and output them on LPD-compliant printers. (For details about the basics of LPD, see "Line Printer Remote/Line Printer Daemon" in Chapter 2; for information about configuring the LPD attributes, see "Changing LPD Attributes" in Chapter 4.)

Although LPR and LPD work together, they are two distinct processes. LPR is the mechanism for sending a print file from a system to an LPD printer, while LPD is the flip side — it receives incoming print streams from an LPR-capable host. The AS/400 supports both processes.

Configuring LPR/LPD

You can implement LPR on the AS/400 in two ways: by establishing a fixed connection between a local output queue and a remote LPD queue via the CRTOUTQ (Create Output Queue) command, or on an ad hoc basis with the SNDTCPSPLF (Send TCP/IP Spooled File) command, also known as LPR.

To configure the AS/400 to support LPD for incoming LPR requests, you can use the CHGLPDA (Change LPD Attributes) command or the CFGTCP (Configure TCP/IP) menu, option 20, option 13. The only parameters for the CHGLPDA command are whether to start the LPD servers automatically and the number of servers to start. You should start at least two LPD servers (the default with the CHGLPDA command) so the system can process multiple incoming print requests. LPD server jobs in subsystem QSYSWRK direct incoming LPD print streams (from an LPR host) to an AS/400 output queue and print them if a print writer is attached to the queue.

Sending spooled files from a local AS/400 using LPR to a remote host running the LPD process requires configuring both the AS/400 and the host. The remote host may be an AS/400, a Unix system, a PC, a network printer interface card or device, or a printer. Many newer printers are network-ready, which usually means they have a network connection (Token-Ring or Ethernet) and can print a variety of data streams, such as Novell Netware, Windows NT, and LPD.

Configuration of the remote host, PC, or printer is system-dependent. Some devices let you use a virtual terminal (and Telnet) to access and configure the device. Other systems may require you to configure LPD on a locally attached terminal or PC. In either case, LPD configuration on the client usually consists of specifying IP address and subnet mask information and the name of the printer queue on the device. These two critical pieces of information are needed when a user creates an output queue on the AS/400 or uses an ad hoc LPR command. Consult the documentation for the host, PC, or printer for device-specific instructions on configuring IP address and printer queue information.

Configuring an Output Queue

Once the device is configured, you can configure the AS/400 to print to that device. Creating an output queue establishes a fixed relationship between the AS/400 and the LPD-capable device. Essentially, you use the CRTOUTQ command to create an output queue, identifying the device with an IP address and printer queue name. The AS/400 then uses LPR to send a spooled file to the designated device.

Figure 5.12 shows the CRTOUTQ prompt screen. For most of the command's parameters, you'll specify values just as you do when creating an output queue for a local printer. The difference between a local output queue and one that handles LPR requests lies in the Remote system and Internet address parameters.

FIGURE 5.12
Create Output Queue — Screen 1

```
                    Create Output Queue (CRTOUTQ)

 Type choices, press Enter.

 Output queue . . . . . . . . . .               Name
   Library  . . . . . . . . . . .   *CURLIB     Name, *CURLIB
 Maximum spooled file size:
   Number of pages  . . . . . . .   *NONE       Number, *NONE
   Starting time  . . . . . . . .               Time
   Ending time  . . . . . . . . .               Time
               + for more values
 Order of files on queue  . . . .   *FIFO       *FIFO, *JOBNBR
 Remote system  . . . . . . . . .   *intnetadr




                                                             Bottom
 F3=Exit   F4=Prompt   F5=Refresh   F10=Additional parameters   F12=Cancel
 F13=How to use this display       F24=More keys
```

On the first CRTOUTQ prompt screen, specify for the Remote system parameter either the host name of the LPD-capable device or special value *INTNETADR, which indicates that you specify an IP address in a later parameter. Whichever value you enter causes the next parameter to be displayed, as shown in Figure 5.13. Enter the name of the print queue configured on the LPD-capable device for the remote printer queue (RTMPRTQ) parameter.

FIGURE 5.13
Create Output Queue — Screen 2

```
                      Create Output Queue (CRTOUTQ)

Type choices, press Enter.

Output queue . . . . . . . . . . OUTQ        > RMTOUTQ
  Library . . . . . . . . . . .                 *CURLIB
Maximum spooled file size:       MAXPAGES
  Number of pages . . . . . . .               *NONE
  Starting time . . . . . . . .
  Ending time . . . . . . . . .
                          + for more values
Order of files on queue . . . . SEQ           *FIFO
Remote system . . . . . . . . . RMTSYS      > *INTNETADR



Remote printer queue . . . . . . RMTPRTQ      *USER



                                                                 More...
F3=Exit   F4=Prompt   F5=Refresh   F10=Additional parameters  F12=Cancel
F13=How to use this display       F24=More keys
```

Rolling forward presents the display shown in Figure 5.14. The parameters of interest on this screen are AUTOSTRWTR, CNNTYPE, and DESTTYPE. AUTOSTRWTR controls whether a print writer should be started automatically for the output queue. I've found that having the system start a writer automatically helps eliminate troubleshooting calls. You can also start a writer at any time with the STRRMTWTR (Start Remote Writer) command, but specifying 1 (for one writer) on AUTOSTRWTR reduces calls from users with printing problems by making sure a writer is started.

The default value for CNNTYPE is *SNA, which you must change to *IP to indicate that an IP connection is to be used for spooled files placed in the output queue. The DESTTYPE parameter determines the type of system to which the spooled file will be sent. Use a value of *OS400 for an IP connection to a remote AS/400 running V2R3 (or higher) of OS/400. LPR print streams destined for a Unix host, a PC, or a network printer or device require a DESTYPE value of *OTHER.

Press Enter to view the next set of parameters (Figure 5.15). The Manufacturer type and model (MFRTYPMDL) parameter here lets you specify the type of printer. Many printers are available, including popular models from IBM, Hewlett Packard, Epson, NEC, Okidata, and Panasonic. You can prompt the parameter for a list of available printers and roll through the screens to find the printer you wish to configure. I suggest selecting an earlier version of your printer if you cannot find an exact match. If your printer is not among those available, you can use the workstation customization special value (WSCST) to customize the printer stream to fit the characteristics of any printer. But realize that workstation customization is not for the faint of heart — check the appropriate IBM documentation before attempting to customize the printer data stream.

FIGURE 5.14
Create Output Queue — Screen 3

```
                    Create Output Queue (CRTOUTQ)

 Type choices, press Enter.

 Writers to autostart . . . . . . AUTOSTRWTR     1
 Queue for writer messages  . . . MSGQ          QSYSOPR
   Library  . . . . . . . . . . .                 *LIBL
 Connection type  . . . . . . . . CNNTYPE       *ip
 Destination type . . . . . . . . DESTTYPE      *other



                                                                  Bottom
 F3=Exit    F4=Prompt    F5=Refresh    F10=Additional parameters   F12=Cancel
 F13=How to use this display        F24=More keys
```

FIGURE 5.15
Create Output Queue — Screen 4

```
                    Create Output Queue (CRTOUTQ)

 Type choices, press Enter.

 Writers to autostart . . . . . . AUTOSTRWTR    > 1
 Queue for writer messages  . . . MSGQ           QSYSOPR
   Library  . . . . . . . . . .                   *LIBL
 Connection type  . . . . . . . . CNNTYPE       > *IP
 Destination type . . . . . . . . DESTTYPE      > *OTHER
 Host print transform . . . . . . TRANSFORM     *YES
 Manufacturer type and model  . . MFRTYPMDL     *IBM42011
 Workstation customizing object   WSCST         *NONE
   Library  . . . . . . . . . . .
 Image configuration  . . . . . . IMGCFG        *NONE
 Internet address . . . . . . . . INTNETADR
 Destination options  . . . . . . DESTOPT       *NONE


 Print separator page . . . . . . SEPPAGE       *YES

                                                                  More...
 F3=Exit    F4=Prompt    F5=Refresh    F10=Additional parameters   F12=Cancel
 F13=How to use this display        F24=More keys
```

Pressing Enter from the screen in Figure 5.15 shows the remaining parameters (Figure 5.16) needed to create an output queue for an LPD-capable printer. At the Internet address (INTNETADR) parameter, near the bottom of the parameter list, you can enter the IP address of the remote printer. This parameter appears when you specify *INTNETADR for the RMTSYS parameter. The next parameter, Destination options (DESTOPT), lets you provide special functions such as multiple copies by specifying destination options for the remote printer. You can leave this value at the default (*NONE) or provide option information to be sent to the remote printer. Refer to the documentation for the remote host or printer to determine the format and syntax of destination options. You can send up to 128 characters (enclosed in apostrophes) to the destination.

FIGURE 5.16
Create Output Queue — Screen 5

```
                    Create Output Queue (CRTOUTQ)

 Type choices, press Enter.

 Writers to autostart . . . . . . AUTOSTRWTR    > 1
 Queue for writer messages  . . . MSGQ            QSYSOPR
   Library . . . . . . . . . . .                     *LIBL
 Connection type  . . . . . . . . CNNTYPE       > *IP
 Destination type . . . . . . . . DESTTYPE      > *OTHER
 Host print transform . . . . . . TRANSFORM       *YES
 Manufacturer type and model  . . MFRTYPMDL       *IBM42011
 Workstation customizing object   WSCST           *NONE
   Library . . . . . . . . . .
 Image configuration  . . . . . . IMGCFG          *NONE
 Internet address . . . . . . . . INTNETADR     > '198.0.0.15'
 Destination options  . . . . . . DESTOPT         *NONE


 Print separator page . . . . . . SEPPAGE         *YES

                                                          More...
 F3=Exit   F4=Prompt   F5=Refresh   F12=Cancel   F13=How to use this display
 F24=More keys
```

A sample CL command to create an output queue might be

```
CRTOUTQ  OUTQ(RMTOUTQ)            +
         RMTSYS(*INTNETADR)       +
         RMTPRTQ(RMTQ)            +
         AUTOSTRWTR(1)            +
         CNNTYPE(*IP)             +
         DESTTYPE(*OTHER)         +
         MFRTYPMDL(*HP4)          +
         INTNETADR('198.0.0.15')
```

Creating an output queue such as this establishes a more or less permanent connection between the AS/400 output queue and the remote printer. When the spooled file goes into a SND (send) state, a connection is made between the AS/400 and the remote printer and the spooled file is sent to the printer.

Establishing a Temporary Connection

In some cases you may wish to establish an ad hoc connection between the AS/400 and a remote printer. For instance, you may want to use temporary connections over the Internet to enable the sales force to access a remote AS/400 over the Internet, run jobs, and direct reports back to their own PCs in the field. Assuming each salesperson has an LPD daemon on his or her PC, (s)he can establish a temporary connection by determining the IP address of the incoming connection and sending a spooled file (via LPR) to that IP address. The SNDTCPSPLF command sends a spooled file to a printer (using LPR) in much the same manner as the SNDNETSPLF (Send Network Spooled File) command uses SNADS to send a spooled file between systems. Figure 5.17 shows the first prompt screen for the SNDTCPSPLF command.

FIGURE 5.17
The LPR (SNDTCPSPLF) Command — Screen 1

```
                     Send TCP/IP Spooled File (LPR)

 Type choices, press Enter.

 Remote system  . . . . . . . . . > *INTNETADR



 Printer queue  . . . . . . . . . > RMTQ



 Spooled file . . . . . . . . . . > QSYSPRT        Name
 Job name . . . . . . . . . . . . > DSP01          Name, *
   User . . . . . . . . . . . . . >   ACCT01       Name
   Number . . . . . . . . . . . . >   063090       000000-999999
 Spooled file number  . . . . . . > *ONLY          1-9999, *ONLY, *LAST
 Destination type . . . . . . . .   *OTHER         *AS400, *PSF2, *OTHER
 Transform SCS to ASCII . . . . .   *YES           *YES, *NO
 Manufacturer type and model  . .   *HP4
                                                               More...
 F3=Exit   F4=Prompt   F5=Refresh   F12=Cancel   F13=How to use this display
 F24=More keys
```

As you can see, several of the parameters are the same as those for creating an output queue. The value for the remote system parameter can be the name of the remote host (or printer) or its IP address. Like the Remote printer queue parameter on the CRTOUTQ command, the printer queue (PRTQ) parameter indicates the name of the printer queue created on the remote printing device.

To identify the correct spooled file entry, you must specify the name of the spooled file (parameter FILE), the name of the job that created it (JOB), and the number of the spooled file (SPLNBR). For the destination type, use the value *OTHER to send the spooled file to a non-AS/400 system and *AS400 to send it to another AS/400. Specify the Manufacturer type and model parameter just as you do for an output queue.

The Destination-dependent options (DESTOPT) parameter on the subsequent screen (Figure 5.18) lets you specify unique or uncommon LPD options for the remote printer. The Delete file after sending (DLTSPLF) parameter lets you specify whether the spooled file is to be deleted after it is transmitted. The default, *NO, retains the spooled file in the output queue after it has been transferred to the remote printer. I generally keep the spooled file on the AS/400 until I am certain it was successfully received.

FIGURE 5.18
LPR (SNDTCPSPLF) Command — Screen 2

```
                        Send TCP/IP Spooled File (LPR)

 Type choices, press Enter.

 Internet address . . . . . . . . > '198.0.0.15'

                           Additional Parameters

 Workstation customizing object      *NONE         Name, *NONE
   Library . . . . . . . . . . .                   Name, *LIBL, *CURLIB
 Delete file after sending . . .     *NO           *NO, *YES
 Destination-dependent options  .


 Print separator page . . . . . .    *YES          *NO, *YES




                                                                       Bottom
 F3=Exit   F4=Prompt   F5=Refresh   F12=Cancel   F13=How to use this display
 F24=More keys
```

Here's a sample CL command you might enter to transfer a file to an LPD-capable printer:

```
LPR RMTSYS(*INTNETADR)            +
    PRTQ(RMTQ)                    +
    FILE(QSYSPRT)                 +
    JOB(063090/ACCT01/DSP01)      +
    SPLNBR(*ONLY)                 +
    INTNETADR('198.0.0.15')
```

The AS/400's LPR and LPD capabilities let it send and receive print files in a TCP/IP environment. However, the use of LPR and LPD is not standard. A base set of capabilities exists in most LPD-capable systems (hosts, PCs, printer interface cards/devices, and network-ready printers), but vendors often extend those capabilities. Watch out for differences, especially in pitch and fonts. Workstation customization, although not a trivial task, can accommodate most vendor-specific differences.

SMTP AND POP3

One of the most popular uses of networks is for e-mail. Over the past five years, e-mail traffic has grown explosively. E-mail has proven to be a successful method of information sharing on both a corporate and personal basis.

E-mail is universal — you can send a message to anyone in the world who has the capability to receive the message. The AS/400 supports both Simple Mail Transfer Protocol (SMTP) and Post Office Protocol 3 (POP3), the tools needed to send and receive e-mail on private intranets and over the public Internet. We discuss the basics of these services in Chapter 2 (see "Mail Transfer — Simple Mail Transfer Protocol (SMTP)" and "Mail Access — Post Office Protocol 3 (POP3)") and their attribute configurations in Chapter 4 (under "Changing SMTP Attributes" and "Changing the POP Server Attributes").

SMTP and POP3 work together, but they provide services exclusive of each other. Basically, SMTP is used to transfer mail between hosts, and POP3 is used to transfer mail from a host to a client, such as a PC.

Simple Mail Transfer Protocol

SMTP is a server process comprising the following four jobs in subsystem QSYSWRK:

- QTSMTPBRCL (SMTP bridge client)
- QTSMTPBRSR (SMTP bridge server)
- QTSMTPCLNT (client SMTP process)
- QTSMTPSRVR (server SMTP process)

These jobs process incoming and outgoing SMTP requests and provide the interface between SNADS and the SMTP process.

Although SNADS is an SNA-based process, it provides the routing and addressing functions for SMTP. SNADS thus interacts with SMTP, which in turn interacts with the TCP/IP protocol. The SMTP bridge client and bridge server jobs provide the interaction between SMTP and the distribution queues and routing table entries SNADS uses.

As mentioned early in this chapter, the presence of OfficeVision/400 or JustMail/400 (a mail-only subset of OfficeVision/400) has no effect on the

SMTP process. If either AS/400-based e-mail product is on the system, the AS/400 can send and receive SMTP-based e-mail and route it to AS/400's mail users, who can then use familiar tools to access the mail. If neither Office-Vision/400 nor JustMail/400 is on the AS/400, users can simply access their mail through one of the many POP3-compliant products.

A name server is important to the SMTP environment, however. The name server is necessary to identify the address for incoming and outgoing mail messages. The alternative to using a name server is to have all systems list all hosts in the host table. Although that may be possible in a private intranet, it is certainly impossible across the public Internet.

You can either install a DNS server or have an Internet Service Provider (ISP) supply this capability. DNS servers have in their configuration records known as MX records, which are used for Mail eXchange. MX records identify the mail servers in different networks that can be used to forward mail if the destination is not reachable directly.

Incoming SMTP mail is sent to the AS/400 using the AS/400's host and domain name specified in the TCP/IP configuration. It is critical that the AS/400 host and domain name reside in both the host table on the AS/400 (CFGTCP menu, option 10) as well as in the local domain and host name entry (CFGTCP menu, option 12). Not having the same information in both locations will cause mail transfers to fail. The AS/400 does not need to "poll" or request mail to be delivered from another mail server — the mail serving process automatically attempts a connection with the AS/400 (based on the host and domain name) and transfers the mail. The process works similarly for outgoing mail. The AS/400, when it must send mail outside the local system, contacts the appropriate name server and either delivers the mail to the remote system directly or forwards it through another mail server.

SMTP–SNADS interaction is used to route the mail to the appropriate user's mailbox. SMTP receives incoming mail and forwards it to SNADS, which then places the mail in the appropriate storage area on the AS/400. Outgoing mail follows a similar process — the user sends the mail to SMTP, which forwards it to SNADS for delivery.

Post Office Protocol 3
POP3 lets a client system (such as a PC) retrieve mail from a mail server (such as an AS/400). The POP3 client opens a connection to the server, checks whether mail is present, and downloads the mail to the client. A configuration option usually lets the user determine whether the mail should be removed from the server when downloaded or retained on the server.

The POP3 server on the AS/400 is a store-and-forward server that stores messages destined for users and forwards the messages when the client system connects to the AS/400. The POP3 server is one of the products in the Any-Mail/400 framework, which enables mail products (other than SNADS) to process mail requests on an AS/400. The ability to add new mail products lets the AS/400 accommodate different client software products, as well as other directory and mail serving products. This capability is part of the Mail Server Framework (MSF). MSF jobs are started with the STRMSF (Start Mail Server Framework) command and run in subsystem QSYSWRK.

Because the AS/400 (in an SMTP and POP3 environment) simply stores, routes, and forwards mail, the content of the messages is not important. In other words, attachments, graphics, and fonts are not of concern to the AS/400. The AS/400 simply stores and forwards the mail message; the client is responsible for the proper display of the message. Even if the user uses Office-Vision/400 to send and receive mail, the content of the message remains unchanged; however, the user may not be able to view the attachments. For instance, because OfficeVision/400 is not a graphical-based product, users cannot view graphics attachments.

Configuration of the POP3 client of course depends on the client software you choose. All clients need two pieces of information: the name of the SMTP server and the name of the POP3 server. These are often the same system, as in the case of the AS/400 providing mail services.

After configuring the client, simply accessing new mail initiates a connection to the AS/400 server and downloads mail. Sending mail is the same process in reverse — the client connects to the AS/400 and delivers the mail to the server.

Chapter 6

Client Configuration

An AS/400 may be a client or a server in a TCP/IP network, depending on whether the AS/400 requests or supplies services. When the AS/400 is a server, it can be accessed by client systems using different software packages. Different clients provide different capabilities, and the configuration of client systems to access the AS/400 depends on the type of client, the client operating system, and the capabilities desired between the client and the server.

In this chapter, we give step-by-step instructions for configuring client software for the following software packages:

- Windows 95
- Client Access using TCP/IP
- RS/6000 using AIX
- WRQ Reflection
- Attachmate

We show actual screen shots for each client package. We also explain client AnyNet configuration for Client Access.

WINDOWS 95 CONFIGURATION

Microsoft includes TCP/IP support in its wildly popular Windows 95 (Win95) operating system. The support is strong, with a solid implementation of TCP/IP that you can use as a base for other products, such as Client Access. Microsoft also includes services such as Telnet and FTP, as well as utilities such as PING (connection verification), NETSTAT (network statistics), and TRACERT (trace route). Although these services and utilities are not up to the standards the AS/400 community expects, they do provide a base level of support.

The main problem with Microsoft's Telnet is that it does not support the 5250 data stream, although it does support VT52/100 type emulation. (Each higher number of VT terminal (52, 100, 220, etc.) provides increased function, particularly in the number of function keys supported.) Many standard 5250 keys (such as Field exit) must be mapped to interesting combinations of VT keys, but the AS/400 does support a VT100 data stream and associated keyboard (see the discussion in "VT100 Terminal Keyboard Mapping" in Chapter 5).

Installation of TCP/IP on a Win95 PC is straightforward, so long as you understand the Microsoft conventions for installing software and the workings of the Control Panel. Several client software packages use Microsoft's TCP/IP stack, so you may need to install it even if you use another client package. Other client packages let you choose whether to use a proprietary stack (which may perform better) or Microsoft's. Let's step through the configuration of TCP/IP under Win95.

Depending on the initial Win95 installation on your PC, you may need to place the Win95 CD in the CD-ROM drive or have access to the original Win95 diskettes. If the manufacturer has preloaded all the Win95 libraries, you can install TCP/IP without the CD or diskettes.

From the Windows desktop, select Start, Settings, Control Panel to display the Control Panel folder (Figure 6.1).

FIGURE 6.1
Control Panel Folder

Double-click Network to open the Network application. A dialog box similar to the one in Figure 6.2 is displayed.

Network is the application from which you configure client software (for Microsoft, Novell, and others), dial-up or LAN adapters to connect to a network, protocols such as TCP/IP, and services such as file and print sharing.

FIGURE 6.2
Control Panel Network Dialog Box

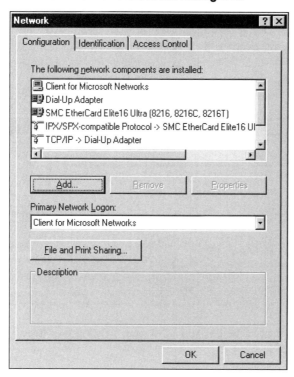

Configuring TCP/IP on a Win95 PC requires adding an adapter and a protocol. Win95 often automatically installs the adapter and the adapter software (drivers) when the modem (for a dial-up adapter) or LAN card (for a LAN) is installed. We do not cover adding an adapter in this book. If the adapter must be added and the drivers installed, review the Win95 online documentation for instructions or pick up one of the many books on the subject.

Here, we concentrate on explaining how to install and configure the TCP/IP protocol. The steps for adding TCP/IP to your Win95 PC (assuming the adapter is correctly installed) are

1. Add the TCP/IP service.
2. Configure TCP/IP.
   - IP address
   - optional DNS server address
   - optional gateway address

3. Test the connection to the AS/400.

4. If you won't use Microsoft's services, add third-party client software.

On the Network dialog box, click Add. A small dialog box (Figure 6.3) lets you select a client, adapter, protocol, or service.

FIGURE 6.3
Select Network Component Type

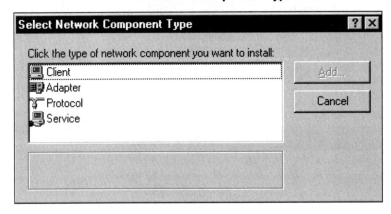

Select Protocol and click Add to display a dialog box like that shown in Figure 6.4.

FIGURE 6.4
Select Network Protocol

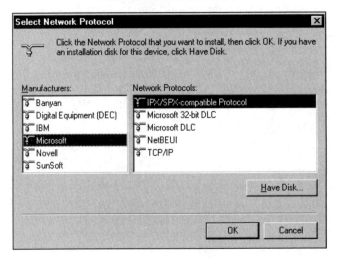

Select Microsoft, and the Microsoft protocols appear in the right pane. The choices are

- IPX/SPX-compatible protocol for Novell Netware support
- Microsoft 32-bit DLC (Data Link Control)
- Microsoft DLC (Data Link Control)
- NetBEUI
- TCP/IP

We want to add the TCP/IP protocol. You may use other protocols for other applications. For instance, a Win95 PC in a Netware environment may use the Microsoft IPX support, while a PC in a Windows NT environment may use the NetBEUI support. More than one protocol can be associated with an adapter.

Selecting TCP/IP and clicking OK installs the TCP/IP protocol to all the adapters on your PC. This is the point in the installation at which, if the required libraries are not on the hard drive, you may need to read the protocol stack programs and files from the Win95 CD or diskettes.

Once the protocol is installed, you must configure TCP/IP for the PC. You'll need to have on hand

- the IP address and subnet mask for the PC, unless the address will be automatically assigned
- the DNS server address (if required)
- the gateway address (if required)

IP addresses may be assigned automatically. Microsoft's Distributed Host Control Protocol (DHCP) is widely used and will automatically assign an IP address (from a group of addresses) to a system that requests an address. Automatic address assignment through DHCP is an excellent method of providing addresses to client systems. Although DHCP is a Microsoft protocol, many vendors (including IBM on the AS/400) provide DHCP server support.

DHCP may be implemented on an AS/400, a Windows NT server, a Win95/98 PC, or other systems that provide DHCP server support. The group of addresses from which a client is assigned its IP address is specified by a system administrator on a DHCP server. Configuring a client (such as a Win95/98) PC to use DHCP is simple — just specify in the client TCP/IP configuration that the IP address will be obtained automatically.

Because DHCP assigns addresses automatically, you won't know the PC's specific IP address. But the specific IP address of a client system is usually unimportant, as most client systems don't provide server processes. However, the IP address of server systems (such as an AS/400) should be fixed and should not be assigned through DHCP.

If you implement DNS in your environment, you need the DNS server address. If you don't use DNS, you must supply host table entries to resolve a name to an address. Of course, you could just use the IP address of the system to which you wish to connect, but DNS does make the job easier.

The gateway address is required if you are in a routed environment and need to specify a gateway to route outside of your LAN.

Let's examine the entries needed for Win95 TCP/IP configuration. When you click OK from the Select Network Protocol dialog box (Figure 6.4), the Network dialog box shown in Figure 6.5 appears.

FIGURE 6.5
Network — Configuration Tab

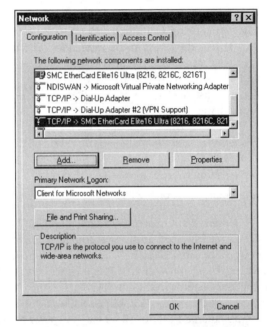

This dialog box shows TCP/IP -> SMC EtherCard, the Ethernet LAN card in my Win95 PC, highlighted. Your selections may be slightly different; choose your Ethernet (or Token-Ring) card. With your selection highlighted, click Properties to bring up the configuration dialog box. The properties you can configure are

- Bindings
- Advanced
- DNS Configuration

- Gateway
- WINS Configuration
- IP Address

You don't need the Bindings, Advanced, and WINS Configuration tabs to configure an AS/400 TCP/IP client — you use only the IP Address, DNS Configuration, and Gateway tabs.

Figure 6.6 shows the IP Address tab. This dialog box lets you indicate whether the network will automatically assign an IP address to the PC or whether a specified address is to be used. If you choose the latter, you must enter an IP address and subnet mask (for information about IP addresses and subnet masks, see "Internet Protocol Addresses" in Chapter 3). Make your selection and click OK, if no further configuration is needed, or switch to the appropriate tab to configure DNS or the gateway.

FIGURE 6.6
TCP/IP Properties — IP Address Tab

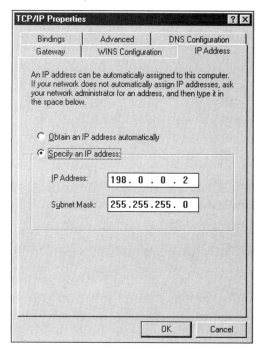

Figure 6.7 shows the DNS Configuration tab. Because DNS is optional, DNS processing is disabled by default. If your network uses DNS services (either from an internal DNS server or an ISP), you must identify the IP address of the server providing the services.

FIGURE 6.7

TCP/IP Properties — DNS Configuration Tab

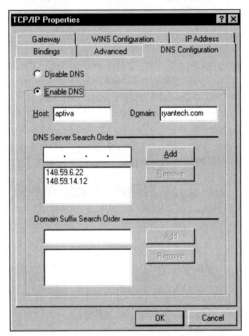

To use DNS, check Enable DNS and specify the name of the host (your PC) and the domain. The DNS Server Search Order box lets you enter up to three IP addresses for DNS servers. The order in which you enter the addresses determines the order in which they will be searched.

On the Gateway tab (Figure 6.8), you can enter up to eight gateways (routers) for routing to other networks. The gateways are used in the order in which they are listed. Normally, one gateway is sufficient.

Once you configure TCP/IP and reboot your PC, you can access the AS/400. First, ping your own IP address to ensure that TCP/IP has been loaded properly and is operational. Then ping the AS/400. If you do not have a TCP/IP shareware utility, simply go to a DOS prompt and type the PING command with the name or IP address of the system you want to verify. You should receive a response similar to that shown in Figure 6.9.

FIGURE 6.8
TCP/IP Properties — Gateway Configuration Tab

FIGURE 6.9
PING Response from an AS/400

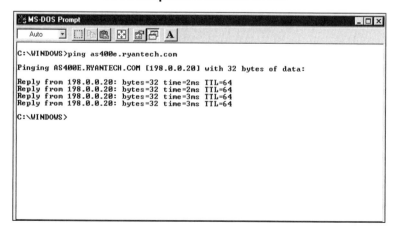

Let's try a Telnet session to the AS/400. Remember that the Win95 implementation of Telnet does not provide a TN5250 data stream, so we look at VT100 emulation, which provides a lowest-common-denominator approach to terminal emulation. Although the keyboard mapping of a straight VT100 client to an AS/400 is not the best, it's certainly workable. We'll look at better emulators later in this chapter.

Invoke a Win95 Telnet session by executing the telnet command with the AS/400's name or address from a DOS window. You'll see the screen shown in Figure 6.10.

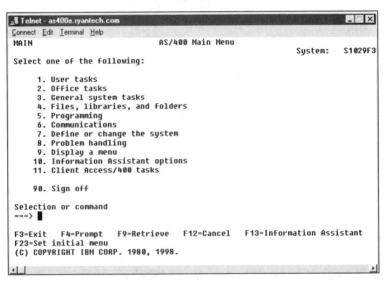

FIGURE 6.10
AS/400 Main Menu from a Win95 Telnet Session

Although the main menu looks just like an AS/400 main menu, the interaction is different. For one thing, the colors are missing — no green letters on a black screen. However, you can change to green on black if you wish to make it look at bit more AS/400-ish. To change the fonts and foreground and background colors, select Terminal on the title bar, then Preferences.

Also, the keyboard mapping between a Win95 Telnet session and an AS/400 terminal is different from other emulators but just the same as any VT100 terminal. Although the mapping is functional, you'll probably find that using a TN5250 emulator provides better interaction between the user, the keyboard, and the application.

CLIENT ACCESS CONFIGURATION

The configuration for Client Access using TCP/IP on Win95 is the easiest yet, requiring just a few simple steps. The first step is to install TCP/IP for Windows

95 as explained in the preceding section. Then install Client Access itself, following the instructions in the IBM documentation.

IBM regularly provides new releases of Client Access. The examples in this section are based on V4R2 of OS/400 and on Client Access Version 3, Release 1, Mod 3 (V3R1M3) and ServicePack level SF45363. New releases of Client Access are not tied to releases of OS/400, and you may have a different release level of one or both. Other versions and ServicePack levels of Client Access may present slightly different displays.

Once you configure TCP/IP and load Client Access, you can configure a connection using TCP/IP to your AS/400. Click Start, Programs, Client Access to open the Client Access folder (Figure 6.11).

FIGURE 6.11
Client Access Folder

Double-click AS/400 Connections to bring up the AS/400 Connections — Primary Environment dialog box. From the Connection menu, select New to invoke the Client Access Add Connection wizard, which steps you through the process of adding a new connection to the AS/400. Click Next to proceed to the Communications screen (Figure 6.12).

FIGURE 6.12
Add AS/400 Connection Communications

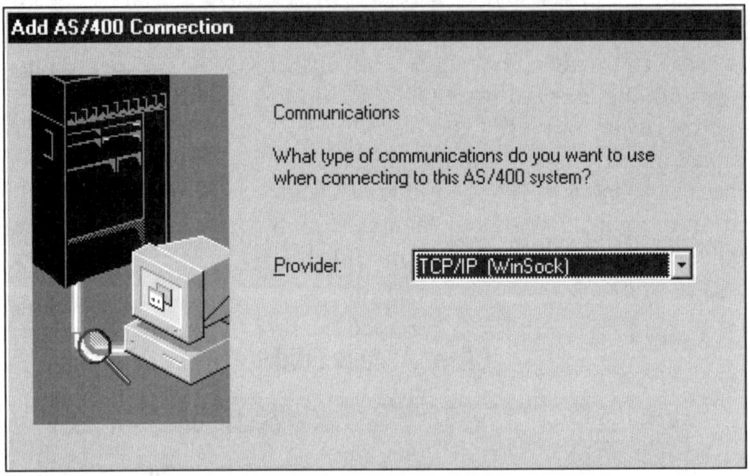

This screen lets you choose the protocol (IBM's term is "Provider") to be used for this Client Access connection. Six choices are available:

- IBM Personal Communications
- IPX/SPX
- Microsoft SNA Server 2.11
- NetSoft NS/Router
- TCP/IP (WinSock 1.1)
- WinAppc Compatible (32-bit)

Choose TCP/IP (WinSock) for your TCP/IP-based connection to the AS/400 and click Next to continue to the System Name screen (Figure 6.13). Enter the name of the TCP/IP system to which you want to connect. Use the fully qualified host and domain name of the AS/400. DNS is not required for a Client Access connection. The HOSTS file (usually located in the Windows directory) can resolve the address from a name. Click Next to proceed to the TCP/IP Address screen, shown in Figure 6.14.

Enter the IP address of the AS/400 using standard dotted decimal notation. If the IP address is not currently in the Windows HOSTS file, a prompt appears asking whether you would like to add the IP address and host/domain name to the HOSTS file. It's a good idea to do so, as PC5250 (the Client Access terminal emulator) examines the HOSTS file first when attempting to connect to an AS/400. Click Next to advance to the User ID screen (Figure 6.15, page 186).

FIGURE 6.13
Add AS/400 Connection System Name

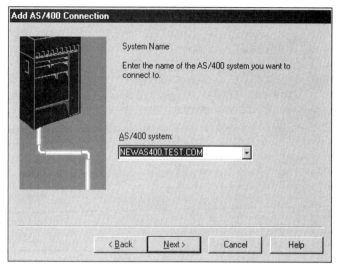

FIGURE 6.14
Add AS/400 Connection TCP/IP Address

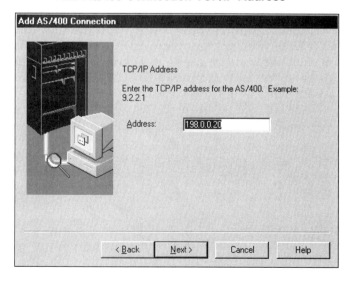

FIGURE 6.15
Add AS/400 Connection User ID

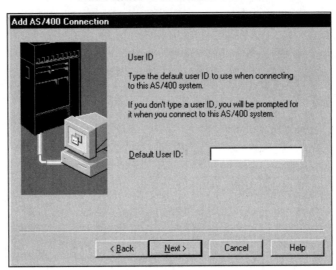

This screen lets you enter a default user ID to be used for accessing the AS/400. I firmly advise you not to, however. When a PC connects to an AS/400, the connection is made through APPC or, as in this case, through the TCP/IP protocol stack. In any case, the user ID and password are used for the initial protocol-level connection. This initial connection determines the security checking for other services, including Client Access shared drives. Resource security is in effect (assuming the AS/400 is at Level 30 security or higher, as it should be), so a service that is not interactive (such as FTP or shared drives) uses this user ID and password to determine the user's right to the object (file or directory) being accessed by the service. Interactive sessions are still controlled by the user ID and password of the person who signs on, but the other services are controlled by the protocol-level connection. Consequently, if the initial protocol-level connection is done with a user ID with a high level of security, users could inadvertently access resources they should not be able to.

Either enter a default user ID or leave this field blank, depending on your organization's standards, and click Next to advance to the Default AS/400 View screen (Figure 6.16). Here, you select the view to be displayed when the user initiates a Client Access connection.

FIGURE 6.16
Add AS/400 Connection Default AS/400 View

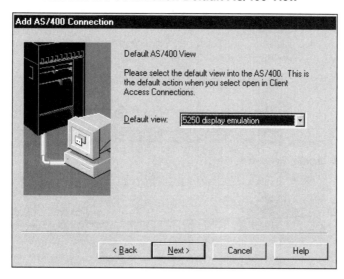

The five available options are

- Graphical access
- AS/400 Operations Navigator
- 5250 display emulation
- Connect only
- User-defined view

You may want to experiment with the different views. Connect only provides just the protocol-level connection, while the others provide different interfaces to the AS/400. Graphical access is a graphically oriented view primarily for operations functions; Operations Navigator is a graphically oriented view of the AS/400 that enables configuration of AS/400 services; 5250 display emulation uses PC5250 to provide green screen access to the AS/400; and the user-defined view lets you associate your own application with the connection. I usually choose 5250 display emulation as the default view. Once a connection has been established, you can change to another view if you wish. When you open a connection, simply choose whatever view you want instead of the default.

Select a default view and click Next to continue to the Congratulations screen in Figure 6.17. This screen lets you verify the connection. When you verify the connection, the PC attempts to locate the AS/400 so you can tell whether you configured the connection correctly (and the animation is amusing). Click Finish to complete the configuration and add this connection to the list of connections.

FIGURE 6.17
Add AS/400 Connection Congratulations

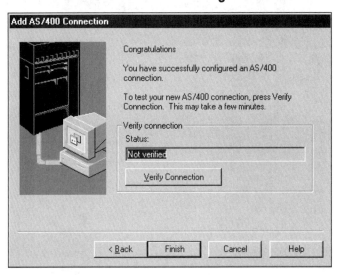

You can now access this AS/400 system either by double-clicking the connection or by selecting the connection, opening the dialog box (with a right click) and clicking Open. In either case, the default view is opened and a connection is made to the selected AS/400.

A TCP/IP-based Client Access connection to the AS/400 provides almost all the functionality you would expect. However, there are two major distinctions between TCP/IP-based Client Access and the APPC counterpart. The TCP/IP connection

- lacks printer emulation
- cannot provide a fixed workstation name

The printer emulation problem is easily resolved either by configuring AnyNet (described in the next section) or by using the AS/400's Line Printer Remote (LPR) capabilities to print directly to a LAN-attached or PC-attached Line Printer

Daemon (LPD) printer. Note that if the printer is directly attached to the PC, the PC must be running LPD. IBM has fixed both of these problems with TCP/IP-based Client Access. All versions of OS/400 after V3R1 and V3R6 can be configured to use a fixed workstation name and provide printer emulation. Check with your IBM representative for the proper PTF and ServicePack levels needed for these features.

The inability to provide a fixed workstation name is more vexing. Without going into a discussion of the merit of this approach, many software packages, whether written in-house or purchased, use a workstation name as a basis for security decisions — the application software examines the workstation name to determine whether the user should have access to resources on the AS/400. The Telnet service definition does not contain an area to specify a workstation name. An incoming TCP/IP terminal session, whether from a VT-style device or from a PC using Client Access, has a virtual device name. The AS/400 chooses this name at random, so a consistent name for a particular workstation is not and cannot be guaranteed. Therefore, software that relies on a fixed workstation name may encounter difficulties with TCP/IP-based Client Access. Using AnyNet also resolves this problem.

CLIENT ACCESS USING ANYNET CONFIGURATION

AnyNet, the AS/400 implementation of IBM's Multiple Protocol Transport Networking (MPTN) architecture, lets you encapsulate one protocol in another. A common use for AnyNet is to provide APPC-based Client Access over a TCP/IP connection. Such a connection is usually used to solve three problems involved with TCP/IP usage:

- TCP/IP-based Client Access does not support printer emulation.
- TCP/IP-based Client Access does not support a fixed workstation name.
- You cannot use APPC Application Programming Interfaces (APIs) with a TCP/IP connection.

AnyNet allows APPC packets (containing Client Access information) to be encapsulated in TCP/IP packets and sent over a network. This feature is useful especially for organizations that have a TCP/IP-based WAN but still need the function provided by APPC-based Client Access.

Of course, everything has its price. AnyNet communication is inherently slower than either APPC or TCP/IP because of overhead associated with packet encapsulation. AnyNet also consumes an additional chunk of the AS/400's resources. IBM continually improves the performance of AnyNet, but it is still slower than a native communications protocol.

The configuration of Client Access using AnyNet is a combination of APPC and TCP/IP-based Client Access configuration and is a bit more complicated.

Begin by installing TCP/IP and Client Access on your Win95 PC as explained in the preceding sections. Then run through the Client Access configuration steps once again, stopping at the Communications screen (Figure 6.12). This time, choose NetSoft NS/Router as the provider and click Next to proceed to the Add AS/400 Connection screen. In the selection box, choose <new> (the default) for a new connection and click Next to proceed to a NetSoft Wizard information screen. Click Next again to start the Configuration Wizard, shown in Figure 6.18.

FIGURE 6.18

Configuration Wizard for AS/400 Workspace Selection

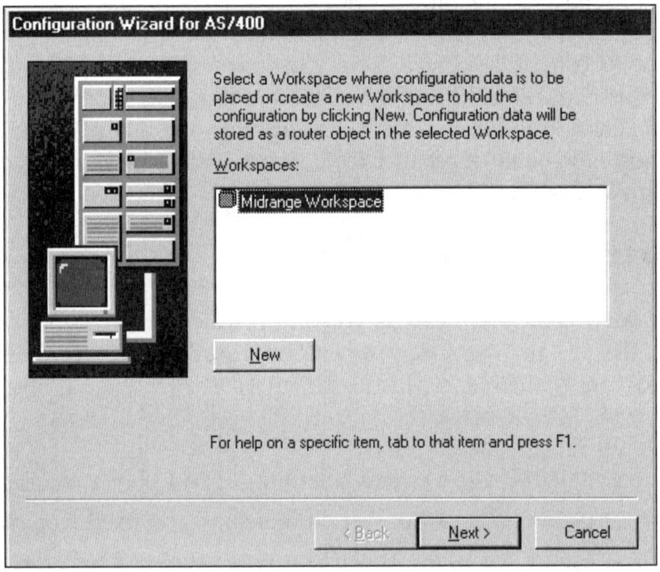

The wizard prompts for a workspace to contain the new configuration. "Workspace" is simply a term NetSoft uses to identify a configuration. Accept the default (Midrange Workspace) by clicking Next. The wizard presents a Select a Link Type screen like the one in Figure 6.19.

Select AnyNet and click Next to continue. The Enter AnyNet Link Information screen appears (Figure 6.20). Enter the name or IP address of the AS/400 to be connected and click Next to continue to the Enter System Information screen shown in Figure 6.21 (page 192).

FIGURE 6.19
Select a Link Type

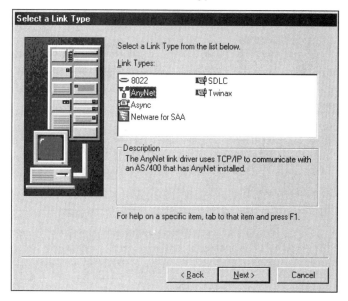

FIGURE 6.20
Enter AnyNet Link Information

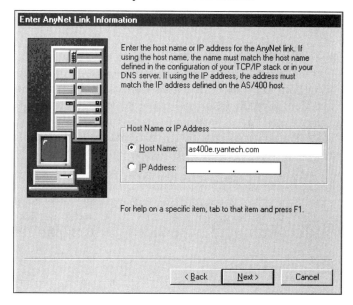

FIGURE 6.21
Enter System Information

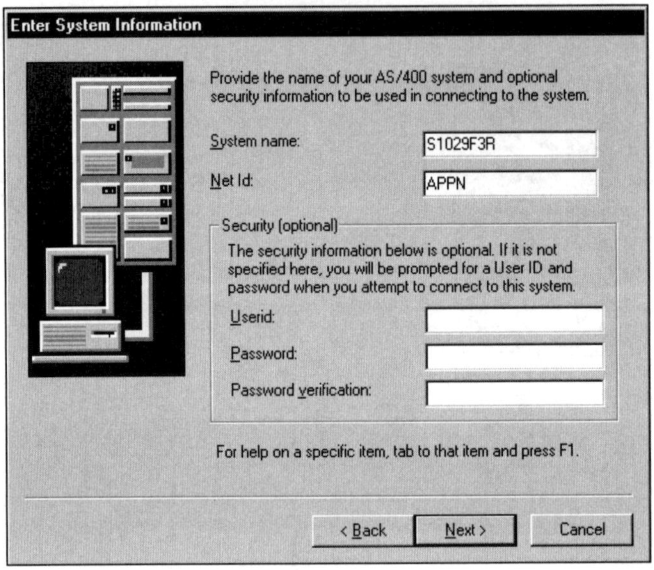

Enter the SNA-based name of the AS/400 — the name of the AS/400 in an SNA (APPC) environment — not the host/domain name. You can determine this name by viewing the AS/400's network attributes and looking for the Local Control Point Name. Click Next to display the Enter PC Information screen (Figure 6.22).

Specify the Net ID for the PC. This should be the same as the network ID of the AS/400, unless special configuration has been done on the AS/400. Specify a name for the PC in the Use a local specific value box and click Next to display the Configuration Summary screen. Review the configuration to ensure the appropriate values have been entered. If there's an error, click Back to correct it; otherwise click Finish. The wizard returns to the Add AS/400 Connection screen and displays the new configuration as the default.

Click Next to display the User ID screen shown in Figure 6.23. As in the Client Access configuration, you may enter a default User ID to be used to access the AS/400. For security reasons, I prefer not to enter a default ID. Either enter a default ID or leave the field blank, and then click Next to advance to the Default AS/400 View screen in Figure 6.24 (page 194).

FIGURE 6.22
Enter PC Information

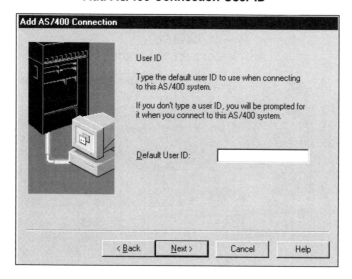

FIGURE 6.23
Add AS/400 Connection User ID

FIGURE 6.24
Add AS/400 Connection Default AS/400 View

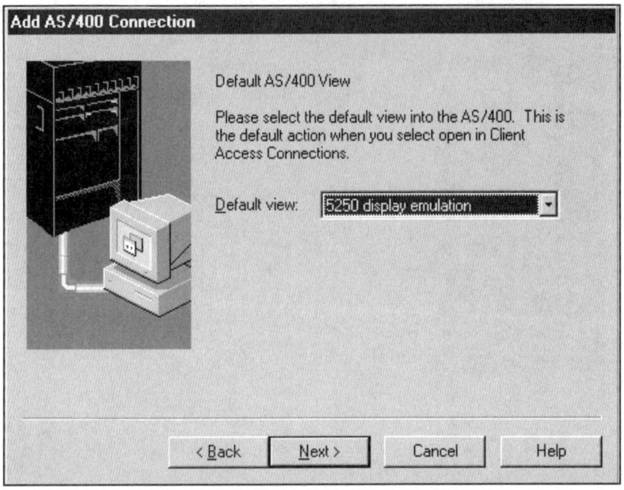

Here you can select the view to be displayed when the user initiates a Client Access connection. The options are the same as those for Client Access configuration (graphical access, AS/400 Operations Navigator, 5250 display emulation, connect only, and user-defined view). Select the appropriate view and click Next to continue to the Congratulations screen (Figure 6.25).

FIGURE 6.25
Add AS/400 Connection Congratulations

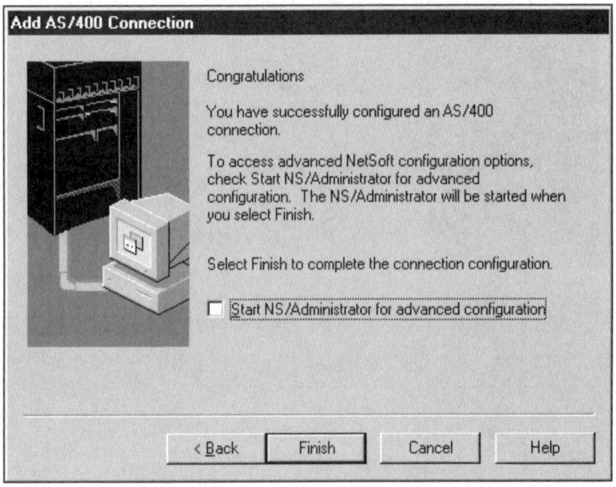

This screen lets you perform advanced NetSoft router configuration. Although advanced configuration is normally not needed, you may wish to use it to enter a specific name for this connection. Otherwise, click Finish to add the AnyNet configuration.

As we mentioned early in this section, AnyNet resolves certain problems with native TCP/IP implementation of Client Access. AnyNet may degrade performance somewhat, but the advantages may outweigh the performance issues.

RS/6000 CONFIGURATION

IBM's RS/6000 Unix-based system is very popular, especially in IBM shops. The RS/6000 uses AIX, a powerful implementation of Unix that borrows from the two major Unix variants — AT&T System V and Berkeley Software Distribution (BSD).

One of IBM's extensions to AIX is the System Management Interface Tool, or SMIT. SMIT is IBM's approach to simplifying the configuration on the RS/6000. You could do the configuration by editing the files that support TCP/IP, but that's a fairly daunting task (even for a Unix system administrator), and SMIT is a much better tool for the job. This section does not discuss the configuration needed to install LAN adapters or licensed program products or do other system administrator tasks. We focus simply on the configuration of TCP/IP on an RS/6000.

From a command line, invoke SMIT with the smit command (or the smittty command on a TTY-style device). You'll see the display in Figure 6.26 (the display is graphically oriented on the RS/6000 system console).

FIGURE 6.26
System Management Interface Tool (SMIT) Main Menu

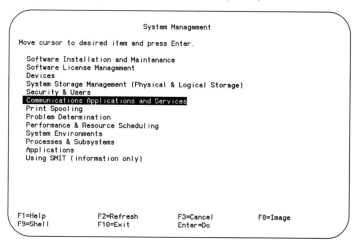

```
                           System Management

Move cursor to desired item and press Enter.

    Software Installation and Maintenance
    Software License Management
    Devices
    System Storage Management (Physical & Logical Storage)
    Security & Users
    Communications Applications and Services
    Print Spooling
    Problem Determination
    Performance & Resource Scheduling
    System Environments
    Processes & Subsystems
    Applications
    Using SMIT (information only)




F1=Help            F2=Refresh         F3=Cancel         F8=Image
F9=Shell           F10=Exit           Enter=Do
```

Using the cursor keys, move the highlight bar to the Communications Applications and Services selection. Press Enter to proceed to the Communications Applications and Services screen. Move the cursor to TCP/IP and press Enter to display the TCP/IP menu of choices shown in Figure 6.27.

FIGURE 6.27
TCP/IP Menu

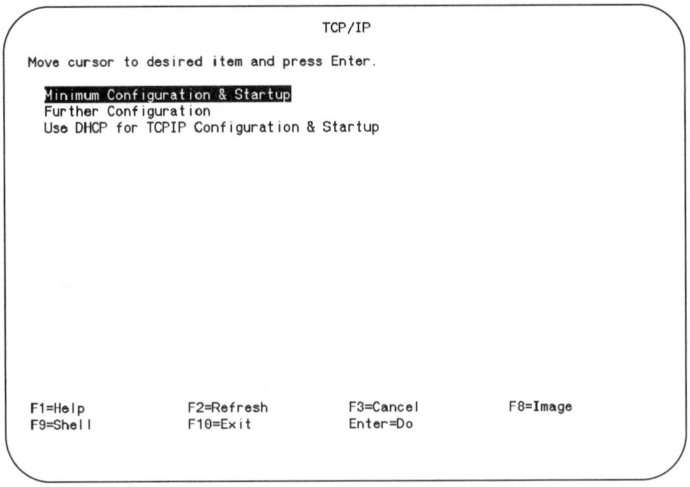

```
                                  TCP/IP
     Move cursor to desired item and press Enter.

     Minimum Configuration & Startup
     Further Configuration
     Use DHCP for TCPIP Configuration & Startup












     F1=Help            F2=Refresh        F3=Cancel        F8=Image
     F9=Shell           F10=Exit          Enter=Do
```

The menu presents three choices. The Minimum Configuration & Startup option provides all you need for the base TCP/IP configuration. This option is the equivalent of selecting the following options on the CFGTCP menu:

- interface setup (option 1)
- default gateway (option 2)
- host name specification (options 10 and 12)
- nameserver configuration (option 13)

The Further Configuration option supports functions such as establishing static routes, setting up DNS services, working with the client and server processes, and starting and stopping the TCP/IP processes. The Use DHCP for TCPIP Configuration & Startup option lets you specify that the RS/6000 will receive its IP address from a DHCP server in the network. We discuss the base configuration options.

Select the Minimum Configuration & Startup option to view the display in
Figure 6.28.

FIGURE 6.28
Available Network Interfaces

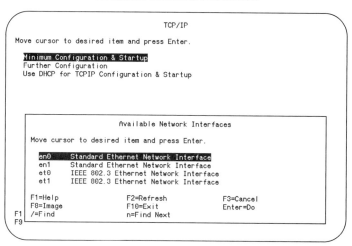

Select the network interface (adapter) you wish to configure. Generally, most
RS/6000 systems (like most AS/400s) have a single network interface. Selecting
the interface produces the entry screen for the minimum configuration values
(Figure 6.29).

FIGURE 6.29
Minimum Configuration Entry Screen

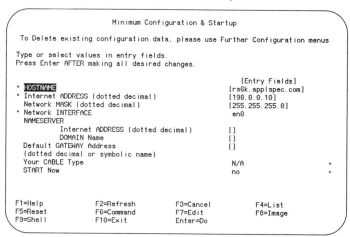

Items with an asterisk (*) can be prompted. The parameters for RS/6000 configuration are as follows:

- HOSTNAME — the fully qualified name for the RS/6000. You can specify additional names under the Further Configuration options.

- Internet ADDRESS — the IP address assigned to the system, in dotted decimal format.

- Network MASK — the subnet mask, in dotted decimal format.

- Network INTERFACE — the interface selected on the previous window.

- NAMESERVER — the dotted decimal address of the DNS server, including the domain name.

- Default GATEWAY Address — the address of the default route for packets destined for outside of the local network. You can specify either an IP address or a system name.

- Your CABLE Type — the type of cable that connects the RS/6000 to the network. You can usually leave this value as N/A, but if you encounter problems, set the cable to bnc for a BNC connection (thinnet), dix for a thick Ethernet connection, or tp for twisted pair.

- START Now — specify whether the TCP/IP processes should be started when you configure the connection. The Further Configuration option lets you start and stop the processes, like the STRTCP (Start TCP/IP) and ENDTCP (End TCP/IP) commands.

After entering the configuration information, press Enter to change or establish the TCP/IP configuration. Using the Minimum Configuration & Startup option invokes the mktcpip command on the RS/6000.

Telnet and FTP processing on an RS/6000 are similar to processing on any ASCII character-mode device such as a PC. You'll likely find the RS/6000's support for TN3270 emulation quite useful. A 3270-style device is similar to a 5250-type device and more closely simulates AS/400 colors and keyboard mapping than does VT emulation.

THIRD-PARTY CONNECTIVITY PRODUCTS

Several third-party products provide connectivity from a PC to an AS/400. Here we examine two of them: Reflection from WRQ and Rally! from Attachmate.

You might ask why anyone would want a non-IBM product — isn't Client Access enough for everyone? Different reasons apply under different circumstances, but a few stand out:

- Price — some products provide equivalent functionality at a lower price, especially with volume purchases.

- Function — other products may provide more (or at least different) functions than IBM's products.

- Flexibility — Client Access lets you connect to AS/400s, but other products (or families of products) may let you connect to multiple host systems.

- Technology —IBM is not known for producing leading-edge products or products that embrace new technology, and third-party vendors often respond to needs in the marketplace before IBM does.

Regardless of your reason for considering a non-IBM product, make sure it fulfills your needs before you buy. I have no personal preference regarding third-party products; I use several different ones depending on the type of connectivity I need and what my clients have installed. Contact manufacturers — they are always happy to explain why their products are the best!

The following sections explain the configuration of Reflection and Rally! Most vendors support several protocol and connectivity types, but we explore only the configuration for the TCP/IP-based products. An interesting related question, though, is which TCP/IP stack should you use? Vendors may have their own stacks and may say theirs are better than Microsoft's. That might even be true, but I prefer to maintain only the stack from the operating system vendor. If the operating system or the underlying TCP/IP interface is changed, the responsibility of providing support for the communications protocol falls to the operating system vendor.

WRQ Reflection Configuration

WRQ's Reflection for IBM product provides host connectivity and data exchange between an IBM host and a PC. Reflection supports both AS/400s and mainframes over a variety of connection types, including Client Access, AnyNet, Microsoft SNA Server, Novell Netware for SAA, NetSoft NS/Router, and Telnet. WRQ also offers Reflection for AS/400, which provides 5250 emulation only.

Reflection requires a WinSock-compliant TCP/IP protocol stack. Installing Reflection is similar to installing most Win95 applications: Put the CD-ROM in the drive and click Run on the Start menu. Find the SETUP.EXE application on the CD and execute the setup utility.

In the first dialog box that appears, you specify which WRQ product to install. Click Reflection for IBM. The subsequent dialog box suggests that you read the latest README file. Click Continue to display the Welcome screen, then click Next to proceed to the Reflection Folder screen shown in Figure 6.30.

FIGURE 6.30
Reflection for IBM Reflection Folder

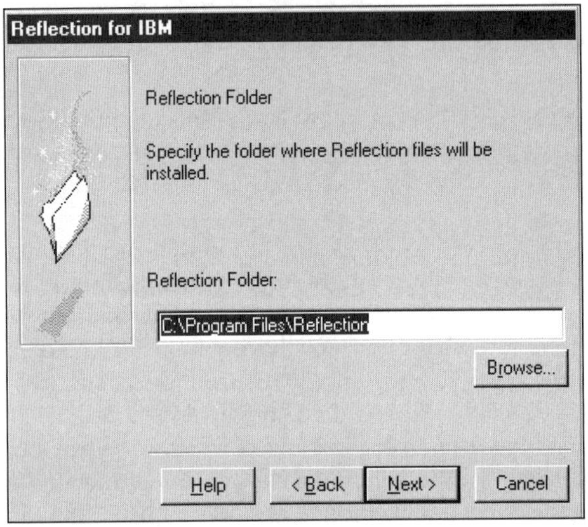

Specify the folder in which to place the Reflection programs and click Next to continue to the User Folder screen (Figure 6.31).

FIGURE 6.31
Reflection for IBM User Folder

Enter the name of a folder in which to place user objects, such as keyboard maps and scripts, and click Next to proceed to the Installation Options screen shown in Figure 6.32.

FIGURE 6.32
Reflection for IBM Installation Options

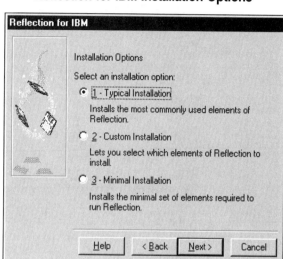

Select the type of installation desired: typical, custom, or minimal. A typical installation is used for most desktop PCs. A custom installation lets you decide which components to install. A minimal installation installs only the base options; this is an appropriate choice for a laptop system. Click Next to continue to the Program Icons screen (Figure 6.33).

This window installs Reflection program icons to the specified folder unless you check "Do Not Create Reflection Icons." Click Next to continue to the Ready to Install screen, then click Finish to install Reflection. Several marketing messages appear, along with a status display. A Setup Successful screen appears when setup is complete.

FIGURE 6.33
Reflection for IBM Program Icons

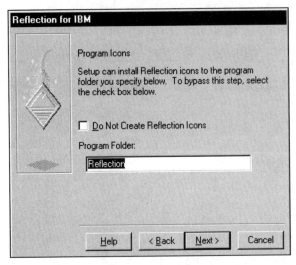

To invoke Reflection, open the Reflection folder and double-click the Host — AS/400 icon. In the dialog box that appears (Figure 6.34), enter the host name or the host's IP address and click Connect.

FIGURE 6.34
Reflection System Name or Address Dialog Box

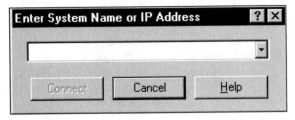

Figure 6.35 shows the AS/400 main menu through Reflection emulation. Several options under the Setup drop-down menu let you customize the screen. For instance, the default status line emulates the 3488 status line; I prefer the 5250 status line (showing my age again). Note the hot spots on the menu — the highlighted areas around the function key definitions. You can "press" a function key by clicking the hot spot with the mouse.

FIGURE 6.35

Reflection's AS/400 Main Menu

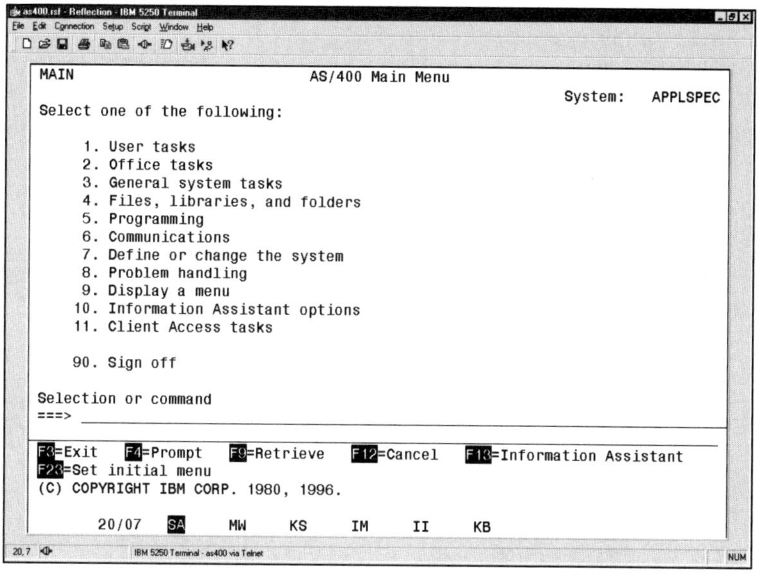

Reflection is a complete terminal emulation product with very good 5250 capabilities and an excellent FTP client. The FTP client has a drop-and-drag feature that makes transferring files between the AS/400 and the client simple.

Attachmate Rally! Configuration

Attachmate's Rally! product delivers AS/400 emulation across a wide variety of connectivity types, including AnyNet, Microsoft SNA Server, Novell Netware for SAA, Synchronous Data Link Control (SDLC), twinax, and TN5250. Rally! requires a WinSock-compliant TCP/IP protocol stack for the TN5250 connection.

To install Rally!, put the CD-ROM in the drive and click Run on the Start menu. Find the SETUP.EXE application on the CD and execute the setup utility. The initial setup screen asks you which product to install. Select Rally! for AS/400 and click Install.

Click Next on the Welcome screen and the appropriate button on the License Agreement screen. The Registration screen (Figure 6.36) appears. Enter a name (and company, if you wish) and click Next to proceed. Click Next again on the Confirm Registration screen.

The Select Install Type screen (Figure 6.37) asks whether Rally! should be installed on the workstation or on a server. The Network Administrator Install option lets a network administrator install Rally! on multiple systems from a file server. Select Local Workstation Install and click Next.

FIGURE 6.36
Rally! User Registration Information

FIGURE 6.37
Select Install Type

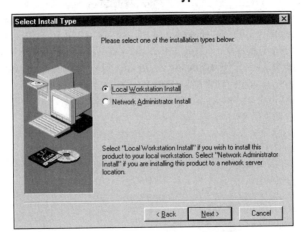

The next screen (Figure 6.38) identifies the directory into which Rally! will be installed. Click Next to accept the default, or click Browse first to select another directory.

From the Setup Type screen (Figure 6.39), select the type of installation: Typical for most desktop PCs, Compact to install only base options (appropriate for a laptop), or Custom to make decisions about the components to be installed. Click Next.

FIGURE 6.38
Select Installation Destination

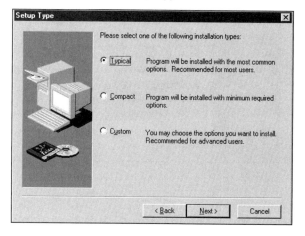

FIGURE 6.39
Setup Type

Figure 6.40 shows the Select Hosts screen, which lets you choose between a standard midrange installation and one that includes APPN support. Select IBM AS/400 Midrange and click Next.

The screen in Figure 6.41 lets you choose to have the setup utility make the necessary modification to the path statement in the PC's AUTOEXEC.BAT file. Either accept the default or select no modification at this time. Click Next to continue.

FIGURE 6.40

Select Hosts

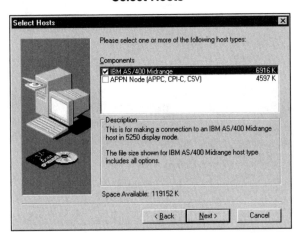

FIGURE 6.41

Path Statement Modification

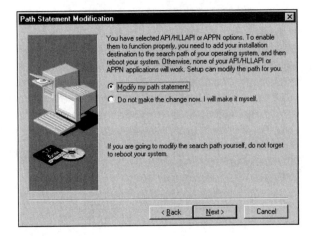

The next screen summarizes the setup. Scroll through the settings to ensure they are correct, then click Next. From the subsequent Confirm Selections screen, click Finish to begin the installation. When all files have been copied and the Information screen appears, click OK to proceed with migration.

The Migration Wizard screen (Figure 6.42) lets you search for and optionally migrate previous versions of Rally!. To maintain configuration settings, you should migrate if a previous version of Rally! is installed. If, as in this example, no previous versions are found, click Cancel to continue.

FIGURE 6.42
Migration Wizard

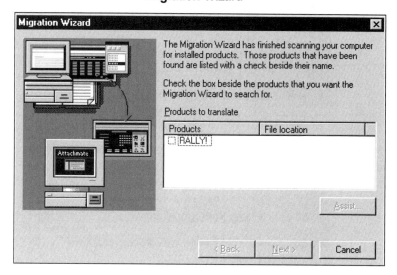

The next screen lets you restart Windows to complete the installation. If you choose No, a "nag screen" reminds you to restart before you run Rally!. Click on the appropriate selection. A Setup Completed screen appears after you restart and lets you view the release notes, return to the desktop, or start Rally!.

To initiate an AS/400 session, open the Rally! folder and double-click Rally! for AS/400. The first dialog box (Figure 6.43) determines whether you want to configure a new session or open an existing (already configured) session. Because this is the first invocation of Rally!, select Creating a new session and click OK.

FIGURE 6.43
Start Rally!

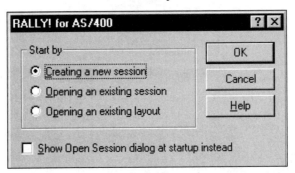

On the New Session Wizard screen (Figure 6.44), choose whether you want to configure a display or a printer session. Click Next.

FIGURE 6.44
New Session Wizard

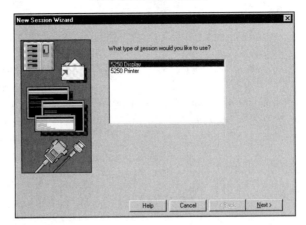

Select the type of connection you want to configure for the session (TN5250 for a TCP/IP connection) in the screen shown in Figure 6.45. Click Next to continue.

FIGURE 6.45
New Session Wizard Connection Selection

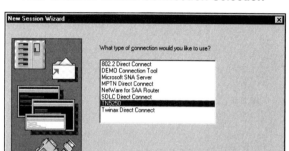

In the Host options screen (Figure 6.46), specify the host name or IP address of the AS/400. You can leave the port (23 for Telnet) and the connection timeout at their default values. Click Next to continue.

FIGURE 6.46
New Session Wizard Host Options

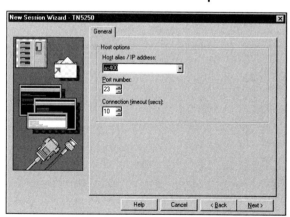

The subsequent screen lets you choose a type of file transfer (Figure 6.47). Select FTP and click Finish. A New Session Information confirmation screen is displayed. Click OK to continue or Cancel if changes are required.

FIGURE 6.47
New Session Wizard File Transfer Selection

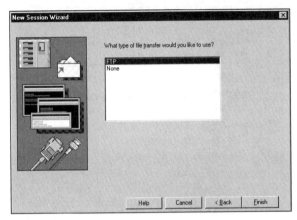

Figure 6.48 shows the AS/400 main menu through Rally! emulation. Rally! is very configurable, letting you change the display type, fonts, and several other options. It also supports hot spots for ease of mouse use. Rally! has a definite AS/400 look and feel. The terminal emulation is flexible, and file transfers are similar to Client Access.

FIGURE 6.48
Rally!'s AS/400 Main Menu

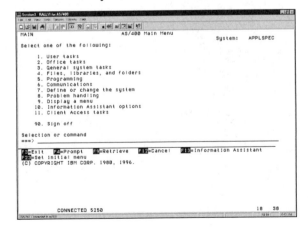

Chapter 7

Controlling the Environment with TCP/IP Exit Points

TCP/IP exit points let you control your networking environment. For example, even after a major rewrite and three new releases, the AS/400's TCP/IP implementation still lacks access logging of File Transfer Protocol (FTP) sessions. Operating systems with built-in logging record every attempt to establish an FTP session as well as the names of transferred files. OS/400 has no built-in logging, so you have no idea who has accessed your system and what files they have copied in or out.

With TCP/IP exit points, you can add logging capabilities to OS/400 FTP. You can also use exit points to provide capabilities such as directing incoming Web traffic to a specific application and providing anonymous FTP access.

This chapter focuses on using TCP/IP exit points to gain maximum control over the TCP/IP environment. We explain the exit point registration facility, as well as each TCP/IP exit point and the exit point interfaces. We include sample CL exit point programs that illustrate the interaction with the FTP server. We also include a program to enable anonymous FTP.

WHAT ARE TCP/IP EXIT POINTS?

An exit point is simply a point in an application at which it can call an external program (an *exit program*) to perform customized processing. V3R2 and V3R7 include four TCP/IP exit points. FTP uses three of these exit points, and the 5250/HTML Workstation Gateway (WSG) function uses the other one. OS/400 versions V4R1M0 and V4R2M0 introduced more exit points. You can expect IBM to increase the number of exit points in the future because exit points provide the opportunity to add processing that may be needed for complex applications or to improve security processing. Table 7.1 lists the TCP/IP-related exit points through V4R2M0, although we restrict our discussion here to the four available with V3R2 and V3R7.

TABLE 7.1

TCP/IP-Related Exit Points

Exit Point	Format	Description
QIBM_QTMF_CLIENT_REQ	VLRQ0100	Validate FTP client request
QIBM_QTMF_SERVER_REQ	VLRQ0100	Validate FTP server request
QIBM_QTMF_SVR_LOGON	TCPL0100	FTP server sign-on
QIBM_QTMT_WSG	QAPP0100	WSG server sign-on
QIBM_QTG_DEVINIT	INIT0100	Telnet device initialization
QIBM_QTG_DEVTERM	TERM0100	Telnet device termination
QIBM_QTMX_SERVER_REQ	VLRQ0100	REXEC server request validation
QIBM_QTMX_SVR_LOGON	TCPL0100	REXEC server logon
QIBM_QTOD_DHCP_ABND	DHCA0100	DHCP address binding notify
QIBM_QTOD_DHCP_ARLS	DHCR0100	DHCP address release notify
QIBM_QTOD_DHCP_REQ	DHCV0100	DHCP request packet validation
QIBM_QTOD_SERVER_REQ	VLRQ0100	TFTP server request validation
QIBM_QZCA_SNMPTRAP	ZCAT0100	SNMP trap routing exit point
QIBM_QZMFMSF_ACT	MSFF0100	MSF accounting exit
QIBM_QZMFMSF_ADR_RSL	MSFF0100	MSF address resolution
QIBM_QZMFMSF_ATT_CNV	MSFF0100	MSF attachment conversion
QIBM_QZMFMSF_ATT_MGT	MSFF0100	MSF attachment management
QIBM_QZMFMSF_ENL_PSS	MSFF0100	MSF envelope processing
QIBM_QZMFMSF_LCL_DEL	MSFF0100	MSF local delivery
QIBM_QZMFMSF_LST_EXP	MSFF0100	MSF list expansion
QIBM_QZMFMSF_MSG_FWD	MSFF0100	MSF message forwarding
QIBM_QZMFMSF_NON_DEL	MSFF0100	MSF nondelivery
QIBM_QZMFMSF_SEC_AUT	MSFF0100	MSF security and authority
QIBM_QZMFMSF_TRK_CHG	MSFF0100	MSF track mail message change
QIBM_QZMFMSF_VLD_TYP	MSFF0100	MSF validate type
QIBM_QZSO_SIGNONSRV	ZSOY0100	TCP sign-on server

An associated exit point interface is used to pass information between OS/400 and the exit program. The information is passed using specific formats (similar to record formats). These formats are simply input and output parameters used between OS/400 and the exit program. As you can see in Table 7.1, both the FTP server and the FTP client validation exit points use the same format (VLRQ0100), indicating that the same information is available for both exit points and that the same exit program could be used for both exit points.

EXIT POINT REGISTRATION

Before you can use exit points, they must be registered with the operating system. Exit points generally are registered when the licensed program product associated with the exit point is installed on the system.

Exit points are registered and programs are associated with the exit points in the OS/400 registration facility. To access the registration facility, execute the WRKREGINF (Work with Registration Information) command. Figure 7.1 shows a sample command display.

FIGURE 7.1

Work with Registration Information Command Display

```
                    Work with Registration Information

  Type options, press Enter.
    5=Display exit point   8=Work with exit programs

                         Exit
          Exit           Point
  Opt  Point             Format     Registered  Text
    _  QIBM_QHQ_DTAQ      DTAQ0100     *YES      Original Data Queue Server
    _  QIBM_QJO_DLT_JRNRCV DRCV0100    *YES      Delete Journal Receiver
    _  QIBM_QLZP_LICENSE  LICM0100     *YES      Original License Mgmt Server
    _  QIBM_QMF_MESSAGE   MESS0100     *YES      Original Message Server
    _  QIBM_QNPS_ENTRY    ENTR0100     *YES      Network Print Server - entry
    _  QIBM_QNPS_SPLF     SPLF0100     *YES      Network Print Server - spool
    _  QIBM_QOE_OV_USR_ADM UADM0100    *YES      OfficeVision/400 Administrati
    _  QIBM_QOE_OV_USR_SND DOCI0900    *YES      OfficeVision/400 Mail Send Ex
    _  QIBM_QOK_NOTIFY    VRFY0100     *YES      System Directory Notify Exit
    _  QIBM_QOK_SUPPLIER  SUPL0100     *YES      System Directory Supplier Exi
    _  QIBM_QOK_VERIFY    VRFY0100     *YES      System Directory Verify Exit
                                                                     More...
  Command
  ===>
  F3=Exit    F4=Prompt   F9=Retrieve   F12=Cancel
```

This command lets you display the exit point and work with exit point programs. You use the ADDEXITPGM (Add Exit Program) command to associate an exit program with an exit point.

At this time, only IBM-defined exit points are available. There is no provision for users to add new exit points to OS/400.

FTP EXIT POINTS

The AS/400's FTP server application includes exit points at which you can integrate custom programs into FTP's logon and command-processing logic. The FTP server monitors each exit point and, if a program is registered for an exit point, calls the exit program and passes information as parameters to it. The exit program processes the information and returns control to the FTP server along with an accept or reject indication and, optionally, user ID and password override values to control the server's subsequent operation. The FTP server then resumes processing.

There are three FTP exit points:

- QIBM_QTMF_CLIENT_REQ
- QIBM_QTMF_SERVER_REQ
- QIBM_QTMF_SVR_LOGON

The QIBM_QTMF_CLIENT_REQ exit point occurs when someone using the AS/400 FTP client application requests an FTP subcommand (e.g., GET, PUT). The QIBM_QTMF_SERVER_REQ exit point occurs when a user accessing the AS/400 FTP server application requests an FTP subcommand. Both exit points use the VLRQ0100 format, which is summarized in Table 7.2.

TABLE 7.2
Format VLRQ0100

Field	Type	Format	Length (bytes)
Application identifier	Input	Binary	4
Operation identifier	Input	Binary	4
User profile	Input	Character	10
Remote IP address	Input	Character	Variable
Remote IP address length	Input	Binary	4
Operation-specific information	Input	Character	Variable
Operation-specific information length	Input	Binary	4
Allow or prohibit operation	Output	Binary	4

The application identifier field indicates the source of the data. This field has a value of 0 when the data comes from the FTP client program and 1 when the data comes from the FTP server program.

The operation identifier field identifies the operation being performed. The possible values are

- 0 — session initialization
- 1 — creating a directory or library
- 2 — deleting a directory or library
- 3 — setting the current directory
- 4 — listing files
- 5 — deleting a file
- 6 — sending a file

- 7 — receiving a file
- 8 — renaming a file
- 9 — executing a CL command

The user profile field contains the profile for the user using the FTP client or server. The remote IP address field contains the address of the remote system in dotted decimal notation, and the remote IP address length field contains the length of the remote system's address.

The contents of the operation-specific information field depend on the type of operation being performed:

- If the FTP client is being used during session initialization, this field is blank — no information is provided.
- If the FTP server is being used during session initialization, the field contains the server's IP address.
- For a directory or library operation (operation identifiers 1, 2, and 3), the field contains the name of the directory or file being used.
- For the file operations (operation identifiers 4 through 8), the field contains the name of the file being used.
- When the operation identifier is 9, the field contains the CL command to be executed.

The operation-specific information length field is self explanatory. The allow or prohibit operation field is an output field and has the following four possible values:

- −1 — Never allow this operation. The exit point program will not be called again in this session.
- 0 — Prohibit (reject) this operation.
- 1 — Allow this operation.
- 2 — Always allow this operation. The exit program will not be called again in this session.

The QIBM_QTMF_SVR_LOGON exit point occurs immediately after a user enters a user ID and an authentication string (i.e., password) to log on to the FTP server. An exit program attached to QIBM_QTMF_SVR_LOGON can control the directories and libraries the user can access. The exit program uses the return parameter to accept or reject the request. You can also override user input values, whatever they are, to values of your choice. This exit point uses the TCPL0100 format, which is summarized in Table 7.3.

TABLE 7.3
Format TCPL0100

Field	Type	Format	Length (bytes)
Application identifier	Input	Binary	4
User identifier	Input	Character	Variable
User identifier length	Input	Binary	4
Authentication string	Input	Character	Variable
Authentication string length	Input	Binary	4
Client IP address	Input	Character	Variable
Client IP address length	Input	Binary	4
Return code	Output	Binary	4
User profile	Output	Character	10
Password	Output	Character	10
Initial current library	Output	Character	10

The application identifier field has a value of 1, indicating the data is from the FTP server program. The user identifier and user identifier length fields return the user name entered at FTP sign-on and the length of the user identifier, respectively, from the USER subcommand.

The authentication string is the password entered at FTP sign-on and is returned from the PASS subcommand.

The authentication string length, client IP address, and client IP address length fields are all self explanatory.

The return code is an output field whose value determines whether the FTP server sign-on attempt should be allowed or rejected, identifies password processing, and determines the current library. Possible return code values are as follows:

- 0 — Reject the server sign-on attempt.
- 1 — Sign on to the server with the supplied user identifier (used as the user profile) and authentication string (used as the password). The user profile and associated password must exist on the AS/400. Set the initial current library to the value in the user profile.
- 2 — Sign on to the server with the supplied user identifier (used as the user profile) and authentication string (used as the password). The user profile and password must exist on the AS/400. Set the initial current library to the value contained in the initial current library parameter.
- 3 — Sign on to the server and override the supplied user identifier and authentication string with values from the exit program. Set the initial

current library to the value contained in the user profile supplied by the exit program.

- 4 — Sign on to the server with the supplied user identifier (used as the user profile) and authentication string (used as the password). The user profile and password must exist on the AS/400. Set the initial current library to the supplied current library.

- 5 — Sign on to the server and override the user identifier and authentication string with values from the exit program. Set the current library to the library associated with the supplied user profile. No further password processing is performed — this value overrides normal AS/400 password processing.

- 6 — Sign on to the server and override the user identifier, authentication string, and current library with values from the exit program. No further password processing is performed — this value overrides normal AS/400 password processing.

The user profile field holds the profile supplied by the exit program, if it supplies a profile. The password field contains the password optionally supplied by the exit program, and the initial current library is the library optionally supplied by the exit program.

Let's look at an example of what a simple exit program can do and how it interacts with the AS/400's FTP server.

Exploring the Server Logon Exit Point

When an exit program is attached to the QIBM_QTMF_SVR_LOGON exit point, the FTP server calls your custom program each time a user attempts to sign on to the FTP server so you can use your own logic to validate or record the logon attempt. With this or any exit program, your program must accept and return certain input parameters and output values. Among the input parameters are the requester's IP address, the user ID, and the authentication string. Among the output values your program must return is a flag indicating logon acceptance or rejection. In the exit program, you can direct the FTP server to either accept or reject the sign-on attempt, and you can also override certain FTP sign-on options.

If your program returns an accept indication, the normal AS/400 security logon process continues. Thus, the exit program doesn't circumvent the AS/400 logon processing, but rather lets you better control the logon attempt. If your program returns a reject indication, the FTP server notifies the user the FTP logon failed, thus letting you provide additional security checking for the FTP server.

Examining the TCPL0100 format in Table 7.3, you can see fairly easily how to use the user profile, password, and initial current library return values.

Depending on the value set for the accept/reject flag, you may need to place a value in one or more of these return parameters. The return parameters let you override the values normally used in the FTP logon attempt.

For instance, by using the value 3 for the accept/reject flag, you tell FTP you are overriding the values for the user profile and password with the values your exit program places in the user profile and password return parameters. With other flag values, you decide whether the initial current library for the FTP session should come from the CURLIB value specified in the user profile object or from the initial current library return parameter. Other return parameters in conjunction with the accept/reject flag let you also dictate the library used as the current library for the session.

Unfortunately, you cannot override the initial current library to an IFS directory or a QDLS folder. Indeed, because the initial current library parameter is only 10 characters long, it seems doubtful that IBM even thought you might want to do so. For the foreseeable future, you're stuck with a library in the QSYS file system as your initial FTP directory.

You should be aware that if your program returns a value of 5 or 6 in the accept/reject flag, no further password validation occurs. Although this seems scary, it's designed to enable anonymous FTP. The authentication string for an anonymous FTP user typically is the user's e-mail address. However, this doesn't usually work as an AS/400 password, which is limited to 10 characters. Thus, you can use values 5 or 6 to bypass password checking. When you enable anonymous FTP, you must have an exit program for the QIBM_QTMF_SERVER_REQ exit point to allow anonymous users to access only your public files and to prohibit use of certain FTP subcommands, such as RCMD (an FTP subcommand that executes a remote command on the server). See "Anonymous FTP" later in this chapter for further discussion of this facility.

The Server Log-on Exit Program

CL program USRFTPLOGC (Figure 7.2) is a sample exit program that can be attached to the FTP server logon exit point QIBM_QTMF_SVR_LOGON. USRFTPLOGC records all FTP logon attempts to a message queue.

FIGURE 7.2

Program USRFTPLOGC

```
/* Program Name: USRFTPLOGC  Copyright 1997 PowerTech Toolworks, Inc */
/* Purpose: This is the FTP server Log-on Exit Point Program to      */
/*          record all FTP log-on attempts to a message queue.       */
/*          Exit point is QIBM_QTMF_SVR_LOGON.                        */
/*          Parameter format is TCPL0100.                            */
/* - - - - - - - - - - - - - - - - - - - - - - - - - - - - - - - - - */
/* Security:    Place in a secure library (i.e., PUBLIC(*EXCLUDE)).  */
/*              Place source code in a secure library.               */
/*              Do not allow retrieval of CL source.                 */
/* Compilation: CRTCLPGM PGM(ASecureLibrary/USRFTPLOGC)    +         */
/*                       SRCFILE(ASecureLibrary/QCLSRC)    +         */
/*                       LOG(*NO)                          +         */
/*                       ALWRTVSRC(*NO)                    +         */
/*                       AUT(*EXCLUDE)                               */
/* - - - - - - - - - - - - - - - - - - - - - - - - - - - - - - - - - */

    PGM   ( &P_AppID   +
            &P_User    +
            &P_UserLen +
            &P_Pwd     +
            &P_PwdLen  +
            &P_IP      +
            &P_IPLen   +
            &P_RtnOut  +
            &P_UserOut +
            &P_PwdOut  +
            &P_LibOut  )

  /* Parameters for exit point interface FORMAT TCPL0100           */

  /* Input parms */
    DCL     &P_AppID    *CHAR   4    /* Application ID (%bin)     */
                                     /* 1 = FTP                   */
    DCL     &P_User     *CHAR 999    /* User ID                   */
    DCL     &P_UserLen  *CHAR   4    /* User ID length (%bin)     */
    DCL     &P_Pwd      *CHAR 999    /* Password                  */
    DCL     &P_PwdLen   *CHAR   4    /* Password length (%bin)    */
    DCL     &P_IP       *CHAR  15    /* Requester IP address      */
    DCL     &P_IPLen    *CHAR   4    /* IP address length  (%bin) */
    DCL     &P_IPLen    *CHAR   4    /* IP address length  (%bin) */

  /* Output parms */
    DCL     &P_RtnOut   *CHAR   4    /* Return code out           */
                                     /* Values are:               */
                                     /* 0=Reject                  */
                                     /* 1=Accept, w/Usrprf Curlib */
                                     /* 2=Accept, w/ &P_LibOut    */
                                     /* 3=Accept, w/UsrPrf Curlib */
                                     /*         and &P_UserOut    */
                                     /*         and &P_PwdOut     */
                                     /* 4=Accept, w/ &P_LibOut    */
                                     /*         and &P_UserOut    */
                                     /*         and &P_PwdOut     */
                                     /* 5=Accept, w/UsrPrf Curlib */
                                     /*         and &P_UserOut    */
                                     /*         Password bypass   */
                                     /* 6=Accept, w/ P_LibOut     */
                                     /*         and &P_UserOut    */
                                     /*         Password bypass   */
```

continued

FIGURE 7.2 CONTINUED

```
DCL        &P_UserOut   *CHAR 10    /* User profile out         */
DCL        &P_PwdOut    *CHAR 10    /* Password out             */
DCL        &P_LibOut    *CHAR 10    /* CURLIB out               */
/* End of FORMAT TCPL0100                                       */

/* Variables for binary conversions */
DCL        &AppID       *DEC  (1 0)
DCL        &UserLen     *DEC  (3 0)
DCL        &PwdLen      *DEC  (3 0)
DCL        &IPLen       *DEC  (3 0)

/* Misc. work variables              */
DCL        &Time        *CHAR  6
DCL        &Date        *CHAR  6
DCL        &Message     *CHAR 256
DCL        &Accept1     *DEC   1    Value(1)
DCL        &MsgQ        *CHAR 10    Value('FTPSVRLOG')
DCL        &MsgQLib     *CHAR 10    Value('USRTCPIP')

/* Message-handling variables        */
DCL        &MsgID       *CHAR  7
DCL        &MsgF        *CHAR 10
DCL        &MsgFLib     *CHAR 10
DCL        &MsgDta      *CHAR 100

MonMsg     (CPF0000  MCH0000)  Exec(GoTo Error)

ChgVar     &AppID      %Bin(&P_AppID)
ChgVar     &UserLen    %Bin(&P_UserLen)
ChgVar     &PwdLen     %Bin(&P_PwdLen)
ChgVar     &IPLen      %Bin(&P_IPLen)

RtvSysVal  QTIME       &Time
RtvSysVal  QDATE       &Date

Chgvar     &Message       +
                     ('FTP Logon'                              +
                     *BCAT %SST(&P_User 1 &UserLen)            +
                     *BCAT 'From IP Addr'                      +
                     *BCAT %SST(&P_IP 1 &IPLen)                +
                     *BCAT 'at'                                +
                     *BCAT %SST(&Time 1 2)                     +
                     *CAT  ':'                                 +
                     *CAT  %SST(&Time 3 2)                     +
                     *CAT  ':'                                 +
                     *CAT  %SST(&Time 5 2)                     +
                     *BCAT 'on'                                +
                     *BCAT %SST(&Date 1 2)                     +
                     *CAT  '/'                                 +
                     *CAT  %SST(&Date 3 2)                     +
                     *CAT  '/'                                 +
                     *CAT  %SST(&Date 5 2))

SndPgmMsg  MsgID(CPF9897)                    +
           Msgf(QCPFMSG)                     +
           MsgDta(&Message)                  +
           ToMsgQ(&MsgQLib/&MsgQ)

ChgVar     %Bin(&P_RtnOut)   Value(&Accept1)  /* Return "Accept" */

Return     /* Normal end of program */
```

continued

FIGURE 7.2 *CONTINUED*

```
ERROR:
    RcvMsg     Msgtype(*LAST)                  +
               MsgDta(&MsgDta)                 +
               MsgID(&MsgID)                   +
               MsgF(&MsgF)                     +
               SndMsgFLib(&MsgFLib)

    /* Prevent loop, just in case          */
    MonMsg     CPF0000

    SndPgmMsg  MsgID(&MsgID)                   +
               MsgF(&MsgFLib/&MsgF)            +
               MsgDta(&MsgDta)                 +
               MsgType(*ESCAPE)

    /* Prevent loop, just in case          */
    MonMsg     CPF0000
```

As you can see, USRFTPLOGC is a simple CL program that accepts the QIBM_QTMF_SVR_LOGON parameter values from format TCPL0100 and assembles a message which it then sends to an AS/400 message queue. Figure 7.3 shows a sample message queue display that might result from running the exit program.

FIGURE 7.3
Sample Display of FTP Server Log-on Requests

```
                           Display Messages

                                          System:    APPLSPEC
Queue . . . . . :    FTPSVRLOG        Program . . . . :    *DSPMSG
  Library . . . :      USRTCPIP         Library . . . :
Severity  . . . :    00               Delivery  . . . :    *HOLD

Type reply (if required), press Enter.
  FTP Logon MICHAEL From IP Addr 198.0.0.2 at 12:46:40 on 01/12/98
  FTP Logon QSECOFR From IP Addr 198.0.0.4 at 12:47:18 on 01/12/98
  FTP Logon FTPUSER From IP Addr 198.0.0.16 at 12:48:39 on 01/12/98








                                                         Bottom
 F3=Exit             F11=Remove a message            F12=Cancel
```

The message queue will contain a record of all FTP server logon requests. Although the output doesn't show whether the logon attempt was successful (because logging occurs before the FTP server performs the OS/400 logon check), it does show each attempt. This information is useful when you want to know who's been logging on to your FTP server. The displayed information includes the requester's user ID, IP address, and the time and date of the logon attempt.

Keep in mind that TCP/IP's limitations mean that none of this information is guaranteed to be true. A hacker can, for example, forge the originating IP address on the logon packet to make the logon attempt appear to originate from another location. However, for nondevious users, you can expect the information to be accurate.

Anonymous FTP

Anonymous FTP is a facility many sites employ to let users who are not known to the system access resources. This facility is used to distribute data that is not sensitive or confidential. The use of anonymous FTP essentially means that the information is available to the general public. This is especially true if the system is attached to the public Internet. Anonymous FTP can be a major benefit in allowing users access to your system, especially when the need exists to transfer standard information to all incoming users.

Anonymous users are generally limited to certain libraries or directories. They are also usually limited as to the type of commands they may use. For instance, to lock an anonymous user to a certain library, you can disable anonymous users' access to the commands that change directories or libraries. You may also wish to prohibit anonymous users from sending files to the AS/400 and from executing CL commands.

A word of caution: Anonymous FTP provides to unknown users an entry point into your system and its resources. Because validation with anonymous FTP is usually nonexistent, these unknown users will be able to obtain data from your system and, if you allow it, send data to your system. Be sure to carefully test your anonymous FTP access to ensure that unauthorized access to sensitive or confidential information is not possible.

The AS/400 supports anonymous FTP. That is, the AS/400 accepts a user ID of anonymous and requests the user's e-mail address as a password. This combination (user ID of anonymous and a password consisting of the e-mail address) is the standard across the Internet for anonymous FTP access. However, to enable anonymous FTP, the AS/400 also requires exit point programs for two FTP exit points: the QIBM_QTMF_SVR_LOGON server logon exit point and the QIBM_QTMF_SERVER_REQ request validation exit point. These exit points are used to ensure that the user accessing the system provides the appropriate password (e.g., an e-mail address) and that the incoming user can access only the files, libraries, and directories that you allow.

Allowing or prohibiting access to FTP commands is accomplished by examining the operation identifier in the VLRQ0100 format. To reiterate, these operation identifiers are

- 0 — session initialization
- 1 — creating a directory or library
- 2 — deleting a directory or library
- 3 — setting the current directory
- 4 — listing files
- 5 — deleting a file
- 6 — sending a file
- 7 — receiving a file
- 8 — renaming a file
- 9 — executing a CL command

To completely restrict anonymous users to a specific library or directory and let them only transfer files from the AS/400, you'll probably want to prohibit anonymous users from executing any FTP commands that establish an operation identifier of 1, 2, 3, 5, 6, 8, or 9. Allowing the commands that establish an operation identifier of 4 (listing files) and 7 (receiving a file) lets anonymous users list files in a specified library (or directory) and transfer files. Both the actions of prohibiting and allowing are done in the exit program associated with the QIBM_QTMF_SERVER_REQ exit point.

The first step in allowing anonymous access is to create a user profile for the anonymous FTP user. Use the CRTUSRPRF (Create User Profile) command:

```
CRTUSRPRF USRPRF(ANONYMOUS) PASSWORD(*NONE) +
          PWDEXPITV(*NONE)
```

This command establishes a user profile that cannot sign on to the system and that will not expire. IBM recommends that the anonymous user be unable to establish an interactive session.

Figures 7.4 and 7.5 show two sample programs for anonymous FTP access. These sample programs are rudimentary and should serve as a guide to developing your own programs — you should incorporate more error checking and security processing in your production anonymous FTP exit programs. CL program ANONYMOUS (Figure 7.4) allows an anonymous FTP user to access the system.

FIGURE 7.4

CL Program ANONYMOUS for Allowing
Anonymous FTP Users to Access the System

```
/* Program Name: ANONYMOUS Copyright 1998 Ryan Technology Resources  */
/* Purpose: This program enables an anonymous FTP user to sign on.   */
/*               Standard user will not be affected.                 */
/*               Exit point is QIBM_QTMF_SVR_LOGON.                  */
/*               Parameter format is TCPL0100.                       */
/* - - - - - - - - - - - - - - - - - - - - - - - - - - - - - - - - - */
/* Security:     Place in a secure library (i.e., PUBLIC(*EXCLUDE)). */
/*               Place source code in a secure library.             */
/*               Do not allow retrieval of CL source.                */
/* Compilation: CRTCLPGM PGM(ASecureLibrary/ANONYMOUS)      +       */
/*               SRCFILE(ASecureLibrary/QCLSRC)              +       */
/*               LOG(*NO)                                    +       */
/*               ALWRTVSRC(*NO)                              +       */
/*               AUT(*EXCLUDE)                                       */
/* - - - - - - - - - - - - - - - - - - - - - - - - - - - - - - - - - */

       Pgm    ( &P_AppID    +
                &P_User     +
                &P_UserLen  +
                &P_Pwd      +
                &P_PwdLen   +
                &P_IP       +
                &P_IPLen    +
                &P_RtnOut   +
                &P_UserOut  +
                &P_PwdOut   +
                &P_LibOut   )

   /* Parameters for exit point interface FORMAT TCPL0100          */

   /* Input parms */
     Dcl      &P_AppID     *CHAR   4    /* Application ID (%bin)    */
                                        /* 1 = FTP                  */
     Dcl      &P_User      *CHAR 999    /* User ID                  */
     Dcl      &P_UserLen   *CHAR   4    /* User ID length (%bin)    */
     Dcl      &P_Pwd       *CHAR 999    /* Password                 */
     Dcl      &P_PwdLen    *CHAR   4    /* Password length (%bin)   */
     Dcl      &P_IP        *CHAR  15    /* Requester IP address     */
     Dcl      &P_IPLen     *CHAR   4    /* IP address length  (%bin) */
     Dcl      &P_IPLen     *CHAR   4    /* IP address length  (%bin) */

   /* Output parms */
     Dcl      &P_RtnOut    *CHAR   4    /* Return code out          */
                                        /* Values are:              */
                                        /* 0=Reject                 */
                                        /* 1=Accept, w/Usrprf Curlib */
                                        /* 2=Accept, w/ &P_LibOut   */
                                        /* 3=Accept, w/UsrPrf Curlib */
                                        /*           and &P_UserOut  */
                                        /*           and &P_PwdOut   */
                                        /* 4=Accept, w/ &P_LibOut   */
                                        /*           and &P_UserOut  */
                                        /*           and &P_PwdOut   */
                                        /* 5=Accept, w/UsrPrf Curlib */
                                        /*           and &P_UserOut  */
                                        /*           Password bypass */
                                        /* 6=Accept, w/ P_LibOut    */
                                        /*           and &P_UserOut  */
                                        /*           Password bypass */
```

continued

FIGURE 7.4 *CONTINUED*

```
Dcl       &P_UserOut    *CHAR  10    /* User profile out  */
Dcl       &P_PwdOut     *CHAR  10    /* Password out      */
Dcl       &P_LibOut     *CHAR  10    /* Curlib out        */
/* End of FORMAT TCPL0100                                 */

/* Variables for binary conversions */
Dcl       &AppID        *DEC   (1 0)
Dcl       &UserLen      *DEC   (3 0)
Dcl       &PwdLen       *DEC   (3 0)
Dcl       &IPLen        *DEC   (3 0)

/* Misc. work variables              */
Dcl       &Accept       *DEC   1    Value(1)
Dcl       &Accept6      *DEC   1    Value(6)
Dcl       &Reject       *DEC   1    Value(0)
Dcl       &Index        *DEC   4    Value(0)
Dcl       &AnonymUC     *Char  9    Value('ANONYMOUS')
Dcl       &AnonymLC     *Char  9    Value('anonymous')
Dcl       &AnonLib      *Char  4    Value('ANON')

/* Monitor and ignore any error messages. */
MonMsg    (CPF0000 MCH0000)

 /* Convert binary numbers to decimal  */
 ChgVar    &AppID      %Bin(&P_AppID)
 ChgVar    &UserLen    %Bin(&P_UserLen)
 ChgVar    &PwdLen     %Bin(&P_PwdLen)
 ChgVar    &IPLen      %Bin(&P_IPLen)

 /* Initialize to accept any user. This is important for   */
 /* 'non-anonymous' users - standard users.                */
 ChgVar    %Bin(&P_RtnOut)   Value(&Accept)

 /* If the user has entered anonymous as a user id, force  */
 /* the user id to upper case, establish the library for   */
 /* them to use (only library ANON), and check for a valid */
 /* email ID as a password.                                */
 If (%sst(&P_User 1 9) *eq &AnonymUC *or +
     %sst(&P_User 1 9) *eq &AnonymLC) Then(Do)
   ChgVar &P_UserOut &AnonymUC
   ChgVar &P_LibOut  &AnonLib
   ChgVar %Bin(&P_RtnOut) &Reject

   /* If the length of the password is greater than 0, check */
   /* for an '@' sign in the password. If the password was   */
   /* not entered, or if there is no '@' sign, reject.       */
   If (&PwdLen *gt 0) Then(Do)

       ChgVar &Index 1

Loop:    If (%sst(&P_Pwd &Index 1) *eq '@') Then(Do)
          ChgVar %Bin(&P_RtnOut) &Accept6
          ChgVar &index &PwdLen
       EndDo
       ChgVar &Index (&Index + 1)
       If (&Index *lt &PwdLen) Goto Loop
       EndDo

     EndDo

     Return      /* Normal end of program */
```

CL Program VALIDATE for Limiting
Anonymous Access to a Specified Library

```
/* Program Name: VALIDATE  Copyright 1998 Ryan Technology Resources */
/* Purpose: This program restricts an anonymous FTP user to the     */
/*              operations of session initialization, listing files */
/*              in the ANON library, and transferring files from    */
/*              the ANON library. All other actions are rejected.   */
/*              Exit point is QIBM_QTMF_SERVER_REQ.                  */
/*              Parameter format is VLRQ0100.                        */
/* - - - - - - - - - - - - - - - - - - - - - - - - - - - - - - - -  */
/* Security:    Place in a secure library (i.e., PUBLIC(*EXCLUDE)). */
/*              Place source code in a secure library.              */
/*              Do not allow retrieval of CL source.                */
/* Compilation: CRTCLPGM PGM(ASecureLibrary/VALIDATE)        +      */
/*                       SRCFILE(ASecureLibrary/QCLSRC)      +      */
/*                       LOG(*NO)                            +      */
/*                       ALWRTVSRC(*NO)                      +      */
/*                       AUT(*EXCLUDE)                              */
/* - - - - - - - - - - - - - - - - - - - - - - - - - - - - - - - -  */

     Pgm    (  &P_AppID   +
               &P_OpID    +
               &P_UsrPrf  +
               &P_IPAddr  +
               &P_IPAdLn  +
               &P_OpInfo  +
               &P_OpInln  +
               &P_RtnCod  )

     /* Parameters for exit point interface format VLRQ0100          */

     /* Input parms */
     Dcl     &P_AppID    *CHAR    4    /* Application ID (%bin)      */
                                       /* 1 = FTP                    */
     Dcl     &P_OpID     *CHAR    4    /* Operation ID (%bin)        */
     Dcl     &P_UsrPrf   *CHAR   10    /* User ID                    */
     Dcl     &P_IPAddr   *CHAR  999    /* IP Address                 */
     Dcl     &P_IPAdLn   *CHAR    4    /* IP Address Length (%bin)   */
     Dcl     &P_OpInfo   *CHAR  999    /* Operation Information      */
     Dcl     &P_OpInLn   *CHAR    4    /* Operation Info Len (%bin)  */

     /* Output parms */
     Dcl     &P_RtnCod   *CHAR    4    /* Return code out (%bin)     */
                                       /* Values are:                */
                                       /* 0=Reject                   */
                                       /* 1=Accept                   */
     /* End of exit point interface format VLRQ0100                  */

     /* Variables for binary conversions */
     Dcl     &AppID      *DEC    (1 0)
     Dcl     &OpID       *DEC    (1 0)
     Dcl     &IPAdLn     *DEC    (3 0)
     Dcl     &OpInLn     *DEC    (3 0)

     /* Misc. work variables              */
     Dcl     &Anonym     *CHAR   10    VALUE('ANONYMOUS ')
     Dcl     &Accept     *DEC     1    Value(1)
     Dcl     &Reject     *DEC     1    Value(0)
```

continued

FIGURE 7.5 *CONTINUED*

```
/* Monitor and ignore any error messages.               */
  MonMsg    (CPF0000 MCH0000)

/* Convert binary numbers to decimal                    */
  ChgVar    &AppID    %Bin(&P_AppID)
  ChgVar    &OpID     %Bin(&P_OpID)
  ChgVar    &IPAdLn   %Bin(&P_IPAdLn)
  ChgVar    &OpInLn   %Bin(&P_OpInLn)

/* Initialize to accept any user. This is important for */
/* 'non-anonymous' users - standard users.              */
  ChgVar    %Bin(&P_RtnCod)   Value(&Accept)

/* Check for anonymous user.                            */
  If (&P_UsrPrf *eq &Anonym) Then(Do)

     /* If not a directory listing or a transfer from the */
     /* library (ANON), reject the request                */

     If ((&OpID *ne 4) *and (&OpID *ne 6)) Then(Do)
           ChgVar    %Bin(&P_RtnCod)   Value(&Reject)

     EndDo

  EndDo

Return     /* Normal end of program */
```

CL program VALIDATE (Figure 7.5) ensures that the user accesses only a certain library for specified functions. VALIDATE would be attached to the FTP server request validation exit point, QIBM_QTMF_SERVER_REQ. This exit program has no effect on standard users. VALIDATE determines whether the user is an anonymous FTP user. If so, the program ensures that the user can list and transfer files in library ANON only. This program does not have provisions for the IFS and lets users access only the specified functions. Allowing IFS access or access to additional functions is simply a matter of modifying the code to use directories and expanding the list of options. VALIDATE uses the parameter values from the VLRQ0100 format of exit point QIBM_QTMF_SERVER_REQ.

THE WSG EXIT POINT

The WSG lets a user with a Web browser access AS/400 applications. The WSG translates the 5250 data stream on the fly to HTML, enabling the Web browser to display traditional green-screen applications. The WSG exit point is used to allow a user to access an application on the AS/400 without signing on to the system. Of course, the application must take responsibility for ensuring that the incoming connection is from an authorized user. The exit point program determines the user profile that will be used for the session.

The syntax for the WSG is

http://*url:port*/WSG/QAPP0100? *operation_specific_parameter*

where *url* is the uniform resource locator for the Web site, *port* identifies the WSG port (5061 by default), WSG identifies the application, QAPP0100 is the WSG exit point format, and *operation_specific_parameter* is optional information to pass to the application.

The WSG exit point uses format QAPP0100, summarized in Table 7.4.

TABLE 7.4
Format QAPP0100

Field	Type	Format	Length (bytes)
Operation-specific parameter	Input	Character	Variable
Operation-specific parameter length	Input	Binary	4
Client IP address	Input	Character	15
CCSID	Input	Binary	4
Allow operation flag	Output	Character	1
User profile	Output	Character	10
Password	Output	Character	10
Current library	Output	Character	10
Program to call	Output	Character	10
Initial menu	Output	Character	10

The operation-specific parameter field is optional. When specified, it contains the parameters sent to the application called by the Web browser. These parameters may be used to identify the current library, the program to be called, or the initial menu. The operation-specific parameter length field contains the length of the operation-specific parameter.

The client IP address field contains the IP address for the incoming client connection.

The CCSID field contains the coded character set identifier, which is set to 500 for EBCDIC data.

The allow operation flag field can be one of two values:

- 0 indicates that the incoming request is refused and an error message is returned to the browser.
- 1 indicates that the incoming request is accepted. The exit program provides the information for the user profile, password, current library, program to call, and initial menu parameters.

The user profile field contains the profile to be used for the incoming connection. The exit program supplies this information. This parameter is required.

The password field holds the password to be used for the incoming connection. This parameter is also required, and the information is supplied by the exit program.

The current library field contains the name of the library (supplied by the exit program) to be used for the incoming connection. This parameter is optional; if not specified, the value in the user profile is used.

The program to call field contains the name of the program to be called for the incoming connection. The exit program supplies the information. This parameter is optional; if the program name is not specified, the value in the user profile is used.

The initial menu field contains the name of the menu to be used for the incoming connection. This information is supplied by the exit program. If this optional parameter is not specified, the value in the user profile is used.

You can use the WSG exit point to specify a current library, program, or initial menu to be called when a user accesses the AS/400 through the WSG facility. The associated exit point program will be called only when the syntax described above is used. In other words, a request such as http://*url:port*/WSG that does not include the exit point format will invoke standard WSG processing, displaying the sign-on screen and allowing the user to access the system through the standard methods. Specifying the QAPP0100 string (and

Tip!

OS/400 caches exit point programs in memory. When you're developing exit point programs for FTP, it's good practice to "bounce" the FTP servers by using the ENDTCPSVR SERVER(*FTP) (End TCP/IP Server) command to end the server and then STRTCPSVR SERVER(*FTP) (Start TCP/IP Server) to restart it. Bouncing the server ensures that any changes to exit programs will be recognized. Because the server is ended and restarted, the server must retrieve a fresh copy of the exit program when it is requested, thus ensuring that any changes you made to the exit program will be in effect the next time the exit program is used. This procedure is not required for all changes, but it may help you avoid unexpected results.

It's also a good idea to wait for a short time after the server has been started before using the exit program to ensure the initialization is complete. Attempting to access the FTP server before it has completed initialization causes the sign-on attempt to fail, which could be falsely construed to be an exit program error. Ensure that the FTP server is up and running (not in a transition state) before accessing the server, both when testing and in production. There is no good way of "knowing" when the server has completed initialization — it depends on the number of servers being started and the load on the system. However, you can check the QSYSWRK subsystem to ensure that the QTFTPnnnnn jobs are in an ACTIVE state.

optional parameters, separated from the QAPP0100 string with a question mark) as part of the request enables any registered exit point program to be called.

REGISTERING AN EXIT PROGRAM

After you write an exit program for a TCP/IP exit point, you must tell TCP/IP the name of the program and of the library in which it resides. This requires registering the exit program with the WRKREGINF command. Alternatively, you can use the ADDEXITPGM command to register an exit point in batch mode — the parameters are similar to the values entered on the WRKREGINF prompt. On the WRKREGINF prompt screen, page down to the exit point to which your program applies and enter option 8 (Work with exit programs). You then enter the name of the exit program on the screen. Press Enter after entering the exit program name, and bounce the FTP servers to ensure the new exit point program will be known to the system. Then, each time the FTP application reaches the exit point, your program is called.

Depending on the exit point, you may need to restart servers. Exit programs for FTP clients are effective with the next client session. However, adding an exit program for the FTP server requires you to end and restart the FTP servers by executing the ENDTCPSVR SVR(*FTP) and STRTCPSVR SVR(*FTP) commands. Exit programs associated with the WSG take effect as soon as they are registered.

EXIT POINT SECURITY

All exit programs (not just those associated with TCP/IP exit points) provide some type of additional processing. Some exit programs deal directly with system security. Others, such as the FTP exit programs, can bypass AS/400 password validation. Exit programs may also pose other security risks. For example, if the user profile for an FTP server job (which runs under the QTCP user profile) is not authorized to the registered exit program, the profile adopts authority sufficient to call the exit program. Exit programs and the registration facility must be protected from unauthorized users.

Exit programs can be protected with the following steps:

1. Create a secure library owned by QSECOFR with PUBLIC(*EXCLUDE) authority. The only private authority you should grant is *USE authority to user profile QTCP.

2. Create any needed source physical files in the secure library with PUBLIC(*EXCLUDE) authority.

3. Create your exit programs in the secure library with PUBLIC(*EXCLUDE).

4. Remove observability information.

5. Turn CL logging off.

6. Disallow the RTVCLSRC (Retrieve CL Source) command.

Another point to keep in mind is the AS/400's FTP security limitations. As with Telnet, anyone on the Internet can intercept FTP packets containing user IDs and passwords and use them to re-enter your system (a "password replay attack"). You might think FTP isn't as dangerous as Telnet because users are accessing only the files you make available for download — users don't have command access to your system. But the FTP RCMD subcommand lets an FTP user execute any command on the AS/400, making FTP as powerful as Telnet for breaking into your system.

Anyone who can gain access to your AS/400 via FTP can run the RCMD command to execute OS/400 commands under the QTCP user profile, unless you restrict use of the RCMD subcommand via a request validation exit program.

Portions of this chapter were adapted with permission from "Who's Accessing my FTP Server,"
(NEWS/400, June 1997) by Dan Riehl, a technical editor for NEWS/400 and president of Power-
Tech Toolworks.

Chapter 8

TCP/IP Management

Even the best-laid networking plans can go astray. The system administrator for an AS/400 that participates in a TCP/IP network must understand the tools and techniques available for network management. These tools are not traditional AS/400 tools, but tools that have been available in the TCP/IP networking community for years.

The AS/400 applies its object orientation and job-processing methods to managing TCP/IP and troubleshooting network problems. The QSYSWRK subsystem and the TCP/IP jobs that run in QSYSWRK are like any other subsystem and jobs on the AS/400, with the same considerations for memory, pool sizes, and queuing. Examining job logs and message queues (including QSYSOPR and QTCP) and working with the configuration status of lines all use standard AS/400 management methods.

The AS/400 also has industry-standard tools for managing a TCP/IP environment. The PING utility lets you determine whether a route exists to a remote system. The NETSTAT utility provides a great deal of information regarding the interface, routing, and connection. You can use Simple Network Management Protocol (SNMP) as well as third-party management tools for TCP/IP network management, but the AS/400 provides simple, familiar management tools you can use for a fairly high level of support.

In this chapter we cover the AS/400 commands for TCP/IP management. These commands include the WRKCFGSTS (Work with Configuration Status) command, PING, and NETSTAT. We look at problem identification and resolution in the context of standard AS/400 tools and TCP/IP-specific utilities.

TCP/IP TRAFFIC

In "The Client/Server Model" in Chapter 1, we discussed the client/server model used for TCP/IP. Essentially, the client/server model means that a system on the network (the client) establishes a connection with another system on the network (the server). Once the connection is established, packets flow between the two systems, generally with the client requesting services and the server satisfying the requests.

Because TCP/IP is based on a peer model, the roles of the client and server systems may (and often do) change. In other words, a server may request services of another system, thus taking on the role of a client. TCP/IP connections are not based on a hierarchy — any system (with the proper authorization) may request services of another system.

TCP/IP provides connectionless services, meaning that the connection between two nodes on a network is not fixed and packets can use different routes to the same destination. This connectionless feature of TCP/IP is both a blessing and a curse — although TCP/IP enables dynamic rerouting of packets in the event of a network failure, response time is not predictable.

The components of TCP/IP processing on the AS/400 include

- the TCP/IP jobs (running in QSYSWRK)
- the physical connection over the line (Ethernet or Token-Ring)
- the logical connection to the network
- optional SNMP services

We examine each component and identify its tools and system considerations.

TCP/IP Jobs

The AS/400 jobs that make up TCP/IP support are similar to any other job on the AS/400. They run in a subsystem, by default subsystem QSYSWRK. Depending on your configuration, TCP/IP jobs that may be in the QSYSWRK subsystem are shown in Table 8.1.

TABLE 8.1

TCP/IP Jobs in the QSYSWRK Subsystem

Job	Description
QAPPCTCP	provides APPC over TCP/IP (AnyNet) support
QTBOOTP	the bootstrap protocol server, used with network computers
QTCPIP	the controlling TCP/IP process
QTFTPxxxxx	File Transfer Protocol (FTP) servers
QTGTELNETS	the Telnet server (multiple QTGTELNETS jobs may be running in the subsystem)
QTRTDxxxxx	the RouteD server, used for Routing Information Protocol (RIP) support
QTRXCxxxxx	the REXEC server for remote execution processing
QTSMTPCLNT	the SMTP client process, used to receive SMTP packets from a remote mail server
QTSMTPSVSR	the SMTP server process, used to send SMTP packets to a remote mail server
QTSMTPBRCL	the SMTP bridge client, used to interact with SNADS
QTSMTPBRSR	the SMTP bridge server, used to interact with SNADS
QTTFTxxxxx	the Trivial FTP server, usually used with network computers
QTMSNMP	the SNMP server process
QTMSNMPRCV	the SNMP server process
QSNMPSA	the SNMP server process
QTLPDxxxxx	the Line Printer Daemon process for receiving print files from a remote host

continued

TABLE 8.1 *CONTINUED*

Job	Description
QTPOPxxxxx	the Post Office Protocol (POP) server
QTPPANSxxxxx	the Serial Line Internet Protocol (SLIP) support for dial-in (answer) connections
QTPPDIALxxxxx	SLIP support for dial-out (dial) connections
QTHTTxxxxx	the Hypertext Transfer Protocol (HTTP) server process
QTWSGxxxxx	the Workstation Gateway (WSG) server process

The *xxxxx* appended to some of the job names in Table 8.1 indicates that several processes of this type may be running in the subsystem. OS/400 automatically assigns a number suffix to the job name when a new server process is started. The number of server processes running concurrently depends on the number of automatically started processes specified in the server attributes, the number of processes started manually with the STRTCPSVR (Start TCP/IP Services) command, and the number of processes started by OS/400 to accommodate incoming requests or system load.

Figure 8.1 shows a sample WRKSBSJOB (Work with Subsystem Jobs) display for subsystem QSYSWRK with several TCP/IP jobs running.

FIGURE 8.1
Work with Subsystem Jobs for QSYSWRK

```
                       Work with Subsystem Jobs                 S1029F3R
                                                     05/25/98  14:11:36
   Subsystem  . . . . . . . . . . :    QSYSWRK

   Type options, press Enter.
     2=Change   3=Hold   4=End   5=Work with   6=Release   7=Display message
     8=Work with spooled files   13=Disconnect


   Opt  Job        User      Type      -----Status-----  Function
    _   QPASVRS    QSYS      BATCH     ACTIVE            PGM-QPASVRS
    _   QTCPIP     QTCP      BATCH     ACTIVE
    _   QTFTP00948 QTCP      BATCH     ACTIVE
    _   QTFTP01062 QTCP      BATCH     ACTIVE
    _   QTFTP02638 QTCP      BATCH     ACTIVE
    _   QTGTELNETS QTCP      BATCH     ACTIVE
    _   QTWSG05070 QTMTWSG   BATCH     ACTIVE
    _   QTWSG05183 QTMTWSG   BATCH     ACTIVE
                                                                  More...
   Parameters or command
   ===>
   F3=Exit    F4=Prompt   F5=Refresh   F9=Retrieve   F11=Display schedule data
   F12=Cancel
```

One of the jobs that is running, aptly named QTCPIP, is the controlling TCP/IP job. In addition, three FTP jobs have been started — this is the default number of jobs specified in the FTP attributes. One Telnet server process —

QTGTELNETS — is running. It handles all incoming Telnet requests for the AS/400. The WSG process initiated three jobs by default when the WSG process started (the third one would appear if you pressed Roll up (Page down) from the Work with Subsystem Jobs display in Figure 8.1).

Other jobs are also executed in the QSYSWRK subsystem. These jobs include the Mail Server Framework (MSF) job, QMSF, which must be started to enable SMTP and POP3 processing. OS/400 normally starts this job automatically. In addition, the QSNADS subsystem must be operational with the QSMTPQ distribution queue and the TCPIP routing table entry configured.

The jobs that accompany QTCPIP in Figure 8.1 are started in two ways:

- automatically, when the STRTCP (Start TCP/IP) command is issued
- manually, through the use of the STRTCPSVR (Start TCP/IP Server) command

Automatically starting the TCP/IP jobs when the STRTCP command is issued requires that the configuration for the TCP/IP function include the AUTOSTART(*YES) parameter. TCP/IP functions that can be autostarted are FTP, Telnet, SMTP, SNMP, LPD, HTTP, WSG, and POP.

You should start only those TCP/IP functions you need in your environment. There are two reasons for being judicious in starting jobs: to decrease security exposure by offering fewer opportunities to exploit potential security holes, and to avoid wasting system resources monitoring jobs that are not being used. I suggest that you automatically start (by specifying AUTOSTART(*YES)) only the jobs that will be used for core processing and manually start other functions as required.

You can manually start TCP/IP functions by using the STRTCPSVR command. Options for the SERVER parameter are *SNMP, *TELNET, *FTP, *SMTP, *LPD, *HTTP, *WSG, and *POP. The only TCP/IP servers that can be restarted are HTTP, DNS, and DHCP. The restart capability is especially handy when configuring the HTTP server on the AS/400.

Starting the TCP/IP functions starts the associated servers in subsystem QSYSWRK. The job log for QTCPIP (Figure 8.2) shows that the QTCPIP job starts the TCP/IP interface. The interface defines the server's IP address and the associated line. The AS/400 is multihoming: there may be multiple IP addresses for a given interface, and there may be multiple interfaces in a single AS/400 system.

The interface may also be autostarted. If you plan to use TCP/IP as part of your normal networking processes, autostart the interface at IPL. Adding or changing the interface (through the CFGTCP (Configure TCP/IP), ADDTCPIFC (Add TCP/IP Interface), or CHGTCPIFC (Change TCP/IP Interface) command)

FIGURE 8.2
QTCPIP Job Log

```
                          Display Job Log
                                              System:   S1029F3R
 Job . . :   QTCPIP        User . . :   QTCP        Number . . . :   003374

     Job 003374/QTCP/QTCPIP started on 05/18/98 at 15:30:39 in subsystem
       QSYSWRK in QSYS. Job entered system on 05/18/98 at 15:30:26.
     Job 003374/QTCP/QTCPIP submitted.
     QTCPIP job started.
     127.0.0.1 interface started.
     Network server currently being varied on for resource LIN02
     Vary command may not have completed.
     198.0.0.20 interface not started.
     Network server RTRNWS not in the correct state.
     Controller ETHLINET currently on-line.
     Device ETHLITCP currently on-line.
     QTCPIP job starting 198.0.0.20 interface.
     198.0.0.20 interface started.

                                                           Bottom
 Press Enter to continue.

 F3=Exit    F5=Refresh    F10=Display detailed messages    F12=Cancel
 F16=Job menu            F24=More keys
```

lets you specify AUTOSTART(*YES) to automatically start the interface. If needed, the associated line is started when the interface is started.

Other jobs that run in QSYSWRK are the host server jobs. These jobs control host server functions and work with incoming requests that require sockets, such as IPX support. The host server jobs are not needed with TCP/IP. However, because other functions (notably Client Access/400) often need the host servers, I usually start both TCP/IP and the host servers at IPL. A convenient place to start the servers is in the system startup program. The IBM documentation describes the startup program in detail, but basically it is a CL program started up on IPL. The startup program is referenced by system value QSTRUPPGM. To start TCP/IP and the host servers, simply place the following commands in the startup program:

```
STRTCP
STRHOSTSVR SERVER(*ALL)
```

(Note that in V4R2, the STRHOSTSVR command is automatically executed when the STRTCP command is issued.) Depending on the amount of time your system takes to vary on lines and perform internal housekeeping tasks, you may need to introduce delays (with the DLYJOB (Delay Job) command) to ensure that tasks are finished.

In addition to the QTCPIP job log in Figure 8.2, you can look for TCP/IP initiation information in the QTCP message queue. Figure 8.3 shows a display of the messages through the DSPMSG (Display Message) command for the jobs shown in Figure 8.1.

FIGURE 8.3
QTCP Message Queue Display

```
                            Display Messages
                                            System:    S1029F3R
 Queue . . . . . :   QTCP             Program . . . . :   *DSPMSG
   Library . . . :     QUSRSYS          Library . . . :
 Severity . . . :   00               Delivery  . . . :   *HOLD

 Type reply (if required), press Enter.
   Job 002206/QTCP/QTCPIP ended abnormally.
   Job 002217/QTCP/QTFTP00971 ended abnormally.
   Job 002209/QTCP/QTFTP02492 ended abnormally.
   Job 002218/QTCP/QTFTP01069 ended abnormally.
   Job 002219/QTCP/QTGTELNETS ended abnormally.
   STRTCP issued by job 003333/QPGMR/QSTRUPJD.
   Not able to determine if job 003374/QTCP/QTCPIP started.
   QTCPIP job started.
   127.0.0.1 interface started.
   198.0.0.20 interface not started.
   STRTCP completed successfully.
   QTCPIP job starting 198.0.0.20 interface.
   198.0.0.20 interface started.
                                                          Bottom

 F3=Exit            F11=Remove a message          F12=Cancel
 F13=Remove all     F16=Remove all except unanswered  F24=More keys
```

Troubleshooting Jobs That Aren't Running

The TCP/IP jobs in the QSYSWRK subsystem must be running to enable TCP/IP processing. At a minimum, the QTCPIP job must be executing, but other jobs are also usually running to provide support for the different services. If the TCP/IP services you want to enable are not functioning, make sure the appropriate job is running in this subsystem.

If a server process has been running but no longer functions and cannot be seen when displaying the jobs in the QSYSWRK subsystem, check the job log for the missing process. By default, job logs go to the QEZJOBLOG output queue. If this default has been changed for your installation, the job logs will go to the output queue specified in the QPJOBLOG printer file definition. Attempt to identify the problem by examining the job log.

THE PHYSICAL CONNECTION

The physical connection is perhaps the easiest part of the TCP/IP process to manage. The physical connection in most cases uses a LAN line, such as an Ethernet or Token-Ring line. An asynchronous line may also be used for SLIP or PPP support. In any case, the command to manage the physical connection is the WRKCFGSTS (Work with Configuration Status) command. You can either specify the name of the line (WRKCFGSTS *LIN *linename*) or issue the command without specifying a line to see a list of all lines.

Figure 8.4 shows a sample of the WRKCFGSTS *LIN command.

FIGURE 8.4
Work with Configuration Status — Line

```
                         Work with Configuration Status              S1029F3R
                                                         05/25/98   14:16:14
     Position to  . . . . .                   Starting characters

     Type options, press Enter.
       1=Vary on   2=Vary off    5=Work with job   8=Work with description
       9=Display mode status    13=Work with APPN status...

     Opt  Description      Status          -------------Job--------------
       _    ETHLINE         ACTIVE
       _      ETHLINET      ACTIVE
       _        ETHLITCP    ACTIVE          QTCPIP       QTCP        003374
       _    QESLINE         VARIED OFF
       _    QTILINE         VARIED OFF
       _    Q1PLIN          VARIED OFF
       _    RTRPPP          VARIED OFF
       _      RTRPPNET      VARIED OFF
       _        RTRPPTCP    VARIED OFF
                                                                     Bottom
     Parameters or command
     ===>
     F3=Exit    F4=Prompt    F12=Cancel    F23=More options   F24=More keys

     Intermediate assistance level used.
```

This example shows the Ethernet line (ETHLINE) in an active state. The network controller (ETHLINET) and network device (ETHLITCP) are also active. This is the state that enables communications across a LAN line. Note the job associated with line ETHLINE — the QTCPIP job that is running in subsystem QSYSWRK. When TCP/IP is activated (using the STRTCP command), the interface associated with a line is also activated, starting the QTCPIP job and associating the job with the line.

Other states may also be displayed on the WRKCFGSTS screen (Table 8.2).

TABLE 8.2
WRKCFGSTS States

State	Description
Active	Appears when the line is enabled for communications.
Connect pending	May appear when an asynchronous line is being used for SLIP communications.
Damaged	Appears when the communication object (the description) has been damaged. You must usually re-create the object.
Failed	Means the communication object has failed, usually because of a microcode loading error. Vary the device off and back on to attempt to recover from this error.
RCYxxx	Either RCYPND (recovery pending) or RCYCNL (recovery cancelled). These states often indicate a physical problem, such as a cabling problem.
Varied off	The communication object is varied off. Vary the object on to enable communications.
Varied on	The communication object is in a state to communicate with another system, but is not connected to the other system.

There may be other communications object states; check the appropriate IBM documentation for more information. The *OS/400 Communication Management* (SC41-5406-00) manual defines the various configuration states, and the *OS/400 Communication Configuration* (SC41-5401-00) manual describes the configuration of communications objects on the AS/400.

Troubleshooting with WRKCFGSTS

The WRKCFGSTS display is a good place to start troubleshooting a networking problem. Ensure the status of the line is active and the QTCPIP job is associated with the line. Check the obvious potential physical problems before troubleshooting the rest of the connection. Common physical problems you may run across include a bad connection, lack of termination on a network segment, a hub that is not connected to the network, and network components (e.g., wiring, hubs, repeaters) that are close to sources of electrical energy (such as flourescent lights or an electric motor).

THE LOGICAL CONNECTION

The logical connection — the connection formed by stations communicating over the network — comprises a number of different components. The most important component of the logical connection is the ability to send packets, correctly routed, from the source to the destination. An obvious indication of a properly functioning logical connection is a successful service, such as a successful Telnet connection or a successful file transfer. However, sometimes a connection cannot be made. The PING and NETSTAT utilities can help find problems in logical connections.

PING

Testing the logical connection is simple with an AS/400 or any device that supports TCP/IP and has the PING utility. PING (Packet InterNetwork Groper) is used to verify a TCP/IP connection and uses the Internet Control Message Protocol (ICMP). PING essentially sends an ICMP packet to the remote system and, if the connection is successful, receives a return reply. Based on the time the packet was sent and the time it was returned, PING calculates the time for the round trip. This is valuable for two reasons.

If the packet never returns, we know there is no route from the source to the destination system and back again. This does not mean that TCP/IP is not configured correctly; it may very well mean that the routing is not established properly. In addition, the routing from the source system to the destination system may be correct, but the routing from the destination system back to the source system may be wrong.

If the packet does make a successful round trip, the time that it takes to make the round trip may be excessive. A troubleshooting technique is to monitor the time it takes to make a round trip from the source system to a remote system. If the round trip time is significantly different from the average observed times, you may need to examine your network for potential performance or bottleneck problems.

Tip!

One of the first things I do after configuring a system for TCP/IP communications is to ping myself. In other words, I use the PING command and ping the address (or name) of the newly configured system. When the PING command is successful, I know I've configured TCP/IP correctly. A successful PING doesn't necessarily indicate that the system is properly configured to communicate in the network (routing and DNS issues may remain), but it does indicate the TCP/IP protocol is loaded properly.

The AS/400 command to ping a system is VFYTCPCNN (Verify TCP/IP Connection) or, more simply, PING. Both the OS/400 command syntax version (VFTTCPCNN) and the Unix command syntax version (PING) invoke the same program. Entering VFYTCPCNN or PING produces the display shown in Figure 8.5.

FIGURE 8.5
PING Command Display

```
                    Verify TCP/IP Connection (PING)

Type choices, press Enter.

Remote system  . . . . . . . . . RMTSYS



Remote internet address  . . . . INTNETADR

                      Additional Parameters

Message mode:                    MSGMODE
  Response message detail  . . .               *VERBOSE
  Summary, if response errors  .               *COMP
Packet length (in bytes) . . . . PKTLEN        256
Number of packets  . . . . . . . NBRPKT        5
Wait time (in seconds) . . . . . WAITTIME      1
Local internet address . . . . . LCLINTNETA    *ANY
Type of service  . . . . . . . . TOS           *NORMAL
                                                           More...
F3=Exit   F4=Prompt   F5=Refresh   F12=Cancel   F13=How to use this display
F24=More keys
```

The first parameter, RMTSYS, identifies the remote system to ping. You can enter a system name, the special value *INTNETADR (indicating an IP address will be specified), or an IP address as a value for this parameter. The system name specified for this parameter must be found in the host table or in a DNS lookup. Specifying *INTNETADR requires an IP address to be specified in a succeeding prompt. If you specify an IP address for this parameter, the address must be enclosed in apostrophes.

The Remote internet address (INTNETADR) parameter is displayed when you specify *INTNETADR for the RMTSYS parameter. Enter the dotted decimal notation for the address of the remote system with which you want to verify the connection.

The Message mode (MSGMODE) parameter determines how much information is returned. The default value, *VERBOSE, returns a message for every ping, while the *QUIET value returns only the initial and summary messages.

The length of the ICMP packet is determined by the Packet length (PKTLEN) parameter. The default value of 256 bytes is sufficient for most cases. The allowable range is from 8 to 512 bytes.

The Number of packets (NBRPKT) parameter identifies the number of packets that should be sent in this PING transmission. The allowable values are from 1 to 999. The default value of 5 is usually more than enough to determine whether a remote system is reachable and to measure the round trip time. If you are having intermittent network connection problems, you may want to ping the remote system more than five times.

The Wait time (WAITTIME) parameter determines the amount of time to wait before an unreturned packet is considered lost. The default time is 1 second, with a maximum of 600 seconds. For most network connections, including Internet connections, the ping time should be considerably less than 1 second. However, with remote systems that are far away (in terms of routing), you may want to increase this value.

The Local internet address (LCLINTNETA) parameter identifies the local IP address from which to ping. The default value of *ANY, meaning any IP address, is usually sufficient. You may wish to specify the local IP address if your system has multiple network interface cards (NIC) and you wish to test the connectivity between a specific local interface and a device on the network.

The Type of service (TOS) parameter specifies the type of service to be used. Many routers and hosts do not use TOS. The default is usually appropriate.

Although the PING command has several parameters, most uses of PING merely specify the remote system (or IP address) to ping. Figure 8.6 shows the result of a simple PING command from an AS/400 to a PC on the local network.

FIGURE 8.6
Ping from AS/400 to a Windows 95 PC

```
                        Command Entry                          S1029F3R
                                           Request level:    6
Previous commands and messages:
   > ping aptiva
     Verifying connection to host system APTIVA at address 198.0.0.2.
     PING request 1 from 198.0.0.2 took 5 ms. 256 bytes. TTL 32.
     PING request 2 from 198.0.0.2 took 4 ms. 256 bytes. TTL 32.
     PING request 3 from 198.0.0.2 took 4 ms. 256 bytes. TTL 32.
     PING request 4 from 198.0.0.2 took 11 ms. 256 bytes. TTL 32.
     PING request 5 from 198.0.0.2 took 4 ms. 256 bytes. TTL 32.
     Round-trip (in milliseconds) min/avg/max = 4/5/11
     Connection verification statistics: 5 of 5 successful (100 %).


                                                              Bottom
Type command, press Enter.
===> _____



F3=Exit   F4=Prompt   F9=Retrieve   F10=Include detailed messages
F11=Display full      F12=Cancel    F13=Information Assistant   F24=More keys
```

As you can see from the response, the minimum time round trip time was 4 milliseconds, the average time was 5 milliseconds, and the maximum time was 11 milliseconds. The PING command also shows that 5 out of 5 pings were successful.

The AS/400 can ping a system on the network, and a network system can ping the AS/400. Figure 8.7 shows the result of a Win95 PC pinging an AS/400 on the Internet.

Ping from Win95 PC to AS/400 on the Internet

```
C:\WINDOWS>ping lcc

Pinging LCC [198.109.144.21] with 32 bytes of data:

Reply from 198.109.144.21: bytes=32 time=310ms TTL=64
Reply from 198.109.144.21: bytes=32 time=320ms TTL=64
Request timed out.
Reply from 198.109.144.21: bytes=32 time=290ms TTL=64
```

In this example, the round trip time is much longer (an average of 306 milliseconds), and at least one ping timed out. Because TCP/IP is a connectionless protocol and packets are retransmitted if the original transmission fails, the fact that a packet timed out is not a major concern. However, you can see that communications with a remote system will be slower and require more retries than communications with a local system.

NETSTAT Utility

The NETSTAT program is used for network statistics. Just as with the PING command, there is an AS/400 syntax version and a Unix syntax version. The Unix version is NETSTAT, while the AS/400 command is WRKTCPSTS (Work with TCP/IP Status). Using either command (and the default *SELECT parameter) displays the screen shown in Figure 8.8.

The network statistics you can view are

- TCP/IP interface status
- TCP/IP route information
- TCP/IP connection status

You can view these statistics directly without going through the selection screen by using the *IFC (interface status), *RTE (route information), or *CNN (connection status) parameter with the NETSTAT command.

FIGURE 8.8
NETSTAT Command Display

```
                  Work with TCP/IP Network Status
                                              System:    S1029F3R
   Select one of the following:

        1. Work with TCP/IP interface status
        2. Display TCP/IP route information
        3. Work with TCP/IP connection status




   Selection or command
   ===> _____

 F3=Exit    F4=Prompt    F9=Retrieve    F12=Cancel
```

TCP/IP Interface Status
The Work with TCP/IP Interface Status display is shown in Figure 8.9.

FIGURE 8.9
Work with TCP/IP Interface Status Display

```
                  Work with TCP/IP Interface Status
                                              System:    S1029F3R
   Type options, press Enter.
     5=Display details   8=Display associated routes   9=Start   10=End
    12=Work with configuration status   14=Display multicast groups

         Internet        Network          Line        Interface
   Opt   Address         Address       Description     Status
    _    127.0.0.1       127.0.0.0      *LOOPBACK      Active
    _    198.0.0.20      198.0.0.0      ETHLINE        Active




                                                              Bottom
   F3=Exit    F4=Prompt    F5=Refresh   F11=Display line information   F12=Cancel
   F13=Sort by column    F24=More keys
```

This display shows the interfaces currently configured on the system, including
the loopback interface. Options available on this display include displaying the

details of the interface, displaying the routes associated with the interface, starting or ending the interface (with the STRTCPIFC (Start TCP/IP Interface) or ENDTCPIFC (End TCP/IP Interface) command, respectively), and working with the configuration status (WRKCFGSTS) of the associated line. You can also display routing data with this option, but I think the second NETSTAT option (Display TCP/IP route information) provides better information.

Displaying the details of the interface is helpful for problem determination and documentation. Figure 8.10 shows a sample of the details provided for an Ethernet line interface.

FIGURE 8.10

TCP/IP Interface Details

```
                    Display TCP/IP Interface Status
                                                System:    S1029F3R
Interface host name . . . . . . . . . . . . . :  AS400E.RYANTECH.COM
Internet address  . . . . . . . . . . . . . . :  198.0.0.20
  Subnet mask . . . . . . . . . . . . . . . . :   255.255.255.0
  Network address . . . . . . . . . . . . . . :   198.0.0.0
  Host address  . . . . . . . . . . . . . . . :   0.0.0.20
  Directed broadcast address  . . . . . . . . :   198.0.0.255

Interface status  . . . . . . . . . . . . . . :  Active
Change date/time  . . . . . . . . . . . . . . :  05/18/98  15:29:50
Line description  . . . . . . . . . . . . . . :  ETHLINE
Line type . . . . . . . . . . . . . . . . . . :  *ELAN
Type of service . . . . . . . . . . . . . . . :  *NORMAL
Maximum transmission unit . . . . . . . . . . :  1492
Automatic start . . . . . . . . . . . . . . . :  *YES




Press Enter to continue.

F3=Exit    F6=Print    F12=Cancel    F22=Display entire field
```

The display shows the name of the host associated with the interface and the interface's IP address and subnet mask. Also shown are the network and host addresses, which indicate the relationship between the network portion and the host portion of the IP address. The broadcast address indicates the address used to broadcast a message to all devices on the network. The display also includes information about the interface status, the date and time the interface was last changed, the associated line description, the type of line, the type of service, the size of the maximum transmission unit (MTU), and whether the interface will start automatically when the STRTCP command is issued.

The interface status bears some additional explanation. We know that the WRKCFGSTS command displays the status of the physical communication configuration object, usually the line. The interface status display shows the status of the logical interface. The possible status indicators for the logical interface are shown in Table 8.3.

Table 8.3
Logical Interface Status Indicators

Indicator	Description
Active	The interface is active and available to process TCP/IP requests.
Ending	The ENDTCPIFC command has been issued, and the interface is changing to an inactive state.
Failed	A physical error has occurred with the associated line description, and the line has failed.
Failed (TCP)	An error has been detected in the TCP/IP protocol stack Vertical Licensed Internal Code (VLIC). You can end TCP/IP (ENDTCP) and then restart it (STRTCP) in an attempt to recover from this error.
Inactive	The interface has not been started.
RCYxxx	A physical error has occurred with the associated line description.
Starting	The interface has been started and is becoming active.

As I mentioned, it's a good idea to print the interface status for documentation purposes. The printout shows the same information as the display and can be filed away as a record of the addressing information.

TCP/IP Route Information

The TCP/IP route information display is shown in Figure 8.11.

Figure 8.11
TCP/IP Route Information

```
                    Display TCP/IP Route Information
                                                  System:    S1029F3R
   Type options, press Enter.
     5=Display details

         Route             Subnet            Next            Route
   Opt   Destination       Mask              Hop             Available
    _    127.0.0.0         255.0.0.0         *DIRECT           *YES
    _    198.0.0.0         255.255.255.0     *DIRECT           *YES
    _    224.0.0.0         240.0.0.0         *DIRECT           *YES




                                                                 Bottom
   F3=Exit    F5=Refresh      F6=Print list    F9=Command line
   F11=Display route type     F12=Cancel       F13=Sort by column    F24=More keys
```

This display shows the routes known to the AS/400. The information is contained in the AS/400's internal routing tables. Two routes will always be shown:

- a route for the loopback network (127.0.0.0), which will be a direct connection
- a route for the network to which the AS/400 is attached, which also will be a direct connection

Another route also commonly shown (although not on this figure) is the default route, indicated by a route destination of *DFTROUTE. The default route may or may not be a direct connection. Other routes may be shown on the display if the AS/400 is in a routed environment.

Information provided on the Route Information display includes

- the route destination. This is usually a network address but could also be the address of a specific remote system. The possible route destinations are
  — a directly attached network or subnetwork
  — a host system
  — a remote subnetwork
  — a remote network
  — a default route
- the subnet mask of the destination network, subnetwork, or system.
- the next hop IP address. This will have one of two types of values:
  — a value of *DIRECT, meaning that the destination is on the same network as the AS/400
  — the IP address of the router that will route packets to the destination network, subnetwork, or, system
- a route available indication. A value of *YES indicates that the router (or network if directly connected) is active and available. A value of *NO indicates that the route is not available, possibly due to an inactive interface or a nonfunctioning router. IBM indicates that a router in the process of becoming available may not be immediately available to the AS/400 and recommends that you ping the router to cause the system to recognize it.

To obtain more detailed route information, select option 5 for the desired route to produce a display like the one in Figure 8.12. The detailed information is divided into two sections: information about the route and information about the local interface. The local interface information is the same information

FIGURE 8.12
Detailed Route Information

```
                     Display TCP/IP Route Details
                                             System:    S1029F3R
Route information:
  Route destination . . . . . . . . . . . . :   198.0.0.0
  Subnet mask . . . . . . . . . . . . . . . :   255.255.255.0
  Next hop host name  . . . . . . . . . . . :   AS400E.RYANTECH.COM
  Next hop  . . . . . . . . . . . . . . . . :   *DIRECT
  Type of service . . . . . . . . . . . . . :   *NORMAL
  Route available . . . . . . . . . . . . . :   *YES
  Route type  . . . . . . . . . . . . . . . :   *DIRECT
  Route source  . . . . . . . . . . . . . . :   *CFG
  Change date/time  . . . . . . . . . . . . :   05/25/98  11:05:11
  Route maximum transmission unit . . . . . :   1492
  Reference count . . . . . . . . . . . . . :   0

Local interface information:
  Internet address  . . . . . . . . . . . . :   198.0.0.20
    Subnet mask . . . . . . . . . . . . . . :     255.255.255.0
    Network address . . . . . . . . . . . . :     198.0.0.0
                                                        More...
Press Enter to continue.

F3=Exit    F6=Print    F12=Cancel    F22=Display entire field
```

provided in the Interface Status section (see above). The route information consists of the same route destination, subnet mask, next hop, and route available information that appears on the main display, plus the following detail information:

- Next hop host name — the name of the host that provides the route. This may be the name of the AS/400 if the next hop is *DIRECT.

- Type of service — the TOS value.

- Route type — the type of destination to which packets are being routed. Possible values are *DIRECT, for routing to a direct connection to a local network or subnetwork; *HOST, for routing to a specific remote host; *SUBNET, for routing to a remote subnetwork; *NET, for routing to a remote network; and *DFTROUTE, for default routing.

- Route source — the method used to determine the routing information. *CFG indicates that the routing information was manually configured (a static route) through the use of the ADDTCPRTE (Add TCP/IP Route) command or the CFGTCP menu, option 2. A value of *ICMP indicates that the route was learned through ICMP redirection. *SNMP means that the route was discovered through SNMP.

- Change date/time — indicates when the routing table information was last updated. This can be valuable information, especially if a route cannot be found.

- Route maximum transmission unit — identifies the MTU value for the route. This information is either specified (if the route source is *CFG) or learned from the network.

- Reference count — the number of references to this route in the routing table cache.

The Route Information detail display is valuable for determining whether a route exists in the AS/400 routing table. For instance, assume an attempted connection with a remote system is unsuccessful. Your next step might be to ping the remote system to determine whether it is reachable. If the ping is unsuccessful, you can examine the routing table to determine whether a route exists to the remote system. Depending on the routing table information, your troubleshooting path can take you in different directions. If the route is available, the problem might be in the TCP/IP configuration of the remote system, the routing on the remote system (back to the source system), or invalid routing information. If the route is not available, direct your attention to the routers and lines in the network that are logically between the source and the destination systems.

TCP/IP Connection Status

The connection status display (Figure 8.13) gives you access to perhaps the most valuable information NETSTAT provides.

FIGURE 8.13
TCP/IP Connection Status

```
                   Work with TCP/IP Connection Status
                                                    System:    S1029F3R
     Local internet address . . . . . . . . . . . :    *ALL

     Type options, press Enter.
       4=End    5=Display details

           Remote          Remote      Local
     Opt   Address         Port        Port       Idle Time  State
           *               *           ftp-con >  167:14:43  Listen
       _   *               *           telnet     003:41:04  Listen
       _   *               *           as-svrmap  003:41:35  Listen
       _   *               *           1026       167:11:00  Listen
       _   *               *           1027       167:11:00  Listen
       _   *               *           1028       167:10:49  Listen
       _   *               *           1029       167:10:49  Listen
       _   *               *           1030       167:10:49  Listen
       _   *               *           1031       167:10:49  Listen
       _   *               *           1032       167:10:49  Listen
       _   *               *           1033       167:10:49  Listen
       _                                                             More...
     F5=Refresh   F11=Display byte counts   F13=Sort by column
     F14=Display port numbers   F22=Display entire field   F24=More keys
```

The initial connection status display shows the remote address, the remote port, the local port, the idle time, and the state of the local port.

The Remote Address column shows either the IP address of the remote system or an asterisk (*) if the local port is listening for a connection. The Remote Port column shows the TCP/IP port (or port name) of the remote system, if connected, or an asterisk if the local port is waiting for a connection. The Local Port column shows the TCP/IP port (or port name) of the local system. This is the port at which the local system is either connected or listening for a connection. The Idle Time column shows the amount of time since the last activity on the port. The timer starts from the last activity or when the process was started.

The State column shows the state of the local port's connection. Common states and their meanings for a local port are shown below:

- Listen — the AS/400 is listening at the local port for an incoming connection.

- Established — the connection is established and the systems are communicating.

- Closed — the connection has ended.

Other states may be seen during a transition period. These states, which involve sending and receiving acknowledgments to end the connection, include SYN-sent, SYN-received, FIN-wait-1, FIN-wait-2, Close-wait, Closing, Last-ACK, and Time-wait.

The ports (both remote and local) can use well-known names rather than a port number. Remember that TCP/IP server processes listen at certain ports for an incoming connection request. All ports have a specific port number, and well-known ports may also have a name. These names are defined in the service table, which can be modified with the WRKSRVTBLE (Work with Service Table Entries) command. Table 8.4 shows some of the more common default service table entries (well-known name, port, and function) on the AS/400. This is not a complete list. Other well-known names and ports, such as ports for IPX and UDP traffic, may be in the service table.

TABLE 8.4
Common Ports Defined in the Service Table

Service Table Entry	Port	Function
as-central	8470	AS/400 central server
as-database	8471	AS/400 database server
as-dtaq	8472	AS/400 data queue server

continued

TABLE **8.4** *CONTINUED*

Service Table Entry	Port	Function
as-file	8473	AS/400 file server
as-netdrive	8477	AS/400 network drive server
as-netprt	8474	AS/400 network printing server
as-pop3	5110	AS/400 POP3 server
as-rmtcmd	8475	AS/400 remote command server
as-signon	8476	AS/400 sign-on server
as-svrmap	449	AS/400 server mapper
as-transfer	8478	AS/400 transfer server
as-vrtprint	8479	AS/400 virtual printer server
domain	53	Domain Name Service
finger	79	Finger
ftp-control	21	FTP control processing
ftp-data	20	FTP data transfer
lpd	515	Line Printer Daemon
netstat	15	NETSTAT
pop3	110	Post Office Protocol
smtp	25	Simple Mail Transfer Protocol
snmp	161	Simple Network Management Protocol
snmp-trap	162	Simple Network Management Protocol — Traps
telnet	23	Telnet
wsg	5061	Workstation Gateway
www	80	World Wide Web (HTTP)
APPCoverTCPIP	397	AnyNet

Pressing F11 from the connection status screen (Figure 8.13) displays the byte count for the different ports (Figure 8.14).

Displaying the details of a connection (using option 5) provides a wealth of information — three screens' worth. The first screen shows the details of the connection (Figure 8.15).

Tip!

The TCP/IP Connection Status with Byte Counts display is an important troubleshooting aid. If the connection is active and data is being transferred, pressing F5 to refresh the screen should show a change in the byte counts. A connection with an unchanging byte count probably means a recently broken connection (that the system has not yet discovered), a network problem, or a problem at the remote system.

FIGURE 8.14
TCP/IP Connection Status with Byte Counts

```
                    Work with TCP/IP Connection Status
                                                 System:    S1029F3R
  Local internet address . . . . . . . . . . :    *ALL

  Type options, press Enter.
    4=End    5=Display details

        Remote          Remote      Local
  Opt   Address         Port        Port      User       Bytes Out    Bytes In
  _     *               *           as-cent > QUSER             0           0
  _     *               *           as-data > QUSER             0           0
  _     *               *           as-dtaq   QUSER             0           0
  _     *               *           as-file   QUSER             0           0
  _     *               *           as-netprt QUSER             0           0
  _     *               *           as-rmtcmd QUSER             0           0
  _     *               *           as-signon QUSER             0           0
  _     *               *           as-netd > QUSER             0           0
  _     *               *           as-tran > QUSER             0           0
  _     *               *           as-vrtp > QUSER             0           0
  _     198.0.0.2       1043        as-cent > QUSER           158         439
                                                                  More...
  F5=Refresh    F11=Display connection type    F13=Sort by column
  F14=Display port numbers    F22=Display entire field    F24=More keys
```

FIGURE 8.15
TCP/IP Connection Details — Screen 1

```
                    Display TCP Connection Status
                                                 System:    S1029F3R
  Connection identification:
    Remote host name . . . . . . . . . . . . . :    APTIVA
      Remote internet address . . . . . . . . . :      198.0.0.2
      Remote port . . . . . . . . . . . . . . . :      1044
    Local host name . . . . . . . . . . . . . . :    AS400E.RYANTECH.COM
      Local internet address . . . . . . . . . . :      198.0.0.20
      Local port . . . . . . . . . . . . . . . . :      telnet
    Associated user profile . . . . . . . . . . :    QTCP
  TCP programming interface information:
    State . . . . . . . . . . . . . . . . . . . :    Established
    Connection open type . . . . . . . . . . . . :    Passive
  Timing information:
    Idle time . . . . . . . . . . . . . . . . . :    000:00:00.201
      Last activity date/time . . . . . . . . . :      05/25/98   14:47:35
    Round-trip time . . . . . . . . . . . . . . :    .103
    Round-trip variance . . . . . . . . . . . . :    .048

                                                                  More...
  Press Enter to continue.
  F3=Exit      F5=Refresh    F6=Print    F9=Command line    F10=Display IP options
  F12=Cancel    F14=Display port numbers    F22=Display entire field
```

Information displayed includes identification information for the local and remote systems, including the IP address and port. The state and type of connection are also shown. The timing information details show important troubleshooting information similar to the information you obtain using the PING utility. The timing information on this screen also includes the idle time and the last activity time.

Rolling down displays the second detailed connection status screen (Figure 8.16).

FIGURE 8.16
TCP/IP Connection Details — Screen 2

```
                    Display TCP Connection Status
                                          System:     S1029F3R
Bytes out . . . . . . . . . . . . . . . . . . :   208354
  Outgoing bytes buffered . . . . . . . . . . :     0
  User send next  . . . . . . . . . . . . . . :     1076479530
  Send next . . . . . . . . . . . . . . . . . :     1076479530
  Send unacknowledged . . . . . . . . . . . . :     1076479530
  Outgoing push number  . . . . . . . . . . . :     1076479529
  Outgoing urgency number . . . . . . . . . . :     1076479128
  Outgoing window number  . . . . . . . . . . :     1076487841
Bytes in  . . . . . . . . . . . . . . . . . . :   6855
  Incoming bytes buffered . . . . . . . . . . :     0
  Receive next  . . . . . . . . . . . . . . . :     8482179
  User receive next . . . . . . . . . . . . . :     8482179
  Incoming push number  . . . . . . . . . . . :     8482179
  Incoming urgency number . . . . . . . . . . :     8482178
  Incoming window number  . . . . . . . . . . :     8489653


                                                      More...
Press Enter to continue.
F3=Exit      F5=Refresh    F6=Print    F9=Command line   F10=Display IP options
F12=Cancel   F14=Display port numbers   F22=Display entire field
```

This screen shows the number of bytes in and out (from the AS/400 perspective) for this connection. Other details important to the network administrator are the send and receive time and the outgoing and incoming information as expressed in the User send next and Receive next fields. These are sequence numbers for the next byte of data to be sent or received. This information tells the network administrator the sequence numbers the AS/400 is using. When there are network problems, the network administrator can use a network analyzer to show the packets and can then match the sequence number the AS/400 is using to the actual packets on the network. These sequence numbers are actually contained within the IP packets being sent from the AS/400 to the remote system (User send next) and from the remote system to the AS/400 (Receive next).

Rolling down once more shows further information regarding the connection, as in Figure 8.17. The Retransmission information gives the number of segments retransmitted by the AS/400 due to an acknowledgment not being received. Watch this value — if the number of retransmissions is higher than the number that have been historically present for this connection, it could be an indication that there are network problems.

FIGURE 8.17
TCP/IP Connection Details — Screen 3

```
                    Display TCP Connection Status
                                           System:    S1029F3R
Retransmission information:
  Total retransmissions . . . . . . . . . . . . :   0
  Current retransmissions . . . . . . . . . . . :   0
Send window information:
  Maximum size  . . . . . . . . . . . . . . . . :   8712
  Current size  . . . . . . . . . . . . . . . . :   8311
  Last update . . . . . . . . . . . . . . . . . :   8482160
  Last update acknowledged  . . . . . . . . . . :   1076479530
  Congestion window . . . . . . . . . . . . . . :   8712
  Slow start threshold  . . . . . . . . . . . . :   4096
Precedence and security:
  Precedence  . . . . . . . . . . . . . . . . . :   0
Initialization information:
  Maximum segment size  . . . . . . . . . . . . :   1452
  Initial send sequence number  . . . . . . . . :   1076271175
  Initial receive sequence number . . . . . . . :   8475323

                                                       Bottom
Press Enter to continue.
F3=Exit      F5=Refresh    F6=Print    F9=Command line   F10=Display IP options
F12=Cancel   F14=Display port numbers   F22=Display entire field
```

The Send window information identifies the current and largest size of the send window, or the number of bytes that can be transmitted without an acknowledgment. A large send window is an indication that the network is successfully transmitting large packets without the need for retransmission. A small window size means that the system has detected problems and has reduced the window size in an attempt to reduce the number of retransmissions.

The Precedence information is less important — it indicates the priority the application associates with the connection. This value is usually 0, for routine.

The Initialization information identifies the current maximum segment size, the first sequence number sent by the AS/400 for this connection, and the last sequence number received by the AS/400 for the connection. This information may be valuable to a network administrator monitoring the packets on the line.

TCP/IP Administration Menu
You can access many common TCP/IP functions from the TCP/IP Administration Menu. Entering GO TCPADM on any command line displays the menu shown in Figure 8.18.

FIGURE 8.18

FIGURE 8.18
TCP/IP Administration Menu

```
 ┌──────────────────────────────────────────────────────────────────────
 │  TCPADM                      TCP/IP Administration
 │                                                      System:    S1029F3R
 │  Select one of the following:
 │
 │     1. Configure TCP/IP
 │     2. Configure TCP/IP applications
 │     3. Start TCP/IP
 │     4. End TCP/IP
 │     5. Start TCP/IP servers
 │     6. End TCP/IP servers
 │     7. Work with TCP/IP network status
 │     8. Verify TCP/IP connection
 │     9. Start TCP/IP FTP session
 │    10. Start TCP/IP TELNET session
 │    11. Send TCP/IP spooled file
 │
 │    20. Work with TCP/IP jobs in QSYSWRK subsystem
 │
 │
 │  Selection or command
 │  ===> _____
 │  ────────────────────────────────────────────────────────────────────
 │  F3=Exit    F4=Prompt    F9=Retrieve    F12=Cancel
 │  (C) COPYRIGHT IBM CORP. 1980, 1998.
 └──────────────────────────────────────────────────────────────────────
```

Each function on this menu is also available through other OS/400 commands or menus; they are merely grouped together here for convenience. This menu gives you centralized access to the following functions:

- Configure TCP/IP invokes the CFGTCP menu.
- Configure TCP/IP applications calls the CFGTCPAPP (Configure TCP/IP Application) command.
- Start TCP/IP executes the STRTCP command.
- End TCP/IP invokes the ENDTCP command.
- Start TCP/IP servers calls the STRTCPSVR command.
- End TCP/IP servers executes the ENDTCPSVR (End TCP/IP Server) command.
- Work with TCP/IP network status invokes the WRKTCPSTS command (or the NETSTAT utility).
- Verify TCP/IP connection calls the VFYTCPCNN command (or the PING utility).
- Start TCP/IP FTP session executes the STRTCPFTP (Start TCP/IP FTP) command (or the FTP utility).
- Start TCP/IP TELNET session invokes the STRTCPTELN (Start TCP/IP Telnet) command (or the Telnet utility).

- Send TCP/IP spooled file calls the SNDTCPSPLF (Send TCP/IP Spooled File) command (or the LPR utility).

- Work with TCP/IP jobs in QSYSWRK subsystem executes the WRKSBS-JOB (Work with Subsystem Jobs) command.

WHERE TO TURN FOR HELP

Managing and troubleshooting your TCP/IP network is a task that all network administrators will eventually have to undertake. Good network design, a robust and solid physical network, and the use of standard protocols and equipment will help alleviate problems, but networks are dynamic. New applications, data communications equipment, and users are constantly being added to networks. Because more and more AS/400 installations are embracing TCP/IP as the protocol of choice, understanding the basics of network management and troubleshooting is essential.

Several issues are involved with network management in a TCP/IP environment — the physical cabling, the routing and addressing, the applications, the server processes, and the requirements of users. You must understand all of these issues to provide a reliable network. Network problems are often a result of a problem in the cabling or data communications equipment. I usually look at physical issues when a problem is transitory or hard to reproduce. Checking the cabling usually requires expertise not found in most computer rooms — look to an outside vendor to ensure the cabling is reliable. Vendors or data communications consultants have the hardware and software tools to diagnose physical problems. Data communications equipment, though reliable, will fail on occasion. Usually these types of problems are not transitory — a hub or router will fail and no traffic will be transmitted.

Harder problems to solve deal with routing and addressing. These problems may show themselves in a connection that cannot be reached or extremely long response times (especially with PING). A solid understanding of the routing employed in your network will help address these problems. Check the byte counts when problems occur to help determine whether the AS/400 is not sending or receiving packets. Retransmissions may also play a part here, especially if a router is congested in the network and packets need to be retransmitted because of timeout conditions.

Where do you turn when you can't solve your network problems? The manuals mentioned earlier in this chapter help provide some answers. Because TCP/IP support is embedded in the operating system and IBM adds new features with every release, you may need Program Temporary Fixes (PTFs) for your AS/400. IBM support (or your third-party support organization) may also be a resource for you to draw on. TCP/IP is a standard protocol; many consulting companies can assist with TCP/IP-based network problems, even if they have never seen the AS/400. You may need to make the relationship between a standard implementation of TCP/IP and the implementation on the AS/400.

Monitor your network regularly. Understand the processes that are running on your AS/400, and identify the amount of traffic that is normal on your system. Establishing baselines of performance is important in understanding when a problem is occurring on your system. Use the tools identified in this chapter to keep TCP/IP on your AS/400 robust, reliable, and effective.

Chapter 9

The AS/400 Web Server

This chapter begins with a bit of history and then discusses the standard AS/400 Web capabilities. We cover how to configure the AS/400 as a Web server with the WRKHTTPCFG (Work with HTTP Configuration) command, including explanations of the Hypertext Transfer Protocol (HTTP) directives. We examine the 5250-HTML Workstation Gateway (WSG), including functionality, configuration, and rerouting of HTTP access to the WSG, and Common Gateway Interface (CGI) programming. Finally, we discuss the Net.Data (DB2WWW) feature and show actual Hypertext Markup Language (HTML) pages, macros, and screen shots of the resulting output.

THE AS/400 AND THE WEB

The marriage of one of the world's most popular business systems and the newest, most talked-about technology may seem like a strange combination, but it's a natural by-product of the advances IBM has made in the AS/400 arena over the past few years. IBM has been positioning the AS/400 as a server and a full player in the networking and information-sharing arenas for some time now, even while maintaining the solid market share it has enjoyed as a proven performer in many different industries. The bringing together of the old and the new is another step in the direction IBM is taking the AS/400 and the AS/400 customer base.

Let's take a closer look at what is old and what is new. The AS/400 has been on the market since 1988, with its heritage in the System/38 (born in 1978) and the System/36 (born in 1986). Certainly AS/400 technology has been around a while. The World Wide Web debuted in the early 1990s, so it is a comparatively new technology. But the Web is based on TCP/IP, a protocol that has been in use since 1982. The AS/400 has embraced new processor technology (the PowerPC chip) and new releases of OS/400 that can fully participate in a TCP/IP network. The AS/400 as a Web player is an interesting mix of old and new.

HISTORY OF THE WEB

The idea of a hypertext-linked method of exploring information has been around for years, with an early reference in the July 1945 issue of *The Atlantic Monthly* (in an article by Vannevar Bush). The concept of the Web was conceived by Tim Berners-Lee, a researcher at CERN, the European Particle Physics Laboratory. In 1980, Berners-Lee wrote a program (named Enquire) for storing and accessing information. In 1989, he wrote a proposal that suggested linking hypertext documents across the Internet — the basis for the Web. In 1990, Berners-Lee developed a Web browser on a NExT system. His work became available on the Internet in 1991.

In 1993, Marc Andreeson (and others) at the National Center for Super-computing Applications (NCSA) developed a Web browser named Mosaic — the first graphically oriented Web browser. The NCSA also created a Web server. Andreeson left NCSA and started a company named Netscape, which became wildly successful in the burgeoning Web client and server market.

The Web has since experienced tremendous growth. Its first huge expansion occurred in 1993, and shortly afterward Web traffic became the second-highest user of bandwidth on the Internet (with e-mail being the highest user). Although Internet statistics are out of date as soon as they are provided, well over 2 million Web servers are now on the Internet. Most of the information made available on the Internet uses the Web. The Web is the vehicle for electronic commerce, information, and entertainment on the Internet.

THE BROWSER AND THE SERVER

Two components are necessary to provide Web access: a client using Web browser software and a server that uses HTTP to serve Web pages written in HTML. TCP/IP is the protocol that provides the connectivity from the client to the server.

The Web browser client connects to the Web server, usually using well-known port 80. The server responds with the requested page or, if a specific page is not requested, with a welcome or index page. This information is transmitted to the browser, which interprets and displays the HTML page.

Many browsers are available, with Netscape Navigator and Microsoft Internet Explorer the most widely installed. Both support standard HTML pages, and both have advantages and disadvantages. However, the choice of browser seems to be fraught with emotion, and we won't discuss it here other than to say, "Choose the browser that best fits your needs and provides the features you expect." The AS/400 does not support Web browser client software.

Many servers also exist on the market today. The AS/400 has a native HTTP server embedded in OS/400 V3R1 and above. IBM has enhanced the HTTP server with every release of OS/400 and continues to provide the functionality needed for effective Web serving. In addition, ports of Netscape Enterprise server are being readied for the AS/400.

The basic addressing scheme used for HTTP processing is the Uniform Resource Locator, or URL. The URL is the portion of a complete Web address that follows the http:// designator. A URL consists of the system and domain name of the HTTP server, as well as other optional information such as the port to use, the Web document to view or program to execute, and parameter information that can be passed to the Web server.

HYPERTEXT TRANSFER PROTOCOL (HTTP)

The protocol developed to bring Web pages over a network to a Web browser is known as the Hypertext Transfer Protocol. HTTP is a fairly simple protocol used to transmit Web pages between the server and client. Four phases exist in a session between a Web browser client and a Web server:

1. Establishing the connection — the browser attempts to connect to the server using port 80. A timeout error occurs if the server does not respond to the client in a specified amount of time.

2. Requesting a Web page — the browser requests a Web page from the server. The browser may request either a specific Web page or the default welcome or index page. In either case, the Web page is returned to the browser or, if the page is not found, an error message is returned.

3. Displaying the result — the browser either displays the requested page or the error message.

4. Closing the connection — the browser requests that the connection be closed.

An HTTP server provides several functions. HTML document serving is certainly an important component, but some others are

- Multimedia — a mix of visual and audio information
- Logging — tracking the access from clients
- Application support — the ability to execute applications tied to the HTML pages
- Image maps — clickable images that let the user access different pages based on the portion of the image that was clicked

The AS/400's HTTP server has two additional and unique components:

- Access to green-screen applications with the 5250/HTML WSG
- Easy access to DB2/400 through the Net.Data product

Even if the HTTP server is running in the QSYSWRK subsystem, Web access to the AS/400 is prohibited unless HTTP is explicitly configured. The HTTP directives — internal commands that control the Web server — must be established and made active before Web browsers can access the system. Once the HTTP server on the AS/400 is configured, Web browser clients can access the AS/400, and the HTTP server can serve the Web pages stored there.

THE HTTP DIRECTIVES

The HTTP directives provide information that determines the processing of the Web server. We discussed the configuration of the HTTP server itself in Chapter 4, but you must also configure the directives the server needs. The directives may seem a bit confusing (actually, they *are* confusing), but fortunately only a few are needed to enable the AS/400 to be accessed. In the next sections we identify and explain all the HTTP directives; in "A Short List of Directives" (later in this chapter), we come up with a short list limited to those you might actually need.

Configuring the HTTP Directives

You configure the HTTP directives using the WRKHTTPCFG command. Executing this command produces the display shown in Figure 9.1.

FIGURE 9.1
Work with HTTP Configuration Display

```
                      Work with HTTP Configuration
                                                      System:    S1029F3R
         Configuration name . . . . . . . :    CONFIG

     Type options, press Enter.
       1=Add    2=Change    3=Copy    4=Remove    5=Display    13=Insert

          Sequence
     Opt    Number    Entry
     ─      ─────     ─────────────────────────────────────────────────────
     _      00910     #  Map    /test/*      /as400/*
     _      00920     #  Pass   /as400/*     /QDLS/400HOME/*
     _      00930     #  Pass   /httpfile/*  /QSYS.LIB/AS400LIB.LIB/HTML.FILE/*
     _      00940     #  Pass   /doc/*       /QDLS/graphics/*
     _      00950     #  Pass   /file/*      /www/webdata/*
     _      00960     #  Fail   /QDLS/TESTING/*
     _      00970     #  Redirect  /wsg      http://hostname:5061/WSG
     _      00980     #
     _      00990     #  HTTP server CGI programs must find an Exec directive    >
     _      01000     #  This Exec directive refers to a path where the CGI
                                                                    More...
     F3=Exit    F5=Refresh    F6=Print List    F12=Cancel    F17=Top    F18=Bottom
     F19=Edit Sequence
```

IBM ships about 60 to 70 lines of directive statements. Many of the different types of statements are duplicated and show the form of the directives. These directives are all "commented out" — that is, they are not active (a pound sign (#) makes the entire line a comment). Removing the pound sign makes the directive active. I find that I generally have to modify the directives to make them applicable to my needs, but the commented directives help in understanding the syntax of the specific directive. The directives can be grouped into several categories. The directive categories and the directive statements are as follows:

- General settings
  - Hostname
  - Port
  - Enable
  - Disable
- Mapping rules
  - Exec
  - Fail
  - Map
  - Pass
  - Redirect
- File name suffixes
  - AddType
  - AddEncoding
  - AddLanguage
  - SuffixCaseSense
- Accessory programs
  - POST-Script
  - Search

- Directory listings
  - DirAccess
  - DirShowBytes
  - DirShowDate
  - DirShowDescription
  - DirReadMe
  - DirShowMaxDescrLength
  - DirShowOwner
  - DirShowSize
  - AlwaysWelcome
  - Welcome
- Logging
  - AccessLog
  - ErrorLog
  - LogFormat
  - LogTime
  - NoLog
- Time-out conditions
  - InputTimeOut
  - OutputTimeOut
  - ScriptTimeOut

General Settings

The general settings determine overall processing of the HTTP server. You specify the processing methods available for the server in this section. You can also specify the name of the Web server and the port used if you wish.

- The HostName *<hostname>* directive lets you override the Web server's default host name. The default name is the name specified with option 12 from the CFGTCP (Configure TCP/IP) menu. Normally this directive is not needed.

  Example: `HostName www.rtr.com`

Result: This host will be identified as www.rtr.com regardless of the name specified in option 12 of the CFGTCP menu.

- The Port *<port>* directive identifies the port at which the HTTP server will listen for an incoming connection. The default port is 80, which is the standard for Web servers. If this port number is changed, Web browsers using the default port will not be able to access the AS/400. If the port number is to be changed (perhaps for security reasons), the new port number should not be the same as any of the other well-known ports, so use a number greater than 1024.

Example: `Port 2000`

Result: The port for accessing the HTTP server on this system is 2000, not the standard port 80.

- The Enable *<method>* and Disable *<method>* directives cause the HTTP server to accept or reject incoming requests for connection. The incoming requests indicate the type of method being used for the connection. The AS/400 HTTP server supports three methods: GET, HEAD, and POST. The GET method accesses the URL and returns information. The HEAD method accesses the URL but does not return any information. This method may be used for testing URLs for validity. The POST method is used for HTML form processing. The default method processing for the AS/400 HTTP server is to Enable GET, Enable HEAD, and Disable POST. This default processing indicates that information may be retrieved and URLs validated, but form processing is not allowed.

Example: `Disable HEAD`

Result: HEAD processing is disabled. The HTTP server will return Error 403 — Method *<method>* is disabled on this server.

Mapping Rules

The mapping rules map the incoming URL request to the actual Web page that should be served. These rules allow the URL to be different from the actual HTML document (including the path or library name), enhancing security and flexibility. They also shield the Web browser from the file structure that contains the HTML pages, which is helpful because the AS/400's traditional file system (*library/file.member*) is so different from the Unix file system often used with Web servers.

Five mapping rules are available on the AS/400: Exec, Fail, Map, Pass, and Redirect. The HTTP server uses these rules to translate the URL. You can specify multiple rules in the configuration file. The order of the rules is significant: they are read in order and stored in an internal mapping table. An incoming URL is compared to the rules in order. Some directives (Fail, Pass, and Redirect) end rule processing when satisfied. One Map directive may translate the URL into a new string. Another Map directive may then translate that string to yet another string, and so on, until a directive that terminates rule processing is encountered. Be aware that template/replacement string processing is case sensitive. You may want to duplicate directives in both upper and lower case.

The mapping rules translate a URL to a different string. For example, the /sales/ portion of the incoming URL www.rtr.com/sales/ could be translated to /htmldocs/general/sales/index.html, providing a complete URL of www.rtr.com/htmldocs/general/sales/index.html. In this example, the template is /sales/ and the replacement string is /htmldocs/general/sales/index.html. The HTTP server translates the template string (the string for which it is looking) to the replacement string.

Mapping can be used to let the user enter a shorter URL that is easier to remember and to enable the AS/400 Webmaster (the person responsible for administering the HTTP server) to associate that simple URL with the actual path and file name. Another benefit to mapping is that the file location (or even the complete path name) can be changed without changing the incoming URL. The Webmaster can place the documents where (s)he wishes without the user (or a reference on another Web page) needing to change the URL. The mapping rules follow.

- The Exec *<template>* *<replacement>* directive indicates that the server should execute a program on behalf of the browser. The incoming URL is mapped to a replacement string that identifies the library containing the CGI program. All CGI programs on the AS/400 must be located in the traditional file structure, QSYS.LIB, so all Exec directives are mapped to this file system. The library that actually contains the CGI programs must be identified as part of the QSYS.LIB file system. The last part of both the template and the replacement strings must be the wildcard character, an asterisk (*).

  Example: Exec /sales/cgibin/* /QSYS.LIB/RTRSALES.LIB/*

  Result: All incoming requests for CGI program execution for the sales department are mapped to library RTRSALES. The program name is specified in the place of the asterisk in the template string. This rule shows the use of a wildcard statement, indicating that any incoming program name will be mapped to the replacement string using the same program name.

- The Fail *<template>* directive is mainly used for testing. Usually the Pass directives (perhaps in conjunction with Map directives) are used to explicitly grant access; the Fail directive explicitly prohibits access. When a match to the template string is encountered, the HTTP server returns an Error 403 — Forbidden by rule. This error is also produced if there are no Pass or Map directives that match an incoming URL. In other words, misconfigured rules cause this error — one you are likely to see when you first start exploring HTTP configuration!

Example: `Fail /sales/forbid.html`

Result: An incoming URL with the /sales/forbid.html string is rejected and causes an error.

- The Map *<template> <replacement>* directive is often used. This directive maps an incoming URL template string to a replacement string. It's important to understand that the Map directive does not terminate rule processing. Instead, the newly constructed string is used for further processing with other directives. Remember also that a Map directive is not sufficient to allow access to the HTTP server; it must be used in conjunction with another directive, usually Pass.

Example: `Map /sales/ /htmldocs/general/sales/`

Result: The incoming template /sales/ is mapped to the replacement string /htmldocs/general/sales/. Any information following the template string (for instance, an HTML document name) is appended to the replacement string.

- The Pass *<template> <optional replacement>* directive is the most commonly used method of rule processing. This directive checks an incoming URL template string. If it matches a Pass directive template, rule processing is terminated. The replacement string is optional; if used, it is substituted for the template, and the constructed URL is then passed to the HTTP server. A Pass directive is needed to enable access to the Web server. Note: A general Pass /* directive allows access to any file or document on the AS/400. This has obvious security implications and should probably not be used.

Example: `Pass /sales/welcome.html /htmldocs/general/`
`          sales/index.html`

Result: The incoming template /sales/welcome.html is mapped to the replacement string /htmldocs/general/sales/index.html. Because this is a Pass directive, rule processing is terminated and the constructed URL is passed to the HTTP server.

- The Redirect *<template> <replacement>* directive redirects an incoming URL request to another server. Redirect can be used after HTTP processing has been moved to a different server so that no changes are required to the incoming URLs.

Example: `Redirect /sales/* http://www.web.rtr.com/`
`          htmldocs/general/sales/*`

Result: Incoming requests for documents in the /sales/ directory are redirected to another server, www.web.rtr.com, in its htmldocs/general/sales directory.

File Name Suffixes

The file name suffix directives are used to associate a file with a specific extension (on the incoming URL request) to a file with a certain language, to a certain file type, or to a Multipurpose Internet Mail Extension (MIME, a standard for attaching graphics, audio, and other multimedia objects to an e-mail message) encoding method. IBM provides defaults that should match most needs for file association based on file name extension. You may never need to change the file name suffix directives. In fact, IBM doesn't even include examples of these directives in the HTTP configuration file. If you do need to use file name suffix directives, I urge you to consult the IBM documentation for more information about them. The *TCP/IP Configuration and Reference* (SC41-5420) and the *Web Master's Guide* (GC41-5434) are the best manuals for more information regarding all the HTTP directives.

- The AddType *<.extension> <type/subtype> <encoding> <optional quality>* directive is used to specify the data type of files with a specific extension. This enables files, based on their extension, to be associated with applications. For instance, a .mov file would be associated with the QuickTime movie application. Note that the AddType directive can be used in place of the AddEncoding directive — AddType is a superset of AddEncoding.

  Example: `AddType  .avi   video/x-msvideo   binary  1.0`

  Result: Incoming files with an extension of .avi are associated with the Microsoft Video for Windows encoding type.

- The AddEncoding *<.extension> <encoding>* directive associates files with a specific extension to a type of MIME encoding. TheAddEncoding directive is a subset of the AddType directive.

  Example: `AddEncoding .Z x-compress`

  Result: Incoming files with a .Z extension are associated with the x-compress MIME encoding type.

- The AddLanguage *<.extension> <language>* directive is used to associate files with a specific extension to a certain language.

  Example: `AddLanguage .en en_US`

  Result: Incoming files with an .en extension are associated with the U.S. English language.

- The SuffixCaseSense *<Off|On>* directive specifies whether file extension processing is case-sensitive. The default of Off causes the case of the extension to be disregarded for the other file name suffix directives.

  Example: `SuffixCaseSense On`

  Result: The case of incoming file name extensions will be considered.

Accessory Programs

You may not need the accessory programs directives. These directives identify the action to be taken (the CGI script to be executed) if an incoming POST or Search request is not explicitly handled by an Exec directive.

- The POST-Script *<filename>* directive identifies the default script to be used if an incoming POST request is not explicitly handled by an Exec directive.

  Example: `POST-Script /QSYS.LIB/RTR.LIB/DEFPOST.PGM`

  Result: The DEFPOST program will be executed if an incoming POST request is not explicitly handled by an Exec directive.

- The Search *<filename>* directive identifies the default script to be used if an incoming search request is not explicitly handled by an Exec directive.

  Example: `Search /QSYS.LIB/RTR.LIB/DEFSCR.PGM`

  Result: The DEFSCR program will be executed if an incoming Search request is not explicitly handled by an Exec directive.

Directory Listings

The directory listings directives are optional but often used, especially when the browser user may select different Web pages, graphics files, or documents. When you use these directives, be aware that they provide browser access to your AS/400. You can restrict browsing to certain libraries or directories as explained below, but if you don't restrict browsing, a browser user could identify the location of files on your system.

This library or directory browsing is applicable only to an incoming URL request that does not (either explicitly or through mapping) refer to a specific HTML document or CGI program. If a specific Web page or program is specified, regardless of the directory listing directives, only that page will be retrieved or that program executed.

- The DirAccess *<On |Off|Selective>* directive determines directory listing access. A value of On allows directory listing if a file or program is not explicitly specified. A value of Off prohibits directory listing and displays the Error 403 — Forbidden by rule message. A value of Selective displays the directory listing only if a member (using the QSYS.LIB file system) or a file or directory (using the Integrated File System — IFS) exists with the special name wwwbrws. If Selective is the value for the DirAccess directive and wwwbrws is not present, the server sends the browser Error 403 — Forbidden by rule. A library in the QSYS.LIB file system must be specified in accordance with name format 1 (e.g., QSYS.LIB/*library.lib/file.file/member.mbr*).

Example: `DirAccess Selective`

Result: Directory access is allowed only when the incoming URL request does not explicitly specify a file or program and the wwwbrws object is in the specified library or directory.

- The DirShowBytes <*On | Off*> directive specifies whether the size of the object (if the size is smaller than 1K) will be shown on the directory listing. The default for this directive is On.

  Example: `DirShowBytes Off`

  Result: The size of objects smaller than 1K is not shown.

- The DirShowDate <*On | Off*> directive specifies whether the modification date of the object is shown on the directory listing. The default for this directive is Off.

  Example: `DirShowDates On`

  Result: The modification date of objects is shown.

- The DirShowDescription <*On | Off*> directive determines whether the object description is shown on the directory listing. The default for this directive is On. The member description is shown for objects in the QSYS.LIB file system. Objects containing HTML in the IFS provide the object description in the <TITLE> HTML tag.

  Example: `DirShowDescription Off`

  Result: The object description will not be shown.

- The DirReadMe <*Top | Bottom | Off*> directive specifies whether readme type information is shown on the directory listing. The default is Off. If a value of Top or Bottom is used and a member (in the QSYS.LIB file system) or a file (in the IFS) is named readme, the text in the readme object is displayed on either the top or the bottom of the directory listing. This readme information may be used to give instructions to users or to inform them that access is being logged.

  Example: `DirReadMe Top`

  Result: Text in the readme object is shown at the top of the directory listing.

- The DirShowMaxDescrLength <*length*> directive specifies the maximum length of description text to be displayed.

Example: `DirShowMaxDescrLength 50`

Result: 50 characters of descriptive text will be shown in the directory listing.

* The DirShowOwner <*On* | *Off*> directive determines whether the owner of the object is shown. The default for this directive is Off.

Example: `DirShowOwner On`

Result: The owner of the object will be shown in the directory listing.

* The DirShowSize <*On* | *Off*> directive specifies whether the size of the object is shown. This directive controls all objects, whereas the DirShowBytes directive controls only objects smaller than 1K. The default for this directive is Off.

Example: `DirShowSize On`

Result: The size of the object is shown in the directory listing.

* The AlwaysWelcome <*On* | *Off*> directive works with the DirAccess and Welcome directives and directs the processing if a file is not specified on the incoming URL request in the following manner.

  — If the server receives an incoming request (with no file name specified), the AlwaysWelcome directive is set to On, and a Welcome file (discussed in a moment) exists, then the Welcome file is served to the Web browser.

  — If the AlwaysWelcome directive is Off, the URL has a trailing slash (/), and a Welcome file exists, then the Welcome file is served to the Web browser.

  — If the AlwaysWelcome directive is Off, the URL does not have a trailing slash, and a Welcome file exists, the DirAccess directive determines processing.

  — If no Welcome file exists, the DirAccess directive determines processing regardless of the setting of the AlwaysWelcome directive.

The default for this directive is On.

Example: `AlwaysWelcome On`

Result: The Welcome file is displayed if it exists; otherwise, DirAccess processing is performed.

* The Welcome <*filename*> directive identifies the file for the Always-Welcome directive. This directive is used to establish a home page on your AS/400. An incoming request (such as http://www.rtr.com) with no file name specified displays (depending on the setting of the AlwaysWelcome directive) the HTML document specified in the Welcome directive. The HTML document name may be any name, but welcome.html or index.html is often used.

Example: `Welcome /htmldocs/index.html`

Result: The index.html document in the /htmldocs directory is displayed.

Logging

The AS/400 can log incoming requests of the HTTP server. Logging is optional, but I think it's an important function for a Web server. The ability to understand who is accessing data is important to the data owners. For instance, if your organization places marketing information on your Web site, the people in the marketing department probably want to know which product descriptions are being accessed more than others. On a private intranet, it may be important for management to determine which resources employees most need by logging the Web pages they access.

Are there privacy considerations with logging? The log identifies the system name (or IP address) of the client system requesting services, the resource being accessed (Web page or program), the method used (GET, POST), and the date and time of access. Certainly this information identifies the person (or at least the system) accessing the resources. Your security and privacy policies should guide you in your decision regarding logging.

- The AccessLog *<log name> <optional maximum size>* directive identifies the file to be used for logging. The file location is determined by another directive, LogFormat (discussed below). The command to create the log file is CRTSRCPF (Create Source Physical File) — CRTSRCPF QUSRSYS/HTTPACCESS RCDLEN(375), for example. Each time the HTTP server is started, a new member (or file), with a member (or file) name constructed from the date and time, is created to receive the logging information. HTTP logging does not occur if the AccessLog directive is not present in the configuration file. The optional maximum size parameter identifies the maximum size of the logging file (the default value is 2 MB). When the logging file reaches the specified size, it accepts no more log data. If the maximum size is set to 0, the file continues to grow until the HTTP server is restarted.

  Example: `AccessLog  QUSRSYS/HTTPACCESS`

  Result: The HTTPACCESS file in library QUSRSYS will log access information.

- The ErrorLog *<log name> <optional maximum size >* directive identifies the file to be used for logging and is similar to the AccessLog directive. The location of the file is determined by the LogFormat directive just as is the location of the access log, and you create the error log file using the CRTSRCPF command. Each time the HTTP server is started, a new member (or file) is created and named just as is the access log. Error logging does not occur if the ErrorLog directive is not present in the configuration file. The optional maximum size parameter also works just as in the AccessLog directive.

Example: `ErrorLog   /HTTPlogs/errorlog`

Result: The errorlog file in directory HTTPlogs will log error information.

- The LogFormat *<DDS | Common>* directive determines the location and format of the access log and error logs. When LogFormat has a value of DDS, the file is located in the QUSRSYS library and has a file format consisting of three fields with a record length of 375 bytes. A value of Common specifies the file be located in the IFS and have a 375-byte record length with one field.

Example: `LogFormat Common`

Result: The 375-byte, 1-field format is used, and the access log and error log files are located in the IFS.

- The LogTime *<local | GMT>* directive specifies whether the log entries should be time-stamped with the local time (the default) or Greenwich Mean time — GMT. GMT time-stamping may be useful for a global operation.

Example: `LogTime GMT`

Result: Access log and error log timestamps use GMT time rather than local time.

- The NoLog *<template...>* directive indicates whether accesses by specific groups, based on host name or IP address, should be logged. You can use this directive to avoid logging local users to the Web site, instead logging only accesses from Web browsers outside your organization. You can specify multiple templates separated by a space. An asterisk acts as a wild card for any dotted decimal notation octet (in the case of an IP address) or domain name (in the case of a host name). This directive is in effect only when the AccessLog directive is On.

Example: `NoLog *.rtr.com`

Result: No accesses from any host at rtr.com will be logged.

Time-out Conditions

The HTTP server can identify time-out conditions from three sources: input from the browser, output from the server, or a time-out processing a script. The AS/400 HTTP server provides a directive for each condition. You can specify the time for each directive in minutes or hours. One minute is the smallest time interval that can be specified.

- The InputTimeOut *<time specification>* directive specifies the amount of time the server will wait for the client to send information. If the time limit is exceeded, the server sends the client an error message. The default time for this directive is 2 minutes.

Example: `InputTimeOut 10 minutes`

Result: An attempt to send data from the client to the server will time out if unsuccessful in 10 minutes.

- The OutputTimeOut *<time specification>* directive indicates the amount of time to allow for the server to send data to the client. If the time limit is exceeded, the server sends the client an error message. The default time for this directive is 20 minutes.

Example: `OutputTimeOut 1 hour`

Result: An attempt to send data from the server to the client will time out if unsuccessful in one hour.

- The ScriptTimeOut *<time specification>* directive specifies how long to wait for a CGI program to finish execution. If the time limit is exceeded, the server ends the CGI program and sends the client an error message. The default time for this directive is 5 minutes.

Example: `ScriptTimeOut 15 minutes`

Result: A CGI program must be completed in 15 minutes or the attempt will time out.

A Short List of Directives

The numerous directives and long explanation may leave you thinking that configuring the HTTP directives is a large task. However, very few directives are absolutely required; in fact, a single Pass directive is enough to allow access to your AS/400 Web server. More involved and complicated Web server configurations are certainly possible and may be needed for your installation. Let's look at the groups of directives to identify the ones that are usually used.

- General settings — Normally, no changes are needed for this group of directives. The defaults for enabling and disabling methods work fine unless you are using forms, possibly as a front end to a CGI program. In that case, you must Enable POST. The HostName and Port defaults are usually what are needed.

- Mapping rules — The important concept to remember regarding mapping rules is that a Pass directive is usually needed to allow a Web browser to access the AS/400. The Map directive is handy for translating an incoming URL to a string that can then be used with a Pass directive. Fail directives are usually not used, Exec directives are used only for CGI program access, and Redirect is needed only to redirect incoming requests to a new server.

- File name suffixes — These directives are needed only if you are providing content that goes beyond the standard Web server. Most business implementations of the AS/400 Web server do not need to use these directives.

- Accessory programs — These directives are needed only if you do not have an explicit path and file name for incoming search and POST requests.

- Directory listings — These directives can be quite useful. The combination of DirAccess, AlwaysWelcome, and Welcome can be used to provide a home page effect to an incoming browser request. You can use the other directives to provide directory listings if you want your Web site to provide a way to browse a list.

- Logging — You should implement these directives to determine who is accessing the Web site.

- Time-out conditions — Use these directives only if performance issues cause time-outs during access to the Web server.

All told, mapping rules and logging directives are the key to a successful AS/400 HTTP server implementation. The simplest method of serving Web documents from the AS/400 HTTP server is to specify a Pass statement. For instance, the Pass statement

```
Pass  /as400/*    /htmldocs/mktng/*
```

enables any incoming request with URLs in the form of http://*system.domain*/ as400. Those incoming URLs will be changed to http://*system.domain*/ htmldocs/mktng. A document specified on the incoming URL will be located in the htmldocs/mktng directory and served to the Web browser.

Of course, you may need to create a more complex Web server strategy with Map, Pass, Exec, and Redirect directives. Fail directives are generally needed only for testing. Web document serving is accomplished with Pass (and optionally Map) directives, CGI and Net.Data programs need Exec directives, and sending incoming URL requests to a different server requires Redirect directives.

Tip!

Objects (such as Web documents) stored on the AS/400 must have specific authorizations. User profile QTMHHTTP must have READ authorization to objects in the QSYS.LIB file system, or the objects must have public use (PUBLIC(*USE)) authority. Objects in the IFS require public read and execute (PUBLIC(*RX)) authority.

THE 5250-HTML WORKSTATION GATEWAY (WSG)

The AS/400 traditionally uses a 5250 display for interaction with programs and applications. Whether that display is a standard 5250 device, such as a 3486 InfoWindow, a PC using some vendor's terminal emulation software and a twinaxial adapter, or a PC using Client Access across a LAN, the 5250 data stream is a constant. All of these connectivity methods use the same data stream to send information to and from the AS/400.

The language used by Web browsers — HTML — produces output that is actually very similar to the 5250 data stream. In fact, these data streams are so similar that IBM has developed a method of translating the 5250 data stream to an HTML data stream. IBM uses this translation method for the WSG. Any Web browser that can access a properly configured AS/400 can access any traditional green-screen application through the WSG.

The AS/400 WSG server job runs in the QSYSWRK subsystem. The WSG server monitors TCP/IP port 5061 for an incoming request. When the AS/400 receives an incoming request that specifies port 5061, the WSG server starts another job to handle the request. Depending on the contents of the incoming URL and the configuration of the AS/400, the sign-on screen or an application screen may be displayed.

The standard URL for accessing the AS/400 through the WSG is

```
http://system.domain:5061/WSG
```

The 5061 identifies the port to which the incoming URL will be directed, and the WSG indicates that the Workstation Gateway application should be used. Specifying the URL in this form produces the AS/400 sign-on screen (assuming the AS/400 is configured), while a different form of the URL would provide access to an application.

Chapter 7 discusses the WSG exit point. Exit point format QAPP0100 lets you provide access to a specific application. A URL of the form

```
http://system.domain:5061/WSG/QAPP0100?information
```

causes the exit program associated with the exit point to be executed. This program can validate the incoming request, perhaps by IP address or by information passed on the URL. When the incoming WSG request is validated, the program sets the allow operation field in format QAPP0100 to enable automatic login and return a user profile, password, current library, and program to execute to the system. If the allow operation field is not set, an error message is returned to the browser.

WSG Configuration

Configuring the WSG server is detailed in Chapter 4 under "WSG Attributes." The important parameters are AUTOSTART, to automatically start the WSG servers when TCP/IP is started, and DSPSGN, to enable sign-on. Servers can be started with the STRTCPSVR (Start TCP/IP Server) command, but if the DSPSGN parameter does not have a value of *YES, sign-on attempts through the WSG are refused.

You can use HTTP directives to allow users to enter an "alias" URL to access the WSG without knowing the intricacies of the actual URL. An HTTP directive such as

```
Redirect /AS400/* http://system.domain:5061/WSG/*
```

lets users simply specify AS400 in the URL; the Redirect directive transparently reroutes the incoming request to the WSG server.

WSG Operation

Client operation from a browser accessing the WSG is different than accessing an AS/400 with a traditional 5250-style device or a TN5250 emulator; it is also different than accessing Web applications. The WSG makes it appear that the client is connected to the AS/400, when actually the connection is broken after each transaction. The WSG uses virtual terminal APIs to provide the interaction between the client and the server and maintains the connection created with the APIs until the browser signs off the system. Figure 9.2 shows a sample WRKACTJOB (Work with Active Jobs) display from a WSG session.

This combination of a Web browser with a 5250 style device has its drawbacks, however. A WSG connection is much slower than a traditional 5250 connection or a TN5250 connection. You can expect much longer response times when using the WSG. Also, the WSG keyboard is disconnected from the application. In other words, pressing function keys on the keyboard has no effect on the application. Users must access function keys (and other special keys such as Print and Attention) by clicking the displayed function key legend with a mouse. Applications that automatically update a 5250 display do not work correctly with the WSG.

From a Web browser standpoint, the interaction is less than desired. Web browsers traditionally use the Back and Forward buttons to navigate Web pages. These *do not* work with the WSG and can cause utter confusion for the user. Because the browser and the server are essentially disconnected, using the Back and Forward buttons attempts to access a Web page that does not really exist. The flow of the application does not support this type of navigation. Also, because the Web browser must interpret the pages from the server, screens may not be displayed as the creator wished.

The WSG is an interesting product but limited in its usefulness. Experienced 5250 users generally are uncomfortable with the WSG. It's been my

FIGURE 9.2

WRKACTJOB Display from a WSG Session

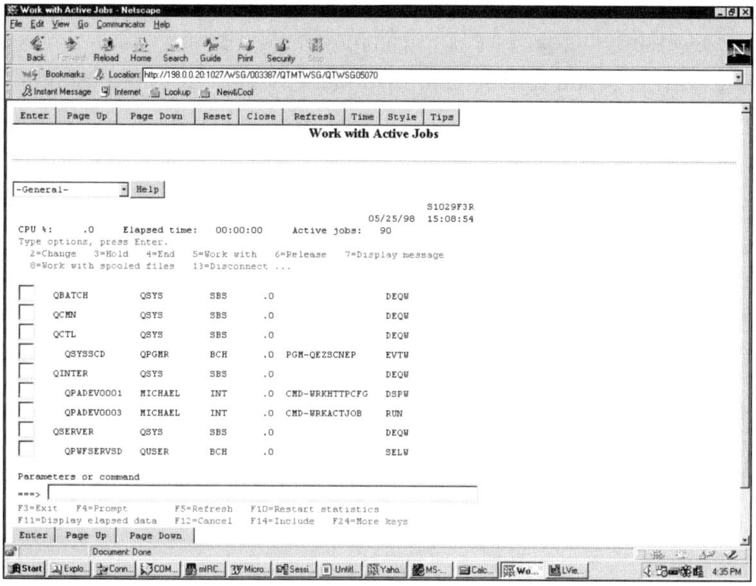

experience that the WSG is best used by inexperienced users or users new to the AS/400. These users do not demand that the interface be as faithful to the 5250 interface as experienced 5250 users do. Several vendors' implementations of Java applets provide much better 5250 emulation than the WSG.

COMMON GATEWAY INTERFACE (CGI)

CGI provides the ability to link programs with the HTTP server, enabling Web users to access programs and data on the AS/400 through the use of HTML screens. CGI is the Internet standard for linking programs with Web servers. CGI programs on the AS/400 can be written in any high-level language. They must be stored in the QSYS.LIB file system, however, because the AS/400 can execute only programs that exist in the traditional file system.

CGI programs usually work with forms created with HTML and displayed on a Web browser. Examples of forms include requests for information, "guest books," and electronic commerce forms for buying products online. The interaction between a Web browser and a CGI program flows as follows:

1. The Web browser requests a form by submitting a URL request to the server. The server sends to the client the form, which contains an action request identifying the program that will process the contents of the form.

2. The client returns the completed form to the server. The process of sending the form to the server causes the CGI program to be executed.

3. The CGI program processes the information contained in the form, often by accessing the database and calling other programs.

4. The CGI program formats information and returns it to the client in an HTML form.

5. The browser displays the form on the client system.

The CGI program receives its input information from the form returned to the server. The information in the form may be returned in environment variables or through the use of standard input. The AS/400 supports both of these methods, although in slightly different ways. Both methods use APIs to receive the information. Interacting with information in environment variables requires the use of the QtmhGetEnv (Get Environment Variable) and QtmhPutEnv (Put Environment Variable) APIs. Interacting with variables using standard input (and output) uses the QtmhWrStout (Write to Stdout), QtmhRdStin (Read from Stdin), and QtmhCvtDb (Parse CGI Input) APIs.

CGI Configuration
Configuring the AS/400 to enable CGI programs is quite simple. Configuration requires creating HTTP directives to enable Exec processing. An Exec directive such as

```
Exec  /cgibin/*  /QSYS.LIB/CGIPGMS.LIB/*
```

identifies the library (CGIPGMS) that will contain any requested CGI programs.

You may also need to enable HTML methods. The HTTP server enables the GET method by default. Another method, POST, is commonly used and must be enabled explicitly in the HTTP configuration if it is to be used. The HTTP directive to enable the POST method is simply

```
Enable POST
```

The difference between GET and POST is in how the form data is returned to the program. The GET method returns the data in the environment variable named QUERY_STRING. Some servers have a limited amount of environment space, and a form that returns a large quantity of data may not be able to return all the data in the QUERY_STRING variable. The POST method transfers data by using standard input and can return an unlimited amount of data.

The HTML document for the form sent to the Web browser must include an HTML tag specifying the form method (GET or POST) and the action to be taken. The HTML FORM tag might look like

```
<FORM METHOD="GET" ACTION="/CGIBIN/MYPROG.PGM">
```

With the Exec statement shown above, this tag causes the server to execute program MYPROG in library CGIPGMS. MYPROG processes the information contained in the form, in this case using the GET method and environment variables. The program would probably return information to the browser using another form. The HTML programming involved with creating forms is beyond the scope of this book, but several excellent references are on the market (see Further Reading for a list of references).

CGI programs provide complete control over input to the application program and output from it. You may need to learn some new programming techniques, such as accepting data from a nontraditional source (an HTML form), using environment variables, and parsing input streams. But once you learn these techniques, you can Web-enable your applications fairly easily. In fact, with the right design considerations, you can provide different interfaces for your application programs.

AS/400 programs usually accept input from a display file. A display file has characteristics in common with an HTML form — both provide input to a program and output to a user; both work with fields; and both provide a mechanism for committing the transaction to the program. The input is ordered in both cases, with both providing the ability to access individual fields in the incoming data stream. Because of these similarities, you can modify existing applications (or develop new ones) that can accept input from either a display file or an HTML form. For example, you could develop a program that processes input from both sources. Such a back-end processing program would simply accept parameters from two different programs — one a traditional display file handling program and the other a CGI program that interacts with an HTML form.

NET.DATA

Although CGI programs provide the most complete control over the interaction between an AS/400 and a Web browser, they can be fairly complicated and require the programmer to learn new techniques. IBM provides a method for accessing the AS/400 database in a manner that requires much less programming (except for HTML and SQL queries) and is transportable across different (primarily IBM) platforms. This method, known as Net.Data, lets you place input data from the HTML form into SQL queries (the input phase) and return the query results in an HTML form for display at the Web browser (the report phase).

Net.Data actually incorporates a CGI interface that processes the HTML form input and the SQL call to the AS/400 database. The program that provides this CGI interface is the DB2WWW program. This program is in library QTCP on a new AS/400, but you should move it to your CGIBIN library — the library that contains your CGI programs. Net.Data processing is controlled by macros (files or members containing a combination of HTML and Net.Data commands and function calls).

The URL request for accessing a Net.Data macro is of the form

```
http://system.domain/QSYS.LIB/DB2WWW.PGM/macro/command
```

This statement invokes the Net.Data processor (DB2WWW) with the specified macro. You could also map a more standard URL to the specific URL form needed for Net.Data to make it a bit easier for the users.

A Net.Data macro incorporates four sections:

- a variable definition section
- the SQL command section
- the HTML input section
- the HTML output section

The variable definition section provides a place in the macro to define any variables needed for processing. In the SQL command section, the SQL command to be executed over the AS/400 database is stored. The input section contains the HTML code delivered to the client browser when the DB2WWW request command is input. The output section contains the HTML statements that will be returned to the client with the result of the SQL database queries.

Net.Data works with the macro processor contained in DB2WWW, enabling the following events to occur between the client and the server:

1. The HTTP server receives the incoming URL, identifies (perhaps after Map processing) that the URL must be processed by DB2WWW, and passes the request to the macro processor.
2. The macro processor examines the input section (HTML statements) of the macro and sends the client the appropriate HTML form.
3. The user enters the information required by the form and submits it for processing. Some forms contain the information embedded within the form and do not require the information to be entered. In this case, the user simply submits the form for processing.
4. The macro processor executes the SQL statements contained in the SQL section over the database.
5. The macro processor then executes the output section, returning the resultant form to the client browser.

Let's look at some sample Net.Data macros. (These macros are courtesy of PowerTech Toolworks, Inc., a Washington-based training and education organization.) Figure 9.3 shows macro EXECMAIN, which uses Net.Data to access the AS/400 database for an indication of stock price.

FIGURE 9.3
Sample Macro EXECMAIN

```
Net.Data Macro   execmain              (Copyright 1997 PowerTech Toolworks, Inc.)

%define TABLE="PRODNET.STOCK"

%FUNCTION(DTW_SQL) getstock () {
SELECT STNOW, STSTRT, STCHG, STDATE, STUPDN FROM $(TABLE)

%REPORT{

    %ROW{
        <Left>
        %IF ("$(V5)" == "U")
            <IMG SRC="images/th_up.gif">Up
        %ELIF ("$(V5)" == "D")
            <IMG SRC="images/th_dn.gif">Down
        %ENDIF

        $(V3) <br>
        <p>
        $(V1) <br>
        <p>
Last Updated $(V4) <br>
        </left>
    %}

%}

%}

%html (main) {
    <html>
    <title>Company Executive Inquiry</title>

    <BODY bgcolor="#ffffff">
        <Center>
        <IMG SRC="images/ptlogo.gif" WIDTH=480 HEIGHT=70 ALT="Powertech">
        <h2>Company Executive Inquiry</H2>
        </center>

        <table width=700>
          <tr>
          <th align="right">
              Company Stock <font size="-2" color="#024AC9">(Delayed)</font><br>
              <font size="-1">
              @getstock ()
              </font>
          </tr>

        </table>

    <center>
        <IMG SRC="images/bar1.gif" vspace="5">
    </center>
    <p>
<center>
```

continued

FIGURE 9.3 CONTINUED

```
<table border="0" width="400">
  <tr>
    <td align="center" valign="top">
      <A href="news.htm"><IMG SRC="images/c_news.gif" border="0"></A>
    </td>

    <td align="center" valign="top">

      <A
href="http://as400.powertech.com/QSYS.LIB/CGIBIN.LIB/DB2WWW.PGM/QSYS.LIB/DB2WWW.
LIB/MACROS.FILE/EXECPROD.MBR/MAIN">
                  <IMG SRC="images/prod_10.gif" border="0"></A>
    </td>

    <td align="center" valign="top">

      <A
href="http://as400.powertech.com/QSYS.LIB/CGIBIN.LIB/DB2WWW.PGM/QSYS.LIB/DB2WWW.
LIB/MACROS.FILE/EXECREP.MBR/MAIN">
                  <IMG SRC="images/reps_10.gif" border="0"></A>
    </td>
  </tr>
</table>

</center>
</body>
</html>
%}
```

The SQL command section (A in Figure 9.3) defines the SQL table (PRODNET.STOCK) to be accessed. Net.Data function getstock is defined to select several variables from the table. The HTML output section (B) defines the output from the Net.Data function. This information is displayed on the Web page as either a thumbs-up (th_up.gif) if the stock price is up (variable V5 = "U") or a thumbs-down (th_dn.gif) if the price is down. The HTML input section (C) displays the Web page and provides the user with buttons to select company news, the top 10 products, or the top 10 sales reps. Figure 9.4 shows the resulting Web page.

FIGURE 9.4

EXECMAIN Net.Data Macro Display

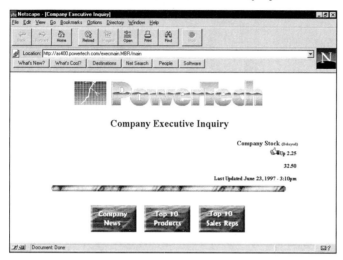

When the user clicks the button for a display of the top 10 products, another Net.Data macro-driven Web page is displayed. That macro, EXECPROD (Figure 9.5), has the same format and flow as EXECMAIN. The definition of the table and the SQL statement appear first (A in Figure 9.5), followed by the report definition (B). The input section (C) of the macro is fairly short; it simply provides the background for the Web page. The main part of the macro is the table contained in the report section; this table contains the output from the Net.Data macro. The macro selects several items from the table and orders the information with two levels of sorting. These table items (columns) then are assigned to the variables specified in the HTML table as variables V1–V7. Figure 9.6 shows a sample of the Web page displayed as a result.

Net.Data provides several advantages over CGI programming, including ease of use and portability to other platforms. Although it does not provide complete control over the program, it can be used when an SQL statement suffices for the data selection and retrieval. See the *Net.Data Programming Guide* at www.as400.ibm.com/netdata for the Net.Data programming manual. This online guide is the complete, up-to-date reference for Net.Data programming.

FIGURE 9.5
Sample Macro EXECPROD

```
Net.Data  Macro  execprod   (Copyright 1997 PowerTech Toolworks, Inc.)

%define TABLE="PRODNET.PRODSUM"

%FUNCTION(DTW_SQL) prodqry() {
SELECT PRDSC, PRAYTD, PRAMTD, PRADAY,
       PRQYTD, PRQMTD, PRQDAY
    FROM  $(TABLE)
    ORDER BY PRAYTD DESC

%REPORT{

<table border=3 width=620 cellpadding=3>
   <td colspan=7 align=center>
   <font size="+1" color="#00AAFF"><b>Top 10 Products</b>
   </font></br>

   <tr>
      <td align=center nowrap>
      <font size="-1">
      <b>Product Description</b></td>
      <td align=center nowrap>
      <font size="-1">
      <b>Y-T-D $</b></td>
      <td align=center nowrap>
      <font size="-1">
      <b>M-T-D $</b></td>
      <td align=center nowrap>
      <font size="-1">
      <b>Today $</b></td>
      <td align=center nowrap>
      <font size="-1">
      <b>M-T-D Qty</b></td>
      <td align=center nowrap>
      <font size="-1">
      <b>Y-T-D Qty</b></td>
      <td align=center nowrap>
      <font size="-1">
      <b>Today Qty</b></td>
   </tr>

   %ROW{
      <tr>
      <td align = Left>  <font size="-1"> $(V1)</td>
      <td align = right> <font size="-1"> $(V2)</td>
      <td align = right> <font size="-1"> $(V3)</td>
      <td align = right> <font size="-1"> $(V4)</td>
      <td align = right> <font size="-1"> $(V5)</td>
      <td align = right> <font size="-1"> $(V6)</td>
      <td align = right> <font size="-1"> $(V7)</td>
      </tr>
   %}

</Table>
%}

%}
```

continued

FIGURE 9.5 *CONTINUED*

```
%HTML (main) {
  <html>
    <title>Company Product Ranking</title>

    <BODY bgcolor="#ffffff">
      <Center>
      <IMG SRC="images/ptlogo.gif" WIDTH=480 HEIGHT=70 ALT="Powertech">
      @prodqry()
    </body>
  </html>
%}
```

FIGURE 9.6
EXECPROD Net.Data Macro Display

SUMMARY

Each new release of OS/400 has provided increasing Web functionality and performance. IBM recognizes that Web processing is here to stay and has successfully wed OS/400 and the AS/400 hardware with the Web. The AS/400's Web processing capabilities provide fully functional HTTP serving from both the traditional QSYS file system and the IFS, and its CGI programming provides complete interaction between the DB2/400 database and HTML Web pages. The AS/400 also provides some platform-unique capabilities — the 5250-HTML WSG, for translating 5250 data streams to HTML data streams that can be read by Web browsers, and the Net.Data product, for using data from Web browsers in SQL queries. Although the WSG is limited, Net.Data provides simple access to the AS/400 database.

Chapter 10

Configuring Advanced AS/400 TCP/IP Functions and Applications

The AS/400 has a complete set of TCP/IP functions available in OS/400 releases V4R1M0 and V4R2M0. This increased TCP/IP functionality brings the AS/400 up to the level of Unix systems, Microsoft NT systems, and other systems that support a high level of TCP/IP capability.

In this chapter, we cover configuration of the following advanced features:

- The Bootstrap Protocol (BOOTP), released in V4R1

- The Bootstrap Protocol/Dynamic Host Control Protocol (BOOTP/DHCP) Relay Agent, released in V4R2

- Distributed Data Management (DDM) over TCP/IP, released in V4R2

- Dynamic Host Control Protocol (DHCP), released in V4R2

- Routing Information Protocol 1 (RIP1), released in V4R1

- Routing Information Protocol 2 (RIP2), released in V4R2

- Remote Procedure Call (RPC), released in V4R1

- Trivial File Transfer Protocol (TFTP), released in V4R1

- Domain Name Service (DNS), released in V4R2

- Point-to-Point Protocol (PPP), released in V4R2

Configuring these advanced AS/400 TCP/IP functions requires the use of Operations Navigator. Select Operations Navigator from the Client Access folder. Select your AS/400 from the list of AS/400s. Select Network, and then select OS/400 to display the list of OS/400 servers. (Note that TCP/IP may be another available selection depending on the version of Client Access you're using. IBM has divided the selections between TCP/IP, which provides configuration support for the standard TCP/IP functions such as Telnet and FTP, and OS/400, which provides support for the advanced function configuration. If you see only a TCP/IP selection, it should include all the standard and advanced features.)

BOOTSTRAP PROTOCOL (BOOTP)

BOOTP provides the ability to dynamically assign IP addresses to workstations and to load the operating system into network computers (network stations). Network stations don't have local disk drives and don't store their operating system on disk. Instead, a server, such as the AS/400 or Windows NT, stores the operating system and downloads it to the network station when the network station attaches to the network, usually when it is powered on. TFTP works hand-in-hand with BOOTP to provide the initial operating system load (IPL) for the network stations.

BOOTP listens at port 67 for an incoming client request. When the AS/400 detects an incoming request, BOOTP interrogates a table on the AS/400 to identify the client (by its Media Access Control — MAC — address) and provide the client with an IP address. The MAC address is the address assigned to the Ethernet, Token-Ring, or (in rare cases) the twinaxial Network Interface Card (NIC). This address is usually the address assigned by the manufacturer but may be overridden in the network station setup.

Once the client has an IP address, TFTP takes over and transfers the network station's operating system image (also named in the table) to the client network station. The network station loads the operating system transferred from the server and can then function in the network. An AS/400 system administrator maintains the table containing the IP address and operating system information through the Operations Navigator interface.

To work with the BOOTP server, from the Operations Navigator list of OS/400 servers, left-click BOOTP, then right-click to obtain the drop-down list. Available choices are Start — to start the server; Stop — to end the server; and Properties — to add, remove, or change network station information. Choose Properties, then switch to the Defaults tab to display a dialog box similar to the one in Figure 10.1.

FIGURE 10.1
BOOTP Properties — Defaults Tab

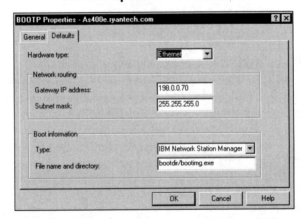

I find that when configuring network stations, most of the information that must be specified for each network station is the same. Thus, I generally first access the Defaults tab so I can specify the information that will be used by many (if not all) network stations in the network. Figure 10.1 shows the default parameters dialog box.

Allowable options for Hardware type are Ethernet, Token-Ring, or Twinaxial. From the drop-down list, choose the appropriate network type. Two pieces of information may be specified for under "Network routing" — the Gateway IP address and the Subnet mask. These two pieces of information identify the gateway system (router) that will enable the client workstation to access a different network. If your network is not connected via routers to other networks, you can skip this section. Under "Boot information," you specify the type of network station and the location of the operating system. IBM currently supports only the IBM Network Station Manager application for network stations, so it is your only option for Type. For File name and directory, specify the location of the operating system to be downloaded to the client workstation when the workstation attaches to the network. This information depends on the type of network station you're using — consult the appropriate documentation for the directory and file name containing the operating system for your specific network station.

Assigning the default values does not add an entry for a network station — it simply makes adding network station information easier. Adding network station information requires using the General tab (Figure 10.2).

FIGURE 10.2
BOOTP Properties — General Tab

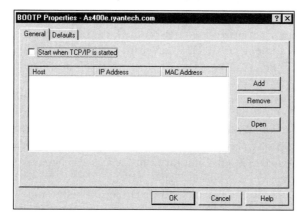

The first box on the General tab determines whether the BOOTP server should be started automatically when TCP/IP is started. Check this box to start the server automatically or clear it if you want to start the server manually. As with all TCP/IP servers, don't start this server unless you need it because any server job requires memory and system resources that shouldn't be expended needlessly. Note you may also specify this option with the CHGBPA (Change BOOTP Attributes) CL command or by using the appropriate menus and selections from the CFGTCP (Configure TCP/IP) command.

Click the Add button to add new network station information. The unique pieces of information you need to specify for each network station are the name of the network station (Host), its IP address, and its MAC address. Click OK to add the new network station's information.

The Remove button deletes an existing network station configuration; and the Open button opens the configuration for a network station, enabling you to change values associated with that specific configuration. Note that this table of network station information could also be maintained with the WRKBTPTBL (Work with BOOTP Table) command.

Tip!

Obtain the MAC address information from the network station itself. If you can't find the MAC address in the network station's documentation, the network station generally identifies its MAC address when powered on: You just need to watch the screens after you turn it on.

BOOTSTRAP PROTOCOL/DYNAMIC HOST CONTROL PROTOCOL (BOOTP/DHCP) RELAY AGENT

The BOOTP/DHCP Relay Agent sends incoming BOOTP requests (such as for a network station) to an address not on the local network. This relay may be needed when there is no BOOTP server on the local network. The BOOTP/DHCP Relay Agent relays or forwards the BOOTP requests to the appropriate network containing the BOOTP server.

To work with the BOOTP/DHCP Relay Agent server, from the Operations Navigator list of OS/400 servers, left-click BOOTP/DHCP Relay Agent, then right-click to obtain the drop-down list. Available choices are Start — to start the server; Stop — to end the server; and Configuration — to add, change, or remove BOOTP/DHCP relay information. Choose Configuration to display a dialog box similar to the one in Figure 10.3.

The first box on the General tab determines whether the BOOTP/DHCP Relay Agent server should be started automatically when TCP/IP is started. Check this box to start the server automatically or clear it if you want to start the server manually. As with all TCP/IP servers, don't start this server unless you need it because any server job requires memory and system resources that shouldn't be expended needlessly. Note that there is no corresponding CL command to perform this task.

FIGURE 10.3
BOOTP/DHCP Relay Agent Properties — General Tab

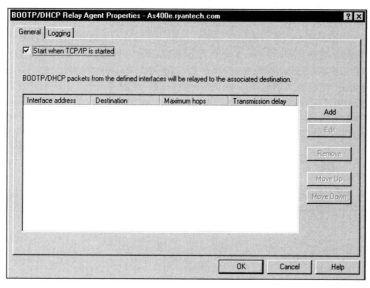

Clicking the Add button on the General tab brings up a dialog box similar to the one in Figure 10.4.

FIGURE 10.4
New Relay Definition Dialog Box

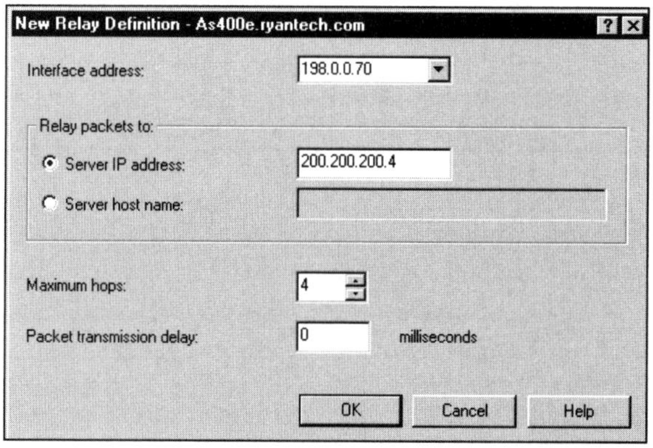

For Interface address, specify the IP address of the router or gateway system on the local network that will forward the BOOTP requests to a BOOTP server on another network. Under "Relay packets to," specify either the Server IP address or the Server host name. The Maximum hops value determines the number of hops (or routers) that can be passed through to reach the destination. The default value of 4 should suffice in most instances; if your network is large and has many routers that must be passed through to reach the destination, you may need to increase this value accordingly. The maximum value is 64 hops. For Packet transmission delay, specify the minimum delay (in milliseconds) before the BOOTP packet is sent to the next destination or hop. Click OK to return to the General tab, then switch to the Logging tab (Figure 10.5) to specify the information that should be logged for BOOTP/DHCP processing.

FIGURE 10.5

BOOTP/DHCP Relay Action Properties — Logging Tab

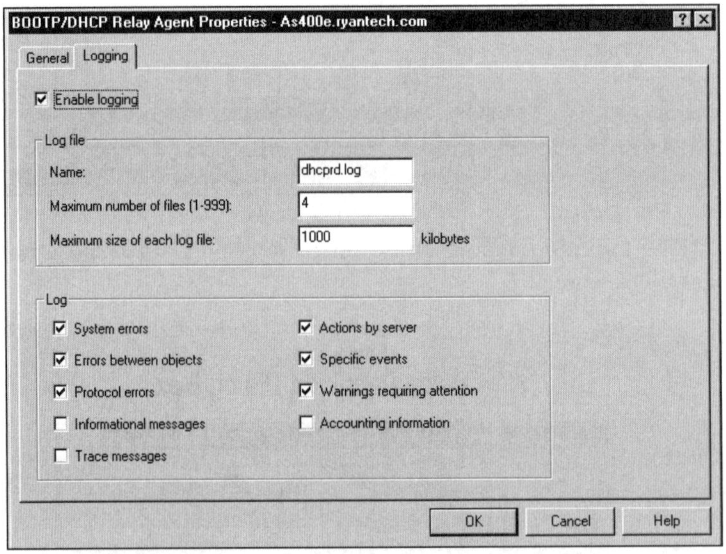

Check the Enable logging box if you want to log any of the following information:

- System errors
- Errors between objects
- Protocol errors
- Informational messages
- Trace messages
- Actions by server

- Specific events
- Warnings requiring attention
- Accounting information

Under "Log file," Name defaults to dhcprd.log, but you may specify the file name and IFS directory where you want the logging information to be kept. "Maximum number of files" and "Maximum size of each log file" work together. When a log file reaches its maximum size, the system creates a new log by appending a number to the file name, creating a new file name. This automatic process continues to the limit specified by in "Maximum number of files." When the maximum number is reached, the oldest file is overwritten by newer information.

Under "Log," check the boxes for the specific information you want logged, then click OK to exit the dialog box.

Distributed Data Management (DDM) over TCP/IP

DDM has been a part of OS/400 for many years. Now the DDM over TCP/IP server permits DDM processing over a TCP/IP connection, enabling the use of DDM files with FTP file transfers.

To work with the DDM over TCP/IP server, from the Operations Navigator list of OS/400 servers, left-click DDM, then right-click to obtain the drop-down list. Available choices are Start — to start the DDM server; Stop — to end the server; and Properties — to add, change, or remove DDM over TCP/IP information. Choose Properties to display a dialog box similar to the one in Figure 10.6.

Figure 10.6
DDM Properties Dialog Box

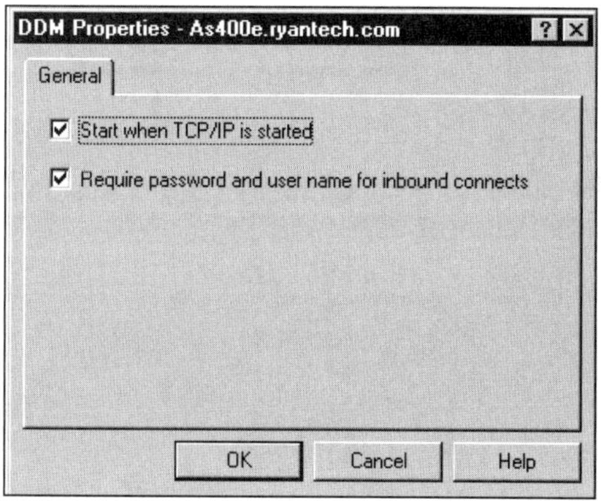

Check "Start when TCP/IP is started" if you want the DDM server started automatically when TCP/IP is started; clear the box if you want to start the server manually. As with all TCP/IP servers, don't start this server unless you need it because any server job requires memory and system resources that shouldn't be expended needlessly. Check "Require password and user name for inbound connects" if you want to require a password and a user name on incoming connection requests. Note that this information may also be entered with the CHGDDMTCPA (Change DDM over TCP/IP Attributes) command. When you've completed this dialog box, click OK to exit.

DYNAMIC HOST CONTROL PROTOCOL (DHCP)

The concept behind DHCP is that the DHCP server contains a pool of addresses in a given address range. These addresses are doled out dynamically to clients when they make a request of the server. DHCP is often used with larger networks and with dynamic networks where clients are often entering and exiting the network. A small or static network may not need DHCP.

As of V4R2, the AS/400 has the capability to perform as a DHCP server, responding to clients' requests for an IP address and supplying the client with one.

To work with the DHCP server, from the Operations Navigator list of OS/400 servers, left-click DHCP, then right-click to obtain the drop-down list. Choose Configuration to start the DHCP configuration wizard (Figure 10.7).

FIGURE 10.7
DHCP Configuration Wizard

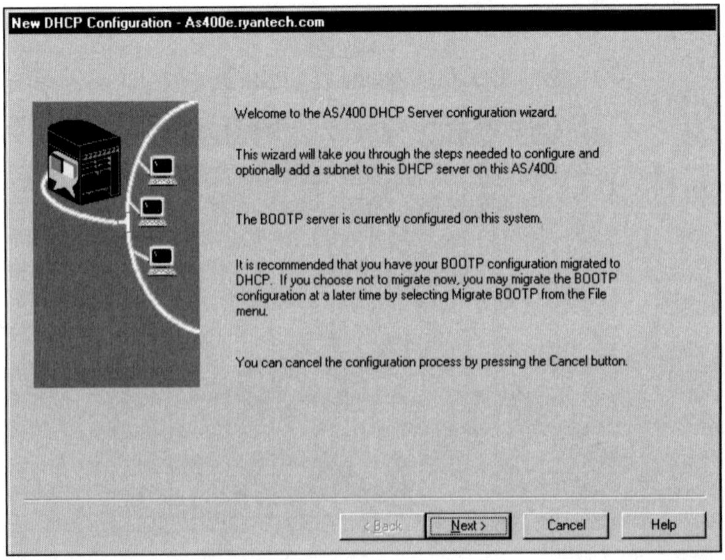

The wizard first determines whether BOOTP is configured on your system. If BOOTP is configured, the wizard asks whether you want to migrate the BOOTP configuration to DHCP. This is normally a good idea because it creates a *single* source of dynamic IP address information on the system. If BOOTP is configured, click Next to continue to the Migrate BOOTP Configuration screen (Figure 10.8).

FIGURE 10.8
Migrate BOOTP Configuration

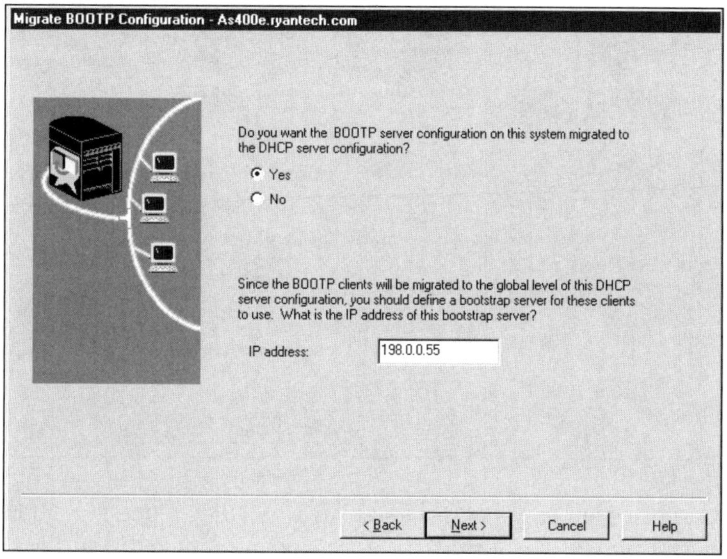

If you want to migrate the BOOTP configuration to DHCP, check Yes and enter the IP address of the BOOTP server in the box provided. Click Next to continue to the Default Lease Time screen (Figure 10.9).

FIGURE 10.9
Default Lease Time

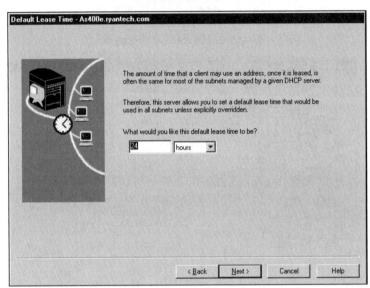

IP addresses are given to client systems when they request an address from a DHCP server. The lease time is the amount of time that a client may keep the assigned IP address when the client is not on the network. While the IP address of a client is generally not important, you can guarantee that a client will retain the same IP address even if the client is not attached to the network. IBM's lease-time default is 24 hours, while implementations on other DHCP servers often provide a default lease time of three days. Specify the desired lease time and click Next to continue to the Create a New Subnet screen (Figure 10.10).

Check Yes when you are configuring DHCP for the first time or when you are reconfiguring DHCP to add a new subnet. Otherwise, check No. Click Next to continue to the Subnet Manages Twinaxial Devices screen (Figure 10.11).

FIGURE 10.10
Create a New Subnet

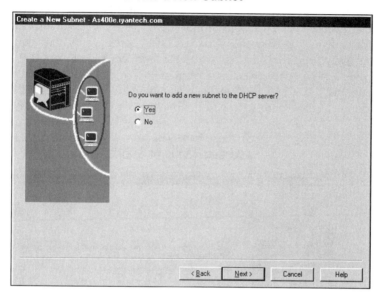

FIGURE 10.11
Subnet Manages Twinaxial Devices

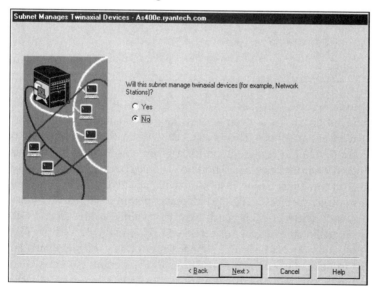

Here you determine whether TCP/IP over Twinax will be used. Check Yes *only* if network stations or PCs connected through twinaxial adapters will be used on the network and must be served from this DHCP server. However, because TCP/IP over Twinax is an ineffective method of communications, you shouldn't use it: TCP/IP over Twinax essentially forces you to buy new adapters for PCs (only from IBM) and also causes a fairly noisy protocol (TCP/IP) to be used over a slow communications medium. PCs and network stations should be connected via a LAN medium such as Ethernet or Token-Ring. Click Next to continue to the Address Range or Subnet screen (Figure 10.12).

FIGURE 10.12
Address Range or Subnet

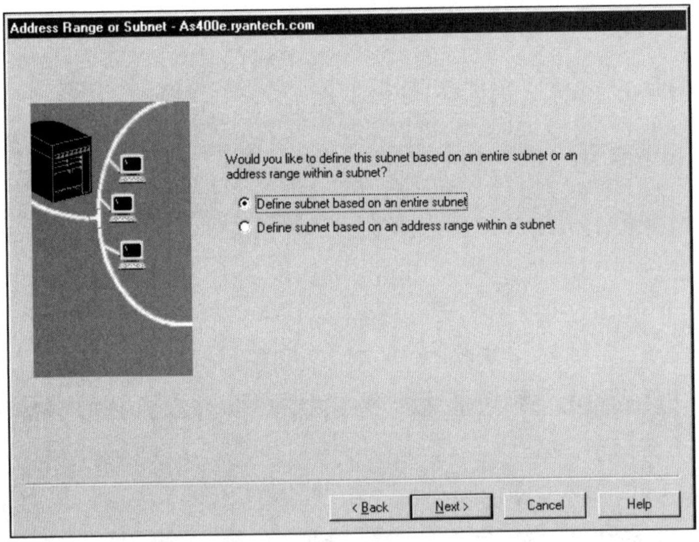

On this screen, you specify whether this DHCP configuration will be for an entire subnet or for a given address range. Usually DHCP will be configured for an entire subnet. This is especially true for the initial configuration of DHCP. Note that the configuration for a given address range is similar to defining an entire subnet; the difference is that specifying an entire subnet assumes all the addresses in a subnet, while specifying an address range enables you to specify a range of addresses within a subnet. To create an entire subnet, check Yes and click Next to continue to the Define Subnet Based on an Entire Physical Subnet screen (Figure 10.13).

Enter a subnet Name and a subnet Description. You must also enter the IP address for an entire subnet — in Figure 10.13, a complete Class C address. In our example, this requires that the last octet of the address be 0, indicating an entire network. Enter the subnet mask for this subnet, and click Next to continue to the Exclude Addresses screen (Figure 10.14).

FIGURE 10.13
Define Subnet Based on an Entire Physical Subnet

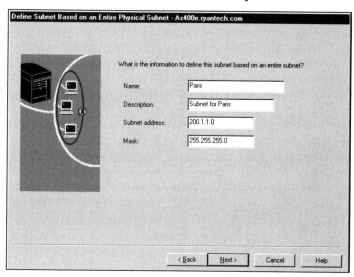

FIGURE 10.14
Exclude Addresses

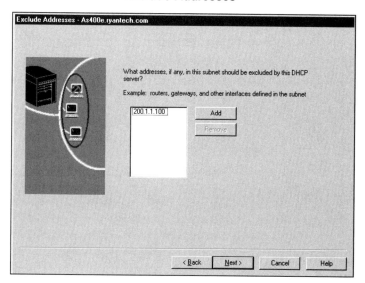

This screen enables you to exclude addresses from the entire subnet or from a range of addresses. Servers, hosts, and data communications devices will usually be excluded from obtaining their addresses from the DHCP server because addresses for these types of devices should be static (see "Excluded Addresses," page 305). Addresses specified here will not be eligible to be given to clients when attaching to the network. Enter any addresses to be excluded and click Next to continue to the Subnet Lease Time screen (Figure 10.15).

FIGURE 10.15

Subnet Lease Time

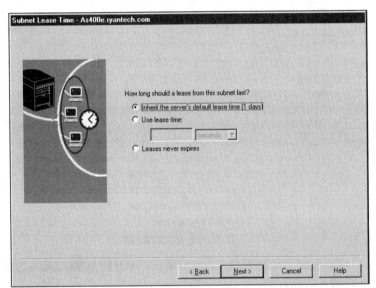

We have already defined the default lease time for the DHCP server. This screen lets you specify a different lease time for a specific subnet or address range. Check "Inherit the server's default lease time" to accept the default value. Check "Use lease time" to specify a different lease time for this subnet or range of addresses. Check "Leases never expire" to specify that a client may keep an IP address for an unlimited time period. Click Next to continue to the Subnet Gateways screen (Figure 10.16).

DHCP can deliver gateway or router addresses to clients that obtain their IP addresses from the DHCP server. The other alternative for devices to know of a gateway address is to specify the gateway address in the client's TCP/IP configuration. If you want to enable DHCP to deliver gateway addresses, check Yes and under "What are the IP addresses ..." specify the IP address(es) of the gateway(s). Click Next to continue to the Subnet Domain Name Server screen (Figure 10.17).

FIGURE 10.16
Subnet Gateways

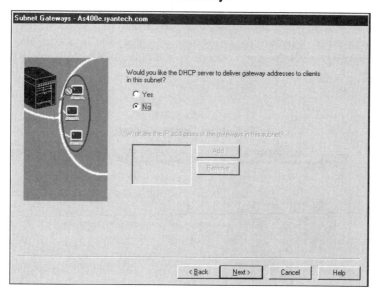

FIGURE 10.17
Subnet Domain Name Server

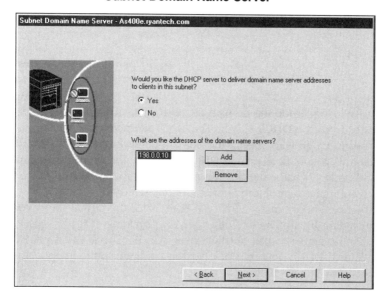

DHCP can provide the addresses of DNS servers to clients that obtain their IP addresses from the DHCP server. The other alternative for devices to know of a DNS server address is to specify the address in the client's TCP/IP configuration. If you want to enable DHCP to deliver DNS addresses, check Yes and under "What are the addresses ..." specify the IP address(es) of the DNS server(s). Click Next to continue to the Subnet Domain Name screen (Figure 10.18).

FIGURE 10.18
Subnet Domain Name

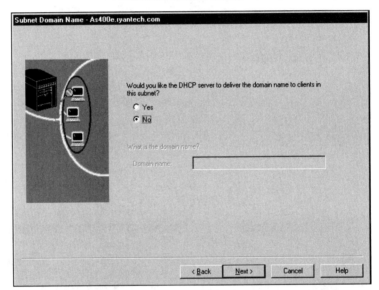

DHCP can provide the domain name to clients that obtain their IP addresses from the DHCP server. The other alternative for devices to know of a domain name is to specify the domain name in the client's TCP/IP configuration. If you want to enable DHCP to deliver the domain name, check Yes and under "What is the domain name?" specify the domain name. Click Next to continue to the More Subnet Options screen (Figure 10.19).

You may specify many additional options for the DHCP server configuration, including IP addresses of other servers providing TCP/IP services, time offsets, and whether to use NetBIOS over TCP/IP. Check Yes if you need to set additional DHCP options. Click Next to continue to the Support Unlisted Clients screen (Figure 10.20).

FIGURE 10.19
More Subnet Options

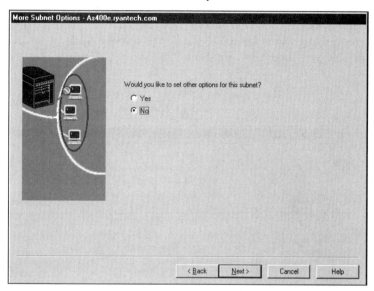

FIGURE 10.20
Support Unlisted Clients

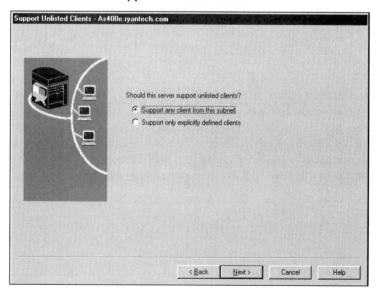

Here you specify whether unlisted clients — that is, clients that are not explicitly known to the DHCP server — should be given IP addresses from the DHCP server when requested. The default of Yes is usually the proper value; however, for increased system security you can check No and provide IP addresses only to clients known to the DHCP server. Check the desired value and click Next to continue to the Start DHCP screen (Figure 10.21).

FIGURE 10.21
Start DHCP

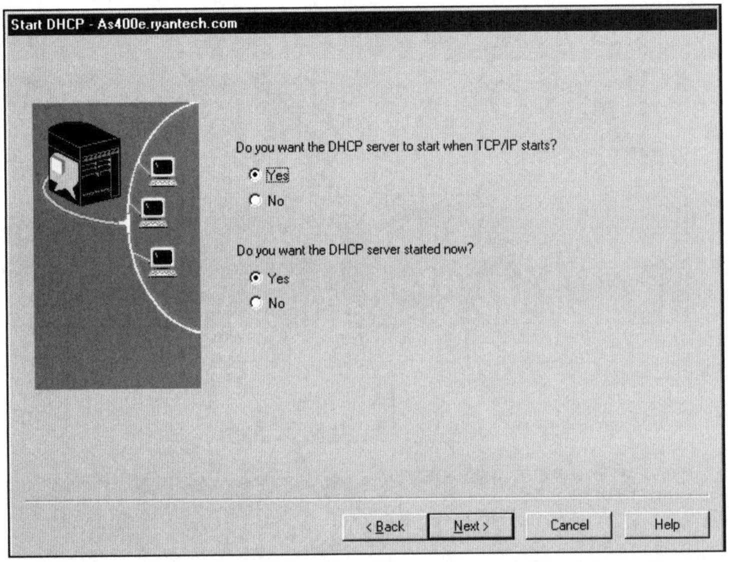

Check Yes if you want to have the DHCP server start automatically when TCP/IP is started on the system. As with all TCP/IP servers, don't start this server unless you need it because any server job requires memory and system resources that shouldn't be expended needlessly. Also check Yes if you want to start the DHCP server immediately, which is useful if you changed the DHCP configuration and want those changes to be effective immediately. Click Next to continue to the New DHCP Configuration Summary screen (Figure 10.22).

FIGURE 10.22
New DHCP Configuration Summary

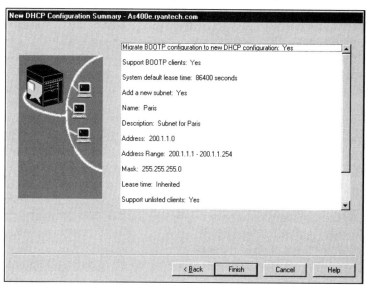

New DHCP Configuration Summary - As400e.ryantech.com

Migrate BOOTP configuration to new DHCP configuration: Yes

Support BOOTP clients: Yes

System default lease time: 86400 seconds

Add a new subnet: Yes

Name: Paris

Description: Subnet for Paris

Address: 200.1.1.0

Address Range: 200.1.1.1 - 200.1.1.254

Mask: 255.255.255.0

Lease time: Inherited

Support unlisted clients: Yes

< Back | Finish | Cancel | Help

This screen displays the configuration information for the newly created DHCP server. Examine the values shown for the configuration. If any values need to be changed, click Back until you return to the appropriate screen, and change the parameters. Click Finish to complete the configuration of the DHCP server on the AS/400.

Excluded Addresses

Excluded from the DHCP pool of IP addresses (even though they are in the address range) are addresses for devices that need a static IP address (that is, servers, such as Windows NT or Netware LAN servers; host systems, such as AS/400s and mainframes; and data communications devices, such as hubs, routers, and switches). These devices need static addresses because other devices often have these devices' addresses specified in their TCP/IP configuration. For instance, because routers serve as gateways to other networks, many devices on a network specify the address of the router as the default gateway. A router's address could change if the address were obtained dynamically, which would make the configured router's address in a device's TCP/IP configuration invalid. Similarly, IP addresses for servers and hosts are often entered into the DNS tables to enable a client to access a server or host by name rather than an IP address. If the IP address were obtained dynamically, the address could change, making the DNS information invalid.

ROUTING INFORMATION PROTOCOL (RIP)

RIP provides a mechanism for routers and hosts to share routing information with other routers and hosts. This shared data includes information such as the IP addresses of the hosts known by that router or host. This information can help in identifying the best route from a source device to a destination device.

The AS/400, depending on the version of OS/400, supports RIP1 and RIP2. Both versions supply the routing information. RIP2 also includes a mask for each route, which provides packet authentication, multicast support, and a subnet mask. Most routers support both versions of RIP, with RIP2 being preferred because it has more capabilities.

The question is, do you want your AS/400 to interact in a RIP environment? I generally prefer to use a router for this type of work because a router is built to accommodate protocols such as RIP and using a router offloads this type of processing from the AS/400 to a lower-cost data communications device. If you are considering RIP, understand that other routers must be in the environment because RIP is a protocol designed to interact with other routers.

To work with the RouteD(RIP) server, from the Operations Navigator list of OS/400 servers, left-click RouteD, then right-click to obtain the drop-down list. Choose Properties to continue to the dialog box shown in Figure 10.23.

FIGURE 10.23
RouteD Properties — General Tab

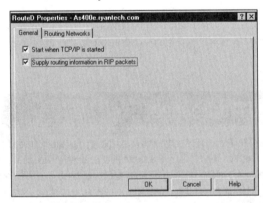

On the General tab of the RouteD Properties dialog box, check "Start when TCP/IP is started" if you want the RouteD process started automatically when TCP/IP is started. As with all TCP/IP servers, don't start this server unless you need it because any server job requires memory and system resources that shouldn't be expended needlessly. Check the "Supply routing information ..." box if you want routing information supplied in RIP packets. This box determines whether the RouteD process should be in effect for all interfaces. You can selectively turn on or turn off RouteD capabilities for a given interface with other RouteD configuration options. You should generally check both options to implement RouteD on your AS/400.

The default RouteD settings enable sending RIP2 traffic and receiving both RIP1 and RIP2 traffic. However, if you need different settings than the defaults, switch to the Routing Networks tab (Figure 10.24).

FIGURE 10.24

RouteD Properties — Routing Networks Tab

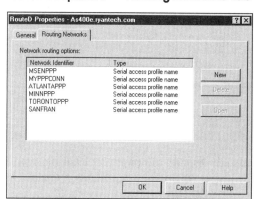

With the New button, you can specify new routes and their characteristics. You may specify a route based on the route's IP address and subnet mask, a host name, or a PPP connection profile, or you may specify options for all routes. The IP address, host name, or PPP connection profile specified here identifies an interface on your AS/400 system. Options for a route that may be specified (or modified with the Open button) include routing information, route redistribution, the metric or hop count, and the RIP community. You may also specify whether specific network addresses should be forwarded to other RIP devices and whether the addresses of specific devices should be forwarded.

REMOTE PROCEDURE CALL (RPC)

RPC is designed to enable a client to issue a call to an AS/400 server. The server processes the request and sends the requested information back to the client. This is the essence of client/server computing. As of V4R1, the AS/400 can perform in an RPC environment.

To work with the RPC server, from the Operations Navigator list of OS/400 servers, left-click RPC, then right-click to obtain the drop-down list. Choose Properties to continue to the dialog box shown in Figure 10.25.

FIGURE 10.25

RPC Properties — Transports Tab

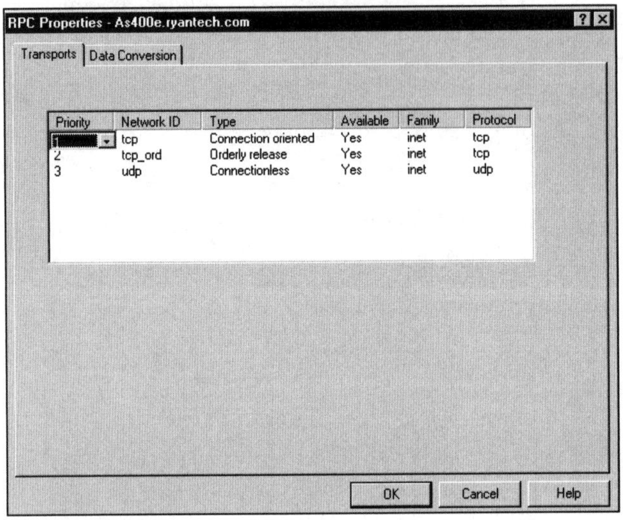

The Transports tab displays the protocols available with RPC: TCP (Transmission Control Protocol), TCP-ORD (Transmission Control Protocol with Orderly Release), and UDP (User Datagram Protocol). In the Priority field, you can specify the order that the protocols should be used in. The only other modifiable field is Available, where you specify whether the listed protocol is available to be used with RPC.

On the Data Conversion tab (Figure 10.26), you can specify the Code Page (ASCII coded character set identifier) to use with each client to ensure that the translation of data between the client and the AS/400 server will be correct. If incoming client requests are from a client that uses a different Code Page than the AS/400 (00819), click Add, then specify the client's IP address and its Code Page.

TRIVIAL FILE TRANSFER PROTOCOL (TFTP)

TFTP — a subset of the File Transfer Protocol (FTP) — is used to transfer information between a client and a server. TFTP is an automated process that has no interactive capabilities. It is often used to transfer configuration information to a router or to transfer the operating system to a network station. On the AS/400, TFTP works with BOOTP to satisfy requests from network stations. When the AS/400 receives a BOOTP request from a client, the AS/400 uses TFTP to transfer the operating system to the client.

FIGURE 10.26
RPC Properties — Data Conversion Tab

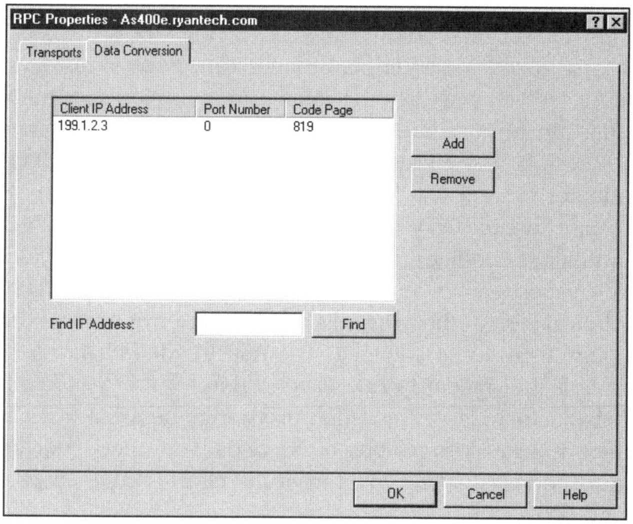

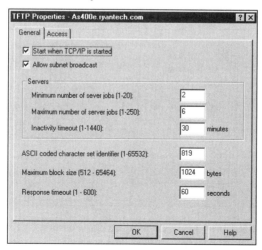

To work with the TFTP server, from the Operations Navigator list of OS/400 servers, left-click TFTP, then right-click to obtain the drop-down list. Choose Properties to continue to the dialog box shown in Figure 10.27.

FIGURE 10.27
TFTP Properties — General Tab

On the General tab, check the first box if you want the TFTP server to be started automatically when TCP/IP is started. As with all TCP/IP servers, don't start this server unless you need it because any server job requires memory and system resources that shouldn't be expended needlessly. Check Allow subnet broadcast to enable sending a broadcast message to all devices on the network. Under "Servers," specify the minimum and maximum number of server jobs that can run on the AS/400 as well as the inactivity timeout. The default values of 2, 6, and 30 respectively are usually sufficient. Increase the maximum number value if you have a high number of incoming TFTP requests. Increase the inactivity timeout value if connections are being dropped because of a timeout condition. Decrease the inactivity timeout value if you want inactive connections to be ended sooner than the default. The remaining values can often be left at their defaults unless you have network considerations that require them to be changed. The ASCII coded character set identifier is 00819, which is the standard Code Page setting for the AS/400. Maximum block size defaults to 1024 — this value may range between 512 and 65464. Response timeout defaults to waiting 60 seconds before a connection is dropped if a response is not received from the client — the values range between 1 and 600 seconds.

On the Access tab (Figure 10.28), you can specify the File access permissions to the directory containing the network station operating system.

FIGURE 10.28
TFTP Properties — Access Tab

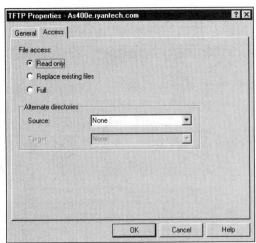

Check the appropriate box depending on whether you want to allow read-only access, the ability to replace files, or full access. Because the purpose of TFTP on the AS/400 is to download the network stations' operating system, this value should probably be left at the default of Read only. Under "Alternate directories," you can specify a different directory for the source directory, which is where the network station operating system will be downloaded to. You may also specify a target directory, which is where information can be transferred to the AS/400 if access is enabled for replacing files or full access. Alternate directories are normally not required. Click OK to establish the characteristics for the TFTP server.

DOMAIN NAME SERVICE (DNS)

The DNS server on the AS/400 provides name resolution for clients. Recall from Chapter 3 how DNS works: a client issues a request to access a host using the host's name; the DNS server resolves the host name to an IP address and passes the IP address back to the client; the client then accesses the host using the IP address (see "Domain Name Services (DNS)" in Chapter 3 for a more in-depth discussion of how DNS works).

Configuring a DNS server can be a daunting task. The most important function of DNS is to resolve host names to IP addresses, and in this section, we step through establishing host names and IP addresses in the AS/400 DNS server. Then we look briefly at the dialog box where you can configure many other DNS server properties.

To work with the DNS server, from the Operations Navigator list of OS/400 servers, left-click DNS, then right-click to obtain the drop-down list. Choose Configuration to continue to the screen shown in Figure 10.29.

FIGURE 10.29
DNS Server Configuration

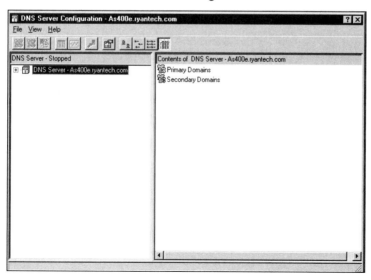

The first step is to create a new configuration. Select the name of the AS/400 you want to configure DNS for, then right-click and select New Configuration. You may receive a message indicating that creating a new configuration will overwrite the old configuration. If you are sure you want to do this (you *do* if this is a new configuration), click Yes to continue. The DNS wizard will appear to guide you through the configuration steps. Click Next to continue to the screen shown in Figure 10.30.

FIGURE 10.30
DNS Root Servers

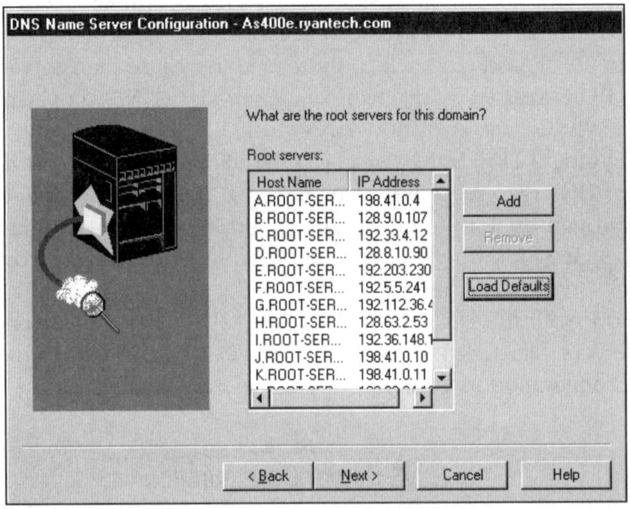

Root servers are the final servers that will be checked for name resolution. There are root servers on the Internet at various locations. If you are not directly attached to the Internet, you don't need to be concerned about root servers. In other words, if your DNS configuration is for your private intranet or if you are using DNS services from an Internet Service Provider (ISP), root servers don't need to be configured on your system. If you are directly attached to the Internet, click Load Defaults to load the root servers that were known to IBM at the time of the operating system release. You may also add individual root servers or remove root servers from the configuration. Click Next to continue to the domain type selection screen (Figure 10.31).

A DNS server may be configured to perform as a primary domain server, a secondary domain server, or a cache-only server. There should be only one primary domain server in a domain, and this server will be updated when hosts are added to the domain or removed from the domain. Check Primary domain server if this is the only DNS server in your network.

FIGURE 10.31
DNS Domain Type

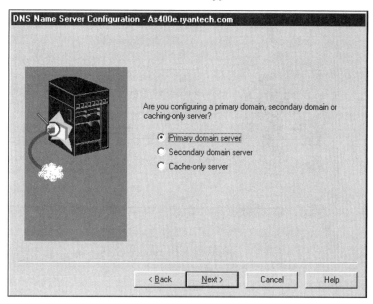

There can be a secondary domain name server as a backup or additional resource for name resolution in your network. Secondary domain servers periodically check the primary domain server for any updates to the configuration. Check Secondary domain server if you have another name server in your network and you want the AS/400 to provide a backup or additional name serving capability.

A cache-only server contacts another name server if the name to be resolved is not in the server's cache. Check Cache-only server if you have other DNS servers in your network and you are configuring the AS/400 DNS solely to speed up the name resolution process. Click Next to continue to the domain name screen (Figure 10.32).

FIGURE 10.32
DNS Domain Name

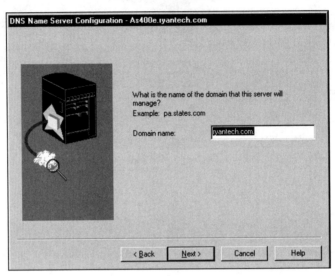

You must specify the name of the domain to be managed in the DNS configuration. The default name provided is the configured domain name on the AS/400. While the default name is usually appropriate, you may change the name if you are providing DNS services for a different domain. Click Next to continue to the host name and address screen (Figure 10.33).

At this point, you specify the actual host names and associated IP addresses. Remember that you don't specify the names and addresses of client systems in DNS, just the names of servers and hosts. Click Add to display a small dialog box where you specify the host name and IP address. Only the host name is needed — not the fully qualified name — because all the hosts are in the same domain, and that domain name was specified on the previous screen. Add the appropriate host names and IP addresses. Check "Create reverse mappings by default" to instruct DNS to automatically create the DNS records that allow the reverse of name resolution — the ability to resolve a name by specifying an IP address. When you finish adding host names and associated IP addresses, click Finish to complete the configuration.

This is the minimum configuration that is required to provide name resolution services for a network. However, as I mentioned earlier, several other records may be added to the DNS configuration. Select the domain you just created, right-click, and choose Properties to continue to the dialog box shown in Figure 10.34.

FIGURE 10.33
DNS Host Name and Address

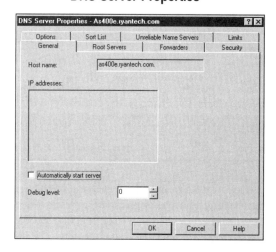

FIGURE 10.34
DNS Server Properties

Many different DNS configuration record types are available. One of the most important is the mail exchanger record (MX record), which provides the logical link between mail servers. From this dialog box, you configure such things as MX records, security information, and other DNS records. However, a full discussion of DNS configuration is beyond the scope of this book. It requires a strong knowledge of DNS and the different record types that are available. For a good reference book on the subject, see Further Reading.

POINT-TO-POINT PROTOCOL (PPP)

PPP is the preferred method of dial-up IP access. Another method, Serial Line Internet Protocol (SLIP) is also available on the AS/400. PPP is a more robust protocol, providing better error detection and recovery. The AS/400 can either dial out to a PPP-capable host (such as an ISP) or allow a PPP device to dial in to the AS/400. Whether the AS/400 is in a dial-out or dial-in role depends on the connection profile being used.

Select AS/400 Network from the Operations Navigator list. Expand the Point-to-Point selection. Two items appear — Connection Profiles and Modems. Let's examine Modems first. Click Modems to display the list of modems that are defined for the AS/400 (Figure 10.35).

FIGURE 10.35
Modem List

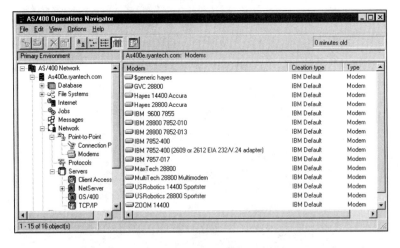

The AS/400 sends a modem initialization string to the modem to establish the operating characteristics, so the appropriate modem selection is important. You actually select a modem for a specific connection profile later in the configuration. Here, you may examine the characteristics of a modem by highlighting the modem entry, right-clicking, and choosing Properties. Modem properties include the initialization string, the reset string, the dial command, and the answer command. You cannot change any of the default modem selections from this screen, but you may create a new modem entry if you need specific characteristics. You also may want to try the $generic hayes modem entry if you have a modem that is not listed. The Hayes AT command set is the standard command for most modems so this entry may provide the modem characteristics you need.

PPP is actually configured in the connection profile. Select Connection Profiles, right-click, and choose New Profile to display the New Point-to-Point Profile Properties dialog box (Figure 10.36).

FIGURE 10.36

New Point-to-Point Profile Properties — General Tab

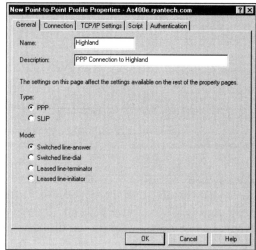

On the General tab, you specify the general characteristics of the connection. For the connection Name and Description, use something that will help you remember the purpose of the connection profile, such as a location or application.

In this example, we will configure a connection profile that puts the AS/400 into a role that allows other devices to dial in to the AS/400. For Type, check PPP as a protocol (you can also configure SLIP here).

The Mode setting affects the other settings available on other screens. The mode determines how the AS/400 will participate in a dial scenario. The different modes are Switched line-answer, Switched line-dial, Leased line-terminator, and Leased line-initiator. For this example, we'll check Switched line-answer, and then switch to the Connection tab (Figure 10.37).

FIGURE 10.37
New Point-to-Point Profile Properties — Connection Tab

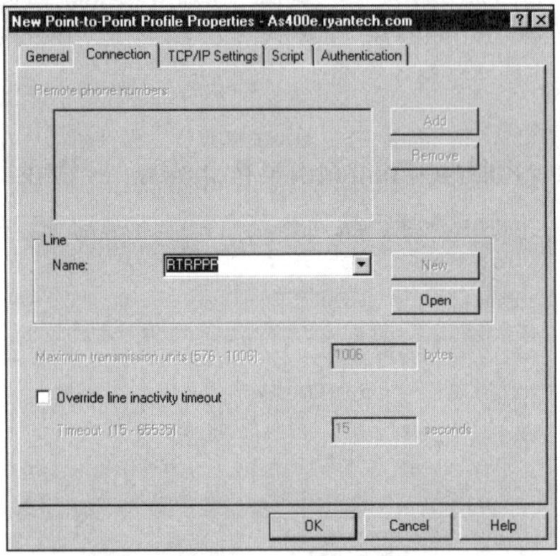

This dialog box provides parameters for all the connection types, based on what is checked for Mode on the General tab. Because we are configuring a switched line-answer connection (a device dials into the AS/400), we see the two parameters that are currently available on the dialog box: Line name and Override line inactivity timeout.

For Line name you need to specify the name of an asynchronous line configured on the AS/400. If an asynchronous line is already configured on the AS/400, display on the drop-down list of line names, and choose the line name you want to use for this connection. If you do not already have a line configured, this dialog box lets you configure a new line. Enter the new line name and click New to continue through a series of dialog boxes that let you create an asynchronous line description on the AS/400.

For Override line inactivity timeout, you specify how long a line may be inactive before it is varied off. This setting overrides the setting in the asynchronous line description. After the line has been selected and changes made to the Override line inactivity timeout (if needed), switch to the TCP/IP Settings tab (Figure 10.38).

In this dialog box, you specify the settings that will be used for a dial connection. Several parameters are available, with more parameters available depending on the choices you make here.

For the Local IP address, you specify the address of the AS/400 for this connection. You may choose from the drop-down list of IP addresses configured on your system or provide a new IP address.

FIGURE 10.38

New Point-to-Point Profile Properties — TCP/IP Settings Tab

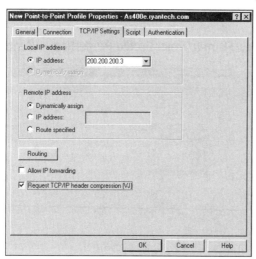

For the Remote IP address, you may check Dynamically assign — to assign an IP address dynamically to the incoming connection; IP address — to assign this IP address to any incoming call that uses this connection profile; or Route specified — to provide a unique IP address for the incoming connection depending on the incoming user name. In most cases you will check Dynamically assigned.

Under "Routing," the Allow IP forwarding parameter is important because it determines whether IP packets can be forwarded across this interface. This parameter is effective only if IP packet forwarding is enabled systemwide. (Configure the systemwide parameter through the CFGTCP — Configure TCP/IP — menu, option 3.) If IP forwarding is enabled for this connection profile and systemwide, IP packets may be forwarded across this interface, meaning that if a PPP connection is made to the Internet, IP packets could be forwarded from the Internet to devices on your LAN — an obvious security exposure. You should closely examine the capability of forwarding packets across a dial-up interface. You may want to provide this capability, but be aware that doing so opens your network (and any networks connected to your network) to packets being forwarded from an external source.

Check "Request TCP/IP header compression" to enable VJ (Van Jacobsen — the "father" of asynchronous communications) compression. If both the sending and receiving systems can use VJ compression, the overall throughput of communications improves because compressed data is being transferred. If either side can't use VJ compression, the connection proceeds without compression.

Switch to the Script tab (Figure 10.39) to specify whether to use a connection script.

FIGURE 10.39
New Point-to-Point Profile Properties — Script Tab

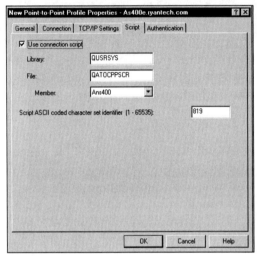

A script is a file that contains responses to prompts issued by the computer to which you are connecting. In the case of an incoming connection to an AS/400 (such as we are configuring), if you choose to use a connection script, the remote system must match the responses that the AS/400 expects.

The default script file is QUSRSYS/QATOCPPSCR. This source file contains several members, with each member a script for a different type of connection. Don't keep the scripts you have modified in this source file; move them to a separate source file that is secure — i.e., one that has AUT(*EXCLUDE) authority. Below is the ANS400 script, which works for an incoming PPP connection to an AS/400:

```
*********************************************************
* SERVER CONNECTION SCRIPT EXAMPLE
* FOR AS/4ØØ WITH LOGIN AND PASSWORD PROMPT
*********************************************************
(PROMPT)
& login:
incoming
& password:
secret
* END OF SERVER CONNECTION SCRIPT EXAMPLE
```

This script requires a specific login string and password to be entered before allowing the PPP connection to be made. The remote system would have a script that would enter the login (incoming) and password (secret) shown in this example. This provides a higher measure of security because the script must validate the connection. The user would still need to sign on to the AS/400 with a user ID and password.

Another use of a script is to assign an IP address to an incoming connection. You may want to do this to ensure proper routing because you have a port restriction or because you have an application associated with an IP address.

A script is not mandatory — you may decide not to use a script if you are not concerned about the potential security exposure. Simply check or clear "Use connection script" to enable or disable script processing for this connection profile.

"Script ASCII coded ..." determines the Code Page to be used for the script. Use the default value of 00819 unless you have other language considerations.

Switch to the Authentication tab (Figure 10.40) to specify the authentication method (if any) to be used for connections.

FIGURE 10.40

New Point-to-Point Profile Properties — Authentication Tab

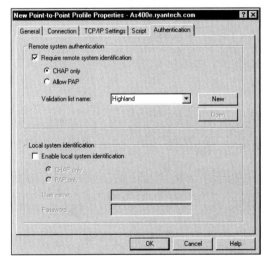

You don't need a connection script if you use authentication because authentication is performed at the connection level. Choose either a connection script or authentication. Authentication options are available for both the remote system to authenticate itself to the AS/400 and to let the AS/400 identify itself to the remote system. Checking "Require remote system identification"

causes the AS/400 to require authentication from the remote system when the remote system attempts a connection. Two options are available: CHAP only or Allow PAP. Both require the use of a validation list. CHAP (Challenge Handshake Authentication Protocol) validates both user IDs and passwords. It encrypts passwords and also changes identifiers to reduce the possibility of a mass password attack. PAP also validates user IDs and passwords but does not encrypt passwords. In addition, PAP is more vulnerable to a mass password guessing attack. The AS/400 supports both authentication protocols — check CHAP if the remote system also supports CHAP because it will provide a higher level of security.

A selection of either CHAP or PAP requires that a validation list be used. A validation list is a list of user IDs, passwords, and authentication protocols (CHAP or PAP). Incoming user information will be authenticated against this list. If a list of validation lists is available, you may choose one from the drop-down list, or you can create a new validation list by entering a list name and clicking New. A dialog box will appear enabling entries to be made to the new validation list (Figure 10.41).

FIGURE 10.41
New Validation List Dialog Box

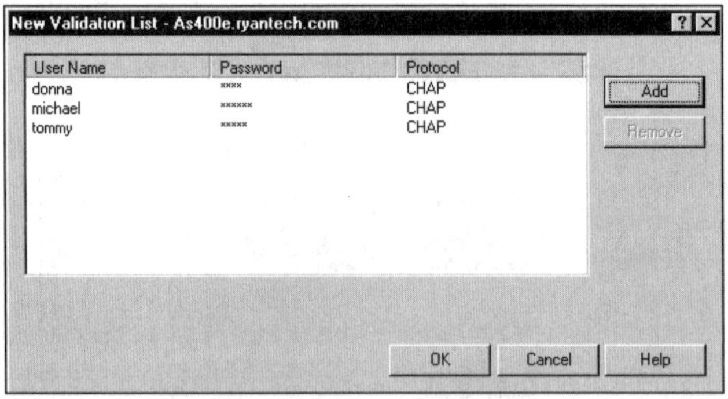

This dialog box allows you to add a user ID, password, and the protocol (CHAP or PAP) for each user authorized to make a connection using this connection profile. Click Add, add the users, and click OK to return to the Authentication tab.

The Local system identification section of the Authentication tab is similar to the Remote system authentication section, but with the direction reversed — this is the user ID and password that the AS/400 would supply when the AS/400 is making a connection to a remote system. If the remote system is using CHAP or PAP as a protocol, you should specify a User name and Password in this section. This user name and password will be supplied to the remote system when this local AS/400 attempts to make a connection.

When you have completed all the entries for a connection profile, click OK to create the connection profile. You may then choose the newly created connection profile, right-click, and select Start to vary on the line on the AS/400 and make it ready for an incoming connection.

SUMMARY

The advanced TCP/IP functions that are supported in V4R1 and V4R2 provide the level of functionality needed for the AS/400 to be a complete partner in a TCP/IP environment. The support for DHCP and DNS enables the AS/400 to serve clients with IP addresses and to resolve host names to IP addresses. Although the AS/400 is not the best router on the market (its strengths lie in transaction processing and database capabilities), RIP1 and RIP2 support lets the AS/400 learn of other networks and provide information to routers (and hosts) about its network. BOOTP and TFTP support provide operating system download support for network stations. PPP support, together with SLIP support, provides the ability for networks or devices to establish a TCP/IP connection to the AS/400 over a dial-up line.

These advanced functions are important, but they are above and beyond the core functions of TCP/IP. These core functions of virtual terminal support with Telnet, file transfers with FTP, electronic mail support with SMTP and POP3, and Web serving with HTTP are the main services used in a TCP/IP environment. The AS/400 provides excellent implementations of all the standard core services. This strong performance in the standard services enables the AS/400 to provide solid support for clients and other hosts that need to share information.

IBM's breadth of support of TCP/IP on the AS/400 is significant. For years, the only way to communicate with IBM midrange (and mainframe) systems was to "talk Blue" — that is, use the IBM-supported SNA and bisynchronous communications. But over the years, IBM has recognized that the communications industry has moved to an open environment that is not proprietary and not owned by any one organization.

TCP/IP embraces this open concept. The TCP/IP protocol suite, as described in this book, enables communication to just about every computer system available. Without difficult-to-use protocol converters, systems can attach to the AS/400 using industry-standard protocols. In addition, the world is open to the AS/400 with TCP/IP. The AS/400 can share information in a number of ways with these different systems. What does this mean to us as AS/400 professionals? Our systems can fully interact in the new computing model — a distributed model of communications where the type of system is not important, but the ability to access the information and the services is critical.

Appendix A

The History of TCP/IP

The United States Advanced Research Projects Agency (ARPA) was created in the early 1960s — the years of the Cold War and air raid drills — to provide research for many government projects. As part of the Department of Defense, ARPA's charter included military projects, and one of its tasks was to create a network that would withstand an attack while enabling the flow of command and control communications between political and military leaders. ARPA fulfilled this task by creating the ARPANet.

The ARPANet implemented pioneering research into packet-switching networks. Interface Message Processors (IMP), forerunners of modern routers, provided an interface between a host and a WAN connection, "knew" of other hosts in the network, and could route messages or packets to the appropriate destination. The first protocol implemented on the ARPANet was the Networking Control Program, or NCP, whose purpose was to create, modify, and end connections from a host to the network. The NCP was designed to allow other services, such as file transfers and virtual terminal access, to use the protocol without having to know the underlying structure. This advance prepared the foundation for packet-switching protocols such as TCP/IP.

In the early 1970s, ARPA (also known as DARPA, for Defense Advanced Research Projects Agency) investigated many methods of communication related to packet-switching networks, including radio, satellite, and cable connectivity methods. At about the same time, Xerox's Palo Alto Research Center (PARC) was experimenting with coaxial cable and packet-switching techniques. PARC's experimentation led to the development of Ethernet networking.

DARPA decided to interconnect ARPANet with other packet-switching networks by developing a protocol that would be common to all networks. In the process, DARPA (in particular Vinton Cerf and Robert Kahn) pioneered work that enabled the development of TCP and IP. Around 1980, the U.S. Defense Communications Agency, which was responsible for the ARPANet at the time, established the TCP/IP protocol suite as the standard protocol for the ARPANet, and by 1983 all ARPANet systems were converted to TCP/IP. The ARPANet was also split into two networks at about this time: the ARPANet for research and the MILNET for military applications. The change from NCP to TCP/IP on the ARPANet (and MILNET) highlighted a need for more organization for the ARPANet, which led to the formation of the Internet Activities Board (IAB), as discussed in the next section.

From the start, universities also played a major role in the development of TCP/IP and the Internet. The original ARPANet network consisted of four sites: the University of California at Los Angeles, the University of California Berkeley, the Stanford Research Institute, and the University of Utah. The growth of the Internet in the early years was primarily due to these and other universities embracing the concept and implementing the Internet on their systems.

Many university computer science departments were using the Berkeley Software Distribution (BSD) variety of Unix created by the University of California at Berkeley. DARPA funded a company, Bolt Beranek and Newman (BBN), to implement BBN's version of TCP/IP into BSD Unix. This integration of BSD Unix and BBN TCP/IP was available at low cost to universities. At about this time (the early 1980s), the Internet was becoming more popular and computers more readily available, with PCs and Apple systems on the market. Students and professors were interested in advancing computer science through networking between universities as well as at the campus and university level. TCP/IP's low cost, availability, and integration with BSD Unix made it the choice for these efforts.

In 1985, the National Science Foundation (NSF) established a network known as NSFNET to allow networks around the country to access major supercomputing centers located in San Diego, California; Boulder, Colorado; Champaign, Illinois; Pittsburgh, Pennsylvania; Ithaca, New York; and Princeton, New Jersey. In addition to being linked together, these supercomputing centers were linked to the ARPANet. In 1985 the NSF funded the connection of the regional supercomputing networks to the NSFNET, further fueling the growth of the Internet. Because the NSFNET also used TCP/IP, the protocol's momentum and the number of systems on which it was used both increased.

As any casual reader of industry trade magazines or even the popular press can see, the Internet has already made a huge impact on society in general and on the information technology industry in particular. Easy, inexpensive Internet access is available to anyone with a PC. Installation of the TCP/IP protocol suite has become simple and relatively painless. The protocol's ease of use is traceable directly to the original efforts of DARPA and NSF to make a protocol that all could embrace.

Figure A.1 shows an abbreviated timeline of Internet and TCP/IP development, courtesy of Robert H'obbes' Zakon of the MITRE Corporation. You can see the complete timeline at

http://info.isoc.org/guest/zakon/Internet/History/HIT.html

FIGURE A.1
Hobbes's Internet Timeline

1957

- USSR launches Sputnik, first artificial earth satellite. In response, U.S. forms the Advanced Research Projects Agency (ARPA) within the Department of Defense (DoD) to establish U.S. lead in science and technology applicable to the military.

1967

- Association for Computing Machinery Symposium on Operating Principles
  - Plan presented for a packet-switching network
  - First design paper on ARPANet published by Lawrence G. Roberts

1969

- ARPANet commissioned by DoD for research into networking. The four original nodes were
  - University of California, Los Angeles: Network Measurements Center
  - Stanford Research Institute (SRI): Network Information Center
  - University of California, Berkeley: Culler-Fried Interactive Mathematics
  - University of Utah: Graphics
- First RFC: "Host Software" by Steve Crocker
- University of Michigan, Michigan State, and Wayne State University establish X.25-based Merit network for students, faculty, alumni

1970

- ARPANet hosts start using Network Control Protocol (NCP)

1972

- International Conference on Computer Communications with demonstration of ARPANet between 40 machines and the Terminal Interface Processor (TIP), organized by Robert Kahn
- InterNetworking Working Group (INWG) created to address need for establishing agreed-upon protocols. Chairman: Vinton Cerf

1973

- Bob Metcalfe's Harvard PhD thesis outlines idea for Ethernet
- Robert Kahn poses Internet problem, starts internetting research program at ARPA. Vinton Cerf sketches gateway architecture in March on back of envelope in hotel lobby in San Francisco.

continued

FIGURE A.1 *CONTINUED*

1974

- Cerf and Kahn present basic Internet ideas at INWG in September at University of Sussex, Brighton, UK

- Vinton Cerf and Robert Kahn publish "A Protocol for Packet Network Intercommunication," which specified in detail the design of a Transmission Control Program (TCP)

1977

- First demonstration of ARPANet /Packet Radio Net/SATNET operation of Internet protocols with BBN-supplied gateways in July

1982

- ARPA establishes the Transmission Control Protocol (TCP) and Internet Protocol (IP) as the protocol suite commonly known as TCP/IP for ARPANet. This leads to one of the first definitions of an "internet" as a connected set of networks, specifically those using TCP/IP, and "Internet" as connected TCP/IP internets.

- DoD declares TCP/IP suite to be standard for DoD

1983

- Cutover from NCP to TCP/IP (January 1)

- ARPANet split into ARPANet and MILNET; the latter became integrated with the Defense Data Network created the previous year.

- Internet Activities Board (IAB) established

- University of California, Berkeley releases the 4.2BSD version of Unix, incorporating TCP/IP

1986

- NSFNET created (with a backbone speed of 56 Kbps)

- NSF establishes five supercomputing centers to provide computing power allowing an explosion of connections, especially from universities. The centers are

  — JVNC@Princeton

  — PSC@Pittsburgh

  — SDSC@UCSD

  — NCSA@UIUC

  — Theory Center@Cornell

1987

- NSF signs a cooperative agreement to manage the NSFNET backbone with Merit Network, Inc.

continued

FIGURE A.1 *CONTINUED*

1988

- November 2: a worm burrows through the Internet, affecting about 6,000 of the 60,000 hosts

- DARPA forms the Computer Emergency Response Team (CERT) in response to the needs exhibited during the worm incident

- DoD chooses to adopt OSI and views use of TCP/IP as an interim

- NSFNET backbone upgraded to T1 (1.544 Mbps)

1989

- Internet Engineering Task Force (IETF) and Internet Research Task Force (IRTF) comes into existence under the IAB

- Number of hosts exceeds 100,000

1990

- ARPANet ceases to exist

1993

- InterNIC created by NSF to provide specific Internet services:

  — Directory and database services (AT&T)

  — Registration services (Network Solutions, Inc.)

  — Information services (General Atomics/CERFnet)

1994

- ARPANet /Internet celebrates 25th anniversary

Hobbes's Internet Timeline Copyright ©1993–1997 by Robert H. Zakon

THE ORGANIZATION OF **TCP/IP** SUPPORT

Development and support of TCP/IP is and always has been a cooperative effort. Other protocols are proprietary and are developed based on how the vendor that owns the protocol perceives the market needs. The Internet has proven to be the great leveler of vendor-proprietary protocols. All major vendors have embraced TCP/IP for both internal networks and the Internet. This was not always the case — in the past, many vendors were critical of the growth of TCP/IP, which is quite different from other major protocols such as Novell's IPX or IBM's SNA. Some, most notably IBM, were reluctant to use TCP/IP rather than their own protocols. But TCP/IP's nonproprietary nature is in large part what enabled the Internet to experience its recent explosive growth, which in turn catalyzed the protocol's broader acceptance.

University involvement in the development of TCP/IP has also been a major contributor to the growth of TCP/IP and the Internet. Since the first integrated version of BSD Unix and BBN TCP/IP was made available to universities at low cost by DARPA, universities have experimented with and enhanced TCP/IP, creating new services and features that have been implemented in the protocol suite.

With the tremendous growth of the Internet and the corresponding growth in the use of TCP/IP, one might think that strong leadership would be required. A leadership group could dictate to the users and implementers of TCP/IP and the Internet and rigidly control development of the protocol and the network. But actually the development and growth of TCP/IP and the Internet is largely managed by volunteers who request comments from people interested in the medium. (The Request for Comment (RFC) process is outlined later in this appendix.)

The Internet Activities Board (IAB) is responsible for overall Internet design, engineering, and management. Both university and vendor representatives sit on the IAB, with the representatives entering and leaving the IAB based on their skills, availability, and interest. New members are appointed by the IAB chairperson, who is elected to a two-year term by the members of the board. A major portion of the IAB's activities is to manage the growth, development, and efficiency of the TCP/IP protocol suite.

The IAB has two task forces: the Internet Engineering Task Force (IETF) and the Internet Research Task Force (IRTF). The IETF is managed by the Internet Engineering Steering Group, which has the responsibility of resolving short- to medium-term protocol and architectural issues of the Internet and TCP/IP. As stated in RFC 1160, which describes the organization of the Internet, the charter of the IETF includes

- responsibility for specifying the short- and medium-term Internet protocols and architecture and recommending standards for IAB approval
- providing a forum for the exchange of information within the Internet community
- identifying pressing and relevant short- to medium-range operational and technical problem areas and convening Working Groups to explore solutions

The IETF is composed of vendors, computer science researchers, network managers, and others involved with the Internet and TCP/IP. At its inception, eight technical areas were identified for the IETF for managing and developing the protocol and the Internet as a whole:

- applications
- host and user services
- Internet services

- routing
- network management
- OSI integration
- operations
- security

As you can see, these areas encompass the development and maintenance of TCP/IP from applications to security. The decisions (and the research and effort that go into them) are made by volunteers rather than by a single entity. I think you'd agree that this is a remarkable business model for the development of one of the most widely used protocols in the information processing industry.

The IETF is composed of a number of working groups or subcommittees formed to address certain issues. These working groups suggest changes to the TCP/IP protocol suite and the architecture of the Internet and propose new standards for IAB or approval.

The Internet Research Task Force (IRTF) takes a longer, more strategic view of the Internet and of TCP/IP. The IRTF provides more of a pure research function, while the IETF's function is more tactical. The IRTF is composed of the same sorts of people who belong to the IETF (e.g., vendors, computer science researchers, network managers). In fact, many individuals are members of both organizations.

THE REQUEST FOR COMMENT (RFC) PROCESS

As mentioned earlier, the development of the Internet and the TCP/IP protocol suite is not accomplished through executive fiat, but rather by acclamation of the people who use the Internet and TCP/IP. People's voices are heard through the Request for Comment (RFC) process, which provides the method for

- identifying needs
- proposing solutions
- building consensus
- changing TCP/IP and the Internet

The RFC process was initiated in 1969 to document the ARPANet protocol suite. RFCs are used to discuss new ideas, document existing standards, and initiate dialogs about TCP/IP and the Internet. RFCs are available from a number of sources on the Internet, one of which is the Internet Network Information Center (InterNIC), a consortium of companies that provide directory and database services, registration services, and information services. InterNIC maintains a searchable archive of RFCs at www.internic.net. RFC 1140 summarizes the status of all the standard RFCs and is updated regularly.

The IETF's working groups create most of the RFCs for the development of TCP/IP and the Internet. When a new standard is created, it goes through a series of levels. The first level is as a proposed standard, indicating that a working group has perceived a need for a change in TCP/IP or the Internet. Proposed standards are made available for comment online.

After review by interested parties, these work-in-progress documents (known as Internet drafts) are either discarded or submitted to the RFC editor for publication. The review by interested parties is facilitated by the Internet: most communication regarding internet drafts and the various levels of standards is accomplished via e-mail or FTP, although the information can be sent through the postal service if necessary.

When a document is selected for publication, it is assigned a standards (STD) number as described in RFC 1311. The Internet Engineering Steering Group (IESG) of the IETF reviews the proposed standard and makes a recommendation regarding further advancement. In the normal course of events, promotion of a document to a proposed standard eventually results in the development a new standard.

A proposed standard requires six months of review before it can be promoted to a draft standard. During that period, interested parties can examine the proposed standard and give feedback to the members of the IETF working group that initiated it. A proposed standard also requires two independent implementations and the recommendation of the IESG before it can be promoted to the next level. Promotion to a draft standard results in creation of a new standard within six months unless major problems are discovered.

A review period of at least six months is required before a draft standard can be promoted to a standard. In addition, operational experience is needed, interoperability of at least two implementations must be shown, and the recommendation of the IESG must be acquired before a new standard is created.

The independent implementations required for proposed and draft standards are done by interested parties, often members of the working group sponsoring the proposed standard. They make their results known to the Internet community, usually sharing the code used for the implementation so that others can attempt to duplicate the results. The interoperability of the implementations (in the draft-standard-to-standard phase) is important to ensure that the standard will operate in the same manner on multiple hardware and software platforms.

Appendix B

Understanding and Configuring the SLIP Protocol

Serial Line Internet Protocol (SLIP) originated in the early 1980s as a simple IP packet-framing protocol and was formally introduced by John Romkey in 1988 (RFC 1055). In the RFC, Romkey made it clear that SLIP is not an Internet standard, but rather a de facto standard for point-to-point TCP/IP serial connections. The RFC describes the protocol as providing "… no addressing, packet type identification, error detection/correction or compression mechanisms." The RFC continues, "Because the protocol does so little, though, it is usually very easy to implement."

SLIP got a boost in 1990, when Van Jacobson defined a compression method for serial connections in RFC 1144. This method, known as Compressed SLIP (CSLIP) or Van Jacobson Compression, shrinks the size of TCP/IP headers, thereby providing faster communications throughput over slow serial connections.

More recently, a new serial communications protocol was born. From 1992 through 1994, several RFCs set the Internet standard for the Point-to-Point Protocol (PPP). PPP addresses the problems inherent in SLIP, and since its introduction has just about done away with SLIP. Most TCP/IP implementations still support SLIP, but PPP has become the method of choice for running TCP/IP over serial lines.

V3R2 added AS/400 support for CSLIP as well as a password authentication procedure implemented via scripts. V4R2 supports PPP as well. Earlier releases of OS/400 must use SLIP for TCP/IP connections through an AS/400 serial port.

You could use SLIP to connect an AS/400 to the Internet via an ISP, but doing so would be extremely dangerous because misconfiguring the AS/400 could result in Internet traffic being routed onto your LAN after only a password check. It's less dangerous to use SLIP to dial in directly to an AS/400 from a remote location because you're not connecting to the Internet; however, even dial-in has exposures. It's up to you to weigh the risks against the benefits and determine whether SLIP meets your requirements. If SLIP is right for you, it can provide an easy and inexpensive method to connect to an AS/400 from home or from any remote location.

A dial-in SLIP connection to the AS/400 supports standard TCP/IP services such as terminal emulation (Telnet or TN5250), FTP for file transfer, and LPR for remote printing. Connecting a remote PC to an AS/400 via SLIP requires minimal equipment. On the AS/400, you need a communications port (your

Electronic Customer Support communications line or communications line adapter 2609, 2612, or 6152 will do), an asynchronous modem, a phone line, and OS/400 V3R2 or V3R7. SLIP currently supports a maximum connection speed of 19.2 Kbps, so any asynchronous V.34 28 Kbps modem should work fine (modem speed will automatically fall back to 19.2 Kbps for SLIP traffic).

On the PC, you need an asynch modem, a phone line, a TCP/IP stack/dialer, and TCP/IP client software. Windows 95 provides a stack/dialer that supports SLIP; the Win95 Resource Kit includes instructions for setting up a SLIP connection. Alternatively, Trumpet Software International offers a good shareware product, Trumpet Winsock, in Windows 3.x and Windows 95 versions. You may be able to get a copy of Trumpet Winsock from your local ISP, or you can download it from Trumpet's Web site (www.trumpet.com). Yet another option is to buy a product that includes a TCP/IP stack/dialer, such as Netscape Gold, WRQ's Reflection Network Series, NetManage's Chameleon HostLink, or Spry's Internet Office. Let the services you require dictate your choice. You can buy simple TN5250 client software for terminal emulation or a product that adds features such as file transfer and printing.

Configuring the AS/400 for a SLIP dial-in connection is a five-step process (steps 2 and 3 are not strictly required, but they do provide some security):

1. Create an AS/400 line description.
2. Create an authorization list.
3. Specify the log-in script member to use.
4. Specify the modem type.
5. Add a TCP/IP point-to-point profile.

You must create the line description for the dial-in connection as a dial-in line. Here is a sample command:

```
CRTLINASC   LIND(SLIPANS) RSRCNAME(LIN011)    +
            ONLINE(*NO) INTERFACE(*RS232V24)  +
            CNN(*SWTPP) VRYWAIT(*NOWAIT)       +
            AUTOCALL(*NO) BITSCHAR(8)          +
            PARITY(*NONE) STOPBITS(1)          +
            DUPLEX(*FULL) ECHO(*NONE)          +
            LINESPEED(19200) MODEM(*NORMAL)    +
            MODEMRATE(*FULL) SWTCNN(*DIAL)     +
            AUTOANS(*NO) AUTODIAL(*YES)        +
            DIALCMD(*OTHER) CALLNBR(*NONE)     +
            INACTTMR(*NOMAX) MAXBUFFER(1500)   +
            THRESHOLD(*OFF) FLOWCNTL(*YES)     +
```

```
XONCHAR(11) XOFFCHAR(13)          +
IDLTMR(1) DSRDRPTMR(6)            +
AUTOANSTYP(*DTR) CTSTMR(25)       +
RMTANSTMR(60) CMNRCYLMT(2 5)      +
TEXT('SLIP *ANS Line')
```

The line description (LIND) name is your choice, and the resource name (RSRC-NAME) should be an RS-232 line on your system.

To provide some minimal security for your SLIP connection, use an authorization list and a SLIP connection script to permit only certain users to connect via SLIP. The following two commands create an authorization list and add a user to the list:

```
CRTAUTL AUTL(SLIP) TEXT('SLIP authorized users')
ADDAUTLE AUTL(SLIP) USER(RMT_USER)
```

When you have a SLIP connection script in place, the AS/400's internal SLIP software checks the authorization list to determine whether a remote user should have access to TCP/IP services on the AS/400. You can write your own script or use one of the IBM-supplied sample scripts in source file QUSRSYS/QATOCPPSCR. Member ANS400 contains the following script:

```
(PROMPT)
& login:
(USERID)
& password:
(PASSWORD)
```

When a remote user requests a SLIP connection, SLIP runs the script to prompt the user for an ID and password. Remember that SLIP doesn't support encryption, so the user ID and password are transmitted as clear text, readable by anyone monitoring your phone line. For more information about writing AS/400 SLIP connection scripts, see the *OS/400 TCP/IP Configuration and Reference*.

SLIP connections require asynch modems. To specify your modem type, issue the CFGTCP (Configure TCP/IP) command and select option 22. The resulting Configure Point-to-Point TCP/IP menu is the main menu for SLIP configuration. Select option 11 to go to the Select Point-to-Point TCP/IP Modem Information screen, which presents a list of supported modems. Identify the type of modem to be used. If the desired modem is not on the list, the $generic hayes modem type will probably work.

You create a point-to-point profile by selecting option 1 from the Configure Point-to-Point TCP/IP menu. From the Work with Point-to-Point TCP/IP menu, again select option 1 to add a new configuration. At the Add TCP/IP Point-to-Point *ANS Profile menu, assign the local and remote IP addresses. If the connection does not go through the Internet, you can use any valid IP address.

Alternatively, the AS/400 SLIP implementation provides an extension that lets the AS/400 dynamically assign IP addresses.

The connection profile requires several pieces of information. Specify the line description you've created, the modem type, the name of the connection script, and the script member file and library. You must also decide whether the AS/400 should provide TCP/IP datagram forwarding. Datagram forwarding is usually not a good idea because of the associated security risk. SLIP allows datagrams to be forwarded among different interfaces on your system — for example, from your AS/400 to the Internet. If another connection is in place between the AS/400 and your local network, datagram forwarding would let your AS/400 transmit packets between the two interfaces. The packets would have to be addressed correctly, but the exposure still exists. You may wish to enable datagram forwarding to allow devices on your network to access another network (such as the Internet) through the AS/400, but you should be aware of the security ramifications.

Before starting SLIP on the AS/400, you must first start TCP/IP using the STRTCP (Start TCP/IP) command. You must also start the TCP/IP servers to be used. You can configure servers to automatically start with TCP/IP, or you can start them manually. To manually start the Telnet and FTP servers, for instance, use the command

```
STRTCPSVR SERVER(*TELNET *FTP)
```

To start SLIP, select option 9 (Start) from the Work with Point-to-Point TCP/IP display, or use the following command:

```
STRTCPPTP CFGPRF(SLIPANS)
```

where SLIPANS is the name of the SLIP configuration profile. To minimize the security exposure, you can limit the time the SLIP connection is available by using the AS/400 job scheduler to run the STRTCPPTP (Start TCP/IP Point-to-Point) and ENDTCPPTP (End TCP/IP Point-to-Point) commands at specified times (for example, on weekdays at 6 p.m. and 10 p.m., respectively).

The AS/400 is ready to accept a call and establish the SLIP connection when the SLIP configuration profile has the status RINGW (ring waiting). You can check the status at the Work with Point-to-Point TCP/IP screen.

The steps involved in configuring your PC for a SLIP connection depend on your TCP/IP software. (The 16-bit Trumpet Winsock is one of the easiest TCP/IP stack/dialers to configure.) But in general, all PC-based TCP/IP software requires the same information from you.

The PC's TCP/IP stack/dialer may let you specify the name of a script file to use when you log in to the host system. If you use a scripted log-in sequence on the PC, you must ensure the script will interact correctly with the AS/400 log-in script. Alternatively, you should be able to specify that you want an interactive log-in prompt at the PC. In this case, the stack/dialer will prompt the user for a user ID and password before connecting. The TCP/IP client software will also need to know the name or IP address of the host. Specify the AS/400's IP address for this parameter.

Troubleshooting information is located in the job log and in spool files generated by the SLIP job. At the Work with Point-to-Point TCP/IP screen, you can use option 14 (Work with session jobs) to view the job log and spool files associated with the SLIP connection.

Once your SLIP connection is running smoothly, you can use Telnet and FTP and access the AS/400's HTTP server, SMTP mail server, and 5250/HTML Workstation Gateway. The simple SLIP connection is a great way to become familiar with the AS/400's Internet/intranet capabilities and experiment with various TCP/IP software.

SLIP can be a convenient and inexpensive way to add dial-in access to your AS/400. But you must be aware of its security weaknesses. SLIP is a minimalist protocol, originally intended as a quick fix for remote access to Internet-connected hosts. Because it was meant only as a temporary solution (until a better protocol came along), SLIP defines no methods for authentication, error checking, or connection recovery. Its replacement, PPP, has such provisions and so is more difficult to implement. Hence SLIP is still often the first remote access protocol to appear in a vendor's new TCP/IP offering (such as IBM's for the AS/400).

SLIP defines no authentication procedures, but vendors often add password security using simple front-end scripting. You can take advantage of the AS/400's support for log-in scripts to add a password requirement yourself, which is enough to deter the average unauthorized user. Along with a log-in script, you should use an AS/400 authorization list so only selected user profiles can log in using SLIP. Another technique is to run the AS/400 SLIP connection only when remote users are likely to want to use it (e.g., during evening hours). Limiting the time SLIP is operational limits the time a hacker has available to try to break in to your AS/400.

Appendix C

Major TCP/IP RFCs

WWW.IETF.ORG

way by which changes are made in the
ite. The following are some of the major
cellent RFC reference at www.faqs.org/
t for each RFC. Although this is not a
specially for those responsible for TCP/IP

main Name Allocation

meline

uthors

Workshop Closed Pages Document:

ns

and TCP/IP Tools and Utilities

ssage Headers

- RFC 2043, The PPP SNA Control Protocol (SNACP)
- RFC 2026, The Internet Standards Process (Revision 3)
- RFC 1939, Post Office Protocol (Version 3)
- RFC 1935, What Is the Internet, Anyway?
- RFC 1925, The Twelve Networking Truths
- RFC 1918, Address Allocation for Private Internets
- RFC 1917, An Appeal to the Internet Community to Return Unused IP Networks (Prefixes) to the IANA
- RFC 1916, Enterprise Renumbering: Experience and Information Solicitation
- RFC 1883, Internet Protocol, Version 6 (IPv6) Specification
- RFC 1882, The 12 Days of Technology Before Christmas
- RFC 1865, EDI Meets the Internet: Frequently Asked Questions about Electronic Data Interchange (EDI) on the Internet
- RFC 1855, Netiquette Guidelines
- RFC 1818, Best Current Practices
- RFC 1661, The Point-to-Point Protocol (PPP)

- RFC 1647, TN3270 Enhancements
- RFC 1646, TN3270 Extensions for LUname and Printer Selection
- RFC 1635, How to Use Anonymous FTP
- RFC 1631, The IP Network Address Translator (NAT)
- RFC 1594, FYI on Questions and Answers: Answers to Commonly asked "New Internet User" Questions
- RFC 1593, SNA APPN Node MIB
- RFC 1591, Domain Name System Structure and Delegation
- RFC 1576, TN3270 Current Practices
- RFC 1531, Dynamic Host Configuration Protocol
- RFC 1463, FYI on Introducing the Internet — A Short Bibliography of Introductory Internetworking Readings for the Network Novice
- RFC 1462, FYI on "What Is the Internet?"
- RFC 1459, Internet Relay Chat Protocol
- RFC 1436, The Internet Gopher Protocol (A Distributed Document Search and Retrieval Protocol)
- RFC 1429, Listserv Distribute Protocol
- RFC 1350, The TFTP Protocol (Revision 2)
- RFC 1336, Who's Who in the Internet: Biographies of IAB, IESG, and IRSG Members
- RFC 1311, Introduction to the STD Notes
- RFC 1305, Network Time Protocol (Version 3) Specification, Implementation, and Analysis
- RFC 1267, A Border Gateway Protocol 3 (BGP-3)
- RFC 1219, On the Assignment of Subnet Numbers
- RFC 1213, Management Information Base for Network Management of TCP/IP-Based Internets: MIB-II
- RFC 1208, Glossary of Networking Terms
- RFC 1207, FYI on Questions and Answers: Answers to Commonly Asked "Experienced Internet User" Questions
- RFC 1205, 5250 Telnet Interface
- RFC 1179, Line Printer Daemon Protocol
- RFC 1160, Internet Activities Board
- RFC 1140, IAB Official Protocol Standards
- RFC 1120, The Internet Activities Board
- RFC 1118, The Hitchhiker's Guide to the Internet

- RFC 1094, NFS: Network File System Protocol Specification
- RFC 1087, Ethics and the Internet
- RFC 1060, Assigned Numbers
- RFC 1058, Routing Information Protocol
- RFC 1057, RPC: Remote Procedure Call Protocol Specification (Version 2)
- RFC 1055, A Nonstandard for Transmission of IP Datagrams Over Serial Lines: SLIP
- RFC 1014, XDR: External Data Representation Standard
- RFC 977, Network News Transfer Protocol
- RFC 959, File Transfer Protocol (FTP)
- RFC 917, Internet Subnets
- RFC 904, Exterior Gateway Protocol Formal Specification
- RFC 903, A Reverse Address Resolution Protocol
- RFC 894, A Standard for the Transmission of IP Datagrams Over Ethernet Networks
- RFC 854, Telnet Protocol Specification
- RFC 822, Standard for the Format of ARPA Internet Text Messages
- RFC 821, Simple Mail Transfer Protocol
- RFC 793, Transmission Control Protocol
- RFC 792, Internet Control Message Protocol
- RFC 791, Internet Protocol
- RFC 783, The TFTP Protocol (Revision 2)

Further Reading

I recommend several books as reference materials for understanding TCP/IP in general and on the AS/400 in particular. The best place to start is with the following IBM manuals:

- *OS/400 TCP/IP Configuration and Reference V4R1* (SC41-5420)
- *Webmaster's Guide V4R1* (GC41-5434)

Here are some other books that I also consider excellent and use regularly:

Albitz, Paul, and Cricket Liu. *DNS and BIND.* Sebastopol, California: O'Reilly and Associates, 1988.

    Probably the best book on the Domain Name System.

Chapman, D. Brent, and Elizabeth Zwicky. *Building Internet Firewalls.* Sebastopol, California: O'Reilly and Associates, 1995.

    This is a great book on network security and firewalls.

Comer, Douglas. *Internetworking With TCP/IP.* Englewood Cliffs, New Jersey: Prentice-Hall, 1991.

    This three-volume series by one of the founders of TCP/IP is among the best on the market.

Hunt, Craig. *TCP/IP Network Administration.* Sebastopol, California: O'Reilly and Associates, 1997.

    Provides some good general information as well as good information on routing and DHCP.

Krol, Ed. *The Whole Internet User's Guide and Catalog.* Sebastopol, California: O'Reilly and Associates, 1992.

    This classic was one of the first Internet books.

Miller, Mark. *Troubleshooting TCP/IP.* New York: M&T Books, 1993.

    This is an excellent guide to the details of TCP/IP, especially from a protocol perspective.

Naugle, Matthew. *Local Area Networking.* New York: McGraw-Hill, 1991.

    This is a good book about the different components of networking in a LAN environment.

Riehl, Dan. "Who Is Accessing My FTP Server?" *NEWS/400,* June 1997.

Glossary of Terms

Agent — The SNMP term for a client.

AnyNet — An implementation of IBM's MultiProtocol Transport Network (MPTN). Enables TCP/IP packets to be encapsulated within SNA packets and vice versa.

APPC — Advanced Program-to-Program Communications. An IBM communications protocol widely used in the AS/400 environment that provides peer relationships between nodes.

ARP — Address Resolution Protocol. The technique used to determine the physical address from a logical address.

ARPA — Advanced Research Projects Agency. The organization that provided the funding, research, and direction for early packet-switching development.

ARPANet — The forerunner of the Internet. The packet-switching network established by ARPA.

ASCII — American Standard Code for Information Interchange. A character set used by most computers except IBM AS/400 and mainframe systems.

ASN.1 — Abstract Syntax Notation 1. The notation used to represent data in SNMP's Management Information Base (MIB).

Block mode — A technique used by IBM AS/400 and mainframe systems for terminal interaction. The contents of the screen (including keystrokes) are sent to the host as a block.

BSD Unix — A version of Unix that contained TCP/IP. The free distribution of this operating system enabled the rapid growth of the Internet.

Canonical form — Another term for the Network Virtual Terminal (NVT) data stream format definition used in Telnet and FTP.

CGI — Common Gateway Interface. A programming method to allow programs to interact with HTML forms.

Character mode — The technique used by PCs, Unix systems, and most non-IBM systems for terminal interaction. Every key pressed is sent to the host individually.

Circuit switching — A method of communication whereby a link (usually a physical line) exists between two or more systems and gives users exclusive use of the circuit until the connection is released. Packets are not routed, but are directly sent between systems.

Datagram — A data message. This term is commonly used to describe TCP/IP data messages.

DIX — Shorthand for the consortium (consisting of Digital Equipment Company, Intel, and Xerox) that developed the original Ethernet standard.

DNS — Domain Name Service. A protocol that returns an IP address when provided with a host name.

Domain — A logical grouping of network hosts within a hierarchy of larger groups of hosts.

EBCDIC — Extended Binary Coded Decimal Interchange Code. A character set used by IBM AS/400 and mainframe systems.

Exit point — A point in an application at which it can call an external program (an *exit program*) to perform customized processing.

Exit program — A program called from an application's exit point to perform customized processing.

FCS — Frame Check Sequence. The checksum field of an Ethernet frame.

Frame — The "container" for a data communications packet. The frame consists of the data communications packet information as well as the physical (hardware) address information and checksum information.

FTP — File Transfer Protocol (or File Transfer Program). The standard TCP/IP method of transferring files between systems.

Hop — An instance of a packet passing from one network to another network (usually through a router) in an attempt to reach the destination.

Host table — A table or file on a system that returns an IP address when provided with a host name; an alternative to DNS.

HTML — HyperText Markup Language. The language used to create Web pages.

HTTP — HyperText Transport Protocol. The protocol used for Web traffic.

ICMP — Internet Control Message Protocol. The protocol used for PING transmissions.

Integrated File System — A series of file systems supported on an AS/400. These file systems approximate the file systems found on systems such as Unix or PCs.

InterNIC — The Internet Network Information Center, the governing body of Internet address and domain name assignment.

IP — Internet Protocol. The routing level of TCP/IP. Unreliable, and can discard packets.

IP address — The address for a TCP/IP connections. Consists of up to 32 bits of information that identify the network and the host's connection to the network.

IPX — Internetwork Packet Exchange. A communications protocol used with Novell Netware networks.

ISP — Internet Service Provider. A vendor of Internet-access services.

LAN — Local Area Network.

LIC — Licensed Internal Code. OS/400 code that resides below the Machine Interface layer.

LLC — Logical Link Control. One of two sublayers of the 802 series data link layer.

LPD — Line Printer Daemon. The counterpart to LPR, used to receive print files from a remote system.

LPR — Line Printer Remote (or Line Printer Requester). A protocol used to send print files to a remote system.

MAC — Media Access Control. One of two sublayers of the 802 series data link layer.

Manager — The SNMP term for a server.

Maximum Transmission Unit — The largest packet size that can be sent over a network.

MIME — Multipurpose Internet Mail Extensions. A standard for attaching graphics, audio, and other multimedia objects to an e-mail message.

MPTN — Multiple Protocol Transport Networking. A cross-protocol networking architecture.

MSF — Mail Server Framework. The IBM framework that enables e-mail applications to interoperate. Post Office Protocol 3 (POP3) is an example of an application that exists within the MSF.

Name format — Different methods of specifying file, library, or directory information on an AS/400 when transferring files using FTP. Name Format 0 is the traditional library/file structure, while Name Format 1 enables access to the Integrated File System.

National Science Foundation — The U.S. government agency that provided the management of the early Internet.

NETSTAT — Network Statistics. Used on TCP/IP-based systems to identify routing and connection information.

NFS — Network File System. A protocol developed by Sun Microsystems that lets networked computers access file systems on other systems.

NIC — Network interface card.

NSFNET — The National Science Foundation-sponsored network that was the middle step between the ARPANet and the Internet.

NVT — Network Virtual Terminal. The base definition of virtual terminal access. Used in Telnet and FTP.

Octet — An eight-bit byte.

OSI — Open Standards Interconnection. A communications protocol that is more widely used in Europe than in the U.S. OSI contains all the components needed in a protocol and is often used as the benchmark to which other protocols are compared.

Packet — A data message. This term is commonly used to describe data messages in a packet-switching network.

Packet switching — A data transmission technique whereby user information is segmented and routed in discrete data envelopes called packets, each with its own appended control information for routing, sequencing, and error checking. Allows a communications channel to be shared by many users, each using the circuit only for the time required to transmit a single packet. Describing a network that operates in this manner.

PARC — Xerox Palo Alto Research Center. The organization that provided early research in the development of packet-switching networks, metaphors such as windowing, and devices such as a mouse.

PING — Packet InterNetwork Groper. A TCP/IP-based service for determining whether a remote system is reachable across a network.

POP3 — Post Office Protocol 3. A standard method for a client to receive e-mail messages from a server.

Port — The fundamental connection point in a TCP/IP network. Server programs listen at ports for incoming connections to process.

PPP — Point-to-Point Protocol. A standard method of transmitting TCP/IP packets over a serial connection.

Protocol — A structured system of messages, commands, and operations that let systems communicate in a network.

RFC — Request for Comment. The process by which Internet and TCP/IP standards and practices are defined.

RIP — Routing Information Protocol. A protocol used by routers to explore and learn of attached systems and networks.

RPC — The Remote Procedure Call module of the Network File System.

Sendmail — The Unix program used to send most e-mail across the Internet.

SLIP — Serial Line Internet Protocol. A nonstandard method of TCP/IP over a serial line that does not provide error correction.

SMIT — System Management Interface Tool. A tool used on IBM RS/6000 systems enabling system configuration and management.

SMTP — Simple Mail Transfer Protocol. A protocol used to send mail messages between systems, especially between servers.

SNA — Systems Network Architecture. An IBM proprietary protocol widely used in business for wide area network connections.

SNMP — Simple Network Management Protocol. A high-level protocol for managing a TCP/IP-based network.

SPX — Sequenced Packet Exchange. A Netware networking protocol.

Subnet — A method of logically dividing a TCP/IP-based network. Used in routing to determine the correct address of a system.

Symmetry — The ability of both the client and the server to negotiate the options for a Telnet session.

TCP — Transmission Control Protocol. The application-based, reliable portion of TCP/IP.

TCP/IP — Transmission Control Protocol/Internet Protocol. The protocol of the Internet. A packet-switching protocol that is widely used and implemented by many vendors.

Telnet — Virtual terminal processing, enabling a user at one system to sign on to another system.

TN3270 — An implementation of Telnet that supports the IBM 3270 data stream.

TN5250 — An implementation of Telnet that supports the IBM 5250 data stream.

UDP — User Datagram Protocol. A protocol in the TCP/IP suite that provides transport services similar to TCP, but without the overhead of error detection and correction. Often used for services that do not require the reliability provided with TCP (e.g., Domain Name Service).

URL — Uniform Resource Locator. A name that identifies the host containing the requested Web page and optionally information to identify or display a specific page.

UUCP — Unix-to-Unix Copy Program. An older method of sending e-mail across a network.

VT100 — A terminal type popularized by Digital Equipment Corporation that is widely used for Telnet implementations.

WAN — Wide Area Network.

WinSock — Windows Sockets. A Microsoft standard that enables TCP/IP services to be used in a Windows environment.

XDR — The External Data Representation module of the Network File System.

Index

New Books in the 29th Street Press Library

THE A TO Z OF EDI, SECOND EDITION

By Nahid M. Jilovec

The A to Z of EDI, Second Edition, gives you the practical details of EDI implementation. Not only does it show you how to cost justify EDI, but it gives you job descriptions for EDI team members, detailed criteria and forms for evaluating EDI vendors, considerations for trading-partner agreements, an EDI glossary, and lists of EDI organizations and publications. And this edition includes all-new information about EDI and the Internet, system security, and auditing. 221 pages.

THE ACCOUNTING SOFTWARE HANDBOOK
Your Guide to Evaluating Vendor Applications

By Stewart McKie

This second edition of *The Technology Guide to Accounting Software* will help you understand how you can apply technologies such as client/server, workflow, imaging, OLAP, and the Internet to deliver effective accounting systems. The accompanying CD contains more than 50 profiles of selected vendors and products. Also included is a detailed step-by-step selection process to help you efficiently arrive at a vendor shortlist for your evaluation. 265 pages.

MASTERING THE AS/400, SECOND EDITION
A Practical, Hands-On Guide

By Jerry Fottral

With its utilitarian approach that stresses student participation, this introductory textbook to AS/400 concepts and facilities emphasizes mastery of system/user interface, member-object-library relationship, use of CL commands, and basic database and program development utilities. The second edition is updated to V3R1/V3R6. Each lesson includes a lab that focuses on the essential topics presented in the lesson. 575 pages.

MCSE RAPID REVIEW STUDY GUIDES

Series Editor: Mike Pastore

You know that becoming a Microsoft Certified Systems Engineer can be lucrative. Still, seeking the certification isn't a goal for the faint of heart. Our Rapid Review Study Guides give you pre- and post-assessments to measure your progress, exam preparation tips, an overview of exam material, vocabulary drills, hands-on activities, and sample quiz questions on CD and in the book. Current titles include *Networking Essentials*, *System Management Server 1.2*, *TCP/IP for Microsoft Windows NT 4.0*, *Internet Information Server 4.0*, *Windows 95*, *Windows NT 4.0 Server*, *Windows NT 4.0 Workstation*, and *Windows NT 4.0 Server in the Enterprise*.

WINDOWS NT MAGAZINE ADMINISTRATOR'S SURVIVAL GUIDE:
SYSTEM MANAGEMENT AND SECURITY

Edited by John Enck

In this first book in our Survival Guide™ series, John Enck has assembled the best articles and authors from *Windows NT Magazine* to share their experience with mission-critical system management and security issues. Topics include tuning, troubleshooting, installation, securing the Internet connection, testing, encryption, task managers, file servers, and more. 359 pages.

WINDOWS NT MAGAZINE ADMINISTRATOR'S SURVIVAL GUIDE:
NETWORKING AND BACKOFFICE

Edited by John Enck

In this second book in our Survival Guide™ series, John Enck has assembled the best *Windows NT Magazine* articles about networking and BackOffice issues. Topics include Remote Access Service, PPTP, assigning IP addresses and IP routing, name resolution, using NT with the Internet, connectivity, implementing MS Exchange, and more. 469 pages.

WINDOWS NT MAGAZINE INSTANT SOLUTIONS:
TROUBLESHOOTING IIS 4.0 AND VISUAL INTERDEV 6.0

By Ken Spencer
Series editor, Sean Daily

Author Ken Spencer has worked with IIS and Visual InterDev since their early preview stages. In the first of our Instant Solutions series of books, he takes knowledge selected from his development and system management experiences and condenses it for you. In a handy problem/solution format, he includes tips for installing IIS and Visual InterDev, tips for optimizing IIS performance, tips for troubleshooting IIS and Visual InterDev security, and more. 168 pages.

Also Published by 29th Street Press

1001 SECRETS FOR WINDOWS NT REGISTRY
By Tim Daniels
For the accomplished user, *1001 Secrets for Windows NT Registry* is the definitive reference for system customization and optimization. Organized into sections that cover networking, applications, system management, hardware, and performance, the book also has an accompanying CD that is packed with innovative registry monitoring and performance utilities. 321 pages.

THE ADMINISTRATOR'S GUIDE TO MICROSOFT SQL SERVER 6.5
By Kevin Cox and William Jones
This book guides database managers and administrators into a thorough understanding of the client/server aspects of the SQL Server 6.5 product, and includes many useful tips for managing security, troubleshooting, and improving performance. 469 pages.

BUILDING AS/400 CLIENT/SERVER APPLICATIONS
Put ODBC and Client Access APIs to Work
By Mike Otey
Mike Otey gives you the why, what, and how-to of AS/400 client/server computing, which matches the strengths of the AS/400 with the PC GUIs that users want. This book's clear and easy-to-understand style guides you through all the important aspects of AS/400 client/server applications. Mike covers APPC and TCP/IP communications, as well as the underlying architectures for each of the major AS/400 client/server APIs. CD with complete source code for several working applications included. 505 pages.

CLIENT ACCESS TOKEN-RING CONNECTIVITY
By Chris Patterson
Client Access Token-Ring Connectivity details all that is required to successfully maintain and troubleshoot a Token-Ring network. The first half of the book introduces the Token-Ring and describes the Client Access communications architecture, the Token-Ring connection from both the PC side and the AS/400 side, and the Client Access applications. The second half provides a useful guide to Token-Ring management, strategies for Token-Ring error identification and recovery, and tactics for resolving Client Access error messages. 122 pages.

CONTROL LANGUAGE PROGRAMMING FOR THE AS/400, SECOND EDITION
By Bryan Meyers and Dan Riehl, NEWS/400 *technical editors*
This comprehensive CL programming textbook offers students up-to-the-minute knowledge of the skills they will need in today's MIS environment. Chapters progress methodically from CL basics to more complex processes and concepts, guiding students toward a professional grasp of CL programming techniques and style. In this second edition, the authors have updated the text to include discussion of the Integrated Language Environment (ILE) and the fundamental changes ILE introduces to the AS/400's execution model. 522 pages.

DATABASE DESIGN AND PROGRAMMING FOR DB2/400
By Paul Conte
This textbook is the most complete guide to DB2/400 design and programming available anywhere. The author shows you everything you need to know about physical and logical file DDS, SQL/400, and RPG IV and COBOL/400 database programming. Clear explanations illustrated by a wealth of examples demonstrate efficient database programming and error handling with both DDS and SQL/400. 610 pages.

DATA WAREHOUSING AND THE AS/400
By Scott Steinacher
In this book, Scott Steinacher takes an in-depth look at data-warehousing components, concepts, and terminology. After laying this foundation, Scott presents a compelling case for implementing a data warehouse on the AS/400. Included on an accompanying CD are demos of AS/400 data-warehousing software from several independent software vendors. 342 pages.

DEVELOPING YOUR AS/400 INTERNET STRATEGY
By Alan Arnold
This book addresses the issues unique to deploying your AS/400 on the Internet. It includes procedures for configuring AS/400 TCP/IP and information about which client and server technologies the AS/400 supports natively. This enterprise-class tutorial evaluates the AS/400 as an Internet server and teaches you how to design, program, and manage your Web home page. 248 pages.

THE ESSENTIAL GUIDE TO CLIENT ACCESS FOR DOS EXTENDED

By John Enck, Robert E. Anderson, and Michael Otey

The Essential Guide to Client Access for DOS Extended contains key insights and need-to-know technical information about Client Access for DOS Extended, IBM's AS/400 product for DOS and Windows client/server connectivity. This book provides fundamental information about how to install and configure Client Access; and advanced information about integrating Client Access with other types of networks, managing how Client Access for DOS Extended operates under Windows, and developing client/server applications with Client Access. 447 pages.

ESSENTIALS OF SUBFILE PROGRAMMING
and Advanced Topics in RPG

By Phil Levinson

Essentials of Subfile Programming teaches you to design and program subfiles, offering step-by-step instructions and real-world programming exercises that build from chapter to chapter. You learn to design and create subfile records; load, clear, and display subfiles; and create pop-up windows. In addition, the advanced topics help you mine the rich store of data in the file-information and program-status data structures, handle errors, improve data integrity by using journaling and commitment control, and manage program-to-program communication. An instructor's manual is available. 260 pages.

IMPLEMENTING AS/400 SECURITY, THIRD EDITION

By Wayne Madden and Carol Woodbury

Concise and practical, this third edition of *Implementing AS/400 Security* not only brings together in one place the fundamental AS/400 security tools and experience-based recommendations that you need, but also includes specifics on the latest security enhancements available in OS/400 V4R1 and V4R2. 424 pages.

INSIDE THE AS/400, SECOND EDITION
Featuring the AS/400e series

By Frank G. Soltis

Learn from the architect of the AS/400 about the new generation of AS/400e systems and servers, and about the latest system features and capabilities introduced in Version 4 of OS/400. Dr. Frank Soltis demystifies the system, shedding light on how it came to be, how it can do the things it does, and what its future may hold. 402 pages.

INTERNET SECURITY WITH WINDOWS NT

By Mark Joseph Edwards

Security expert and *Windows NT Magazine* news editor Mark Edwards provides the quintessential guide to Internet and intranet security from the Windows NT platform. Security is the number one concern of NT users, and this comprehensive book covers network security basics as well as IIS and MPS, and includes specific advice about selecting NT tools and security devices. The accompanying CD-ROM includes security-related utilities, tools, and software packages — firewalls, port scanners, network-monitoring software, and virus detection and prevention utilities. These tools, combined with the tips and techniques in the book, are powerful weapons in your security efforts. 520 pages.

AN INTRODUCTION TO COMMUNICATIONS FOR THE AS/400, SECOND EDITION

By John Enck and Ruggero Adinolfi

This second edition has been revised to address the sweeping communications changes introduced with V3R1 of OS/400. As a result, this book now covers the broad range of AS/400 communications technology topics, ranging from Ethernet to X.25, and from APPN to AnyNet. The book presents an introduction to data communications and then covers communications fundamentals, types of networks, OSI, SNA, APPN, networking roles, the AS/400 as host and server, TCP/IP, and the AS/400-DEC connection. 194 pages.

THE MICROSOFT EXCHANGE SERVER INTERNET MAIL CONNECTOR

By Spyros Sakellariadis

Achieve Internet connectivity using Exchange Server 4.0 and 5.0. This book presents four Internet connectivity models, shows how to set up the Internet Mail Connector with an Internet Service Provider, and illustrates how to monitor Internet traffic. It also includes troubleshooting and reference guides. 234 pages.

THE MICROSOFT EXCHANGE USER'S HANDBOOK

By Sue Mosher

Microsoft Exchange is all about making connections — connections to a Microsoft Mail server, to Exchange Server, to a fax machine, or to online services. Here's the must-have, complete guide for users who need to know how to set up and use all the features of the Microsoft Exchange client product. Includes chapters about Microsoft Exchange Server 5.0 and Microsoft Outlook. 692 pages. CD included.

THE MICROSOFT OUTLOOK E-MAIL AND FAX GUIDE

By Sue Mosher

Sue Mosher explains the setup of individual e-mail services and components, e-mail options and when you might want to use them, and many time-saving techniques that take you beyond the basics. Users at all levels will learn from this comprehensive introduction to Microsoft's next generation of messaging software. The book includes coverage of the Internet Mail Enhancement Patch, Rules Wizard, and special features for Microsoft Exchange Server users. 500 pages.

MIGRATING TO WINDOWS NT 4.0

By Sean Daily

This book is a comprehensive yet concise guide to the significant changes users will encounter as they make the move to Windows NT 4.0. The author, a Microsoft Certified Systems Engineer (MCSE), eases the transition with his enthusiastic presentation of a wealth of tips and techniques that give readers the sense they're receiving "insider information." 475 pages.

POWERING YOUR WEB SITE WITH WINDOWS NT SERVER

By Nik Simpson

Powering Your Web Site with Windows NT Server explores the tools necessary to establish a presence on the Internet or on an internal corporate intranet using Web technology and Windows NT Server. The author helps readers navigate the process of creating a new information infrastructure, from the basics of justifying the decision to management through the complete implementation cycle. 640 pages. CD included.

PROGRAMMING IN RPG IV, REVISED EDITION

By Judy Yaeger, Ph.D., a NEWS/400 *technical editor*

This textbook provides a strong foundation in the essentials of business programming, featuring the newest version of the RPG language: RPG IV. Focusing on real-world problems and down-to-earth solutions using the latest techniques and features of RPG, this book provides everything you need to know to write a well-designed RPG IV program. This revised edition includes a new section about subprocedures and an addition about using the RPG ILE source debugger. An instructor's kit is available. 435 pages.

PROGRAMMING IN RPG/400, SECOND EDITION

By Judy Yaeger, Ph.D., a NEWS/400 *technical editor*

This second edition refines and extends the comprehensive instructional material contained in the original textbook and features a new section that introduces externally described printer files, a new chapter that highlights the fundamentals of RPG IV, and a new appendix that correlates the key concepts from each chapter with their RPG IV counterparts. Includes everything you need to learn how to write a well-designed RPG program, from the most basic to the more complex. An instructor's kit is available. 481 pages.

RPG IV JUMP START, SECOND EDITION
Moving Ahead With the New RPG

By Bryan Meyers, a NEWS/400 *technical editor*

In this second edition of *RPG IV Jump Start*, Bryan Meyers has added coverage for new releases of the RPG IV compiler (V3R2, V3R6, and V3R7) and amplified the coverage of RPG IV's participation in the integrated language environment (ILE). As in the first edition, he covers RPG IV's changed and new specifications and data types. He presents the new RPG from the perspective of a programmer who already knows the old RPG, pointing out the differences between the two and demonstrating how to take advantage of the new syntax and function. 214 pages.

VISUALAGE FOR RPG BY EXAMPLE

By Bryan Meyers and Jef Sutherland

VisualAge for RPG by Example brings the RPG language to the GUI world and lets you use your existing knowledge to develop Windows applications. Using a tutorial approach, *VisualAge for RPG by Example* lets you learn as you go and create simple yet functional programs start to finish. The accompanying CD-ROM offers a scaled down version of VARPG and complete source code for the sample project. 236 pages.

FOR A COMPLETE CATALOG OR TO PLACE AN ORDER, CONTACT

29th Street Press
Duke Communications International
221 E. 29th Street • Loveland, CO 80538-2727
(800) 621-1544 • (970) 663-4700 • Fax: (970) 203-2756

OR SHOP OUR WEB SITE: **www.29thStreetPress.com**

We Want Your Response

Mail it

Fax it

Web it

Complete this form to join our network of computer professionals

We'll gladly send you a free copy of

- ❏ *Windows NT Magazine*
- ❏ *Selling NT Solutions*
- ❏ *NEWS/400*
- ❏ *Selling AS/400 Solutions*
- ❏ *Business Finance*

 Publisher of practical, hands-on technical books for Windows NT and AS/400 computer professionals. Providing help not hype.

Name _____

Title _____ Phone _____

Company _____

Address _____

City/State/Zip _____

E-mail _____

Where did you purchase this book?

❏ Trade show   ❏ Computer store   ❏ Internet   ❏ Card deck   ❏ Bookstore

❏ Magazine   ❏ Direct mail catalog or brochure

What new applications do you expect to use during the next year?

_____

_____

How many times this month will you visit one of Duke Communication's Web sites (29th Street Press, *NEWS/400, Selling AS/400 Solutions, Windows NT Magazine, Selling NT Solutions, Business Finance*)? ___

Please share your reaction to *TCP/IP and the AS/400*

_____

_____

_____

❏ YES! You have my permission to quote my comments in your publications. (initials) _____

[98SCXBOOK]

COPY THIS PAGE AND MAIL TO
29TH STREET PRESS • 221 EAST 29TH STREET • LOVELAND, CO 80538
OR FAX TO (970) 667-2321
OR RESPOND VIA OUR WEB SITE AT www.29thStreetPress.com